60

FARRAR
STRAUS
GIROUX

ALSO BY THOMAS BENDER

Toward an Urban Vision:
Ideas and Institutions in Nineteenth-Century America

The Making of American Society (coauthor)

Community and Social Change in America

New York Intellect: A History of Intellectual Life in New York,
from 1750 to the Beginnings of Our Own Time

The University and the City:
From Medieval Origins to the Present (editor)

Budapest and New York: Studies in
Metropolitan Transformation, 1870–1930 (coeditor)

The Anti-Slavery Debate: Capitalism and Abolitionism
as a Problem in Historical Interpretation (editor)

Intellect and Public Life: Essays on the
Social History of Academic Intellectuals in the United States

American Academic Culture in Transformation (coeditor)

City and Nation (coeditor)

Rethinking American History in a Global Age (editor)

The Education of Historians for the Twenty-first Century (coauthor)

A NATION
AMONG NATIONS

A NATION AMONG NATIONS

AMERICA'S PLACE IN

WORLD HISTORY

THOMAS BENDER

HILL AND WANG

A DIVISION OF FARRAR, STRAUS AND GIROUX

NEW YORK

Hill and Wang
A division of Farrar, Straus and Giroux
18 West 18th Street, New York 10011

Copyright © 2006 by Thomas Bender

Printed in the United States of America
Published in 2006 by Hill and Wang
First paperback edition, 2006

The Library of Congress has cataloged the hardcover edition as follows:
Bender, Thomas.
A nation among nations : America's place in world history /
Thomas Bender.— 1st ed.
    p.   cm.
Includes bibliographical references and index.
ISBN-13: 978-0-8090-9527-8 (hardcover : alk. paper)
ISBN-10: 0-8090-9527-0 (hardcover : alk. paper)
1. United States—History.   2. United States—History—Philosophy.   I. Title.

E178.B428 2006
973—dc22

                                                            2005052808

Paperback ISBN-13: 978-0-8090-7235-4
Paperback ISBN-10: 0-8090-7235-1

Designed by Jonathan D. Lippincott

www.fsgbooks.com

9   10   8

FOR DAVID AND SOPHIA

CONTENTS

PREFACE AND ACKNOWLEDGMENTS

This book proposes and then elaborates a new framing of U.S. history. It rejects the territorial space of the nation as the sufficient context for a national history, arguing for the transnational nature of national histories. National histories are part of global histories; each nation is a province among the provinces that make up the world. For most of human history most peoples lived in societies and polities other than the nation-state. Most of the post-Columbian history we call American preceded the emergence of the United States as a nation-state. This book places the American experience in its larger context so as the better to understand it. In addition, it aims to encourage a more cosmopolitan sense of being an American, to have us recognize the historical interconnections and interdependencies that have made America's history global even as it is national, provincial even as it shares in the general history of humans on this planet.

Writing this book has required that the author stretch well beyond the special expertise of his training and specialized professional experience, especially pronounced among historians of the United States. That means that I have had to rely more than usual on fellow scholars. The notes acknowledge the published work on which I was especially dependent. Here I wish to thank some of the scholars who helped me in person, though even this list omits many who directly and indirectly educated me on various occasions. Although I began formal work on this book in the summer of 2001, I know I am drawing on reading and the professional exchanges of a whole career. I cannot directly acknowledge all of that here except to say that I deeply appreciate the intellectual generosity I have found in academe as well as in my relations with friends and intellectuals outside the academic world over the years.

It has been my good fortune to have Elisabeth Sifton as my editor for this book. From the point the idea for it emerged, when it was still quite vague, she embraced it. Her confidence, encouragement of boldness, and positive reactions to each chapter have meant a great deal. Her sharp eye and pencil, along with her fine sense of the language, have touched nearly every paragraph, much to their benefit.

I did a large part of the work on this book at the New York Public Library, where I was the Mel and Lois Tukman Fellow at the Cullman Center for Scholars and Writers in 2002–2003. That center provided a wonderfully sustaining intellectual community, and I wish to thank especially Peter Gay, its then director, and two fellows, Stacy Schiff and Philip Steinberg, who read what I wrote there and offered very helpful suggestions. Eric Foner of Columbia University not only read an early version and offered wise counsel, as always, but also assigned some chapters to his graduate class, thus multiplying the commentary I received from uptown. I finished the book at the Center for Advanced Studies in the Behavioral Sciences, which provided a beautiful setting and uninterrupted time.

I have presented portions of this book as lectures at a number of institutions. Most important were the seminars at the École des Hautes Études en Sciences Sociales in Paris in January 2004, when I had the invaluable opportunity to present several chapters to foreign scholars of the United States. I thank François Weil for arranging my appointment as a *directeur d'études associé*, and his colleagues for their interest and insight. I am thankful as well for the opportunity to present some of my ideas to a group of American studies scholars at Hokkaido University in Japan, a meeting arranged by Jun Furuya in March 2004. Greg Robinson generously arranged for me to present this work at the Université du Québec à Montréal and at McGill University, and I thank him for those valuable discussions. The invitation to present an Annenberg seminar in the history department at the University of Pennsylvania resulted in an extremely valuable conversation; I want especially to thank Sarah Igo, Nancy Farriss, Steven Feierman, Jonathan Steinberg, and Kathleen Brown, who supplied me with specific bibliographical references to overcome various ignorances on my part. I want to thank those who participated in discussions at Harvard University; the State University of New York at Buffalo; the University of Rochester; the University of Wisconsin, Madison; the University of Maryland; Michigan State University; the University of Texas, San Antonio; the University of California, Davis; Santa Clara University; Yale University; Columbia University; and my own, New York University, where I presented a portion of the work to the Atlantic History Workshop, and organized summer seminars on the theme for the NYU Faculty Network of historically black colleges and for the Gilder Lehrman Institute seminar for high-school teachers. I also presented material at a conference titled "Rethinking America in Global Perspectives," jointly sponsored by the American Historical Association, the Community College Humanities Association, the National Endowment for the Humanities, and the Library of Congress. These discussions were extremely illuminating for me, as was the opportunity to present my ideas to the readers (hundreds of them!) of the College Board's AP U.S. History Test. My ideas on how to deal with transnational themes benefited enormously from the remarkable Friday Seminars of the International Center for Advanced Studies at NYU, and I want to thank everyone involved. Indeed, without the experience of my several years as director of ICAS I could not have even begun to imagine such a book as this one. For thirty years now NYU has supported my scholarship and teaching; that support has not only been material but, more important, NYU surrounded me with lively students and colleagues.

Several NYU colleagues read chapters and shared bibliography with me: I thank especially Molly Nolan, from whom I have learned so much over many years, Marilyn Young, Walter Johnson, Manu Goswami, Martha Hodes, Chris Otter, Barbara Krauthamer, and my former colleagues Louise Young and Robin D.G. Kelley. Several other individuals not already noted warrant special mention: Jorge Cañizares-Esquerra, Arif Dirlik, Florencia Mallon, Steve J. Stern, Colleen Dunlavy, Susan Sleeper-Smith, Selçuk Esenbel, Jeffrey Herf, and the seventy foreign and American participants in the La Pietra meetings in Florence, Italy, in 1997, 1998, 1999, and 2000 on the internationalization of American history.

I received smart, imaginative research help from two NYU students: Emily Marker, an undergraduate who did research in French materials for me, and Marcela Echeverri, a graduate student in Latin American history who did research in that field for me. The English-language library on the history and culture of Japan at the International House of Japan was an unexpected and invaluable resource, and I wish to thank the librarians there for their assistance. Marc Aronson pointed me toward connections between British credit, India, and the American crisis.

This book is dedicated to my two children, David and Sophia, who have enriched my life in ways that go beyond words. For that I am, as any parent would be, forever indebted to them. But I thank them here specifically for expanding my temporal and geographical horizons. Sophia has pulled my sense of history back to the ancient world, while David, with his extraordinary knowledge of the polities and peoples of the modern world, has expanded my sense of historical geography to the ends of the earth. Gwendolyn Wright, a vital presence and shining light through both pleasure and pain, has contributed to my life as well as this book in her own special ways.

A NATION
AMONG NATIONS

INTRODUCTION

———⌾———

This book proposes to mark the end of American history as we have known it. *"End"* can mean both "purpose" and "termination," and both of those meanings are necessary to introduce my themes. First I mean to draw attention to the *end* to which national histories, including American history, have been put. Histories are taught in schools and brought into public discourse to forge and sustain national identities, and they present the self-contained nation as the natural carrier of history. I believe this way of writing and teaching history has exhausted itself. We need a history that understands national history as itself being made in and by histories that are both larger and smaller than the nation's. The nation is not freestanding and self-contained; like other forms of human solidarity, it is connected with and partially shaped by what is beyond it. It is time to stop ignoring this obvious dimension of a national history. Nineteenth-century nationalist ideology became embedded in the development of history as a discipline, but it obscures the actual experience of national societies and produces a narrow parochialism at a time when we need a wider cosmopolitanism.

National histories, like nation-states, are modern developments. The first national history of the United States, David Ramsay's *History of the American Revolution*, was published in 1789. In fact, Ramsay held off publishing it until the Constitution was ratified.[1] History—and especially history in the schools—contributed mightily to the acceptance of the nation as the dominant form of human solidarity during the next two centuries. It became the core of civic education in schools and other institutions devoted to making peasants, immigrants, and provincial peoples into national citizens. A common history, which involved both common memories and a tacit agreement to forget certain differences, was intended to provide a basis for a shared national identity.

This conception of the citizen was absolute; it was supposed to trump all other sources of identity. Regional, linguistic, ethnic, class, religious, and other forms of solidarity or connection that were either smaller or larger than the nation were to be radically subordinated to national identity. Moreover, national territory was to be firmly bounded. To sustain the idea of a national citizen or subject, the national space and population were presumed to be homogeneous. In return, the modern nation-state promised to protect its citizens at home and abroad. One artifact that marks both the importance of borders and the promise of protection is the passport—a nineteenth-century innovation.

The leaders of the new nation-states naturalized the nation as the most basic, obvious form of human solidarity, and they were helped by historians. Although this elevation of the nation is still quite new, everyone has become so comfortable with the notion as to refer routinely to events that occurred a thousand years ago within the present borders of France as "medieval French history." In this age of talk about globalization, multiculturalism, and diasporas, clearly our experience does not match up to such nationalist assumptions. Life is simply more complex. Historians know this as well as everyone else.

It is often said that the persistence of the demonstrably false nineteenth-century ideological framing of history can be explained by the absence of an alternative. My aim in this book is to offer another way of understanding the central events and themes of American history in a context larger than the nation. Unlike notions of American "exceptionalism," this framing insists that the nation cannot be its own historical context. In fact, it presses context to its ultimate terrestrial limit: the globe itself. Here the major themes and events of American history, including such distinctively American events as the Revolution and the Civil War, are examined in a global context. To go beyond the nation is not necessarily to abandon it but to historicize and clarify its meaning. "To stand outside of the filiation of history and the nation-state," the historian Joyce Appleby has written, "is not to disparage it but, rather, to get some purchase on the powerful presuppositions that have shaped our thinking."[2]

In the past few years some of the most innovative and exciting scholarship in American history has been framed in ways that do not necessarily tie it to the nation-state—work on gender, migrations, diasporas, class, race, ethnicity, and other areas of social history. If this scholarship has not succumbed to the nationalist framing, neither has it altered or displaced it. It has grown up beside the older default narrative that we all carry around in our heads. It has brought forth new knowledge about previously unstudied or insufficiently recognized groups and themes in American history, but it has not changed the dominant narrative structure. The unitary logic of national history seems to have kept at bay new scholarship that could be transformative. Too often this new scholarship is bracketed (literally so in textbooks) rather than integrated. Much is added, but the basic narrative stays the same. That is why textbooks get longer and longer, more and more ungainly, and less and less readable, with the old nineteenth-century narrative buried under the mass. This narrative must be challenged more directly.

About a decade ago I began to think more seriously and quite differently about the way American history has been written, to say nothing about the way I was teaching it. What concerned me was not the then-much-contested question of the politics of history, at least not in the narrow sense of supporting or opposing this or that side in the so-called culture wars.[3] Nor was it about favoring liberal or conservative interpretations, for on the issue that concerned me there was no difference. The problem for me was more fundamental and methodological: it seemed to me that the default narrative I carried around in my head limited my capacity to understand the central themes of American history. What were the true boundaries of America's national experience? What history did the United States share with other nations? How would the use of a wider context change the core American narrative? I began to rethink two aspects of that core narrative: its unexamined assumption that the nation was the natural container and carrier of history; and its neglect of the truth that space, no less than time, is fundamental to historical explanation, that history plays out over space as well as over time.

American history was taught to me and to you as if it were self-contained. Recent changes in the school history curriculum highlight the problem rather than solve it. In the interest of better preparing our youth for citizenship in a multicultural nation in a globalized world, most states now require schools to offer world history courses. That appears to be an effective curricular change, but in practice the new curriculum subverts the good intentions that prompted it. Most world history courses do not include American history. Somehow the world is everything but us. America's interconnections and interdependencies beyond its borders are rarely captured in these courses, and the revised curriculum reinforces the very split between America and the world that contemporary citizenship must overcome.

If Americans tend to think of something "international" as being "out there," somehow not connected with them, we historians of the United States bear some responsibility for this misperception. The way we teach history, with our disciplinary commitment to the nation as the self-contained carrier of history, reinforces this parochialism. We assume this nationalism, but we do not argue it. If historians want to educate students and the public as true citizens, they must think more profoundly about the way they frame national histories, which we must keep, but in ways that reveal commonalities and interconnections.

Strangely enough, many scholars who study foreign nations and regions—area studies specialists—have shared and reinforced the binary approach that puts the United States and the rest of the world in two different boxes. American studies and area studies programs developed at the same time in American universities, but until very recently they did not acknowledge that each was an interacting part of the same global history. Thus we have limited our understanding of other parts of the world, and missed the ways other histories have been part of our own. Americans need to be more conscious of being a "part of abroad," as the New York *Journal of Commerce* observed in the auspicious year of 1898.

This book elaborates two nested arguments. The first is that global history commenced when American history began, in the decades before and after 1500. The second follows directly from the first: American history cannot be adequately understood unless it is incorporated into that global context. It then becomes a different kind of history with more explanatory power. It reconnects history with geography. It incorporates causal influences that work across space as well as those that unfold over time. It enriches our understanding of the historical making and remaking of the United States. It is, moreover, the only way to map and appraise the changing position and interdependencies that connect the United States today to the other provinces of the planet.

At the end of the nineteenth century Max Weber famously defined the nation-state as the possessor of a legitimate monopoly of violence. Evidence surely supports this definition, which is necessary but not sufficient. The nation also depends on the population's embrace of a national identity. Nationalism and national identity are founded largely on a sense of shared memories. Making and teaching such shared memories and identities were the work of historians and of national history curricula, generously supported to promote the formation of national identities and national citizens. But we need to recover the historicity of the prior and coexistent forms and scales of human solidarity that compete with, interact with, and even constitute the nation. A national history is a contingent outcome, the work of historical actors, not an ideal form or a fact of nature. It is the outcome of interplay and interrelations among historical social formations, processes, and structures both larger and smaller than the nation. Recently social historians have greatly illuminated those "smaller" histories within the nation; now the larger ones are emerging, too.

Thinking of the global dimensions of a national history, historians must step outside the national box—and return with new and richer explanations for national development. They can better recognize the permeability of the nation at boundaries, the zones of contact and exchange among people, money, knowledges, and things—the raw materials of history that rarely stop at borders. The nation cannot be its own context. No less than the neutron or the cell, it must be studied in a framework larger than itself.

This book examines the United States as one of the many provinces that collectively constitute humanity. The story I tell begins around 1500, when oceanic seafaring for the first time connected all the continents and created a common history of all peoples. The beginning of American history was part of the event that made global history. I end with the twentieth century, when the United States loomed larger in global events than could ever have been imagined at the beginning of the story.

The American nation-building project has been unusually successful. But the history of that success cannot and ought not be used to sustain a claim of historical uniqueness or of categorical difference. Whatever the distinctive position of the United States today, it remains nonetheless only one global province interconnected with and interdependent with every other one. The history of the United States is but one history among histories.

The clamor of debate about multiculturalism and globalization has encouraged talk of the decline of the nation-state and the possibility of a post-national history. But I do not believe the nation is likely to soon disappear. True, nation-states have done terrible damage to the human community, but they are also the only enforcer available to protect human and citizen rights. The nation must remain a central object of historical inquiry so long as we understand history to include both the analysis of power in society and the clarification of ethical responsibility within the human community. My purpose here is not to dismiss national history but to propose a different mode for it, one that better respects the empirical record and better serves us as citizens of the nation and the world.

A considerable scholarly literature has recently been produced that in various ways challenges the old way of teaching national histories. There have even been manifestos that call for alternative approaches, including two for which I am responsible.[4] They were both directed exclusively to my disciplinary peers, academic readers and professional historians, and they both called for something different without actually doing it. This book is addressed to a wider audience, and it actually does what the manifestos propose.

Rather than nibble at the edges of the default narrative, this book examines five major themes in American history and reinterprets them as parts of global history. To do this significantly changes—and in my view enriches—our understanding of those themes. I might have addressed other themes, but the ones I selected are central, and no general history of the United States can omit any of them.

The first chapter explores and redefines the meaning of the "age of discovery." What precisely is new about the New World? That chapter, which establishes the beginning of global history, sets the stage. The next chapter, taking its cue from a comment made by James Madison at the Constitutional Convention, extends the chronology and geography of the

American Revolution, placing it in the context of the competition among the great eighteenth-century empires and especially the "Great War," the global conflict between England and France that lasted from 1689 to 1815. Developments outside the territorial United States were decisive in the American victory against Great Britain and in the development of the new nation. Equally important, the revolutionary crisis of British North America was but one of many around the globe, all deriving from the competition among empires and the consequent reform of them.

Next I place the Civil War in the context of the European revolutions of 1848. Lincoln watched and admired the European liberals who were forging a link between nation and freedom and who redefined the meaning of national territory, and they watched him, understanding that the cause of the Union, especially after the Emancipation Proclamation, was central to their larger ambitions for liberal nationalism. These new understandings of nation, freedom, and national territory were played out on every continent, and often violently.

Most Americans hesitate to acknowledge the centrality of empire in their history, let alone to see that the American empire was one among many. But the imperial adventure of 1898 was not, as is often argued, an accidental and unthinking act, and in my fourth chapter I explore the ways in which empire had been on the national agenda for decades. There is a striking continuity in purpose and style from America's westward expansion to its overseas colonization in 1898. Equally continuous was a policy of extending foreign trade in agricultural and industrial goods and, in the twentieth century, access to raw materials and securing American investments abroad.

My fifth chapter concerns American progressive reform, social liberalism, and the claims of social citizenship in the decades following 1890. With a wide-angle lens, one cannot but recognize that American progressive reform was part of a global response to the extraordinary expansion of industrial capitalism and of large cities at that time. A global menu of reform ideas was available to all. That they were selectively and differently adopted and adapted, nation by nation, shows the importance of national political cultures within the larger, shared global history.

This last point is crucially important. I am not saying there is only one history, or that the American Revolution is like other revolutions of its time. Nor do I say that the Civil War was no different from the emancipation of serfs in the Russian and Habsburg empires or the unification of Germany and Argentina. Nor do I argue that the American empire was indistinguishable from those of England, France, or Germany; or that progressivism in the United States was like progressivism in Japan or Chile. Yet there are family resemblances we have missed, and we have also missed the self-aware communication about common challenges that historical actors on every continent had with one another.

It is not just that all national histories are not the same. More important, the extension of context enables us to see more clearly and deeply exactly what is unique about the national history of the United States. Its major events and themes look different; their causes and consequences get redefined. And then we can better understand the legacy of the past for our present.

The United States has always shared a history with others. To acknowledge that literally makes us more worldly, and it makes our history more accessible to foreign scholars and publics. It makes us more open to interpretations of our history coming from historians and others beyond our borders. It will, I hope, better educate us and our children to the kind of cosmopolitanism that will make us better citizens of both the nation and the world. Surely it will move us closer to the cosmopolitan moral integrity that the anthropologist Clifford Geertz has well expressed for us:

> To see ourselves as others see us can be eye-opening. To see others as sharing a nature with ourselves is the merest decency. But it is from the far more difficult achievement of seeing ourselves amongst others, as a local example of the forms of human life locally taken, a case among cases, a world among worlds, that the largeness of mind, without which objectivity is self-congratulation and tolerance a sham, comes.[5]

This kind of history is not entirely novel. It is a recovery of history as it was envisioned by some of my predecessors a century ago. They were among the many intellectuals and men and women of goodwill who sustained a hopeful internationalism and cosmopolitan values, which resulted in the foundation of various international organizations devoted to peace and uplift. There was a great awareness of global connections, and global thinking was quite pervasive.[6] The 1890s were a decade when transnational developments were as striking as they were to us in the 1990s, and the percentage of foreign investment even greater.

Historians of that era also shared in the presumption that national histories were part of a larger universal history. The intellectual foundations for this understanding of history had been laid by the German philosopher G.W.F. Hegel in the early nineteenth century, but American historians mostly absorbed it in diluted form through their emulation of German historical scholarship, most notably that of Leopold von Ranke, who clearly understood that his particular histories were part of an implicit universal history. The first generation of professional historians trained in the United States was more worldly than the post–World War II group who emphasized American "exceptionalism," and this earlier generation was typically trained in European as well as American history. With their passing, American history became more self-enclosed, a development accelerated by the Cold War.[7]

When, in the 1890s, historians presumed that the Atlantic world shared a history, their unifying theme was, unfortunately, racist. They included in the domain of history only those parts of the world that were organized into nation-states, thus leaving out Africa, most of Asia, and what we now call the Middle East. And the transnational history studied and written by Americans then traced the special Anglo-Saxon gift for political life. Herbert Baxter Adams and his students in the famous historical seminar at The Johns Hopkins University studied the development of American democratic institutions from the medieval forests of Germany, through England and English legal institutions, to the rocky but evidently nourishing soil of New England. It was a kind of genetic history, with history tracking the "germ" of democracy.

Frederick Jackson Turner rejected this metatheory of Adams, his mentor. Instead, he famously proposed his still influential frontier hypothesis at the World's Columbian Exposition in Chicago in 1893. In powerful and almost poetic language he rejected the Atlantic transit of democracy. Rather, he claimed, American democracy was the product of the frontier experience. "The true point of view in the history of this nation," he declared, "is not the Atlantic coast, it is the Great West."[8] While he broke the Eurocentric genetic chain, he did not, as many of his followers did, endorse the idea that national histories, American or otherwise, were self-contained. A point of view is not the same as a method. Two years earlier, in "The Significance of History," which was based on a talk he had given to teachers, Turner elaborated on the importance of historical and geographical contexts larger than the national one. "In history," he observed, "there are only artificial divisions" of time and space. One must take care not to cut off the fullness of either the axis of time or the axis of space. "No country can be understood without taking account of all the past; it is also true that we cannot select a stretch of land and say we will limit our study to this land; for local history can only be understood in the light of the history of the world." "Each [nation] acts on each . . . Ideas, commodities even, refuse the bounds of a nation." He added, "This is true especially in the modern world with its complex commerce and means of intellectual connection."[9]

Turner was not alone in the 1890s. Henry Adams's great *History of the United States During the Administrations of Jefferson and Madison* (1889–91) is a powerful example of a history that moves between local, national, and larger transnational contexts. Adams begins the first volume with regional portraits of the social and intellectual condition of the new nation in 1800, and he concludes the final volume with a similar account of the nation in 1815. But in between, he reveals a nation embedded in a larger Atlantic world, and as a historian he shifts his position from place to place to best reveal and explain actors and acts beyond the borders of the United States that are part of its history. The cosmopolitanism that enabled Adams to write such a history was part of his family history and biography. He was, after all, the great-grandson of John Adams, who with Benjamin Franklin negotiated the Treaty of Paris that ended the war of American independence; the grandson of John Quincy Adams, who negotiated the Treaty of Ghent, which ended the War of 1812; and the son and private secretary of Charles Francis Adams, Lincoln's ambassador to the Court of St. James's. Moreover, he was a distinguished historian of European history. His exquisitely crafted *Mont-Saint-Michel and Chartres* (1904) remains a classic for its celebration of the architecture, social organization, and spiritual devotion of medieval European culture, and he would later publish three memoirs of his travels in the South Pacific.

In 1895, W.E.B. DuBois completed his Harvard dissertation, published a year later as *The Suppression of the African Slave-Trade to the United States of America, 1638–1870*. This work was a forerunner of Atlantic history and the concept of the "Black Atlantic." All the continents with Atlantic shores were part of DuBois's history of this fundamental, even central aspect of U.S. history, since they were all connected by the slave trade and the institution of slavery. DuBois's recognition of the global developments of the 1890s, like Turner's, no doubt encouraged the global perspective that marked his scholarship and political activities throughout his long career. In an address to the graduating class of Fisk University in 1898, he sketched out the broad connections that were making human history singular:

> On our breakfast table lies each morning the toil of Europe, Asia, and Africa, and the isles of the sea; we sow and spin for unseen millions, and countless myriads weave and plant for us; we have made the earth smaller and life broader by annihilating distance, magnifying the human voice and the stars, binding nation to nation, until to-day, for the first time in history there is one standard of human culture as well in New York as in London, in Cape Town as in Paris, in Bombay as in Berlin.[10]

After World War I, this worldly impulse among historians went into decline, though the aspiration was not entirely lost. In fact, in 1933, when most nations, including the United States, were turning more nationalist in the midst of the crisis of the Great Depression, Herbert E. Bolton, a Berkeley historian of Latin America, titled his presidential address to the American Historical Association "The Epic of Greater America" (later published in *The American Historical Review*). He took his colleagues in U.S. history to task for their tendency to study the "thirteen English colonies and the United States in isolation," an approach that, he pointed out, "has obscured many of the larger factors in their development, and helped to raise up a nation of chauvinists." He proposed a much larger framing of history not only to make better citizens, but also "from the standpoint of correct historiography." He insisted—in the spirit of Turner, whose notion of the frontier Bolton had applied to the Spanish frontier in North America—that "each local story will have clearer meaning when studied in the light of the others; and that much of what has been written of each national history is but a thread out of a larger strand."[11]

Much was lost when this perspective atrophied in the interwar and war years and was dismissed after World War II. It is important to recover it for the civic and historiographical reasons Bolton noted, and to renew it with the historical questions of our time. We must also move beyond the Atlantic world or the Western Hemisphere. If we can begin to think about American history as a local instance of a general history, as one history among others, not only will historical knowledge be improved, but the cultural foundations of a needed cosmopolitanism will be enhanced. We do not want to reinforce a narrow and exclusive notion of citizenship. The worldly history promoted by Adams, Turner, DuBois, and Bolton will encourage and sustain a cosmopolitan citizenry, at once proud nationals and humble citizens of the world.

1

THE OCEAN WORLD AND

THE BEGINNINGS OF AMERICAN HISTORY

———— ∞∞ ————

Until recently the basic narrative of American history began with a chapter on exploration and discovery. That formula has changed—but only slightly. With the belated acknowledgment that earlier migrants, the first American peoples, had already been living in the Western Hemisphere for thousands of years when Christopher Columbus arrived and when the Pilgrims established Plymouth Plantation, the theme of the typical first chapter has been changed to emphasize European "contact" with Americans or, in some versions, the European "invasion of America." These rephrasings offer a truer interpretation of the encounter but do not change the story much. Either way, the extraordinary events of the fifteenth and sixteenth centuries are reduced to being a prequel to an American national history. Likewise, to begin with the migration of the first Americans across an Asian-American land bridge, which should change the frame of American history, amounts in practice to no more than a prelude, acknowledged and then dropped. The proto-nationalist and linear narrative persists, shaped and misshaped by its teleological anticipation of the later emergence of the United States. Thus reduced, this early phase of American history loses much of its significance and capacity to explain later developments. And the usual story about "settlement" that follows "discovery," "contact," or "invasion" is not only linear but very narrowly channeled.

The event that occurred in 1492, whatever it is called, was about space, oceanic space. Space was redefined, and movement across oceans made possible entirely new global networks of trade and communication. Recognizing this spatial aspect of American beginnings enlarges our story. The actual "discovery" was greater in significance than the exploration of a landmass unknown to Europeans or even than the beginnings of the United States. The real discovery was of the ocean, which entered history, creating a new world.

The consequences of discovering an oceanic world shaped the history of every continent. On every continent a new world emerged, with consequences for each. The story of North America and of the United States is part of that larger, more important history, not vice versa.

While all the educated classes of the European Renaissance knew the earth was spherical, the world as they understood it did not include the oceans. It was not yet global. For Christendom, indeed for adherents of the Abrahamic religions more generally, the Afro-Eurasian world that was unified by the Mediterranean Sea was an "island world" inhabited by the descendants of Adam and Eve, the human family. God, it was thought, had on the third day commanded the sea to pull back, exposing a portion of the earth's surface for the use of humans.[1] This biblical cosmology was illustrated on the border of one of the most famous surviving maps of the era, that of Fra Mauro of 1459.[2] The great fourteenth-century North African Muslim historian and philosopher Ibn-Khaldun made the same point in words: "The water withdrew from certain parts of [the earth] because God wanted to create living beings on it and settle it with the human species."[3] Beyond the ocean was an unknown, often terrifying space. It was even regarded as a kind of anti-world. Map borders often showed monstrous beings beyond the ocean, and countless medieval accounts and encyclopedias described them. This "other" located beyond the human world was present in the daily iconography of Christianity, routinely carved into the tympana of European cathedrals, where they still attract our notice.[4]

Meanwhile, the greater part of Afro-Eurasia had been unified by the Mongol Empire in the thirteenth century, and its extent facilitated expansive trade. This vast empire reinforces the point being made here: this was a land empire, limited by the sea, and when the Mongols attempted an invasion of Japan in 1281, the combination of superior Japanese seamanship and a terrific storm resulted in their disastrous defeat.

The later significance of Columbus—though he did not grasp it—was that his voyages opened an extraordinary global prospect, first for Europeans and in time for us all. After Columbus, as the Mexican historian Edmundo O'Gorman wrote in 1958, it became possible for humans to see for the first time that "the whole surface of the terraqueous globe, both water and land, . . . is a continuous whole."⁵ The relation of land and water was revolutionized. The world and the earth (or planet) were made one. Human understanding of the world could now grasp its global dimensions, and in 1540 a Spanish humanist, Juan Maldonado, writing in Latin, offered a fantastic account of a flight to the moon, from which he visualized the entire surface of the earth. A dozen years later Francisco López de Gómara—in his *Historia General de las Indias* (1552)—explained that "the world is only one and not many."⁶ This vast expansion of the terrain of humanity enlarged the horizon of human ambition.

The people of all continents, not only Europe, learned over the next century that "the world is an ocean and all its continents are islands."⁷ Global awareness and communication, which we may think of as the striking development of our own time, preceded America and made it possible. Within a quarter century of Columbus's final voyage, the world had been encompassed. Centuries later, Admiral Alfred Thayer Mahan, friend and adviser to Theodore Roosevelt, succinctly described the significance of this: the ocean ceased to be a barrier and became "a wide common, over which men may pass in all directions."⁸ Ironically, given this celebration of the human commons, Mahan was architect of the empire that, he believed, should consolidate America's strategic and commercial domination of the ocean.

The territory that later became the United States participated in the oceanic revolution, was one of its consequences, and shared its larger implications. Much of the meaning of American history is therefore entangled with this reinvention of the world, entangled in histories it shares with other peoples. Each, however, experienced this common history in its own particular way. Though for centuries what became the United States was marginal to those histories, in time, especially in our own time, not only is it very much at the center, but it is a powerful engine of global historical change. So the history of the United States is not and cannot be a history in and of itself. Its context until well into the twentieth century was the ocean world. And it cannot be appraised except as a part of this revolution in human existence—a revolution comparable in significance to the invention of agriculture or cities.

Thinking he had reached the Asian shores of the known world,

Columbus did not refer to the "new world," though he occasionally used the phrase "*otro mundo*," "another world."[9] It was the humanist scholar Peter Martyr who—in a letter of 1493—first employed the phrase "*novus orbis*."[10] More famously, Amerigo Vespucci, another humanist from Florence who was serving as the Medici agent in Lisbon, used the term "Mundus Novus" in an account of a voyage that brought him to the Western Hemisphere—initially a letter written upon his return in 1502 to his Medici patron and subsequently published.[11] This earned him recognition on the famous Waldseemüller map of 1507, which showed the hemisphere as a simple, distinct entity. On this map, one finds for the first time the word "America," the letters stretching roughly from today's Central America to Brazil, the area where Vespucci is supposed to have first seen the "New World."

Vespucci is fairly credited with recognizing that this new world had large implications for European cosmology. He grasped that he had seen "things that are not found written either by the ancients or modern writers."[12] By 1498, Columbus, too, had an inkling of this idea. The letter in which he used the phrase "another world" bears fuller quotation, for it shows Columbus, no less than the humanist, considering the lands he visited as "another world from that in which the Romans and Alexander and the Greeks labored to gain dominion."[13] But neither of them understood the significance of their discovery, which was not in the land they saw, but rather in the ocean that had made it accessible. They both missed the revolutionary transformation of the ocean from a barrier into a connector of continents, a medium for the global movement of people, money, goods, and ideas. By 1519–22, when Ferdinand Magellan (or his crew, since he did not survive the voyage, and one of his five ships, *Victoria*) circumnavigated the globe, the dimensions of this new ocean world had been fully experienced: the world was global, and it was unified by its oceans.

Rather quickly this new world included a novel form of power. Vasco da Gama's actions in South Asia might be seen as pointing quite directly to the foundations of a new kind of imperial power. His arrival in Calicut, on the Malabar Coast of southwestern India, in May 1498 shocked no one. He was greeted there by Moorish traders from Tunis, who knew of Christendom and spoke both Castilian and Genoese. By the end of the summer, da Gama had met there a Jewish merchant from Poland who spoke He-

brew, Venetian, Arabic, German, and a little Spanish.[14] Moreover, da
Gama had known about Calicut before he embarked; a key entrepôt for
the spice trade managed by Muslim merchants, it was his destination.[15]
And the merchants he met in Calicut knew about Europe. Da Gama found
cities and an active commercial and political life in the Indian Ocean region, unlike Columbus in the "new world." This notable point was made
by the Portuguese king in a somewhat gloating letter to Ferdinand and Is-
abella of Spain in 1499: his explorers, the king wrote, found "large cities,
large edifices and rivers, and great populations among whom is carried on
all the trade in spices and precious stones, which are forwarded in ships . . .
to Mecca, and thence to Cairo, whence they are dispersed around the
world. Of these [they] have brought [back] a quantity."[16]

Da Gama's arrival was not significant for the discovery of unknown
places or cultures; his having sailed around Africa was not unimaginable
to traders used to seaborne commercial relations on the east coast of
Africa. It was important, as the king's letter indicated, for commerce. But
we must recognize a larger historical significance in da Gama's presence
in the Indian Ocean. His second voyage, a few years later, marked the incorporation of the ocean into the domain of state power. He returned
with heavily armed ships, establishing a military regulation of the Indian
Ocean. With such militarization, the sea became a place of power as well
as of movement. The beginnings of modern "sea power" can be traced to
this moment.[17]

For the various societies populating the shores of the Indian Ocean
whose ships plied its waters, the ocean had been an edge and a passage.
Now it was a field for the exercise of power over the "essential social interactions of trade."[18] Ever so quickly oceans became a medium for the
lineaments of European power, which would in time enable the establishment of a series of European colonial empires in Asia. Sea power, invented
by the Portuguese in Asia, became, as Mahan later argued, a dominating
form of state power—the product and also the security of empire—well
into the twentieth century. And the contests among empires for oceanic
trade and naval power were, as we shall see, the context for the American
Revolution and the later emergence of the United States as a world
power.

It was trade, not militarism, that drew the attention of Adam Smith to the creation of the oceanic world. In *The Wealth of Nations* (1776), Smith wrote that "the discovery of America, and that of a passage to the East Indies by the Cape of Good Hope, are the two greatest and most important events recorded in the history of mankind." Smith was sympathetic to the American colonies, which were moving toward revolution as he wrote. He supported their opposition to British imperial fiscal and trade policies, against which his famous book was directed. But he did not ascribe world-historical importance to the American resistance. No Tom Paine he. For him, the big historical event between 1400 and 1800 was the oceanic interconnection of the continents, which opened "a new and inexhaustible market" that, Smith believed, promised to transform the world. "It gave occasion to new divisions of labor and improvement of art, which, in the narrow circle of ancient commerce, could not have taken place."

Smith's was not a simpleminded celebration of what we would today call the globalization of capital and trade. He acknowledged uncertainty about the ultimate effects of the emerging global economy. While it was clear to him that the effect of global trade on Europe was to increase both "enjoyments" and "industry," he worried about the future. He recognized and was critical of the enslavement and exploitation that accompanied the expansion of trade. "To the natives . . . both of the East and West Indies, all the commercial benefits which can have resulted from those events have been sunk and lost in the dreadful misfortunes they have occasioned."[19]

However expansive Smith's appraisal of the oceanic revolution, he captured its implications only in part. The geography of trade shifted from the Mediterranean Sea and the Indian Ocean to the "ocean sea," and this displacement was enormously consequential for the peoples of southern Europe, the Levant, Africa, central and South Asia, and the Americas. In 1300 much of Islamic Africa and the Mongol land empire embracing China, the Middle East, and India was flourishing, with greater wealth, power, and art than European Christendom. This contrast dramatically altered with the oceanic revolution. Had Portuguese and Spanish sailors not ventured out onto the ocean and established oceanic trade connections that included both the Americas and Asia, Christendom would have remained marginal in world history, on the periphery of the Afro-Eurasian world.[20]

The oceanic revolution coincided with a vital and creative moment in European thought and culture—the Renaissance, the "New Science," the Protestant Reformation, and Catholic renewal. These revolutionary innovations, too, affected the expansion of Europe. The relation of European values and these cognitive developments to the expansion of Europe's maritime reach and trade are much contested by economic and cultural historians, but the outcome is unmistakable: several emerging nation-states in western Europe were enriched and empowered, while others, Native Americans and Africans, paid a horrific price.[21]

Deadly diseases carried from Europe killed as many as three out of four Americans, perhaps nine out of ten in the Caribbean and Southern Hemisphere—the greatest human demographic disaster in the historical record.[22] In this biological exchange, Europeans contracted syphilis, a global event that makes the additional point that the age of discovery contains a still unwritten but important history of gender relations and sexuality.[23] The European quest for land in the Americas confronted those Native Americans who survived the diseases of initial contact with a multi-century battle for physical, cultural, and political survival. And the European search for labor on that land resulted in the sale of between eleven and twelve million Africans into the gruesome Atlantic slave trade—many of whom perished in transit or soon after. The result was, among other things, a demographic crisis for the peoples of Africa and the Americas.[24]

The era of oceanic exploration was a time of curiosity, of appraising peoples.[25] Cultures were compared, contrasted, and even partially inhabited. Languages were learned. When the Christians of Europe ventured out onto the ocean, they also invented anthropology—the study of the condition of being human.[26] Increasingly formalized knowledge was incorporated into their conceptions of colonization, and it facilitated dispossession, slavery, and even genocide. And mistakes about the cosmological position, character, and intentions of others in the new global world could be immediately consequential: the Aztecs, who were initially uncertain about the religious significance of Cortés and his Spanish soldiers, paid dearly for their hesitation. Perhaps the arriving Europeans miscalculated on Roanoke Island, thus accounting for the still unsolved mystery of the disappearance of the English settlers between 1587 and 1591.

Big questions were asked. Were the beings found beyond the ocean

God's people? Or were they an "other" belonging to the netherworld, the negation of the Christian world? Were they humans or monstrous beings, like those decorating the cathedrals? If they were not the children of Adam and Eve, who were they, and what rights did they have? Were there multiple creations? To discover an *otro mundo*, a world with other peoples, forced people to reconsider what was human. These questions would be revisited well into the nineteenth century, whether one was seeking to mount claims to human rights or to offer defenses of racism, slavery, and colonialism.

THE ISLAND WORLD

In the centuries before Columbus, the peoples of Afro-Eurasia, oblivious to the Western Hemisphere, thought of themselves as inhabiting the entire world *tout court*. The human world as they knew it was an island surrounded by an ocean. For the Greeks this was the *oikoumene*, or "human house."[27] Beyond this house, according to Dionysius, a Greek geographer writing in the first century of the Common Era, was the "vast abyss of the ocean" that "surrounds earth on every side."[28] "Ocean" is a Greek word meaning the "great outer sea" that encompassed the earth, which the Greeks believed was spherical. The Mediterranean was the "inner sea" at the center of this island world.[29] The word "Mediterranean" derives from Greek and Latin roots that mean "middle Earth/land," while in Arabic, the other great Mediterranean language, the sea was named by a word with a similar meaning, *al-Abyad al-Mutawasit*, "the middle white sea."[30]

The Greeks knew much of this world and had mapped it. It is they who named the Indies, by which they meant "all lands east of the Indus."[31] With their sophisticated understanding of geometry, they estimated what the globe's circumference was with remarkable accuracy. Strabo, the Greek historian and geographer who lived in the age of the Roman emperor Augustus, even understood the concept of sailing west to get to the East. Citing the third-century B.C. geographer Eratosthenes, he observed, "If the Atlantic ocean was not an obstacle we might easily pass by sea from Iberia to India, still keeping the same parallel."[32]

At the time of Jesus considerable trade and communication already connected the whole of Afro-Eurasia. The Roman writer Seneca noted that "all boundaries have shifted," for the "all-travelled world lets nothing remain in its previous station: the Indian drinks from Araxes' cold water, the Persians drink from the Elbe and the Rhine."[33] Between 200 B.C. and A.D. 400 trade routes linked the Roman Empire and the Han dynasty in China (much later denoted the Silk Road). There was so much early contact that the Western name for China came from the dynasty that preceded the Han, the Xin. Cross-cultural interactions extended from the China Sea to Britain, from the Caucasus to North Africa and South Asia. Culture, goods, and diasporic communities of traders traversed these long distances.[34]

Although the curricular story of "Western civilization" in our schools makes much of the fall of the Roman Empire, in fact from the fifth century A.D. onward the Mediterranean world flourished, whether under the rule of Constantinople or the Omayyad dynasty in Damascus.[35] Vital trade between and among several Muslim kingdoms and dynasties and Christian traders, especially the Venetians, brought prosperity to all participants. Later, when Sultan Mehmet II conquered Constantinople in 1453, the foundations were laid for a vast Ottoman Empire that came to surround much of the Mediterranean, reaching into Europe, Africa, and Asia. Mehmet II envisioned Constantinople as an Islamic successor to Rome, the center of "the empire of the world."[36] Worldwide trade and the cultural exchanges that accompanied it were facilitated by the Muslim dynasties, reaching a high point with the reign of the Ottoman sultan Suleiman the Magnificent (1520–66). Through their participation in this trade Europeans recognized both their dependence on the Muslim traders and the wealth that direct trade with Asia promised. Arab science also gave them maps and technologies that would enable their exploration of possible sea routes to the East.

The oceanic revolution was to transform the relations of the Atlantic powers to Mediterranean ones and, indeed, of Christendom to Islam. Over time, oceanic trade marginalized the Mediterranean world and weakened the Islamic empires. No wonder that Ottoman leaders, even though not explorers themselves, had great interest in the Portuguese and Spanish voyages; the first illustrated book published in the Ottoman Empire, in Istanbul, was Mehmet Efendi's *Book of the New World* (1583).[37]

But at the time of Columbus, the Atlantic Ocean was, as Fernand

Braudel remarks in his great history of the Mediterranean, an "annex" to the inland sea. The Mamluks and Ottomans, along with lesser Muslim dynasties, held this world together. Extended trade routes in the Mediterranean formed the core of the world's "dominant economy."[38]

The Ottoman Empire nearly circled the Mediterranean but, like the Roman and Byzantine empires before it, was basically a land empire. And while the Red Sea, Indian Ocean, and South China Sea sustained important maritime trade, perhaps surpassing that of the Mediterranean in volume, it was coastal, not oceanic.[39] The great Ottoman trade links were caravan routes that with the help of coastal shipping reached as far as Java in the east, Turkestan and Mongolia to the north, Poland and Hungary to the west, and into today's Eritrea and sub-Saharan Africa to the south. Ottoman trade with western Europe, a source of wealth for both Europe and the Ottomans, was typically carried west from Istanbul and other Ottoman ports in Venetian or Genoese ships.

Touching nearly all other empires, dynasties, and kingdoms of its time, the Ottoman Empire was at once extensive and paradoxically insular.[40] It not only connected the three divisions of the Afro-Eurasian island world but also constituted a civilization that encompassed the whole. Part of Islam's historical significance derives from the fact that for Muslims following these trade routes across Eurasia, Islam afforded a common reference point that facilitated trade, travel, and cultural communication while granting autonomy to a vast number and variety of minority cultures and peoples. At a time when Roman Christianity was a distinctly European religion, persecuting heretics and inattentive to eastern and Coptic Christians scattered in a wide arc of the Levant and eastern Europe, Islam embraced a range of peoples and gave local space to diverse religions and cultures.[41]

When the great Muslim traveler Ibn Battuta undertook his extended journeys between 1325 and 1354—estimated at more than seventy thousand miles—his experience was quite different from the Italian Marco Polo's adventure fifty years earlier, in 1271–95. Marco Polo had gone from a known culture into the unknown; there was no cultural continuity and very little knowledge that connected Venice to the court of the great khan in China. By contrast, Ibn Battuta, who began in Tangier, the place of his birth, remained largely within Dâr al-Islam ("the abode of Islam"), a single cultural universe marked by established lines of communication.

For example, early in his journey, in Alexandria, he met a "pious ascetic" who said: "I see that you are fond of travelling through foreign lands." Battuta affirmed the point, and the man continued: "You must certainly visit my brother Farid ad-Din in India, and my brother Rukn ad-Din in Sind, and my brother Burhan ad-Din in China, and when you find them give them greetings from me." Ibn Battuta reported that his "journeys never ceased until I had met these three that he named and conveyed his greetings to them."[42] Marco Polo's more isolated European culture did not provide him with the resources necessary for such a conversation and such contacts.[43]

The Ottomans did not want to assimilate or reform the cultures of the minority groups within their empire; they were satisfied with and depended on collecting taxes from them. They also sought non-Muslim male children who could be enslaved and serve the sultan; sometimes these men became powerful officials. On these terms, the Ottomans established a *"pax turcica"* that enabled a caravan trade converging on Istanbul to grow eastward for silk from China and, on more southern routes, pepper and spices from Southeast Asia; to the west it connected with Europe, mostly through Italian intermediaries who carried trade along the Atlantic coast and as far north as the Baltic Sea, and from Africa to the south came gold and slaves.[44]

The scope and energy of Islamic mercantile and artistic activity far exceeded anything in western Europe in the fourteenth and fifteenth centuries. Indeed, the centers of wealth and artistic activity in Europe owed their vitality to commercial and cultural relations with the Ottoman Empire. The system worked, but that the Muslim traders were profiting richly from the trade was painfully evident to the Europeans. Moreover, the line between legitimate business practices and piracy was difficult to draw in both the Muslim and the Christian worlds.[45] So the merchants of Europe resented their dependency; they felt captured by these trading patterns even as they profited from trade with the Ottomans and, to a lesser extent, with the Safavid, Mughal, and Songhai empires and from the China trade that passed through Ottoman hands.

Thus it was not their superior wealth or technology or civilization that accounts for the Europeans' expansion across the oceans. I am prepared to argue the opposite: that a sense of weakness, marginality, and inferiority impelled them toward invention and boldness on the high seas.

This interpretation of the discovery of the ocean world takes the beginnings of European settlement in North America away from a simple progressivist narrative of Western civilization triumphant and culminating with the United States. It can fairly be argued—and has been—that Europe's emergence was the consequence of its interaction with the societies of Africa, Asia, and America *after* 1492.[46]

Europeans felt besieged by the richer, expansive Islamic world. The well-known moment when the Spanish expelled the Muslims from Spain in 1492 has encouraged an easy assumption that the Islamic world then was both unitary and weakening, but that was not at all the case. Islam contained many societies, and the dynamic Ottoman and Mughal empires were reaching the height of their power. Even as Muslims lost the Iberian Peninsula, other Muslims were gaining a foothold in central Europe, establishing Ottoman power in Hungary and Austria. Indeed, Captain John Smith of Jamestown fame had, before his adventure in Virginia, fought with the Hungarians against the Ottomans and as a consequence spent time in an Istanbul jail.

The Ottomans were confident, sure of their power and cultural accomplishments. From the Ottoman perspective large parts of Europe were marginal, just as central Asia or sub-Saharan Africa was to Victorian Englishmen.[47] Genoa and Venice, however, were both well known and respected in the eastern Mediterranean; these cities had acquired great wealth in connecting the Ottoman trade with western Europe. The Genoese presence in Constantinople is still evidenced by the Galata Tower they built there, while the city-state of Venice was the center of Mediterranean commerce in the fifteenth century. Venetians focused on the eastern Mediterranean and the caravan routes available to them there, but the Genoese, being squeezed out (largely because they had joined the failed defense of Constantinople against the onslaught of Mehmet II in 1453), sought new opportunities and alternative routes, turning first to the Maghreb and then out onto the Atlantic. A Genoese map published in 1457 shows a European ship in the Indian Ocean, suggesting their ambition to find another path to the East.[48]

In these ventures they collaborated with the Iberians, especially the Portuguese. The Genoese merchant and maritime community in Lisbon was substantial, including Christopher Columbus in the 1480s, and it helped to fund Portuguese exploration and commercial enterprises.

Genoese also supplied exceptionally skilled sailors, who partially manned the Portuguese ships that sailed the African route to the Indies. And when the Portuguese developed sugar plantations, they did so in collaboration with the Genoese.[49]

This moment on either side of 1500 reveals a remarkable conjuncture in the history of capitalism and of the global economy. When the Italians invested in developing an oceanic economy to gain leverage in their Mediterranean trade relations with eastern markets, they were laying a foundation for the displacement of the earlier economy that had served them and the Ottomans so well. Equally important, by investing in sugar production and deciding to use African slaves, they laid the groundwork for the "plantation complex" that was to transform the global economy again in the seventeenth and eighteenth centuries.[50] The two together enabled North Atlantic economies to achieve dominance with a global reach in the nineteenth century.[51]

The European move onto the ocean had huge geopolitical consequences, shifting power to the North Atlantic. The Mediterranean world, with its connections to overland trade routes, lost its centrality,[52] and the Ottoman Empire progressively lost territory, decade by decade, in the eighteenth and nineteenth centuries. Some historians have interpreted this as a decline of the Ottoman Empire but these losses carried the possibility of strengthening the center. In any case, the fracturing of Ottoman authority on the periphery produced a power vacuum that European diplomats of the time called the "Eastern Question."

An Austrian diplomat in 1721 famously characterized the Ottoman Empire as the "sick man of Europe,"[53] but the Ottoman fate was determined not so much by its religion and culture as by its having been a land empire in an age of oceanic commerce and sea power. In fact, the Ottoman dynasty outlasted the Habsburg dynasty's Austro-Hungarian Empire by a few years, the second being dismembered at the 1919 Paris Peace Conference, and the first, reduced in size, surviving until the revolution led by Kemal Atatürk brought it to an end with the establishment of the Turkish Republic in 1923. The weakening of each of these largely agrarian, land-based empires is a geopolitical story, not a cultural or religious one, and it began in the seventeenth century, when they were first challenged and eventually displaced by new state formations. The future belonged to nations whose sailors and merchants mastered the ocean and its commerce.[54] Small trading nations with small home territories often found success in this new world.

GOING GLOBAL

Beginning in the twelfth century, people around the world, on every continent, began to benefit from a process of global warming. The result was population growth, more extensive empire building, and new levels of cultural vitality.[55] In the fourteenth century the Empire of Mali was at its height, recognized for its wealth and power throughout the Mediterranean world. Across the Atlantic, the Aztec Empire consolidated its power, ruling over a vast region of client states with a capital, Tenochtitlán, that in 1325 had perhaps a quarter-million residents; it was the world's largest city when Cortés arrived early in the sixteenth century.

But the fourteenth century was not kind to Europe or China. These two parts of the island world suffered devastating losses of life from famine and the plague. If the Mongol conquests had established safe trading routes that brought new levels of prosperity, the great caravans following them across central Asia spread the terrible Black Death. More than sixty million Chinese died, and Europe lost one-third of its population.

No one knows exactly how it began. It seems likely, however, that social disruptions following the roaming conquests of the Mongols made many societies susceptible to this devastating contagious disease. It is certain that their trade routes became channels for its worldwide distribution. It was carried from Southeast Asia, where it probably began, to China, and across central Asia to Europe. The plague disrupted regular trade, and the caravan routes became identified as conduits of the Black Death. The spread of the plague was one reason that Europeans began looking in the fifteenth century for alternatives to the land routes to the East. Perhaps the sea would be safer.

In the fifteenth century Europe's new energy was revealed in its commitments to exploration and increases in long-distance trade, and also in artistic, scientific, and technological innovation. Such developments can rarely be explained, but perhaps the innovations were a response to the challenge of Islam as well as to the disruptions of established social prac-

tices and cultural assumptions that the plague had caused. Yet this striking new social energy was evident not only in Europe. There were indi-
cations of it from China to Portugal, from the Aztec Empire to the
Ottoman, Safavid, and Mughal empires in central Asia, to the Songhai
Empire in West Africa. While Europe brought its new energy to the
ocean, the house of Osman consolidated its massive Ottoman land empire, and the Muscovy Empire began its expansion to the east, reaching
the Pacific in 1639.

Looking for the most likely leader of the move onto the ocean in the
early fifteenth century, one would not have focused on Europe. The Chinese, not the Portuguese, might have seemed to be the most likely to en-
compass the globe by sea and establish a global trading empire. The great
Chinese fleets then had ships far larger than those of Columbus (four hundred feet long to the mere eighty-five feet of the *Santa María*) that were
exploring the coasts of Southeast Asia, South Asia, and East Africa. It has
been proposed that Zheng He, a Muslim eunuch who was a powerful
Chinese admiral, circumnavigated the globe between 1421 and 1423, almost exactly a century before Ferdinand Magellan's voyage.[56] Whatever
the full extent of this early Chinese move onto the ocean and of the
client-state trading partners Zheng He established, Chinese policy
shifted in 1433: as the result of internal political and fiscal changes, government subsidies for such maritime activities ended, and without government support, which was essential for the very large ships, private
traders turned to regional trading in smaller ships.[57]

Even with this reduction of maritime activity, China remained the
economic engine of Asia. Its robust economy (and, to a lesser extent, the
economies of other Asian empires) prepared the Asian foundation that
made the ocean actually work as a field for global commerce.

The Ming dynasty (1368–1644) had witnessed a transition to a "silver
economy" by the end of the fifteenth century. The reason for this development was partly government policy (making silver legal for paying taxes
in the 1430s), but silver was also needed for China's growing economy
and seems to have had significant value as an economic "good" as well as
a medium of exchange. As a result, silver came to have a much higher
value (compared with gold or any other measure) in China than anywhere
else in the world; between 1540 and 1640, its value was 100 percent
higher than in Europe. Japan had supplied China with silver, but China,

with about a quarter of the world's population and perhaps 40 percent of its economy, had an enormous demand for it, and the demand was eventually supplied by the silver mines of America, which between 1500 and 1800 produced roughly 85 percent of the world's silver; between 1527 and 1821, as much as half of the output went to China. This animated not only the Chinese economy but global commerce as well. When the Chinese relaxed restrictions on maritime trade in 1567, the Asian demand for silver and the global flow of bullion increased dramatically, perhaps doubling almost instantly.[58] As a result, an apparently inexhaustible market emerged for the seemingly limitless production of the silver mines of Mexico and Peru.

The movement of silver from Acapulco to Manila (founded in 1571 precisely to manage this trade) created a global economy built on Pacific as well as Atlantic sea-lanes.[59] Without silver from the Spanish colonies in South America and the Ming dynasty's policy that gave it trade value in exchange for the sophisticated manufactured goods from China and, to a lesser extent, India, it is unlikely that Europeans could have become such successful global traders.[60] But silver now became the currency of the global trading system and Europeans the well-rewarded intermediaries. Without these Asian developments, the prospects for settlement and development in the Americas would have been less promising; public or private investments there would not have been made. Spain's success in the New World therefore depended not only on its securing control of the mines of Peru and Mexico from the disease-weakened Native Americans but also on the expanding economies of Asia.[61] Ironically, the flow of silver into China caused rapid urbanization and speculation there, and inflation made China ever more dependent on the constant flow of silver, which meant that the Ming dynasty became vulnerable to the inevitable interruptions in the global movement of bullion. The resulting economic and social instability seems to have contributed to its collapse in 1644.[62]

In his history of capitalism in the early-modern period, Fernand Braudel declares that Portugal was "the detonator of an explosion which reverberated round the world." Having conquered the Moors in their part of the Iberian Peninsula in 1253, the Portuguese also consolidated a surprisingly modern state, accomplishing what Braudel calls a "bourgeois revolution" in 1385. If the phrase is anachronistic, the point holds: the newly established monarchy was organized in alliance with Portugal's mercantile class, and the result was a market-friendly state. Lisbon was an outward-looking, cosmopolitan city eager for trading opportunities.[63]

Evidently influenced by Genoa, the Portuguese focused on trying to find a way around the Venetian and Ottoman monopolies over the Mediterranean and land routes to the Indies.[64] This focus was one reason why they declined Columbus's petition for a transatlantic voyage. The other was their better knowledge of geography. Following ancient Greek estimates of the circumference of the earth, they thought correctly that Columbus had underestimated it by 20 percent, an error, the Portuguese rightly understood, that would make it unlikely that his plan would bring him to Asia.

They had grasped early that "if you are strong in ships, the commerce of the Indies is yours," as their advocate for the sea, Prince Henry the Navigator, put it. They were strong in ships, and they captured the seaborne pepper and spice trade for more than a century.[65] Portuguese progress down the west coast of Africa was not dramatic; it was incremental and persistent. Portuguese sailors and merchants were as cautious as they were skilled.[66] In 1415, the Portuguese established an African claim at Ceuta, just south of Gibraltar; their first fortified trading post in West Africa came in 1445 on the coast of present-day Mauritania. They did not stop there. They sailed south, dreaming of the east, and established more such enclaves, called *feitoria* in Portuguese and corrupted into the English "factory."

It is often said that Europeans limited themselves to coastal enclaves in Africa because of the problem of local diseases there. That was surely a factor, but so was the strength of the polities they encountered.[67] It is worth noting that the first Portuguese territorial colonization was at São Tomé and other offshore islands that they found uninhabited. The enclaves the Portuguese established on the mainland took little land and demanded only limited authority because the African polities, with their coastal navies and possession of the home ground, were able to negotiate from a position of strength. Historians are increasingly realizing that Europeans did not dominate on the ground; in this early phase, empire was shaped by accommodation and by the mutual pursuit of economic or other interests.

Before the arrival of the Portuguese in the 1490s, the Indian Ocean had been the center of a vast system of trading cities connected to all known regions of the island world. The city of Malacca, founded in 1380, had as many as fifty thousand inhabitants at the start of the sixteenth century, and a Portuguese visitor declared that as a center of trade it "has no equal in the world."[68] A trans-regional trade system between the Indian Ocean and the Mediterranean, linked by the Red Sea, went back to ancient times, when the Egyptians had built a canal from the Nile to the Red Sea. This trade, encouraged and facilitated by the Ottomans, was known to the Portuguese, but only indirectly.

Portuguese ambitions in India were initially contested by the Muslim rulers there, whose power was equal to that of the Portuguese. But they did not press the issue, since they had more important strategic interests elsewhere, while the Portuguese were determined to establish themselves. It has been speculated that had these Indian Muslims displaced the early Portuguese enclaves, any Christian "factories" in India might have been postponed indefinitely.[69] Instead, they traded with the Europeans. Now the Portuguese had direct access by sea to the Mughal Empire and the trade of the East, and for about a century they monopolized the European market for pepper and spices.[70]

The Portuguese also anticipated the later development of the Atlantic sugar economy. During the Crusades, Christians had discovered the sweetness of sugar, originally a product of Bengal but long manufactured in the Levant. Production of this delicious luxury now moved across the Mediterranean, initially under the auspices of an expansive Islam, which brought its cultivation as far as Spain. Later Italian investors expanded its cultivation, and sugar production was established in Cyprus, Sicily, and the Maghreb. In the fifteenth century the Portuguese collaborated with Italian investors and growers to develop sugar plantations on the Atlantic islands of Madeira and São Tomé, while the Spanish established plantations on the Canary Islands.

Both Arabs and Europeans used African slaves in this work. Agricultural slavery was a novelty, which may have been propelled by the labor shortages produced by the legacy of the Black Death.[71] It is important also to keep in mind, however, that between 1530 and 1780 at least a million white Christian Europeans, mostly from the Balkans and Caucasus, were enslaved by the Muslim Arabs of the Barbary Coast. Most of these slaves, typically captured in various conflicts, were put to work in cities and towns or on ships as sailors.[72] The difference in the *mode* of unfree labor imposed on Europeans and Africans warrants emphasis. Slavery in Muslim societies was generally not agricultural. Europeans were familiar with a different form of unfree agricultural labor, serfdom, but they did not employ it on sugar plantations in the Americas. Serfdom was a form of village or communal labor, while slavery in the emerging plantation complex was based on individual slaves, though they typically worked in gangs. Gang labor as a form of slavery had not existed in Africa or the eastern Mediterranean or the Muslim world, except in the salt marshes of the Tigris-Euphrates valley.[73]

The new pattern of unfree labor in the Mediterranean and the Atlantic islands was thus a major innovation. It pointed toward the industrial organization of the future, not back to the patterns of slavery known in African villages. Here was the root idea of the plantation system that was later to develop on a large scale in Brazil and later yet on the Caribbean islands.

PEOPLE FROM THE SEA

The oceanic revolution touched peoples of all continents in many ways—cultural, cosmological, and economic. Every continent experienced the unprecedented arrival of an unexpected people from the sea—and these seafarers came to know other peoples. On every continent, the arrival of the harbingers of a new world elicited a similar phrase: they were always the people from the sea; the Chinese called them "ocean barbarians."[74]

The novelty of the seaborne arrival of the Europeans was greater for Americans than for the various peoples of Afro-Eurasia who already had trading relationships, even if at a distance, with other continents. The shock of the new is evident in the words of an ordinary fisherman from a shore village who was taken in 1519 to the Aztec capital to report to the ruler, Montezuma, who wanted information about the landing of Cortés. He told him, "When I went to the shore of the great sea, there was a mountain range or small mountain floating in the midst of the water, and moving here and there . . . My lord, we have never seen the like of this."[75]

The native peoples of the Western Hemisphere, the first Americans, had been isolated from the island world. While they had extensive north-south trading networks, they had not ventured out onto the ocean. Given that the Aztecs did not deploy the wheel for mercantile purposes (using it only on children's toys) and the Incas had only llamas as beasts of burden, they might have considered making more extensive use of maritime transport, but they did not, keeping to coastal navigation mostly devoted to fishing, not trade. But with the arrival of the Europeans they were pulled into the ocean world. The new world of America formed by the arrival of the Europeans offered opportunities for new trade and new items of trade, including manufactured iron implements and textiles, to say nothing of weapons. Also, alliances were possible. Very early, for example, the Tlaxcalans on Mexico's Gulf Coast recognized in Cortés an ally who might (and did) enable them to strike back at the Aztecs who had turned them into a client people. As it turned out, the Spanish profited from the alliance more than the Tlaxcalans did, a pattern that would be repeated.

Unlike the Western Hemisphere, Africa had all along been part of the island world, with plenty of trade and intercultural relations with Asia and Europe. All three shared the Mediterranean trade routes, and the Swahili port cities on the east coast of Africa opened out to the Indian Ocean.[76] Da Gama had recognized their importance and lingered there before going on to India. Along various routes, African gold and slaves went to the Middle East, Europe, and Asia, but communication between sub-Saharan Africa and the Mediterranean world was limited; west equatorial Africa was on the distant periphery of the Muslim trading empires.[77] Still, caravans of five thousand and more camels regularly traversed the Sahara, carrying goods as well as Muslims going on the pilgrimage to Mecca. "Ships of the desert" from the Maghreb coast crossed the Sahara to Timbuktu, connecting the Mediterranean with the Niger River, giving access to the network of trade routes in West Africa.[78] But the Atlantic was a barrier for Africans, as it was for Americans and Europeans. The opening of the oceans made a new world for them as for everyone else.[79]

The North African kingdom of Morocco was more involved with the sea than were other parts of Atlantic Africa, and in 1603 King Ahmad al-Mansur suggested to Queen Elizabeth of England that they jointly colonize America. Both monarchs, he pointed out, reviled the Spanish, and they could together expel them from America and "posesse" the land and "keep it under our dominion for ever." He presumed that England would not find the "extremetie of heat" in the Spanish Empire in America suit-

able, and suggested that the actual settlement be undertaken by Moroc-
cans rather than the English.[80] It did not happen, of course, yet that such
a proposal could be made suggests the previously unimagined possibilities prompted by the oceanic revolution.

When the Portuguese arrived on the Guinea coast in the early fifteenth century, the geography of trade and patterns of cultural contact
shifted, as did the material conditions of trade. The experience of personal
movement itself changed dramatically; being a passenger on an ocean-
going vessel is quite different from being one on a "ship of the desert."
Ships can carry far more and larger goods than caravans can, and the
number of intermediaries is greatly reduced, likewise the number of taxing jurisdictions. But even this considerable change in the material culture of trading did not immediately suggest the magnitude of the
transformation that followed the arrival of the "men from the sea," as
West Africans called Europeans.

Yet the shock of difference when European met African was less than
we might expect. Portugal and Kongo had similar rates of agricultural
productivity and similar living standards; both had dynastic kingdoms
organized by kinship and clientage; trade and political relations were well
managed. The cosmologies of the Europeans and Africans were profoundly different, however. For example, in the Kongo cosmology white
people were believed to live under the ocean, which made it plausible to
have white men arrive from the sea. And while Afonso, the Christian
king of Kongo in the early sixteenth century, had extensive diplomatic
relations with Portugal, France, and the Vatican, they were conducted, as
Wyatt MacGaffey has observed, "on the basis of a shared and double misunderstanding." The cosmologies differed, but the frameworks of interpretation were complementary.[81] There were enough seeming parallels in
the cultural repertoire of the two peoples that pretending convergence allowed for fruitful miscommunication.

Similar patterns of interaction occurred in North America, where the
Nahuatl speakers of Mexica could communicate and trade with Europeans on the basis of false assumptions about each partner's fundamental
concepts.[82] The interaction of Europeans and Native Americans in the
Great Lakes region operated similarly. A "middle ground" was established where conversants incorrectly but usefully deployed items from the
cultural repertoire (as they understood it) of the other.[83]

Africans and Portuguese recognized and embraced new opportunities to trade a variety of goods. The incremental changes associated with the new oceanic world had cumulative consequences. By the early sixteenth century it was clear that trade was transforming not only the economies but the societies involved, and the changes accelerated. Soon Europeans and Africans were drawn increasingly into a monstrous trade in human bodies. King Afonso of Kongo had early doubts; in a letter to the king of Portugal in 1526 he wrote, "We cannot reckon how great the damage is and so great, Sire, is the corruption and licentiousness that our country is being depopulated."[84]

That was only the beginning. The Portuguese and then the Dutch and British began trading for slaves, and innumerable individual decisions made by Africans and Europeans created a system of exchange that expanded over the next three centuries to dimensions beyond all expectations and even comprehension. This commerce in human beings brought power and wealth to a few African traders; the nobility of Kongo was able to live in a "grand style."[85] More important, the trade brought misery and death for millions of Africans. In Africa itself it weakened social institutions—from family, to clan, to village, to economies and polities. The loss of so many men skewed the gender ratio, promoting polygamy but also increasing the number of dependents for each provider.[86] There was also a multigenerational process by which African craftsmen lost their skills. In 1500 Portugal imported West African cotton textiles; by 1600 the flow had reversed.[87] That a trade as large as that in slaves could be managed in Africa by Africans is a discomfiting but real testament to the effectiveness of African social institutions, but its success—the export of more than eleven million people, plus the children they would have contributed—impoverished the institutional life of West and Central Africa.[88]

There was also a much older slave trade to the east, from East Africa, the Sahara, and the Red Sea regions to various Muslim societies. Conjectures about numbers are less secure, but during the first thousand years of Islamic slavery (650–1600), between four and five million Africans may have been enslaved; estimates for the period 1600–1900 range from four to six million.[89]

Not initially but very soon and then exclusively, Europeans looked to Africa as a source of human bodies. At first the Portuguese took African slaves to supplement the declining supply of white slaves from the Caucasus, but gradually the quest for labor evolved into a racial system of slavery. It is worth noting that in 1500 Africans and persons of African descent were a minority of the world's slaves and by 1700 a majority.[90] The numbers are important, but so are the differences in the experience of slavery. Unlike the white or African slaves in the Muslim world, by 1700 (before then for many) Africans in the Atlantic world were treated more as units of labor than as humans, a reduction that not only was morally repulsive but also tragically narrowed the image and meaning of Africa. The legacy of slavery, which necessarily looms so large in our collective historical memory, obscures a fuller history and richer knowledge of Africa and Africans and still clouds our understanding.

Thus it comes to many as a surprise that in the fourteenth century Africa represented wealth. The continent was known for its crafts and famed for its gold, which sustained the powerful empires and court cities of the interior. The Mediterranean world's main source of gold was the Empire of Mali, which extended more than a thousand miles east to west. The mythic story was told and retold of Mansa Musa, the Malian ruler legendary for his wealth. When he traveled to Mecca for the hajj in 1324, the gold he brought with him—and spent—during his time in Cairo flooded Egypt's economy, resulting in a devaluation of gold specie by perhaps as much as 25 percent and producing financial havoc. By reputation he was known and respected in Europe; a Catalan mapmaker in 1375 portrayed him as a European ruler in dress and the accoutrements of power.[91]

Had Europeans explored the African interior in the fourteenth century when the Empire of Mali was at its peak, rather than a century or more later when Mali had overexpanded and then declined, might the image of Africa have been more positive and the history of Europeans and Africans different? Having heard so much about Mansa Musa's wealth, the beauty of his court, and the power of his empire yet finding so little may have disappointed the Europeans and prompted them to exaggerate all that seemed to be missing, encouraging their conclusion that Africans lacked civilization and were incapable of political life.[92]

Whether for this or other reasons, Europeans invented a new name for Africans. No historian has satisfactorily explained why the Portuguese resorted to the word "Negro" (which was incorporated into the English language by the mid-sixteenth century, the *Oxford English Dictionary* citing its first known use in 1555). But the consequence of using this neologism can be understood all too well. Older names—Africans, or Moors, or, oldest of all, Ethiope—referred to a place and to a history. But "Negro" dissolved historical identity, and color replaced culture. The new name effectively denied the history and culture of Africa's people and distinctive polities. It undermined African claims to history, civilization, religion, culture, or, finally, as Cedric Robinson has emphasized, any "humanity that might command consideration." The ideological utility of this term is transparent: it was developed in concert with the creation of the Atlantic slave system.[93]

The rise of the slave trade produced new coastal cities, shifting energy away from the old internal trade routes and craft centers. At the same time, specie from the New World swamped the gold trade of Mali and the Sudan, which led to further decline.[94] These historically contingent developments facilitated the invention of the "Negro" and the European notion of a homogeneous Africa, an Africa that was no more than a source of slaves in the minds of slavers and, tragically, of many later critics of the slave trade.[95]

The Portuguese in East Africa and Asia did not mainly seek territory, since they were traders who wanted to establish trading posts. The Portuguese negotiated to establish *feitoria*, or fortified enclaves, at Sofala (East Africa), Hormuz (Persian Gulf), Goa (India), and Malacca (Malay).[96] Soon they were profiting immensely from the Indian Ocean trade—enough to consider the Western Hemisphere, which early on might have been theirs for the taking, of only secondary importance. But they did not transform Lisbon into a great European capital of global trade and banking, a failure to exploit the flow of capital associated with its trade that would in time prove costly. Power and wealth gained through trade in the Indian Ocean went to more northern cities, nearer the major markets—first Antwerp and later Amsterdam.[97]

When Amsterdam used its wealth, mercantile skill, and naval power to establish its presence in the Indian Ocean, it displaced the Portuguese. The Dutch East India Company, established in 1602, quickly became one of the world's largest and wealthiest business enterprises. Amsterdam, capital of a small, federated, and newly independent state, was the last city able to build an empire as Venice and Genoa had done.[98] True, the British Empire was launched and managed from London, but seventeenth-century London's economy was built on its position at the heart of a dynamic national economy.[99] The future of European empires would now belong to strong nations.

Portugal's century was the sixteenth, Amsterdam's the seventeenth. Causality is implied in this succession: the Dutch pushed the Portuguese aside, but that is only part of the explanation. When the political and economic elites in Japan, Burma, the eastern Ottoman Empire, and Oman withdrew support from the Portuguese, they became more vulnerable to the Dutch challenge.[100] The first Dutch ship reached Japan in 1600, and beginning in 1601 the Dutch began trading directly and regularly with Canton (Guangzhou). Two years later, they landed in Ceylon and in 1605 captured the Portuguese fort in Malacca, making it the first base for the Dutch East India Company. Like that of the Portuguese, their interest was trade, not territory, and they established their trading posts without making territorial claims. They founded Batavia (today's Jakarta) in 1619, but the Dutch population there remained very small, much smaller than the substantial community of Chinese merchants who were settled there.

One cannot but be struck by how few were the Europeans who established and sustained these first "empires" in the East Indies. And this points to an important truth: these empires were the result less of overwhelming force than of accommodation by local rulers and elites. The colors of empires on maps misleadingly imply a demographic and institutional presence of the European power abroad, suggesting firm and geographically extensive control did not exist. These early European empires were less about force than about negotiation, even if not always between equals.

The Dutch like the Portuguese particularly valued their interests in the East Indies, but the Atlantic beckoned. In 1621 the Dutch *West* India Company was established to compete with the Portuguese in Africa and America—mainly in hopes of gaining a position in the slave trade and in the sugar colonies. The Dutch accomplished both objectives. And such was the global context of the settlement of New Amsterdam on Manhattan Island.

Americans and American histories tend to put the Dutch settlement of New York at the start of a linear development of what would become the American metropolis. But that appropriates for American history what in fact belongs to Dutch history and to the history of oceanic commerce and capitalism. New Amsterdam was part of a global Dutch commercial strategy, and the settlement on Manhattan was on the periphery of the periphery of the empire. Not only were East Indian interests more valuable and more visible from the Dutch point of view; but even in the Americas, Manhattan was minor compared with the far more important and profitable Brazilian sugar colony of Pernambuco, which they had wrested from the Portuguese. If the nineteenth-century American fable has it that the Indians sold Manhattan to the Dutch for the equivalent of twenty-four dollars, it is doubtful that the Dutch valued it at much more. They fought bitterly in global wars to hold on to their Brazilian, African, and Asian possessions but made little effort to maintain control of New Amsterdam when challenged by the English in 1664. In 1665 and again later, after recapturing the city in the Third Anglo-Dutch War, the Dutch returned New Amsterdam to the English, demanding instead Surinam, which they had also captured.

France, a large territorial state, was slower to move out onto the ocean. Before the end of the seventeenth century, however, the French, too, had a global empire, with holdings in South Asia, the Caribbean, and North America. As for the Russians, who had been moving east across Siberia toward America, they mainly wanted animal furs—first sable, until they exhausted it, and then sea otter. They established semi-military settlements where they could create a brutal regime to "harvest" sea otter by means of "forced commerce" with the Aleuts. This had a devastating impact on the Aleut community, whose numbers were reduced from 200,000 in 1750 to about 2,000 in 1800.[101]

Why, one wonders, was the American experience so much more brutal than other long-distance intercultural and market exchanges? And why did European territorial possession become so important there, and so quickly? For several centuries, Christendom had traded with Islam without settlement, save for small "trade diasporas." Europeans seemed to have no particular interest in exploring the land crossed by their caravans or, in the Indies, the hinterland of their "factories." (Later, of course, Europe's policies in Asia and Africa would be quite different.) Yet in America mapping and settlement were achieved within fifty years of Columbus's voyage.[102] There seem to be two broad reasons, with a few added corollaries.

First, the Americas seemed to be unpopulated or underpopulated. There is a tragic truth to this, for the very first European diseases to arrive in the Western Hemisphere substantially depopulated it, most dramatically in the Caribbean Islands and southward. This thinness of population seemed to the Europeans to be matched by a thinness of civilization—notably in the Caribbean, where their initial contact was made and lasting impressions formed. To them, this underpopulation and lack of "civilization" legitimated their conquest and taking possession.[103]

The English especially tended to measure both civilization and proprietary claims by the presence or absence of agriculture. If the Indians did not cultivate the land, they had no right to it. While it is true that Native Americans relied heavily on the hunt, many tribes with whom the English came into contact did in fact cultivate the land, but gender blindness among other things seems to have blocked this from English view. Agricultural work was something men did in England, but men in America hunted, and the English did not recognize gardens and fields tended by women as agriculture.

A shortage of labor to extract wealth from the New World—literally, in the case of the mines of Peru and Mexico—seemed to demand some strategy of building population there, whether by voluntary settlement or by force. The latter method, in the form of racial slavery, became the principal solution; between the mid-fifteenth and the mid-nineteenth centuries more Africans than Europeans crossed the Atlantic to the Americas. Among women before 1800 the ratio of Africans to Europeans was even higher. Only in New England was the sex ratio among Europeans balanced.[104]

These conditions were in striking contrast to the situation in Asia. India and China not only were manifestly well populated—China already had one-fourth of the world's population—but showed evidence of old, historical civilizations, even if Europeans thought of them as decayed or, worse, decadent.[105] And it was of practical importance that these countries had well-known and highly valued goods to trade. Urbanization was probably more advanced in China, India, and the Arab trading regions than in Europe.[106] Their substantial coastal cities were filled with merchants prepared for trade. And, finally, while smallpox killed natives in the Western Hemisphere, malaria threatened Europeans in Africa and Asia.

The English had additional reasons for settling in North America. Seventeenth-century England was experiencing an increase in population (a premonition of a later demographic transition, which in the nineteenth century produced a modern rate of population growth in industrializing England). Without an adequate understanding of either economics or demography, the English were not sure what was happening, but immediately visible evidence seemed to indicate overpopulation and consequent poverty. Later Adam Smith explained that long-distance trade might produce metropolitan prosperity (or, as we would now say, jobs), but the idea of disposing of some of the population elsewhere appealed to various early proponents of colonization and colonists. Moreover, a substantial disaffected religious minority was ready to leave England for a new place where they might worship more freely. These strongly committed Protestants might perform an additional service as a northern bulwark to limit the expansion and influence of Catholic Spain in the New World.

As this last point indicates, religion was a very important part of the colonial adventures of Spain, France, and England. The oceanic revolution laid the foundations of modern capitalism, but the initial impulse and sustaining commitment for the early colonizers was in large part religious. Both Catholics and Protestants understood the Western Hemisphere to be providential—something God had reserved for Christians. And that implied the obligation to pursue Satan and convert unbelievers to the one true faith. This is evident in the clerical discourse of Protestant England, Holland, and Scandinavia, as well as among their imperial competitors the Roman Catholic French, Spanish, and Portuguese.[107]

Beginning with the initiation of the annual departure of Spanish galleons from Acapulco to Manila in the 1570s, the New World of the Americas linked the Pacific and Atlantic oceans. I have emphasized trade connections, but culture, too, encompassed the two realms. A striking expression of this is found in a massive painting that hung over the main door of a seventeenth-century Cuzco church, which showed a Jesuit carrying Christianity to Asia. The Jesuit mission to the Pacific became part of the "lived religion" of Peru, a place we may identify with the Atlantic because of the Spanish influence there, but of course its coast is on the Pacific.[108] Later, an important Russian presence (more substantial in the North Pacific than we usually realize) underlined the Pacific dimensions of the American experience.

In the eighteenth century, Europeans explored the Pacific Ocean, which covers one-third of the earth's surface, in the interests of science as well as trade. Inspired by Linnaeus, naturalists hoped to map a "global botanical system." Major expeditions were mounted by Admiral Louis-Antoine de Bougainville for the French, and Alessandro Malaspina led an expedition for Spain in 1789–94. Malaspina, who modeled his expedition on Captain James Cook's three between 1768 and 1779 and knew of Bougainville's expedition, too, collected scientific information and established Guam and the Marianas as focal points for trade, science, and navigation in the South Pacific, much as Cook had earlier done under British auspices at Hawaii.

Geological and botanical knowledge was often linked to the commercial ambitions of the imperial powers, but with Cook's first voyage, sponsored by Sir Joseph Banks of the Royal Society, the natural-history agenda was heightened and made more specific. The expedition included non-English naturalists and went beyond the national exclusivity and rivalry of so much of the earlier mercantilist-inspired exploration. The discoveries made by Cook and others of the small islands of the South Pacific encouraged an awareness of ecological changes. Just as contact with new peoples in the sixteenth century prompted the invention of anthropology, these scientific voyages prompted a critical discussion about climatic and ecological issues. Modern environmentalism was born, it seems, in the eighteenth-century phase of imperial enterprise, as scientists discovered in the self-contained colonial spaces of small islands—almost laboratories—evidence of the social and ecological costs of incorporation into European commercial empires.[109]

Cook's third voyage made Hawaii known to the Atlantic world at about the time of the American Revolution. Tragically, Cook was murdered there, but afterward the island became a magnet, drawing together a wide range of people—some, like missionaries, with a purpose; others, like the sailor Herman Melville, not yet a writer, wanderers. In the nineteenth century it was a key communications center for two great enterprises: Pacific commerce and the scientific understanding of the ocean world. At Honolulu, a cosmopolis in the center of the world's largest body of water, one could find scientists and sailors, merchants and missionaries, whalers and naval officers exchanging information about opportunities for trade, natural-history findings, and ethnographies of the Pacific societies.[110] Early on it was identified as being in the American orbit, though: as early as 1805 a British sea captain referred to the island as an American "commercial hive."[111]

As is so evident today, immigration follows trade routes and capital flows. Transpacific trade invited transpacific migrations. In fact, the first Chinese and Filipinos to settle in what is now the United States shipped out of Manila as crew on a returning galleon and jumped ship in Acapulco, worked for a while in Mexico City, and in the 1760s made their way to the bayous of Louisiana, then a Spanish colony, where they established the oldest continuing Asian-American community in North America. It was incorporated into the United States when Thomas Jefferson purchased Louisiana from the French in 1803.[112]

I hope it is clear at this point just how much a global perspective disrupts and reframes the usual narrative of American history, which conventionally sees American development as a continuous process of westering from the northeastern colonies.[113] In fact the initial settlements in what is now the United States were in Florida (St. Augustine, 1560), Virginia (Jamestown, 1607), and New Mexico (Santa Fe, 1610),[114] and from the beginning the territory that became the United States touched both the Atlantic and the Pacific and was shaped by a multiplicity of historical processes. People and influences arrived in it from all points of the compass and settled in every region.

During the sixteenth and seventeenth centuries no one could envision a single polity being formed in this huge continental space.[115] The early settlements were points on a map of European global quests for wealth and power. There was no path, no way of imagining one, that promised a new society or a new nation in North America. The English arriving on the northeastern coast were not bold imperialists or particularly capable settlers. The New World was, after all, new to them, and they responded to it with considerable uncertainty and fear. The native peoples, more often than not, set the agenda in the first interactions: accepting the arrival of the English, they helped them to survive in the New World they knew so well. English appreciation of their own limitations did not last more than a half century, but that is more than a moment, and it warrants our recall.[116]

The Americas as a whole—the north-south divide was not yet firm—were a singular space marked by multiple sites of contestation and showing on many imperial grids. No one had a sense of being present at the "origin" of a new country. Space was more important than time. Settlers and imperial authorities were more aware of the points of the compass and of the territory claimed by different religious confessions than of the development over time of their new colonial establishments. History as it was made was marked by lateral glances, with the various actors worried about encroachments from the others. Religious rivalry between Protestant and Catholic powers combined with imperial strategies and commercial considerations to determine the opportunities and tactics at any given moment.

ATLANTIC CREOLES

Premodern trade in the Afro-Eurasian island world, whether across land routes or on the sea-lanes of the Mediterranean and Baltic seas and the Indian Ocean, was undertaken by family firms and a myriad and sequence of small operators.[117] Only in the seventeenth century did the Dutch, English, and French develop highly capitalized joint-stock companies. Nor was trade regulated by states, as it would be later, under mercantilist principles. At various nodes of the trading networks were cosmopolitan centers where merchants congregated into overlapping trade diasporas.

Not surprisingly, this familiar, infinitely flexible mode of conducting long-distance trade was transferred to the new oceanic trade pioneered by the Portuguese. Not requiring substantial settlement or territorial acquisition, it was quite simple. Diverse traders, each tied to a trade network in his homeland that gave him his market, congregated in coastal cities, where the mix could be quite cosmopolitan; in the port cities of Gujarat and Malacca, for example, one could find Africans, Persians, Armenians, Arabs, Jews, Portuguese, Genoese, Dutch, English, and Hanseatic merchants.

It is unlikely that most of these merchants went abroad intending to become permanent expatriates, but many stayed on, and the longer they did, the more valuable they were to the family enterprise and to their networks back home. Their "local knowledge" and local contacts were crucial to the development of oceanic long-distance trade. A worldwide market is not impersonal and anonymous, not even in the twenty-first century.[118] Europe's oceanic trade with the East Indies and with Africa and the Americas was managed by individuals with personal knowledge of and ties with their counterparts on-site and at a distance.

The Portuguese and Dutch oceanic enterprises were, then, not empires of settlement but empires of outposts. Only Spain managed to acquire a giant land empire before the eighteenth century.[119] In 1600 fewer than ten thousand Portuguese were living in the whole Indian Ocean region. Substantially fewer English were in India, probably no more than two thousand in 1700. By the end of the seventeenth century the Dutch had more agents abroad, but their numbers do not compromise the point: trade empires were the work of small diasporic communities dotting the coasts of very large continents. So empire at this stage was thin on the ground and very informal.

Trans-regional commerce depended on bicultural (or multicultural) "brokers" who had the linguistic skills and cultural adaptability to negotiate the social aspects of trade across cultural differences. In recent years, scholars have shown that sailors, many of whom were familiar with and comfortable adapting to many local cultures, became skillful cultural brokers. They were used to living cosmopolitan lives, both in port cities and on shipboard, where sailors from all continents constituted a typical crew. Some historians would go so far as to describe the world of the sailing ship as a multicultural world of republican equality, which is said to be a source of the republican ideologies that were so important in the age of Atlantic revolutions, including the American Revolution.[120]

While not wholly wrong, such claims are certainly extravagant. The contradictions experienced on shipboard were many. Sailors lived in a republican world, true, but it was very complex and marked by a very strict hierarchy, with many different domains of power and expectation. It was far more deeply and intricately multicultural than our current understanding of the term. Discipline could be brutal, yet there were important demonstrations of a communal spirit (as in the equality of access to ship stores). When sailors went ashore, they entered an alternative world where the ship's hierarchical authority was attenuated and the opportunities for subversion of it, including a seemingly boundless sexual freedom, were striking, but not necessarily transformative. Capacities for quickly reading local circumstances and adapting to cultural difference were highly developed and valued. Mistakes were often costly.[121]

Similar capacities could be acquired on land, for the Atlantic economy produced cosmopolitan settlements around the "factories" or trading posts on many continents. Again, multilingual cultural brokers were vital, and more often than one might expect they were African or Euro-African. Predictably, Africans were especially important in their own lands, but they could be found in considerable numbers in other parts of the Atlantic littoral. While there were a hundred or so Portuguese merchants in the capital of Kongo in 1550, perhaps ten thousand Africans were in Lisbon, mostly slave but perhaps a thousand of them free, all doing a variety of jobs in government offices, hospitals, noble households, farms, and crafts shops. At least that many were in Mexico City at the end of the sixteenth century.[122] Just as the ocean offered new opportunities for venturesome western Europeans, so, too, in its initial phase it opened a wider world for Africans. Historians are only now discovering that some Native Americans, too, went out onto the Atlantic. For example, the instance of Paquiquineo, who departed the Chesapeake region in 1561 and returned nine years later, has been reasonably well documented.[123]

Two matters bear emphasis here. First, of course, is the geographical distribution of Africans, but perhaps more important is their diversity of experiences and work. Some were free, but even the enslaved majority of African Creoles at first experienced slavery more as it was in the Islamic societies of the Mediterranean. A great difference between slavery in the Mediterranean, where slave occupations and ways of living were various, and slavery in the Atlantic plantation system was the uniformity of experience in the latter. Compared with the mostly urban experience of slaves under Islam, where females as well as males had places in a complex society, the plantation regime prized male labor and narrowed the existence of all the enslaved; human labor was commodified, routinized, and invariant.[124]

But New World slavery followed more than one pattern. While the Portuguese, the Dutch, and finally the English (especially in the Caribbean) developed plantation slavery with its work gangs, slavery in the Spanish colonies differed. If the Dutch and English mobilization of capital and rationalization of labor pointed toward modern capitalism, the Spanish world, including its slavery, was more baroque. Slaves were found, in the Islamic pattern, in the cities; they were used in the mines, too, however. And, as one might expect with Spain's authoritarian system of administration, slavery was a matter of interest to the Spanish state and Church, more than it was in the Protestant English situation, where master-slave relations were deemed a private matter.[125]

Under Spanish auspices a distinctive, now largely forgotten pattern of slavery emerged in northern Mexico, including the territories of what to-day is the southwestern United States. (A similar form of slavery was es-tablished in Argentina as well.)[126] This system had its roots in a convergence of Spanish and Native American practices, which shared dif-ferent but congruent traditions of honor, violence, and captivity. Native Americans had long captured and enslaved enemies, and women and children were often gifted or captured in this context. This kind of enslavement mattered not only for labor—the key issue in the Atlantic plantation system—but also for status, as a symbolic form of honor. The Spanish, who from their familiarity with Muslim slave practices knew a similar form of bondage, adopted the Native American system. Since the Spanish Catholic Church affirmed in 1537 that Indians were rational be-ing with souls and thus could not be enslaved, Indian slavery in Mexico was partially masked as a rescue from heathen life and a chance to work (quite literally) toward Christian salvation. It was a system in which social relations between master and slave could be close, including even mar-riage, which meant that different members of a single family might be slave or free; cousins might be masters over other cousins. This slavery not only predated the enslavement of Africans in the mid-Atlantic settlements near the Chesapeake Bay in the seventeenth century but, located as it was far from Mexico's authorities and formal economy and, later, from the U.S. federal government, continued well beyond the Civil War. The U.S. gov-ernment did not bring it to an end until the late nineteenth century.[127]

But let us return to the Atlantic littoral, which for a century or more sustained a distinctive slavery system. The Atlantic trading economy, be-fore the plantation regime was established, required and rewarded cul-tural brokers. Many of them were Africans and Euro-Africans, products of marriage and other sexual unions between Portuguese men, who readily crossed racial boundaries in seeking mates, and African women.[128] Both Euro-Africans and Africans became culturally competent in multiple con-texts. Africans were used to a multilingual world and thereby special lin-guistic skills; not only did they learn many European (and other) languages, but largely invented a Creole one of their own. By the six-teenth century Africans, slave and free, and mixed-race sailors in Lisbon and in African cities were speaking a Creole language with a distinctive grammar that was a fusion of Portuguese, Bini, and Kongo. This "Guinea speech" or "black Portuguese" constituted an Atlantic lingua franca.[129]

The historian Ira Berlin has recently brought to light the numer-ousness and importance of "Atlantic Creoles." These Africans or Afro-Europeans lived cosmopolitan lives in key communication points—in Lisbon and Seville, in Elmina in Africa, and in Bridgetown, Cap Français, Cartagena, Havana, Mexico City, and San Salvador in the western At-lantic.[130] This geography is important. By recognizing the spatial dimen-sion of history as well as its chronological one, the usual narrative is disrupted. Before plantation slavery a more complex world existed: slave and free, black and white, with boundaries that were difficult to define. It was a liminal world, which is to say malleable. It offered space for alter-native experiences. Skin color in this Atlantic Creole world was impor-tant but not wholly determinative, which makes the contingency of race as a historical construction clearer and more important; that the institu-tionalization of Atlantic slavery took so long becomes a fact of great sig-nificance. One recognizes that in this early phase other racial and labor formations were possible. For perhaps as long as a century, slavery on the Atlantic littoral was quite similar to Mediterranean slavery—mostly ur-ban, with many occupations and varied experiences, many chances for up-ward mobility, and the distinction between white and black, free and slave less marked. The dissolution of this early Atlantic pattern can be observed in seventeenth-century Virginia, but in Brazil some Atlantic Creoles survived into the nineteenth century, mediating between African Islamic communities in Bahia and those in Africa.[131]

Many of the first Americans similarly became cultural brokers, an-other kind of Atlantic Creole. These American cultural brokers, like Africans, had to be linguistically agile, culturally adaptable, with a head for business and a cosmopolitan understanding of markets and goods. In addition to their cultural and economic functions, these "fitt & proper Persons to goe between" were called on as political negotiators between colonial officials and Native American leaders.[132] Some of them were Europeans who "went native." Others were Native Americans who ac-quired knowledge of the Europeans. Squanto, Pocahontas, and, much later, Sacajawea, the Shoshone Indian guide and interpreter for the Lewis and Clark expedition, are widely known—however swathed in myth. Many Indian women became translators and, because of their traditional importance in maintaining ties among groups, offered vitally important contacts for European traders. Women often found opportunities at the interstices of the two cultures, with Christianity sometimes establishing a space for them there. Kateri Tekakwitha, an Iroquois who converted to Christianity (and took her name from Saint Catherine of Siena), like others became a spiritual teacher, finding a voice and a way around the power of the male shamans.[133]

The most famous (or infamous) cultural intermediary in what became Spanish America was Malinali—or Doña Marina to the Spanish. Born a princess in the southern part of Mexico, she was sold by her mother and new stepfather (who, like her actual father, was a cacique, or Indian king) to a Huastec Maya. In 1519, at the age of fourteen, she seized an opportunity that changed her life and helped to transform her world. When one of Hernán Cortés's translators failed to understand a local language, she presented herself as a translator; before long, she was Cortés's concubine and an adviser as well. (One might note that her first child with Cortés, Martín Vallejo, died fighting corsairs in the Mediterranean—which gives us some idea of the mobility within the sixteenth-century ocean world.) Her motives were no doubt complex, but she was briefly the most powerful woman in the Western Hemisphere, and her place in Mexican history is understandably controversial. In the nineteenth century, as Mexican nationalism developed, La Malinche became an epithet for traitor.

If she was an exceptional case, she well illustrated the ambiguous, even ambivalent, position of the *indio ladino*, as a native Andean who in the sixteenth century became competent in Spanish was called. Ladinos were marginal individuals with insecure identities. The first of them were captives, but in time they voluntarily chose the role (or opportunity). These women and men, drawn from a variety of social backgrounds, worked as guides, political and legal interlocutors, translators, or evangelical agents of the Church. Educated in Spanish schools, they often became indigenous historians and chroniclers. The first ladinos were ethnic Andeans, but later mestizos were more nearly bicultural.[134]

In North America, too, one found such cultural brokers of mixed parentage. In areas of French colonization, where there were many more male than female Europeans, French men took Indian mistresses, concubines, and wives. The result of these *mariages du pays* were culturally ambidextrous Franco-Indian children. But English and Dutch men were much less likely to establish unions with African or Indian women. The

English were quite uneasy with racial mixing, and it was less of an issue because the ratio of men to women in their settlements, especially in New England, was more nearly equal. But this led to less intercultural understanding. The rare English couplings with Native American women were not so permanent, because the men usually moved on instead of creating a bicultural family, and the children were unlikely to grow up in a bicultural family: when the father moved on, the matrilineal American tribes incorporated the children.[135]

While Atlantic Creoles often lived in towns, the North American cultural brokers were usually found in small inland settlements or near trading posts.[136] Wherever they were, they faced the challenge of fitting into a new culture without losing their inherited one. And while their liminal world brought freedoms and opportunities for initiative, it could render them suspect and vulnerable.[137] These cultural brokers were vital actors, whether in the vicinity of African "factories," near trading posts and woodland trails in North America, in seaports of Europe, or in various types of settlements in South America and the Chesapeake region.

Some of the cities of the Atlantic littoral were large by the standards of the day. On the west coast of Africa in what is now Ghana, Elmina, founded by the Portuguese in 1482, had a population of between fifteen thousand and twenty thousand persons by 1682, significantly larger than either Boston or New York. The goods managed in the African trade by cultural brokers in such a community ranged from agricultural products and fish to textiles and metalwork. But with the growth of the plantation economy in the seventeenth century—with its seemingly insatiable demand for human bodies to supply labor—commerce and human experiences were reduced. The diversity of activities and experiences that had made complex human identities possible within slavery became rare. The loss of this richness of human experience was one of the least recognized but most violent aspects of the development of the plantation regime in the Atlantic world.

Skills of the Atlantic Creoles were not valued in this new and brutal economy. Indeed, their worldliness produced uneasiness and even fear. Planters on the sugar islands generally wanted slaves directly from Africa—typically young and inexperienced males—who, they thought, would submit to the imposition of the discipline of plantation slavery more easily. For this reason many Atlantic Creoles ended up in marginal slave societies where the planters could not pay the high prices paid by their counterparts in the Caribbean sugar islands—such as the settlements on the Chesapeake Bay, where there is evidence of free and enslaved Africans of just this sort of background.[138]

The most fully documented and thus well known of these Africans are a couple, Anthony and Mary Johnson. The records of Jamestown, Virginia, indicate that one "Antonio a Negro" was sold in 1621 to the Bennett family, on whose plantation he worked for a dozen years. Soon after Antonio landed, "Mary a Negro Woman" arrived in Virginia. Both had talents and industry that were appreciated, and they were allowed to farm independently. They purchased their freedom and land, and they married. As a free woman, Mary conferred freedom on their children, who were baptized. When freed, Antonio anglicized his name. Over the years, his property included slaves, and he possessed legal rights that allowed him to sue a white planter. The Johnsons passed their estate on to their heirs. Both as a slave and later as a slave owner, Anthony worked with white and black, slave and free, and his and Mary's social life crossed these lines. By the eighteenth century, this would no longer be possible. But in the seventeenth century slavery was ill defined or not yet formally institutionalized, although there were indicators of racial differentiation that marked women especially. In 1634, for example, African women were "tithed," making it harder for them to purchase their freedom. As Englishwomen were increasingly protected from work in the fields, African women were deployed as "field laborers." Most important, by 1662 perpetual bondage for the children of enslaved women was established. (In Barbados, children of enslaved African women may have been held in perpetual bondage as early as 1636.) And that became the foundation of slavery in British North America and, later, the United States.

We shall never know how many Anthony and Mary Johnsons there were. But in the mid-seventeenth century on the eastern shore of Chesapeake Bay, several small communities of free blacks had grown up. In one county about one-third of the black population was free. Many of these Africans may have lived in cosmopolitan port cities, and they might well have realized, better than their white counterparts, how terribly isolated and parochial life in the Chesapeake region was. The very existence of their communities, no matter how small, ran against the logic that justified the emerging racial slavery there. By understanding the world of the

Johnsons, one is compelled to recognize how the meaning of race was socially constructed over time. In the earlier social formations, color was recognized as one of many overlapping and significant social identifiers of Africans; there was also lineage, religion, market success, and regional leadership.

The fluid quality of society in early-seventeenth-century Virginia and Maryland, combined with the still incomplete definition of legal slavery, meant that there was no strict connection between race and slavery. The resulting social space enabled the Atlantic Creoles to develop a world and a way of life—difficult because of discriminatory laws and social practices, but not impossible.[139] In other words, their actual experience in the Atlantic littoral did not predict the future of Atlantic slavery. It was reminiscent of the historical pattern of slavery in the Mediterranean, where slaves were as likely to be whites from the Caucasus as blacks from Africa and where free laborers and laborers under varying degrees of coercion interacted and worked together.[140]

THE PLANTATION COMPLEX

The development of a plantation economy, beginning in the sixteenth century, transformed Africa, America, Europe, and Asia, too. It displaced the old silk trade and shifted the increasingly dynamic center of the world economy westward to the Atlantic, marking an advance at the expense of Venice, the Ottoman Empire, and Mediterranean and Asian traders who relied on land routes from the Mediterranean eastward.[141]

The Atlantic economy supplied eager European consumers with mildly addictive drug crops like tobacco and coffee, along with sugar, the last two having been introduced to Europeans as luxury items by the Arabs—sugar from Syria and coffee from Yemen. The Atlantic plantation system transformed these three commodities into items of general consumption. By the eighteenth century, the market for them and for other products of the plantation economy seemed endless, as Europe, led by the British and their North American colonies, became more and more consumption-oriented. Investors prospered, and capital for further economic development accumulated in the metropole. The governments found funding and motive to develop sea power. The Americas had lucrative export crops and developed a society based on a system of labor exploitation of Africans, and Africa suffered the transport of eleven million of its people to the New World.[142]

This new economy, or "plantation complex," had its beginnings in the Atlantic islands off the European and African coast, but it was fully realized first in Brazil, where the Portuguese and later the Dutch established sugar plantations.[143] (The Dutch subsequently brought this brutal regime to Southeast Asia.)[144] By the eighteenth century, the British and, to a lesser extent, the French had developed extraordinarily productive and inhumane regimes of plantation slavery in the Caribbean.

Agricultural innovation was not characteristic of seventeenth-century Europe. Yet the plantation system was remarkably novel, anticipating modern industrial practices. A sugar plantation was an integrated economic unit whose profitability depended on new levels of managerial capacity and a very large labor force being kept at work steadily and with unprecedented intensity. It was a "ferocious" mobilization of agricultural labor.[145] And from the beginning, but especially from the eighteenth century onward, its product was sold into a growing consumer society, first in Anglo-America and then throughout the Atlantic world.

Plantation labor and long-distance trade drew firm lines and distinctions where ambiguity had ruled before: between black and white, slave and free, European and Indian. The recognition of internal differences (and identities) among Africans, Europeans, and Native Americans diminished. Or, put differently, a new sequence of contacts and patterns of differentiation played out in the oceanic world and created the modern identities of African, European, and Native American.

It was the development of oceanic trade that made the plantation complex possible. Because sugar has no nutritional value, it is not a subsistence crop, and local demand is limited; it is necessarily an export crop, but with the advent of a global market it became a valuable agricultural commodity. Reduced to juice on the plantation, the sugar product had a very high ratio of value to bulk, making it an ideal cargo.

Until the development of the Atlantic plantations, production of sugar had been modest, with a small luxury market. But beginning with Madeira, the Canaries, and São Tomé and then extending to Brazil and the Caribbean islands, quality and efficiency were improved, and then the market expanded seemingly without limits. Although its production and trade were centered on the Atlantic, sugar connected all continents, reaching from the Pacific coast of Peru to Bengal.[146] Silver went to Asia to purchase textiles for European markets and to Africa for slaves. Nutritional foodstuffs from North America supplied plantations that could not sustain themselves without these imports. North Americans were also active traders in slaves as part of the triangle that sent molasses north from the sugar islands, rum to Africa, and slaves to the Caribbean. There were different but complementary demands for males and females in the global slave market: young males were sought for the grueling field work on New World plantations; young female slaves were preferred in Africa and in the Mediterranean world as domestic servants and concubines.

The slave system in the southern colonies of British North America developed in a specific historical and geographical context—later than in the Caribbean, and not closely associated with sugar, since the soil and climate would not sustain sugarcane. This development is central to American history, but it was not central to the larger development of the plantation complex.[147] Indeed, its distinctive qualities derive from its peripheral position within the world of Atlantic slavery.

That slavery should become a fundamental feature of the colonies that became the United States was far from being among the initial intentions of those colonies' proponents. They held a different vision, at once religious, militaristic, and utopian. For Sir Walter Raleigh and Richard Hakluyt, the promoters of the first English settlement at Roanoke, Virginia, in 1585, the benefits were two. First, English colonies would challenge or at least limit Catholic Spain's claims in the Western Hemisphere. In weakening and even displacing the benighted Spanish, the English would create an alternative to Spanish cruelty. Also, when Hakluyt petitioned Queen Elizabeth for her support, he spoke of a haven in Virginia for the idle poor of England and for "the naturall people there" who would be treated with "all humanitie, curtesie, and freedome." Far from imagining a future founded on slavery, then, the English colonial projectors promised to bring freedom to America. But by 1587, with the disappearance of the remaining settlers an unsolved historical mystery, the experiment collapsed. Roanoke marked, if it did not quite cause, the failure of a dream, no doubt unrealistic from the start. Yet it took the better part of a century after that before racial, inheritable slavery was formally established in the Chesapeake region. If in the imaginary utopia of the sixteenth century freedom was the desired alternative to slavery, by the end of the seventeenth the two were linked in what has been called an "American paradox": white freedom founded on the enslavement of blacks.[148]

Sugarcane in the Western Hemisphere was initially grown in Santo Domingo, with shipments to Europe beginning in 1516, but the first great New World center of production was Brazil. By 1526, sugar from Brazil was arriving in Lisbon, and the whole century, dominated by Portugal, belonged to Brazilian sugar. The Dutch West India Company, created in 1621 in part to compete with the Portuguese in Africa (for the slave trade) and America (in sugar production), established trading posts near the headwaters and mouth of the Hudson River, but these were of a far lesser priority. Farther south, the Dutch became the initial source of the plantation techniques, tools, slaves, and credit that helped to establish the plantation system in the Caribbean.[149]

The British, too, envisioned wealth from sugar. They brought cane to Jamestown in 1619, but it would not grow there (later, tobacco became Virginia's principal cash crop), and they had better luck on Barbados in 1627. England was the principal European market for sugar, where it was used to sweeten tea and coffee, Asian drinks that became popular in the British Isles at this time. The British aggressively expanded their sugar empire, establishing or capturing more colonies and importing more slaves than their rivals. Within a century they dominated the Atlantic sugar market.[150] Neither slavery nor sugar production was a novelty, but the seaborne interrelationship of land, labor, and markets on three continents constituted a new, systematic pattern of relentless expansion.[151]

The question of the relation of slavery to capitalism is a vexed one. In a brilliant and eloquent book, *Capitalism and Slavery* (1944), Eric Williams argued that the deployment of slave labor provided the foundation for the development of industrial capitalism in Britain. His argument stresses capital formation, but the eighteenth century's rapidly expanding consumer market was vital in generating profits. One could also argue that emergent capitalism transformed slavery into the brutal system that characterized the sugar islands. It does seem that slavery and capitalism were mutually constitutive, and it may well have been this combination that enabled western Europe to lead the world into the era of industrial capitalism. Taking a global perspective, the historian Kenneth Pomeranz argues that the key to European modernization was its investment in slavery: "the fruits of overseas coercion helps explain the difference" between the urban and industrial development of Europe and of China, each of which seemed to have had the same internal resources.[152]

The similarity of sugar plantations to modern industry is also striking. The plantation seems to anticipate modern industrial organization in respect to its high capitalization, strict labor discipline and division of labor, unified control of raw materials and processing, careful scheduling, and the coordination of production and demand. Sidney Mintz describes the Caribbean plantations as a "synthesis of field and factory." To read a contemporary description of a Barbadian plantation, written by a planter in 1700, is to recall images of late-nineteenth-century steel mills:

> In short, 'tis to live in a perpetual Noise and Hurry, and the only way to render a person Angry, and Tyrannical, too; since the Climate is so hot, and the labor so constant, that the Servants [slaves] night and day stand in great Boyling Houses, where there are Six or Seven large Coppers or Furnaces kept perpetually Boyling; and from which with heavy ladles and Scummers they skim off the excrementitious parts of the Canes, till it comes to its perfection and cleanness, while others as Stoakers, Broil as it were, alive, in managing the Fires; and one part is constantly at the Mill, to supply it with Canes, night and day.[153]

A comparison of sugar plantations and cities should invite our attention as well. Neither is self-sufficient. Both require the importation of food. Neither could sustain their populations and in the early-modern period required a constant flow of in-migrants, whether voluntary (the usual case with cities) or forced (as on the plantations).

Slavery in the Chesapeake region was different, developing as it did after the Caribbean sugar economy had matured. The number of slaves in the territory that became the United States was quite small in the seventeenth century, though the system expanded rapidly with the expansion of substantial tobacco exports. However central to U.S. history, in the context of Atlantic slavery it was a late and atypical arrival.[154]

There was a real and consequential transition in the American South from the seventeenth-century world of the Atlantic littoral to the later plantation system, but the result did not replicate conditions on the sugar islands. Still, as the seventeenth century turned into the eighteenth, enslaved Africans in the North American colonies "worked harder and died earlier."[155] Family life weakened, and access to the market such as had been available to the Anthony Johnsons was closed off. Free blacks became anomalous, and neither slave nor free black could claim the protection of the law. The hard edge of slavery—discipline through violence—was prevalent and visible. An undercurrent of "seething animosities," always liable to break out into violence, characterized social relations between master and slave. Color defined status to a high degree as the words "Negro" and "slave" became synonymous.

Whereas the Chesapeake world of the Atlantic Creoles could have been described as a "society with slaves," in the eighteenth century the region had become a "slave society" whose very foundation was racial slavery. Under such circumstances, the blending of cultures characteristic of the Atlantic Creoles was neither considered desirable nor actually possible. The plantation became a site "for a reconstruction of African life." Instead of learning the languages of the planters or joining churches, the circumscribed slaves drew upon their memories to develop an African culture in America, with their own distinctive customs, religious practices, and burial grounds.

The differences between Caribbean slavery and that of the southern United States are most obviously demographic. The proportion of enslaved blacks to free whites was very high in the West Indies, much higher than in the southern United States. The percentage of slaves on the sugar islands went as high as 95 and never below 75. In most parts of the United States, including the South, whites were in the majority, and the scale of mainland plantations was different, too. All Caribbean sugar plantations had at least fifty slaves, and two or three hundred per plantation was not unusual. In the United States, however, as late as 1850, almost half the slaves belonged to planters who owned more than about thirty slaves. Although "gang" labor increased, the gangs were smaller in North America, and, save for Louisiana, there was no "Boyling House." Diverse crops were cultivated in the American South, and many plantations fed their slaves from their own crops.

Mortality rates differed strikingly. Slavery in the sugar islands was a death sentence. Indeed, many planters found it more economical to work slaves literally to death and then import new ones.[156] In contrast, the enslaved population of the United States not only maintained itself by natural increase but actually grew. This meant that in the British West Indies the number of blacks freed from slavery at the time of emancipation amounted to only one-third of the total that over the years had been imported, while in the United States eleven times the number originally imported were freed. A different statistic makes the same point: today the United States, which received 6 percent of all the slaves brought from Africa to the Americas, is home to about 30 percent of persons of African descent in the Americas.[157]

These differences produced contrasting legacies of racism, but I want to focus on one that derives directly from these demographic contrasts. It is a perverse paradox that the most disturbing characteristics of Caribbean slavery may have produced a less problematic racial legacy. The high mortality rate in the West Indies helped to sustain the African culture of those who survived, since the constant immigration of Africans to replace those who died meant that a continuous stream of new African arrivals maintained a sense of African culture, providing a sense of continuity and keeping available traditional cultural resources.

More important was the overwhelming majority of blacks over whites in the West Indies. With no more than 5 percent of the population white, it was functionally inevitable that in the post-emancipation society blacks held many occupations and social positions. That meant that being black in the Caribbean was not synonymous with being in a minority, as it was in the United States. While in the United States one legacy of slavery has been that the white majority defines itself in opposition to black people, that is not the case in the Caribbean. As a result, as Mary Waters writes, "American society is a fundamentally racist society," while the British Caribbean has societies "where there is racism."[158]

If we extend the spatial context of American history, then, the central narrative is changed not only in its geographical position but in its content, too. Certain marginal elements in the traditional story move to the center while others become less significant. Perhaps most important of all, the frame is large enough to appraise the relative significance of the various themes.

The conventional account of the beginning of American history rightly addresses religion, utopian ideas and ideals, economic opportunity, and escape—whether from religious persecution or poverty—but there is much more to it than that. Other equally important themes—capture, constraint, and exploitation—become clear in the larger narrative. Since many more Africans than Europeans made the Atlantic transit in the seventeenth and eighteenth centuries, it is difficult to reduce their story to the margins or even to call it an unfortunate exception to a benign story. By 1820, in fact, five times more Africans than Europeans had come to the Americas. This means that slavery is central to American history, and it also means that the history of the Americas cannot be the story solely of white colonizers and immigrants.[159] That said, one must also acknowledge the point well made by the distinguished Colombian historian and diplomat Germán Arciniegas: although the darkest aspect of the history of America is slavery, it was because of America and in America that humankind initiated a discussion of the problem of slavery.[160]

Nor is U.S. history a linear story of progress or a self-contained history. The beginnings of the United States, as we have seen, are the product—quite contingent and unpredictable—of many histories, several of them global in scope. And these histories converge on the oceanic connection that links the mobility of money, people, and goods to the themes of slavery, racism, and capitalism. These powerful developments were brought together in a protracted global event. U.S. history, and Americans themselves, have ever since been entangled with their transnational histories and legacies.

2

THE "GREAT WAR" AND
THE AMERICAN REVOLUTION

———— ∞∞∞ ————

The Declaration of Independence promulgated by the thirteen colonies was the first time a people had formally and successfully claimed "independence" from the imperial power that had ruled them.[1] Since 1500, history seemed to work in the other direction, toward the accumulation of new territories or concessions. The ocean world invited global contests for more territory, trade, and power, but the struggles also created the conditions for and accounted for the success of the audacious claim by British Americans to a "separate and equal Station." And it was this proposition that the revolutionaries "submitted to a candid World" on July 4, 1776.

Carl Becker famously observed in 1909 that the American Revolution was a double contest: about home rule and about who would rule at home.[2] In fact, it was a triple contest. It was part of a global war between European great powers, it was a struggle for American independence, and it was a social conflict within the colonies. Here I shall emphasize the first and largest of these three, for it is too little known and quite important, as no less a contemporary than James Madison recognized. Speaking behind the closed doors of the Constitutional Convention in Philadelphia, Madison observed that throughout history great powers tended to seek the destruction of each other, often to the advantage of weaker nations:

Carthage & Rome tore one another to pieces instead of uniting their forces to devour weaker nations of the Earth. The Houses of

Austria & France were hostile as long as they remained the great powers of Europe. England & France have succeeded to the pre-eminence & to the enmity. *To this principle we owe perhaps our liberty.*[3]

Madison's point, if we take it seriously, invites us to reframe the story of the Revolution, extending both the chronology and the geography of the explanatory context.

The struggle between England and France for hegemony in Europe and the riches of empire was played out on a global scale between 1689 and 1815. The prolonged cycle of wars between them was known as the "Great War" until what Americans call World War I made the earlier one the *first* "Great War." The British colonies in North America were mostly on the periphery of these wars, but they reaped rewards from that larger conflict, the most important of which was independence. The global conflicts brought troubles as well: trade regulations were imposed by the global empires; changing alliances and naval strategies made the oceanic commerce that was the principal source of income both dangerous and uncertain. When the French withdrew from Canada as a result of the Seven Years' War (1756–63), the colonists welcomed the new security, but there were new sources of instability, too: it emboldened the Americans, and the English became concerned about the administration and cost of their dramatically expanding empire.

After its independence was secured by the Treaty of Paris (1783), the United States, with its large merchant marine, hoped for international recognition as a neutral power in the oceanic world. The profits from global trade could be and at times were considerable, but so were the risks. Too often the American desire for commerce with all nations was denied by either Britain or France or both. The difficulties were evident in the new American republic's first two wars, both fought to protect American commerce, the first against the Barbary States of Algiers, Morocco, Tripoli, and Tunis (1801–1805), the second and more dangerous against Great Britain itself (1812–15). Without British protection in the eastern Mediterranean, which they had lost with independence, American ships were prey in waters patrolled by pirates based in North Africa.[4] The second war came after decades of difficulty in an oceanic world dominated by the great powers; the situation became intolerable when the

Napoleonic Wars reached their climax. The continual presence of Franco-British rivalry in the domestic and foreign affairs of the new nation restricted its practical independence, and American reactions to foreign presences and entanglements shaped and misshaped U.S. politics and economy. Great power rivalries had helped the Americans win their independence and their freedom, and now they threatened the very survival of the vulnerable republic.

Most historians of the revolution and new nation have largely ignored this international context. For example, when, in his widely and long admired volume *The Birth of the Republic* (1956, 1977, 1992), Edmund Morgan, one of the most distinguished historians of colonial America, sets the scene with a description of Lexington Green, where the "shot heard round the world" was fired on April 19, 1775, the larger context he describes is "the history of the Americans' search for principles." Gordon Wood, another leading historian of the era, introduces the crisis of the 1760s as a sudden English intrusion into a colonial venture sustained by "benign neglect." "Great Britain thrust its imperial power" into a society that had become distinctive in its social practices and values, and this "precipitated a crisis within a loosely organized empire."[5]

There is nothing wrong with these framings, but the narrative is so tightly focused, with the English and imperial constitution at the center of the story, that it obscures the larger context that, among other things, encouraged the colonists to expand their rhetorical claims from the "rights of Englishmen" to the "rights of man."[6] Only by claiming these rights and declaring independence could they expect the foreign help necessary for success.[7] Nor can one grasp what seems obvious to a European, that, as the French historian Jacques Godechot has written, a civil war was quickly transformed into an international one with global implications, fought on a global scale, from Lake Champlain to the West Indies, from southern England to the Cape of Good Hope and the Coromandel coast of India.[8]

Americans at the time were aware of these international implications, more so than historians have been since. In 1777, before the colonies sealed their alliance with France, some Americans asked themselves whether it was reasonable, or even morally right, to draw France into what would surely expand into a war among the European powers.[9] They need not have worried. France had its reasons, as Madison knew: revenge for the British victory in the Seven Years' War was crucial, but also, France feared that if the English and Americans settled their differences, they might mount a joint assault on France's West Indian possessions.

For contemporaries elsewhere, it was clear that the American Revolution was embedded in a longer sequence of global wars between France and England.[10] The battles fought between 1778, when France allied itself with the North American rebels, and 1783 touched every continent, and the major French objectives were not in America but elsewhere. In the 1770s, the average Frenchman probably had a clearer idea of Turkey and India than of the British American colonies.[11] The French wanted to reverse their losses in the Seven Years' War, which, in their view, had given Britain too much power within the European balance of powers, and they wanted to regain influence in India and the slave-trading depots at Gorée and the Senegal River.

These French ambitions explain the logic of their support for the Americans, and account for the secret aid for the Americans managed by the dramatist Pierre-Augustin Caron de Beaumarchais. While he was staging his new play *The Barber of Seville* and before there was any formal French alliance, he was already funneling substantial funds from the French king to the Americans. He seems to have been moved to act partly out of sympathy with the Americans' republicanism, but he mainly undertook this work to avenge earlier French losses to the English. The Marquis de Lafayette initially joined the American cause for the glory of it and "hatred of the British."[12]

But British North America was not the main theater of this war. In 1779, for example, the French army that crowded onto five hundred Spanish ships in a joint effort to invade England was vastly larger than any army commanded by Washington in North America. (His largest command was of sixteen thousand troops at Yorktown, half of whom were French.) Spain, an ally of France but not formally an ally of the Americans, was focused on Gibraltar, which it had lost to Britain in 1704. The massive invasion plan, something of a comedy of errors, was aborted.[13] When the war ended in 1783 in a series of separate treaties, the French "rejoiced not so much because the United States was independent as because England had been humbled."[14] But this was true only in North America. Overall, the British were anything but humbled, and it was this larger truth, not simply the American victory at Yorktown, that determined the shape of the peace. Neither France nor Spain had achieved its initial war aims, and Britain came out of the war in command of the sea and more powerful than before.[15]

One can say that global trade implies global wars, yet this seeming truism became practically true only when the rules of war and statecraft were transformed between the seventeenth and the eighteenth centuries. In 1559, Spain and France had agreed that conflicts "beyond the line" that for both of them marked the limit of Europe (which extended to the Azores) would not be taken as a basis or a reason for hostilities in Europe. When the Treaty of Westphalia (1648) had legitimated national boundaries and protected them from violation, much of the rivalry among European states for land or territory played out in relation to their colonial possessions. By the eighteenth century, however, the old phrase "peace beyond the line" ceased to have meaning. The Dutch were the first to consider colonies integral to a war with other European powers: the Treaty of Breda (1667), which concluded a war involving England, the Dutch Republic, France, and Denmark, was the first multilateral peace settlement that had as much concern for extra-European as for European affairs. Indeed, it was in this agreement that the Dutch let the English keep New Amsterdam or, as it had been renamed, New York, while they held the former English possession of Surinam. Then, in 1739, two European powers went to war over a non-European issue for the first time, when Britain challenged Spain's claim to search ships in the Caribbean— a war known in England as the War of Jenkins' Ear.[16] Global empires now implied global wars—and global politics.

Jacques Turgot, Louis XVI's minister of finance, recognized that the boundaries of the political world had become "identical with those of the physical world."[17] Balance-of-power politics was similarly extended globally. "The balance of commerce of the nations in America," a French diplomat had observed in 1757, "is like the balance of power in Europe. One must add that these two balances are actually one." When France entered the Seven Years' War, Foreign Minister Choiseul declared that "the true balance of power really resides in commerce and in America." To weaken Britain in America, he concluded, would shift "considerable weight in the balance of power."[18] By 1776, it was widely understood that conflict in any part of an empire was not contained, nor was it exempt from global power considerations. That is why and how the Amer-

ican Revolution became part of a world war of more than a century's
duration.

GLOBAL EMPIRES

In the Atlantic and Indian oceans, dominance in the two linked enterprises of commerce and naval power had passed from the Portuguese to
the Dutch and then, by the end of the seventeenth century, to the English. Spain and France were land-based powers with territorial empires—
Spain's much more extensive one distributed across the globe. But Spain
made less of it, and the Iberian monarchy lost its initial advantage and
had become a secondary power. The armies of Louis XIV, by contrast, rose
to dominance on the Continent. Though France was slow to develop a
maritime empire, by the mid-eighteenth century *outre-mer* France was
considerable, with outposts in India, most importantly at Pondicherry; in
Madagascar, off the East African coast; and in West Africa, with small
trading posts at Gorée and along the Senegal River. In the Americas,
France laid claim to the great expanse of what is now Canada, of value for
its fur trade and fisheries. And ever since 1697, when Spain had ceded the
western half of the island of Hispaniola to France, in St. Domingue (today's Haiti) it had the jewel of the Caribbean sugar islands, as well as several other small island colonies there.

By nineteenth-century British standards England's colonial empire
was still modest. But the secret of British imperial and commercial success lay in the Royal Navy, not in the amount of colonized territory. At
the outset, Sir Walter Raleigh had articulated the rule that would under-
gird British power. "Whosoever commands the sea," he observed, "commands the trade of the world; whosoever commands the trade of the
world, commands the riches of the world, and consequently the world
itself."[19]

Earlier types of naval power relied on a combination of fortified ports
in key locations, as well as convoys protecting ships with valuable car-
goes; this was the case with the Spanish galleons. But after the War of the
Spanish Succession (1702–13) Britain initiated a more ambitious strategy
to ensure the safety of all sea-lanes necessary for British commerce; this
policy required massive, continuing investment in the Royal Navy.[20] The

British therefore dramatically increased both taxes and debt, and created the Bank of England. This state formation, which the historian John Brewer has called the "military-fiscal" state, was both the foundation and the product of a century of war that enabled an island nation to become a world power. It was extraordinarily successful, but it placed heavy burdens on the imperial structure. Between 1680 and 1780 the British military establishment (mostly the navy) trebled in size and expenditures. These fiscal and administrative challenges were handled with remarkable political consensus, skill, and efficiency.[21] But when the Seven Years' War vastly increased the empire and the cost of maintaining it, the British tried to shift some of the costs of their new military-fiscal state to their colonies. That was when tensions rose. Conflicts in India and North America threatened the empire at the very moment of its apparent success. Likewise in France and Spain military investments increased, and the imperial bureaucracies were reformed. And here, too, the debts, taxes, and administrative reorganizations produced instability. Domestic and colonial tensions led to revolution in France in 1789 and in St. Domingue two years later, while new fiscal demands and regulations triggered rebellions and insurgencies in Spanish and Portuguese America.

So this growing fiscal crisis was global, driven by the increasing military expenditures due to greater global integration and to developments in military technology; conflict and preparing for it became more expensive. The first signs of strain actually appeared in the Ottoman Empire, beginning in the 1690s. Within a century the pressure on its state finances had reached a crisis point, the result of war with the Russian Empire on the north shores of the Black Sea and the Crimean region, of conflict with the Habsburg Empire in Europe, and of the challenges of the French occupation of Egypt in 1798. In addition, demographic growth caused inflation that further reduced tax revenues that were already in decline because of the shift of trade out onto the oceans. Once the British drove Napoleon's army out of Egypt, its governor, Mehmet Ali, began acting independently, though maintaining allegiance to the sultan, while Serbia in 1804 and Greece in 1821 (having already revolted over land distribution in the 1770s) claimed independence.[22]

Britain's victory in the Seven Years' War greatly expanded its empire, and colonial issues became more present in the minds of political and administrative leaders in London. The empire seemed newly comprehensive, with the metropole and colonies together constituting a single global entity.[23] Arthur Young, writing in 1772, explained, "British dominions consist of Great Britain, Ireland, and divers colonies and settlements in all parts of the world."[24] Yet a distinction was often made between the "empire" in the Americas and the "establishments" in Africa and Asia.[25] That said, it was undeniable that Bengal was considered an integral part of the British Empire, even if its administration was delegated to the East India Company, which presumed sovereignty there. Thus Edmund Burke in 1777 declared that "the natives of Hindustan and those of Virginia" were each equally part of the "comprehensive dominion which the divine Providence has put in our hands."[26]

This increase in the size, wealth, and power of the British Empire worried Spain and Portugal. To protect themselves, they would need to enact similar reforms. José de Gálvez, visitor general of New Spain (1765–72) and minister of the Indies (1775–87), brought the empire closer to the metropole and increased trade within it through a policy of *comercio libre*, which offered economic stimuli and an increase in tax revenues without challenging the political status quo by taxing at home. These commercial and administrative reforms not surprisingly caused instability in the colonies during the 1780s. And in Portugal, Sebastião José de Carvalho e Mello, who became the Marquês de Pombal in 1769, was an authoritarian administrator who, having energetically directed the rebuilding of Lisbon after it had been destroyed in the great earthquake of 1755, then turned to strengthening the Portuguese Empire. Here, too, there were rebellions, notably in Pernambuco and Rio de Janeiro, both of which resisted centralizing reforms.[27]

The tensions within each empire easily developed into revolt, for the colonial system depended on the cooperation of local elites, which typically expected a significant degree of autonomy, more often customary than official. The empires' local officials tended to soften the edges of imperial rule, making pragmatic adjustments that often increased their own power more than the crown's. With great variations among the empires and among different colonies in the same empire, it is fair to say that local populations helped to shape the imperial systems that ruled over them.

After the Seven Years' War, when new fiscal and administrative policies disrupted these established and comfortable patterns, protest and rebellion followed. More was usually involved than administration and taxation. The growth in world trade was putting new pressures on local social life. The merchants at the nodes of global trade were becoming very rich, and this made for a double problem: changing power relations among local elites, and their efforts to assert authority within the empire commensurate with their new high status. Even at the periphery of an empire, people were developing a sense of their communities' identity, perhaps even a proto-nationalist feeling, and they were often committed to preserving their traditions and privileges and to loosening their ties to the metropole. In some cases these new political cultures were simply the precipitate of social experiences over time, but in others, as with Mehmet Ali's satrapy in Egypt after 1805, the greater administrative and political autonomy prompted stronger attachments to the colony at the expense of the empire.[28]

Historians writing on the American Revolution have recently been paying attention to the sense of difference, distance, and distinction that developed in British North America; it might fairly be considered an emergent form of nationalism.[29] But one sees the same phenomenon within the older empires of the Middle East and South Asia. Similar tensions weakened the Safavid Empire in Iran; Mughal authority in India began to fragment as early as the 1720s. Often the new local movements were restorative in spirit, sometimes associated with religious revitalization, as one sees with the Sikhs, who resisted efforts of the Mughal elites to exact greater taxes from them. Followers of Muhammad ibn Abd al-Wahhab in Arabia resisted both the religious and the secular authority of the Ottomans throughout the late eighteenth century, and the Wahhabi sect sought autonomy in order to preserve what they claimed was a purer Islam.[30] The Incas' rebellion in Peru in 1780 was another indigenous effort to restore an older politics. In North America, "Pontiac's Rebellion," coming after the defeat of the French in the Seven Years' War, aimed to push the British out of the Ohio Valley, but Pontiac's military campaign was partly sustained by a widely held restorative impulse among Native Americans of the region to strengthen and confirm their own identity. He often deployed the language of the "Delaware Prophet," an Indian visionary who exhorted tribes to stay away from European trade and goods and held out the dream that the whites would go away.

Empires in the eighteenth century were filled with uncontrolled, even unmapped areas, and even in places under formal organizational control, constant negotiations were required to sustain them. Though one should not exaggerate the agency or power of the colonized, one must acknowledge that empire depends on the tacit consent and cooperation of local elites. British imperial power collapsed in North America when the colonists withdrew their cooperation; at the same time in India, there were tensions yet local leaders found power and profit by remaining within the empire. It is doubtful that the British could have maintained their authority had the populace refused to go along, even though the governor-general in India had plenty of political and administrative power, as well as military support, more than any North American royal official. Coercive power was real in the eighteenth-century empires, but it was not the whole story.[31]

The sequence of wars that constituted the Second Hundred Years' War began in 1689 when King Louis XIV of France, worried about the increasing power of Britain, tried to prevent William of Orange, a Protestant, from assuming the English crown. Beyond defending the succession, the English assembled the Grand Alliance (Holland, Spain, Sweden, Savoy, and the electors of Bavaria, Saxony, and the Palatinate) against France, which had grown in territory and power under the Sun King. The prolonged conflict thus began with echoes of the seventeenth century's religious wars and dynastic politics, but over the next decades it modulated to a struggle over a secular "balance of power." In a commentary published a year after the Treaty of Ryswick (1697) ended the first phase of this long struggle, Jacques Bernard, building on the notion of a "Ballance" among the "Kingdoms and States of *Europe*," observed,

> In the present Circumstances of *Europe*, all any single State should reasonably wish, is, to be in a Condition to prevent Surprize from a Neighborhood, and to have a Power sufficient to defend itself *for some time*; and then doubtless those Potentates whose Interest it is that the Aggressor should not, by the Ruin of another, grow too powerful, will come to the Assistance of the Oppressed.[32]

After the end of the War of the Spanish Succession in 1713, relative peace between France and Britain lasted until 1744. The significance of this period is seldom examined in histories of colonial America, but it was the absence of war that permitted the policy described after the fact by Edmund Burke as "benign neglect." During those years the population of British America expanded, as did its economy and trade; and the standard of living rose. Americans were incorporated into a transatlantic consumer economy, and one of the rights they fought for in 1776 was the right to sustain their new standard of living.[33] The popularity of tea drinking was a visible symbol of this developing consumerism: a new social ritual, dependent on an import from Asia, and managed by women who could show their cosmopolitanism in their knowledge of the proper etiquette and accoutrements of tea service.[34]

The political institutions of British America developed, too, notably the representative assemblies or lower houses of the colonial legislatures, which became social and political foci of the new elites. It is no accident that sixteen of the seventeen complaints against England enumerated in the Declaration of Independence referred to policies or actions that compromised the power of these legislative bodies.[35]

American political development followed no established imperial model, since there was none. The British Empire had no general plan or structure; patterns of rights, authorities, and regulations were variable. Moreover, much work of the empire was conducted under business auspices, as in the East India Company. With each political jurisdiction so idiosyncratic, transatlantic misunderstandings were not only possible but predictable.[36] This situation is sometimes contrasted with the more statist, thereby more uniform imperial practices of Spain and France. The point is well taken, but the formal state powers of the French and Spanish empires as evinced on the ground differed from those of the British Empire less than is usually supposed. Whatever the structure at the center, all empires were fairly thin on their periphery, though the colors that fill territory on maps make them seem solid. In all cases there was unavoidably a great deal of local autonomy. Neither the technology nor the concept of modern state administration was available.

The diversity within empires also worked against the notion so central to the modern nation-state: of a citizenry with uniform rights and obligations. In fact, to take only the Atlantic portion of the British Empire, we find a mix of incommensurable rights, privileges, and traditions. Ireland and Scotland had different constitutional relations to England and to local powers, each unlike the American one. Parliament and crown were extremely reluctant to confer full economic or political rights beyond England proper, as the British Americans discovered; Ireland, so close yet so far, discovered the same.[37] So the complexity and internal differentiation within the empire nourished local political cultures and identities that eventually challenged imperial ambitions.

It is often remarked that Britain's conquest of Ireland was a "warm-up" for its settlement of North America in the seventeenth century, but it should be added that Ireland's constitutional conflicts with England in the eighteenth century paralleled those of the Americans.[38] One might have expected the Irish to sympathize with the Americans, but Ireland's linen trade suffered greatly when the American colonies adopted their strategy of refusing to import such goods from the British Isles; so the Irish supported the crown against the American rebels and, in an instance of supposed mutual convenience, proposed to the English that the twelve thousand English troops stationed in Ireland be dispatched to fight in North America.[39]

The British response to the Irish resistance movement some years later, led by Henry Grattan's Protestant Volunteer Army, included trade concessions in 1779 and, in 1782, a restoration of the independence of the Irish Parliament in domestic matters (though it continued to exclude Catholics). Interestingly, this kind of British response (partly a reward for Ireland's earlier support against the Americans) might have worked had it been offered to the Americans during the crisis in the 1760s, but by the 1780s it was impossible. And in Ireland it restored order only briefly; after another rebellion in 1798, led by the Society of United Irishmen and directly aided by France, again to spite England, Britain abolished the Irish Parliament and replaced it with the Legislative Union of Great Britain and Ireland under the United Kingdom in 1801.

It is worth keeping the Irish experience in mind, for it shows that the constitutional issues at the center of most narratives of the American Revolution were not unique and in fact were all but inevitable in the world of empires during the first great age of rights talk. The resistance and ultimate rebellion of the North American colonists were unique only in their precociousness, in their being first, and in the dimensions of their ultimate success. The striking point is that resistance movements appeared on every continent in the second half of the eighteenth century. Historians have largely missed the global character of this phenomenon.

Academic divisions of labor discourage a wider view; study of more than one empire in a single narrative is rare, even different parts of the same empire. The volume on the eighteenth century in *The Oxford History of the British Empire*, for example, has not a single chapter that addresses the Atlantic and Asian parts of the empire within one frame.[40]

Of course, each anti-imperial resistance movement was idiosyncratic. Yet the similarities warrant speculation that global trade and global war, and the mobility of people and ideas which both promoted, were all important, perhaps causal factors. Enlightenment ideas traveled, and so did news of specific challenges to imperial authority, whether in the metropole or on the periphery. And this information circulated far beyond a narrow elite; it has been shown that it was available to African-Americans in the Caribbean, slave and free.[41] "The force of events," C. A. Bayly has recently written, "ricocheted around the globe."[42]

In the late eighteenth century peoples on every continent experienced in varying degrees a multidimensional historical transformation. They all felt the effects of the long-distance trade that the oceanic revolution made possible—altering economic relations, changing daily life, and unsettling traditional social practices, hierarchies, and patterns of prestige. The new mobility and mixing of peoples did the same. A new worldliness developed, thanks to the circulation of people, knowledge, and goods. These changes created both motives and spaces for new kinds of conflict, and they invited responses.[43] Some were reactionary, seeking to restore, others would nervously embrace the new, and sometimes the impulses to restoration and invention went hand in hand.

In South Africa the Boers, Dutch settlers who had been farming there for generations, disputed Dutch land and trade policies, while in Java the issues were taxes and control of labor. The Ottoman bureaucracy faced resistance in Cairo in 1785–98, and its imperial politics became even more frayed in the wake of Napoleon's failed invasion of Egypt. The result: After 1805 Mehmet Ali, officially governor of Ottoman Egypt, operated virtually independent of his nominal imperial overlord, the sultan. At the same time Greek nationalist resistance to Ottoman rule culminated in a full-blown independence movement that achieved success in the 1820s. The slave revolt against French authorities in St. Domingue in 1791 ignited fires of potential revolt on nearby Jamaica, where British colonial authorities clashed with the free blacks (called Maroons) in 1797–98. A

complex, widespread Inca rebellion against Spanish power in Peru was
led by the ladino Tupac Amarú in 1780; a year later a similar uprising,
the Comunero revolt, occurred in New Granada (present-day Venezuela,
Panama, Ecuador, and Colombia). And there were crises in the metropole,
not only the hugely consequential French Revolution in 1789, but a series of failed revolutions throughout Europe.[44] Events in the metropole
could spark and sustain colonial resistance (as in St. Domingue); con-
versely, colonial resistance could amplify metropolitan political tensions,
as with the riots in London provoked by the radical John Wilkes, much
admired and financially supported by the colonists for his attacks on min-
isterial oppression and corruption.[45]

In the North Atlantic world, the challenges to the old, imperial social
forms and cultural values were driven by and in turn promoted an embrace of individualism. The age of revolution was, as Alexis de Tocqueville insisted in his classic accounts of the French Revolution and of
democracy in America, part of a larger history of modern individualism
that sustained claims for equality and autonomy. While this could not be
said of the values driving Mehmet Ali in Egypt or Tupac Amarú in Peru,
it was evident in many crises, including others in the Ottoman and Spanish empires. With some exceptions, there is a large historical narrative
that embraces the American Revolution and other contemporaneous conflicts and revolutions, particularly those making claims of universal human rights.[46]

It is also clear that the cycles of war produced within the empires an
almost insatiable need for revenue, at the same time as liberal ideas of improved governance prompted imperial reform (even for Spain). Newly en-
ergetic and self-consciously rational imperial administrators, armed with
aggressive tax policies, prompted resistance all over the globe.[47] For example, the Spanish policy of *comercio libre* established in the 1770s was not
free trade in the spirit of Adam Smith, but a strategy for expanding trade
within the empire by reducing regulations and abolishing the requirement that commerce pass through Spain. It was analogous to Britain's decision in 1772 to allow the East India Company to ship tea directly to
North America without stopping first at London, and in that instance favoring the company with a tax rebate. After the administrative reforms,
trade increased in the Spanish Empire and so did tax revenues. But the
spread of merchant capitalism unsettled established social patterns and

undermined inherited economic and political practices everywhere. In the 1780s, protests extended from New Granada to Peru, and the principal targets were tax collectors and merchants; the similarities to events fifteen years earlier in British America are striking.

In June 1781, twenty thousand *vecinos* marched to the capital of New Granada shouting, "Long live the king! Death to bad government!" Leaders denounced the officials who had arrived in 1778 to apply Spain's new commercial and fiscal measures. Like the British North Americans in the 1760s, these protesters were not seeking independence. They were loyal to the king but disliked administrative tyranny. The archbishop of Bogotá negotiated an agreement between the government and the rebels—the "Capitulations of Zipaquirá"—which decreed an amnesty and canceled enforcement of the offending fiscal policies.[48]

In Peru a larger rebellion led by Tupac Amarú, a distant descendant of an Inca ruler whom the Spanish had executed in 1572, began in 1780 with a message placed on the wall of a customs house threatening death to "duty collectors" and "court clerks": "Long live our great monarch—long live Carlos III and may all duty collectors die." Mestizos and Indians broke into armories, customs houses, and the homes of prominent officials, much as the mobs had destroyed the home of Governor Thomas Hutchinson in Boston and intimidated customs officials and those appointed to administer the Stamp Act.[49]

While taxes were a significant issue, this rebellion—which soon became a full-scale insurgency—was fundamentally the result of a clash of political ideas and practices. Tensions had been building since the 1740s, but now changes in the economy and administration were undermining the established political practices of both natives and Creoles. Although Tupac Amarú had been educated (at the Colegio de San Francisco de Borja in Cuzco), his ideas were not those of the Enlightenment, nor were they based on religious principles or common-law precedent, as was the case in North America. His followers were inspired by indigenous ideas, by Inca notions of good rule that were more communal than liberal.[50] Tupac Amarú complained of taxes and regulations that exploited Indians, but, more radically, he proposed to reclaim his hereditary right as "Inca-King of Peru."[51]

At first Creoles supported the rebellion. They hated the imperial reforms that José de Gálvez, the former visitor general, had set in motion, and the way that the new visitor general, José Antonio de Areche, filled offices with *peninsulares*, who they thought were of lower social standing and too often "relatives, favorites, and dependents" of Gálvez. Yet Gálvez had believed that the Creoles could not impartially administer because of friendship and family ties, so he had reduced their proportion in administrative offices by one-third. Unlike the Indians, New Spain's leading Creoles drew upon European arguments, as one might expect, notably those developed earlier, in 1771, by the Mexican jurist and poet Antonio Joaquín de Rivadeneira, who said: "The appointment of natives [meaning Creoles] to the exclusion of foreigners is a maxim derived from the natural reason which governs hearts." Foreigners would only seek to enrich themselves, and knew nothing of the people, laws, or customs in America.[52] Yet the Creoles backed away from supporting the rebels, for basically they despised and feared Indians, who in any case lost their initial enthusiasm for an alliance. Each had different, sometimes conflicting issues, and they feared that alliance would contaminate their core agendas.[53]

Although the insurgency was put down within a year, the challenge to empire was substantial, and stability was slow to return to Peru's highlands. The Spanish were aware of how vulnerable their American empire was. An unsigned note, presumably written by a high colonial official, complained that "Gálvez has destroyed more than he has built . . . his destructive hand is going to prepare the greatest revolution in the American empire."[54] One of the king's ministers later reflected in his memoirs that the "entire vice royalty of Peru and Part of the Rio de la Plata was nearly lost in 1781–1782."[55]

There were revolts in Brazil, too. In 1789 Joaquim José da Silva Xavier, or "Tiradentes," as the part-time tooth puller was popularly called, sought to create an independent republic in Minas Gerais in emulation of the new United States. The rebellion failed, but this correspondent of Jefferson is well remembered in Brazil. Along with other small rebellions, especially at Pernambuco, it pressed Portugal's colonial officials to recognize the instabilities that reform was producing and to ease off some of the regulations. As in British North America, the protests were directed against novel policies that were disrupting established habits of unofficial but important local autonomy.

Tensions in British India were very similar. The rival French in India were effectively removed in 1757 when the British seized the French out-post Chandernagore and then, far more important, defeated the nawab of Bengal at Plassey, which consolidated their control over the Bengal terri-tories, making it all but impossible for the Bengal leaders to play off any European ally against the British. As a result, the East India Company, the agent of English power and rule in India, became more absolute and more demanding.[56] Soon it had achieved a level of control that would have pleased the British authorities dealing with the North American colonists. Robert Clive, who had led the outnumbered British forces to victory at Plassey, claimed for the Company more authority than that al-lowed India's indigenous governments, asserting sovereignty backed by effective power. As parliamentary leaders lectured the British Americans, so Clive insisted to the Indians that sovereignty was not divisible: all power "must belong either to the Company or to the Nabob," and he was certain it had come to rest with the Company. "The power," he assured the Company directors, "is lodged where it can only be lodged with safety to us." The "sinews of war are in your own possession"; the Com-pany had achieved "absolute power" in Bengal.[57]

The East India Company's work had gone well beyond mere trade, having become "partly Commercial and partly Military." It offered local rulers pensions and military services in return for taxes, a strategy that encouraged the rulers to disband their armies and made them more de-pendent. Clive was convinced that no native ruler could presume to have "hopes of independence." That was probably true, but power was not the whole story of empire. It was also true that Indian merchants and politi-cal elites saw an advantage in continuing their relationship with the Company and through it with Britain, but this did not mean they did not continue to value autonomy.

Appropriate forms of power and administrative practices continued to be difficult to negotiate and were often disputed. The more the East India Company needed funds, the more it increased its demands for taxes, so re-bellion was always a possibility. This meant the Company had to invest more in military preparedness, which in turn worsened the military-fiscal crisis. When in 1772 the Company lost its battle against deficits and could not pay its debts, it went to London for a fiscal rescue plan, which included a loan, more government oversight, and a change in trade regu-lations designed to increase Company revenue. The government allowed the Company to ship its tea directly to America, dropping the regulation that the ships stop at London en route to pay taxes. As became clear when the tea arrived in Boston, the privilege granted the East India Company exacerbated the problems in America.

The Company's financial crisis warrants further discussion, for it reveals the pressure that imperial expansion placed on the British financial system and the global interactions at work behind the Boston Tea Party. The territories that Britain gained in America and Asia not only meant increased costs for administration and defense but also represented a large new field for investment. They drew heavily on available capital, with implications for credit relations throughout the empire. The British colonies in North America had always been chronically short of local capital, and the expansion of consumerism in the mid-eighteenth century worsened their balance of trade and credit relations with the metropole. Debt climbed substantially, especially among Virginia planters, including Thomas Jefferson. To maintain the trade with the Americans despite the mounting debt, Scottish merchants and bankers resorted to financial innovations that proved unsound; overextension throughout the British banking system resulted in the 1772 credit crisis. The Bank of England tightened credit, calling in debt throughout the empire, and stopped its advances to the East India Company. Not only could the Company not meet its obligations, but it needed more funds to cover the cost of what Edmund Burke described as "a disastrous war against Hyder Ali" in Mysore—and this is when Parliament stepped in. Meanwhile, the Americans, especially the Virginians, had their own debt crisis but got no aid and for that reason felt solidarity with the Boston radicals. The simultaneous crises in Britain, India, and North America were, in fact, one crisis. While Americans were right to resent the British policy that favored the East India Company at their expense, they failed to grasp that their own demand for consumer goods on credit was at least partly responsible for the imperial credit crisis that resulted in Britain's partial export of the East India Company's problem to North America.[58]

The armed rebellions in Mysore and elsewhere were put down, showing the strength of the Company's authority in India, but it was not absolute. In any case, rule in India depended on Indian administrative expertise, just as it was financed by Indian taxation and relied on Indian soldiers in the Company's employ. And in the years after the Seven Years'

War there were continuous tensions; in 1781–82, when the British were negotiating with the Americans, they found themselves much less secure in India than was supposed in the theory that Clive had so confidently articulated after his victory at Plassey.

A CONTINUOUS WAR, 1754-1783

The war that brought independence to the thirteen colonies began in "Indian Country." We may tend to visualize relations between North Americans and Europeans as organized along a frontier line, but Euro-American and Amerindian interaction was pervasive throughout the colonies; a better geographical image might be that of a doughnut, with the center marking "Indian Country," or what we today identify as the Ohio, eastern Mississippi, and Tennessee River valleys. The Indians were surrounded by French settlements to their north and west, by the British on the east and the Spanish to the south. They had multiple opportunities for alliances that played off one European empire against another, and by the mid-eighteenth century they had become quite adept at this. While their relations were in general best with the French, who understood the etiquette of diplomacy well and were not too land-hungry, they were careful not to be taken for granted by any one power.[59] They also held the balance of power between the British and the French.[60]

British schemes to expand into the Ohio Valley became clear in 1747 with the chartering of the Ohio Company, which was to settle the area and build a fort there. It was granted 200,000 acres by the Privy Council two years later. Other, even more extensive land claims were made by the colonial governments of Virginia and Pennsylvania. The French, with at least passive support from the Indians, responded by developing a line of forts. In 1753, the governor of Virginia dispatched George Washington, then twenty-one years old, to discourage this activity. He was captured by the French, released, and sent back to Virginia. The British saw this as a defeat, and the authorities in London decided to respond with force.

British troops and supplies arrived in 1754 and the war commenced. Two years later hostilities were extended to European territory, England and Prussia were allies on one side, and France with Austria and, later, Spain on the other. Indeed, there was no "peace beyond the line," and a

conflict over control of the Ohio Country—the hole in the doughnut—
became the first global war fought on every continent.[61]

It is noteworthy that the British at first focused on the American theater and deployed substantial military resources there. For more than a
decade, they had been placing a higher value on their North American
colonies. This was not because, as in the past, the colonies were an important source of ships, naval supplies, and sailors in a century of conflict,[62]
but because London recognized the commercial implications of the
colonies' growing prosperity and rising living standards. The colonies
were possible targets for new taxes, but even more important, they were a
market for English manufactures.[63] This suggested a redefinition of empire. Unaided by Adam Smith, British colonial authorities came to see
the North American colonies as a consumer economy as well as an extractive one. Thomas Pownall, who had been lieutenant governor of New Jer-
sey and governor of Massachusetts, developed this idea in a pamphlet first
published in 1765 and often reprinted.[64]

One can get a sense of the global extent of the Seven Years' War by a
simple list of its major campaigns and battles.[65] Land battles were fought
in North America and in central Europe; the sea war touched all parts of
the world. Though it is called the Seven Years' War, a name that well describes the European conflict of 1756–63, it was in fact a twelve-year war
for the Americans, beginning in 1754 and, with Pontiac's Rebellion
(1763–66) as a kind of coda, continuing nearly three years after the
Treaty of Paris brought the European aspect to a close in 1763. During
these years there were military campaigns in Nova Scotia (Acadia), the
Hudson River–Lake Champlain corridor and the Mohawk Valley, the Up-
per Great Lakes, the Southeast (in the Cherokee War), and the Caribbean.
The war was also fought in Minorca, Bengal and the Coromandel coast,
Manila, West Africa (along the Senegal River), Gibraltar, and the coast of
France.

In the earlier conflicts between France and England since 1689 victory
claims had been inconclusive. But in this war there was no doubt of the
British victory.[66] Although in Europe the war ended with the *status quo
antebellum*, France recognized that even without a loss of territory its position had diminished. The Prussia of Frederick II (the Great) had
emerged as the foremost military power on the Continent. And in the
colonies France had lost decisively, in both North America and India. Ex-

cept for its settlement of Algeria in the 1830s, France did not again acquire an overseas empire until the 1870s and after—in the second wave of European imperialism.[67] The Amerindians lost badly, too, since with France removed from North America, they could no longer play off the rival European powers against each other. Britain, by contrast, was now dominant not only in North America and India but also on the ocean routes that sustained world trade.[68]

An outburst of British maritime exploration in the Pacific followed, including especially the famous voyages of Captain James Cook. Britain's expanded imperial interests in the Pacific and Indian oceans made it easier, when the time came, to relinquish political control of the thirteen colonies while maintaining trade relations with them. Meanwhile, France commenced planning for a war to recoup its losses, investing especially in rebuilding its navy, which was to be a decisive force in the American Revolutionary War.[69] Spain, an ally of France, had gained nothing in the Seven Years' War and had almost lost both the Philippines and Cuba, so it was prepared to join France. (The British capture of Manila and Havana at the very end of the war had not been known at the Paris peace table and had not been part of the British negotiating strategy; and they were returned.) For the Europeans, then, the Treaty of Paris ending the war was only a pause in a conflict that continued. No one then knew the auspices of the next phase, but it turned out to be the American Revolution.

There was continuity for other participants as well. For the Native Americans, the possibilities once offered by the hole in the doughnut were narrowed, as a single line gradually came to separate them from the Euro-Americans, who pressed constantly for more land. With the formation of the new American nation—and especially in the South in the nineteenth century—the pressure intensified, for the use of enslaved black laborers made Indian land all the more valuable.[70]

In British America the issues that came to define the revolutionary crisis were immediate results of the Seven Years' War and of changing expectations on both sides of the Atlantic. It was also in the Seven Years' War that Americans first gained military experience; more broadly, a new sense of nationalism gripped the Americans. That was true in England, too, but in the colonies the war encouraged British Americans to become more self-consciously *American*.[71] At the peace negotiations ending the Seven Years' War, Choiseul, the French foreign minister, noted that the removal of the French from North America might imply the eventual removal of the British, too.[72] He was right.

Such was the context for a series of initiatives directed to the American colonies by the British government. Not unlike the policies it imposed on India at about the same time, these were intended to reform colonial administration and increase much-needed revenue. These measures are familiar to us, being standard fare in the grade-school history of the American Revolution. But at the time they were novel and provocative for the North American colonists.

The transfer of territory from France to Britain in North America was vast—Acadia, Cape Breton, Canada, the islands of the Gulf of St. Lawrence (except St.-Pierre and Miquelon), and all its territory east of the Mississippi River except New Orleans (that to the west had been secretly ceded to Spain in 1762). The task of organizing this territory marked the beginning of a new administrative activism. A proclamation of 1763 established English law over the territory, and it also organized the "Indian Country" as part of "Quebec." Both decisions must have seemed the obvious ones to make in London, but organizing Indian Country had its own complexities. The British immediately faced the rebellion of Pontiac, who captured a string of British forts before he was finally defeated at Detroit. Also, the British colonists, always land-hungry, had presumed the land now assigned to Quebec would naturally become theirs in time, but when the British authorities formally organized the government of Canada with the Quebec Act (1774), they included Ohio Valley lands that Massachusetts, Connecticut, and Virginia claimed. And Parliament, which to the leaders of the thirteen colonies by then seemed bent on extinguishing their rights as Englishmen, established in Quebec a highly centralized French-style colonial administration. To boot, in an unusual act of intercultural sensitivity and political realism, the English government recognized the rights of Canada's French Catholics, which worried the often virulently anti-Catholic Protestants in the thirteen colonies. It must have seemed to the colonists that Britain had become the guardians of a policy and French-speaking Catholic society they had defeated in the just concluded war.[73]

Where the British saw a chance to increase imperial revenue, to reform inefficiencies in the colonial administration, and to discipline a constantly complaining colonial population, the Americans—steeped in the

libertarian thought of the English Whig tradition and deeply suspicious
of executive power—saw what seemed at times to be a conspiracy. Corrupt politicians, they feared, were attacking rights that derived from
English common law and from the political developments in the previous
decades of "benign neglect," which had allowed the colonial legislatures
to claim new prerogatives.[74] With such different frames of reference and
interpretation, misunderstandings and conflicts were inevitable. As the
Americans explained in the Declaration of Independence, "Governments
long established should not be changed for light and transient causes,"
but the miscalculations of the British led the Americans to conclude that
"when a long train of abuses and usurpations, pursuing invariably the
same Object evinces a design to reduce them under absolute Despotism,
it is their right, it is their duty, to throw off such Government . . . "

Of course, the high ground of the Declaration of Independence was
not in practice so high, nor were the abuses so destructive. The British
colonists who complained about taxes were the least taxed in the Atlantic
world. And the men who claimed to stand for universal principles of
equality and freedom could not imagine women in political life, enslaved
a fifth of the population, and hardly gave a second thought to taking possession of land of the Native Americans. Yet even an abbreviated recount-
ing of the sequence of English measures between the end of the Seven
Years' War and the Declaration of Independence shows that their extravagant fears had a plausible basis, though we know they were misplaced.
The English wanted more control over the colonies and more revenue
from them, neither aim being devious or beyond the pale of reasonable
public policy. The colonists confused political ineptitude with conspiracy.

The American Revenue Act of 1764, more generally known as the
Sugar Act, was intended to raise revenue for imperial defense. Put differently: the plan was to shift to Americans part of the costs of global power
previously wholly borne by British taxpayers, since the government hesitated to increase debt or further raise taxes at home. This strategy marked
a first: it was the first law ever passed by Parliament designed specifically
to raise money for the crown in the colonies. It specified that duties
would be paid on what might be considered luxuries but were in fact
widespread goods in the colonies' growing consumer economy—
including refined sugar, coffee, and Madeira wines. As important as the
duty rates was the promise of enforcement, with a revitalized customs

service and new vice admiralty courts where defendants had fewer rights. It was in response to this policy that in Boston, on May 24, 1764, the famous principle of no taxation without representation was first voiced. Going beyond words, the colonies then adopted a policy of non-importation.

The particularly impolitic Stamp Act followed in 1765; its requirement of stamps on publications and legal documents struck especially hard at newspaper editors, lawyers, merchants, and land speculators, a rather formidable opposition. If the Sugar Act had been the first colonial revenue act, the Stamp Act was the first to tax economic activities internal to the colonies, inviting the colonists to observe the distinction between internal and external taxation, which they immediately did, for the Stamp Act produced both riots in the streets and a sustained public discussion of political theory that lasted for twenty years. The colonists endlessly debated what a viable political form for their lives could be, in a discussion driven at once by interests and by ideals, by local circumstances and by the republican, liberal, and religious ideas about authority and polities that were circulating internationally.[75] It eventuated, as we all know, in the Constitution and *The Federalist Papers*, the two most distinctive and distinguished works of practical politics and political theory achieved by Americans.

Because so much American commentary on the work of the founders emphasizes the uniqueness of this accomplishment, we might usefully pause for a moment to note that while their debate began in defense of distinctively English rights, they increasingly drew upon a large body of Enlightenment ideas that were circulating as far east as Moscow and Vienna and as far south as Buenos Aires. The work of eighteenth-century progressive politics was to select and adapt the ideas that were appropriate to local traditions, circumstances, power relations, and aspirations.[76] Coastal and central Europe responded differently to the Enlightenment. Ocean commerce had transformed the feudal structures of society and politics differently and more fully in the coastal nations than in the interior. Central and Eastern Europe, cut off from transforming ocean commerce, developed into large land-based states, which lacked the substantial bourgeoisie of the maritime cities. Enlightenment ideas did not as a consequence find their audience among the bourgeoisie so much as within the large class of state officials. The liberalism of Joseph II in the

Habsburg Empire strengthened central power as it created a more meritocratic state administration and advanced agricultural reform.[77] Similar developments occurred elsewhere under absolute monarchies. While in Joseph II's Vienna or Catherine the Great's St. Petersburg or Frederick the Great's Berlin the new politics might mean "enlightened absolutism," in Philadelphia it meant republicanism.[78] The significance of the Americans' revolution and constitution also varied, incidentally, depending on local circumstance. The British saw the American contribution as constitutionalism and suffrage, while in France the focus was on rights and state power. For the Swiss and, later, the Argentines and the Germans at the Frankfurt Assembly, it was federalism.[79]

Popular resistance to the Stamp Act forced its repeal in 1766, but the British did not back off the principle. A declaratory act that accompanied the repeal asserted Parliament's power to make laws binding the colonists "in all cases whatsoever" (repeating, incidentally, the language of the earlier Irish Declaratory Act of 1719). Nonetheless, the Townshend Duties, imposed a year later, accepted the American distinction between "internal" and "external" taxation, and set import duties on tea, paper, paint, glass, and lead. Again there were elaborate new enforcement mechanisms, including a new court. And again protest. The colonists' nonimportation policy, an intercolonial activity, helped to promote a sense of colonial separateness, identity, and unity, and the protests continued the colonists' education in political theory. Now they argued that it didn't matter whether or not a tax was internal or external: the relevant distinction, as John Dickinson put it in his famous *Letters from a Farmer in Pennsylvania to the Inhabitants of the British Colonies* (1768), was between Parliament's acknowledged right to regulate trade, which could involve incidental taxation, and any supposed right to impose revenue taxes, which he denied. Again Parliament reconsidered, and the Townshend Duties were reduced.

But the colonies remained astir. The cities, dependent on maritime trade, suffered in these years, with increasing impoverishment, social tension, and conflict. None suffered more than Boston, which became the hotbed of resistance.[80] Boston reacted dramatically—literally theatrically—to the Tea Tax of 1773. Boston radicals costumed as Mohawk Indians boarded an East India Company ship and dumped 342 chests of the Company's tea into Boston Harbor.

By the spring of 1774, London, determined to bring the colonies under control, had enacted a series of laws known as the Coercive Acts, directed especially at Boston. The port was closed, and the Massachusetts government was effectively suspended. The Administration of Justice Act gave new powers and legal protection to colonial officials, strengthening their hand in challenges to imperial authority.

Later, in September 1774, the first Continental Congress met, with twelve colonies sending delegates. At this point, several colonial leaders, including James Wilson of Philadelphia, John Adams of Massachusetts, and Thomas Jefferson of Virginia, like the rebels in New Granada and Peru who were soon to resist the Spanish reforms, had developed the idea that while the colonies owed allegiance to the king, they were not subject to the authority of Parliament. That move carried the colonists to within a single step of independence. The Declaration of Independence, which took that step, was framed as a separation from the king and from the principles of monarchy.

All the while, British troops had been assembled in Massachusetts. On the night of April 18, 1775, the patriot Paul Revere rode from Boston to warn the farmers in Lexington and Concord that the British were coming. The next day the famous shots were fired at Lexington Green. The colonists were in open rebellion, even war. A month later, the Continental Congress named George Washington commander of the Continental army. As 1775 turned into 1776, the Congress established the Committee of Secret Correspondence, charged with seeking the help of "friends" in Europe. Thus far, the dispute had been within the frame of the British Empire. Only the colonies' claim of independence would internationalize it and draw in France and Spain. Tom Paine's *Common Sense*, published in January 1776, made the first call for separation from England. In the context of the conflict with the metropole, his savage attack on the principle of monarchy was less important to the colonists' European friends than his declaration of the absurdity of an island ruling a continent. King Louis XVI agreed secretly to give a million livres (equal to a million British pounds) to the Americans, and the Spanish joined him with roughly the same amount. These funds, transmitted to the colonists by Count Beaumarchais through a phony company that laundered the money, made it possible to buy crucial military supplies— among other items, 80 percent of the gunpowder used by the colonists in the first year of the war.

The war did not go well at first, and the French were reluctant publicly to back a loser. But the British defeat at Saratoga in October 1777, by which time the French and Spanish navies were rebuilt and ready, was enough to enable Benjamin Franklin to persuade the French to ally themselves with the Americans against the British. A formal alliance was signed the following February, and soon thereafter France brought Spain into the anti-British coalition. French provision of matériel, troops, and especially sea power was decisive in the American victory.

1783

At the peace table in 1783 the French contribution to the defeat of Great Britain seems not to have been fairly recognized. The Treaty of Paris gave much to the Americans—surely more than the Spanish would have preferred, since they recognized the land-hungry ex-colonists as a potential threat to their interests in North America—but very little to France, save the considerable pleasure of having helped deprive Britain of a valuable colony. Though the French had significant military and political initiatives under way in India designed to promote a revolt of Indian princes against Britain at the time of the peace talks, there were no known positive results (and indeed there were to be none). So the French did not expect to restore their former influence in India, nor did they ask for the restoration of Canada.[81] They did, however, regain their slave-trading posts on the Senegal River and Gorée.

Spain did no better. Its principal objective in allying with France had been to get Gibraltar back, but it failed in this, though Britain returned East and West Florida to avoid further discussion of Gibraltar—thus abandoning ten thousand British Loyalists who had fled there in 1782–83.[82] Land transfers among England, Spain, and France were few and small, mostly in Africa, Asia, and the Caribbean. Surprisingly perhaps, the most contentious issue that was settled by the negotiators concerned cod fishing and drying rights off the coast of Newfoundland.[83] The Dutch, who entered the war late but whose free-trading Caribbean island of St. Eustatius was a vital source of military supplies for the colonists, made a separate agreement, by which the British returned to them the forts, ports, and cities they had captured in Southeast Asia in return for a

Dutch promise not to interfere with British navigation in Asia or Africa.[84] Oddly enough, the big winners were the new United States and its former colonial ruler, which consolidated its position as a world power, even as it lost the thirteen colonies.[85]

The fighting in North America had ended at Yorktown in October 1781, but the diplomatic efforts to arrive at a final peace treaty were protracted. The result was not one but three separate treaties. The treaty between Britain and the Americans was signed in Paris, the two with France and Spain in Versailles on the same day. These multiple treaties were less problematic than the limited capacity of the Confederation Congress to be a responsible signatory to them. By ratifying the Treaty of Paris, the Congress placed obligations on the British but could not bind its own constituent states. With so much power reserved to the states in the confederation structure of the new American government, it could only "earnestly recommend" to them that they abide by the treaty's provisions.[86] This made it difficult to hold Britain to its commitments, especially those pertaining to forts in the west. A major reason for favoring the Constitution in 1787 and the provision in it making international treaties superior to all state laws was to rectify this weakness in international diplomacy inherent in the continental system and in the Articles of Confederation.

The proliferation of treaties is symptomatic of the seemingly puzzling results of the war. Although their European allies were indispensable to the Americans' military success, their rewards were not commensurate. Many revolutionaries (and even more succeeding generations) were prepared to attribute the happy result to the work of Providence. More likely, as James Madison suggested at the Constitutional Convention, great powers had their own interests. The Comte de Vergennes, well experienced in European diplomacy, preferred the orchestration of a complex balance of power to French aggrandizement.[87] For him in 1783 the American war was not the most pressing diplomatic issue. He was more concerned with the Eastern Question. The weakness of the Ottoman Empire created a power vacuum that might tempt either Prussia or Russia to expand its influence there, which would upset the European balance of power. Vergennes knew that Russia was preparing for war against the Turks; he needed to extricate France from war with Britain in order to be able to counter Russia in the east. And he worried about French vulnerability in the West Indies.[88]

The American peace commissioners—John Adams, Benjamin Franklin, and John Jay—were able negotiators, though Adams and Jay were somewhat provincial in outlook and not always diplomatic.[89] Franklin was by far the most effective, bringing unmatched resources of reputation, knowledge, and personal charm to the work of diplomacy: in France he was widely credited for the peace.[90] Cultural nationalism had not yet developed enough to disrupt the cosmopolitan republic of letters that made learned men like Franklin "citizens of the world." His reputation as a scientist knew no geographical or political limits; the encyclopedist Denis Diderot considered him the very model of the experimental scientist. (That he was one of the most admired and honored figures in the Atlantic world rankled the exceedingly jealous Adams.) The respect granted Franklin, which he carried into every conversation, and his commitment to "Simplicity and Good Faith" (his own phrase) enabled him to win the trust of the English and French negotiators.[91]

The Americans also benefited from the idea of empire held by Lord Shelburne, who preferred "trade to dominion."[92] As secretary of state from 1766–68, Shelburne had pressed for reconciliation with the colonists; when he failed to get support from either the king or the cabinet, he had resigned. He returned to office in 1782, and it fell to him to negotiate the treaty and to reconcile King George III to the independence of the United States. Anxious to ensure the continuation of trade with the Americans, which had doubled between 1758 and 1771, Shelburne thought of the peace treaty not only as the end of the war but also as the first step toward a postwar rapprochement that would serve commerce and weaken the Franco-American alliance.[93] His strategy worked: trade between the Americans and the British was not only restored but dramatically expanded, reaching a volume in the 1790s twice that of the 1760s, though unhampered free trade was not established until 1815.[94] In 1783 his strategic vision was not grasped or appreciated by rival parliamentary factions, and he fell from power, never to return.[95] Ironically, it was his vision (and Adam Smith's) of a free-trade empire that brought even greater global power to Britain in the nineteenth century.

Vergennes did not live to see the results of his contribution to American independence or to France. He died in 1787, before the Americans finally devised an adequate form of government and enshrined it in the Constitution. It was also before King Louis XVI, having accumulated an unmanageable debt—a long time in the making but tipped toward the crisis point by the cost of the American war—was forced to call the States General in 1789, the precipitating event of the French Revolution.[96]

The Treaty of Paris was a disaster for the Amerindians. Not all but many Indian tribes supported the British against the Americans, and surely they recognized that there would be a price to be paid for having backed the losers. But they could not have imagined that the British would completely abandon them. There was no Native American representative at the peace table, and the British signed over "Indian Country" (the trans-Appalachian west to the Mississippi River) to the new American government without consultation. Neither Indians nor Indian possession of these lands was even mentioned in the treaty. The magnitude and meaning of this silence become clear when one realizes that most of the territory transferred to the Americans by the British was in fact Indian Territory. The European populations were concentrated on the coasts, Atlantic and Gulf, while the Ohio Country and Great Lakes region were unknown to most Americans. English was rarely heard on the Mississippi River.[97]

The Indians were "thunderstruck" when they learned the terms of the treaty, all the more so because by 1783 they had achieved "military ascendancy" over the settlers in Kentucky, which should have placed them in a position to negotiate.[98] Little Turkey, a Cherokee leader, both puzzled and angry at the result, commented: "The peace makers and our Enemies have talked away our lands at a Rum Drinking." The results were apparent soon enough. In a message to the Spanish governor of St. Louis in 1784, representatives of the Iroquois, Shawnee, Cherokee, Chickasaw, and Choctaw tribes declared that the Americans were "extending themselves like a plague of locusts in the territories of the Ohio River which we inhabit."[99] They resisted with surprising success for a while, but with the Louisiana Purchase and the British evacuation of their forts in the Ohio Valley after the War of 1812, the Indians were without allies; by 1844, less than 25 percent of the Indians who had lived east of the Mississippi in 1783 were still there.[100]

The exclusionary vision of the future that placed Native Americans outside an ever-expanding United States had its origin, as we have seen, in the resolution of the Seven Years' War, when, instead of being recognized as a part of the new society being created in North America, Indians were placed outside it—beyond some frontier line. Referring to the

Indians in a letter to Congress in 1783, George Washington explained, "We will . . . establish a boundary line between them and us."[101] Over time, this idea of a place or non-place for the Native Americans was realized. In the 1780s, Indians were a part of everyday life for most Euro-Americans; they were still, in the 1820s and '30s, at the center of American consciousness and politics. But by the 1840s they had been pushed beyond the Mississippi and were thought of as exotics if they registered at all in the daily life of the American nation.[102] The logic had been set out in Andrew Jackson's famous presidential justification of the destruction of the historical patterns of Indian life:

> The benevolent policy of the Government . . . in relation to the removal of the Indians beyond the white settlements is approaching a happy consummation . . . Humanity has often wept over the fate of the aborigines of this country, and Philanthropy has been long busily employed in devising means to avert it, but its progress has never for a moment been arrested, and one by one have many powerful tribes disappeared from the earth . . . But true philanthropy reconciles the mind to these vicissitudes as it does to the extinction of one generation to make room for another . . . Nor is there anything in this which, upon a comprehensive view of the general interests of the human race, is to be regretted . . . What good man would prefer a country covered with forests and ranged by a few savages to our extensive Republic, studded with cities, towns, and prosperous farms, embellished with all the improvements which art can devise or industry execute, occupied by more than 12,000,000 happy people, and filled with all the blessings of liberty, civilization, and religion?[103]

This removal of the Indians, one of the most tragic chapters of American history, was part of a pattern of social differentiation and isolation between the Revolution and the Civil War that reduced the complexity of daily experience in many ways. Distinct but strangely similar efforts were made to banish the poor and eccentric to asylums, to send emancipated African-Americans abroad and tighten the regulation of those who were still enslaved, and to restrict the domain of women to the new terms of suburban domesticity.

Many historians date the beginning of the so-called Second British Empire from this period and from lessons learned in England's controversy with the Americans. The emphasis of British imperial policy shifted to trade rather than territorial governance. When territorial rule was exercised, notably in India, it was typically accomplished without representative institutions. The American experience taught colonial administrators how much trouble such institutions were. They also distinguished between European colonials (as in Australia and Canada) and non-Europeans, the nonwhite "others" whom they confidently ruled in an authoritarian manner without representative institutions, relying on force when necessary.[104] The British had always thought of Asians and Africans as inferior, yet imperial officials had often collaborated with indigenous rulers. In the quarter century following American independence this changed. Asians, Eurasians, and Africans were denied meaningful positions of authority.[105] Consider the example of Lord Cornwallis: after his surrender at Yorktown ended the war in America, he was dispatched—after brief service in Ireland—to India, where as governor-general he had authority far greater than any governor had possessed in the American colonies but typical of English rulers in India in the century to come.[106]

British interest in Asian trade had been growing before the American Revolution, and after 1783 Asia replaced the Atlantic as the focus of British mercantile imperialism. The Caribbean was no longer a "British lake." Some have described this shift as the essential background for the success of the British movement to abolish slavery.[107] Others emphasize the China trade as the key development in shifting British interests away from the Caribbean and North America. In either case, the geopolitical orientation further extended Atlantic connections into global ones. The shift to the east brought India into the emerging global cotton economy, especially after the American Civil War, and laid the foundation for the nineteenth-century trade that carried opium from India to China.[108]

Americans, too, expanded their vision of the world and began trading with India and China. The worldliness of the moment is captured in an election sermon of 1783 delivered by Ezra Stiles, president of Yale College. Given the theme of the sermon, one should note that in 1718 the college at New Haven had been renamed for the Boston-born Elihu Yale, who had made a gift to the school at the suggestion of Cotton Mather. Yale had become rich as a high official of the East India Company (he had been governor of Fort St. George in Madras in 1687, though he lost the position because of administrative irregularities), and against this worldly background Stiles spoke for the worldliness of the new republic.

> This great American Revolution will be attended to and contemplated by all nations. Navigation will carry the American flag around the globe itself; and display the thirteen stripes and new constellation at Bengal and Canton, on the Indus and Ganges, on the Whang-ho [Yellow River] and the Yang-yse-kiang; and with commerce [America] will import the wisdom and literature of the east . . . There shall be a universal travelling to and fro, and knowledge shall be increased. This knowledge shall be brought home and treasured up in America; and being here digested and carried to the highest perfection, may reblaze back from America to Europe, to Asia and to Africa, and illumine the world with truth and liberty.[109]

THE AGE OF ATLANTIC REVOLUTIONS

There is no definitive list of the movements that could be called Atlantic revolutions, but historians—R. R. Palmer, Jacques Godechot, George Rudé, and Franco Venturi among them—have made diverse efforts to come up with one, using definitions of various degrees of precision and imprecision. They always include the two other successful eighteenth-century revolutions, of course, France and Haiti, to which we should add the many independence movements in Spanish America during the early nineteenth century. But one should also include failed and ambiguous eighteenth-century cases—ranging from Peru, Poland, Ireland, Sweden, and Belgium to Geneva, Bavaria, Savoy, Milan, and Naples, where in most cases the independence movements could not sustain themselves once France had withdrawn military support.[110]

It is often and rightly said that while the American Revolution was "a crucial event in American history," compared with the French Revolution one can see few "traces elsewhere" of direct influence, save perhaps for its most notable documents (the Declaration of Independence, the Constitution, and *The Federalist Papers*).[111] Yet it had its impact in the eighteenth century; until the events in France, the success of the Americans stood for revolution through the whole Atlantic world, edging the word toward its modern political meaning. Before the seventeenth century, revolution referred to the rotation of planets or to past events of change driven by impersonal forces doing the work of God. There was a considerable discussion of revolution in seventeenth-century England, prompted by the civil war in the middle of the century and the Glorious Revolution near the end. These discussions, most notably John Locke's social contract argument that so influenced both the Declaration of Independence and the American resort to constitutional conventions, were more about the right of revolution and its legitimation than about its process or its transformative qualities. John Adams, writing to his wife, Abigail, on July 3, 1776, after he and Franklin had made their suggestions to Jefferson for the final revisions of the Declaration of Independence, speaks in a more modern key, making revolution more actual, place-specific, and the result of human initiative, the work of human actors:

> When I look back to the Year 1761, and recollect the argument concerning the Writs of Assistance, in the Superior Court, which I have hitherto considered as the Commencement of the Controversy, between Great Britain and America, and run through the whole Period from that Time to this, and recollect the series of political Events, the Chain of Causes and Effects, I am surprised at the Suddenness, as well as the Greatness of this Revolution.[112]

A similar understanding of revolution as exemplified by the Americans is evident in the first book to describe the event, which appeared two years later in France. Emphasizing the contemporaneity of it and the human agency involved, the author of *Abrégé de la révolution de l'Amérique angloise* (*Summary View of the American Revolution*) (1778) referred to the *"révolution actuelle"* and to the revolutionaries as *"coopérateurs."*[113]

The American Revolution was of interest both in Spain and to the Creoles in Spanish America. While Spain was effectively an ally of the Americans against Britain, the revolutionary rhetoric posed a serious ideological difficulty. In addition, the American demands for free trade after 1783 challenged its commercial system, and the costs of the war posed revenue problems. Spain's subsequent reform of its own trade regulations and taxation complicated its already tense relation to its colonies.[114] For the Creoles, however, the mere existence of the new American republic was important. The writings of Thomas Paine, John Adams, George Washington, and Thomas Jefferson became widely known, and translations of the Declaration of Independence and the Constitution were quickly made.[115] Indeed, the American presidential system of government was eventually emulated throughout Latin America and to this day distinguishes governments in the Western Hemisphere from those in Europe.

The Creole elites of Spanish America worried that the radicalism of the French Revolution offered more equality than they wanted in their own societies, and the more radical it became, the less they liked it. Such a revolution in Spanish America would, as the historian John Lynch observes, "destroy the world of privilege they enjoyed."[116] Francisco de Miranda, a Venezuelan political leader who had been in New York and Philadelphia at the end of the American Revolution and in Paris during its revolution, observed in 1799: "We have before our eyes two great examples, the American and the French Revolutions. Let us prudently imitate the first and shun the second."[117] The American Revolution had the advantage of ending monarchical privileges without mobilizing the lower classes (as in France) or producing a slave revolt (as in Haiti).

For Europeans who embraced Enlightenment ideas, the American Revolution suggested the shape of things to come. It seemed to announce a new era of liberty, and it gave new authority to critics of traditional hierarchies of authority. The Americans offered an example of the Enlightenment in action. Europe, they believed, was moving in the same direction. The crisis that Enlightenment *philosophes* felt in Europe, many thought, was pointing toward the birth of a new society based on liberty and citizen sovereignty. The new United States was an important anticipation of this hoped-for development.[118] In 1790, Lafayette gave Thomas Paine the key to the Bastille with instructions to carry it to George Washington. In delivering it, Paine wrote of its symbolism, no doubt reflecting Lafayette's opinion as well as his own: "The key is the symbol of the first ripe fruits of American principles translated into Europe . . . that the principles of America opened the Bastille is not to be doubted and therefore the key comes to its right place."[119] Of course, Paine simplified the sources of the French Revolution. But in 1790 his views on the presence of America in European history were not unusual.

The idea of revolution as social upheaval was not at issue here; that debate would come later. It was the enactment of a new form of government based on new principles of sovereignty that defined this eighteenth-century understanding of revolution. When the French king called the States General into session in 1789, it was to resolve issues about the national debt, but given the well-known ideology of the American Revolution, the king could be seen as implicitly acknowledging the sovereignty of the people when he resorted to this representative body. Indeed, this notion, so central to the American Revolution, was explicitly claimed by the representatives when they formed themselves into the French National Assembly.

The connections between the American Revolution and the Haitian one are complex and reciprocal, though of course the French Revolution was far more important to the events in St. Domingue. Indeed, the revolutionaries there, particularly Toussaint L'Ouverture, referred directly to the rights pronounced by the French National Assembly, wanting to extend to Haiti the 1791 legislation that conferred citizenship on *gens de couleur*. Black slaves were revolting against a white master race and claiming a place for themselves among nations. The Haitians thus forced a practical universality onto the universalist rhetoric of the French Revolution, expanding the meaning of the French claims and making their own revolution the most radical of all. It was an extraordinary event.

A regiment of free blacks from St. Domingue had fought as French allies with the Americans in the siege of Savannah in 1779, where these soldiers gained military experience and confidence. It is likely that they also imbibed some of the libertarian rhetoric of the American Revolution.[120] And then, when war broke out between France and St. Domingue in 1791, the Adams administration—largely motivated by the complex diplomacy among France, Britain, and Spain—maintained trade relations with St. Domingue, supplying the revolutionaries with indispensable naval support, food, and arms. So the American Revolution contributed its part to the rebellion in St. Domingue.

News of events in St. Domingue traveled rapidly.[121] Africans in the New World, whether slave or free, felt solidarity with the revolution, which no doubt inspired hope in them.[122] Knowledge of this history was maintained as part of an oral tradition; in the 1820s the African-American press in the North carried news of Haiti, and free blacks regularly celebrated Haiti's independence day. The free black David Walker spoke for many when he wrote in his famous *Appeal to the Colored Citizens of the World* (1829) that "Hayti [is] the glory of the blacks and terror of tyrants."[123]

Thus when slaveholders in the United States and elsewhere spoke of "French ideas," they had more than Paris in mind. Haiti represented French excess in an especially worrisome form.[124] For slaveholders the Haitian Revolution sent out shock waves that extended from South Carolina to Bahia; everywhere in the New World slave masters thought they perceived a new "insolence" among their slaves.[125] Fear formed a transnational solidarity of white planters and political elites. Simón Bolívar, the liberator of Spanish America, openly opposed slavery, but he shared Jefferson's terrible discomfort with the Haitian Revolution.[126] Francisco de Miranda, who preferred the American to the French Revolution, declared in 1798 that he would rather have no revolution at all than have a Haitian one:

I confess that much as I desire liberty and independence in the New World, I fear anarchy and revolution even more. God forbid that the other countries suffer the same fate as Saint Domingue . . . better that they should remain another century under the barbarous and senseless oppression of Spain.[127]

Among blacks, the Haitian story was a focus for a transnational or diasporic identity, which enabled them to imagine a history in which the world might be turned upside down.[128] But the inspiration of Toussaint L'Ouverture was not entirely imaginary; there is concrete evidence of the influence of the Haitian example in slave revolts at Bahia (1798), Havana (1812), and Charleston (1822), among others. Denmark Vesey, who expected support from Haiti for the Charleston uprising, had quoted from the Declaration of Independence, knew the history of St. Domingue, and planned his rebellion for Bastille Day, July 14.[129]

How radical was the American Revolution? The question emerged rather quickly in American political debate and has continued to be much contested among historians. It has no final answer, for it depends on one's definition of radical and one's time frame for appraising the results of the revolutionary action. Bernard Bailyn once referred to the "transforming radicalism of the American Revolution"; as Abraham Lincoln understood it, that radicalism would play itself out over time, all the way to the present, including the civil rights movement of the 1960s.[130] Yet the Revolution has mostly been celebrated in the United States and elsewhere for its moderation, for its respect for traditional rights and the rights of property, and for not challenging inequalities of wealth, race, or gender.

Still, it was radical in its own time. Leopold von Ranke, the German historian and founder of modern, scientific history, had no doubt of the revolutionary implications of the American movement for independence. Writing in 1854, he identified its radicalism with the idea and practical application of the sovereignty of the people.[131] That was indeed radical in its time, even if the idea of the people as sovereign had been developing within the British parliamentary tradition for some time.[132] And it is also true that the concept was far from completely realized in 1776 or 1789. Still, it was a novel relocation of sovereignty—even unsettling for those committed to it. John Adams recorded his feeling that these were "new, strange, and terrible Doctrines." But he embraced them, pleased that it meant that "the People" were "the Source of all Authority and Original of all Power." It was a remarkable opportunity for a people "to erect the whole Building with their own hands."[133]

However important the notion of popular sovereignty, it should be acknowledged that it had some less than positive side effects. If the sovereignty of the people enabled all citizens to share in the politics of the nation—admittedly more or less fictively[134]—this formal equality erased certain ambiguities that had once allowed for the diffusion of political participation, if not of formal rights. When white males were declared sovereign—and the 1790 naturalization law affirmed the "free white person" (assumed to be male) as normative[135]—then those who were not were more sharply excluded: women, Indians, slaves, and free persons of color.[136] It is notable that the question of citizenship for *gens de couleur* and women was debated in the French National Assembly, while in the United States citizenship for blacks was out of the question, and in the Constitutional Convention citizenship for women was not mentioned, despite Abigail Adams's plea to her husband, John, to "Remember the Ladies."

Two other political consequences of the Revolution strike me as revolutionary. The first, based on the assignment of sovereignty to the people, is the extraordinarily important yet seldom noted shift from "subject" to "citizen," a general development in the Atlantic world that began between 1776 and 1791 and continued into the nineteenth century—with the decline of monarchies.[137] And the weakening of the religious sanction for monarchies opened the way to the separation of church and state, as radical a concept as any—and still discomfiting for many in the United States and elsewhere.

If the political innovations of the American Revolution are impressive, what about its character as a social revolution? It seems to fall in the middle of the Atlantic revolutions in this regard. A new society for whites was already in the making in British North America, and the consensus on the racial boundary made the liberty proclaimed in the Revolution less subversive of the existing social order and therefore less destructive than the French Revolution. One could say that the North American revolution accelerated and legitimated social changes already well under way, while in France the older and stronger structures invited more violent attack. So, as J. Franklin Jameson long ago pointed out and Gordon Wood has recently argued, various democratizing developments in the American Revolution were cumulatively significant, but American society was not shaken to its roots.[138]

The American Revolution nonetheless dissolved traditional hierarchies more than did the Spanish-American revolutions, though the strategic decisions made by the Creole leaders might have predicted a radical experience: they mobilized mixed-blood Creoles, slaves, free blacks, and Indians in their fight for independence. But strong traditions of hierarchy and a refusal to empower these groups led to the establishment of authoritarian governments. Strong military force was maintained with armies that were able and willing to return these groups to a condition of powerlessness.

The patriots in North America did not look for allies among their slaves or Indians. While African-Americans fought in the Battle of Bunker Hill, in deference to southern concerns the Continental Congress forbade blacks to bear arms. When the British offered freedom to blacks who joined their army, the Congress reversed itself, but the five thousand blacks who were enrolled on the patriot side were mostly unarmed and assigned to logistical roles. While the British abandoned their Indian allies at the peace table, they did free thousands of slaves who joined them—transporting them to Canada and the West Indies. But the Americans did not emancipate those who contributed to the revolutionary cause, and the number of slaves in the United States after the peace was larger than in 1776.[139] Still, the practice of politics—the political culture—was friendlier to democratization in North America than in South America. Social and political developments in the United States—driven in part by competing elites and a two-party system—were within decades opening opportunities for white males, but such was not the case in the newly independent South American countries.[140]

Without question, the most radical New World revolution was the Haitian one.[141] Toussaint L'Ouverture made the strongest claim for universal human rights in the age of Enlightenment, and the slaves of African descent whom he led to freedom created the second republic in the New World. He tested the limits of liberty and citizenship, the new universals of the Enlightenment, unlike earlier slave rebels who had been restorationist or secessionist—the Maroons of Jamaica, for example.[142] It turned out, alas, that he found the limits. Europeans and Euro-Americans were not prepared to accept his claims, and thus bounded their own universals.[143]

In fact, the violence in Haiti, the social disorder, and the post-revolution collapse of its economy seriously set back the emerging abolitionist movement. For more than a century racists used Haiti as an argument against emancipation and, in the United States, against efforts to achieve racial justice during Reconstruction and the Jim Crow era.[144] In contrast, Frederick Douglass, the former slave who was American ambassador to Haiti in 1889–91, reminded Americans in 1893 of its continuing importance: "With all her faults, you and I and all of us have reason to respect Haiti for her services to the cause of liberty and human equality throughout the world."[145]

History moves in strange ways, and paradoxically the Haitian Revolution actually resulted in an expansion of slavery. It also led to the development of a sugar economy in Louisiana and in Cuba, which replaced Haiti as the world's leading sugar producer.[146] In the southern states, whites feared slaves familiar with events in St. Domingue and possibly full of revolutionary ideas, and they passed laws in the 1790s limiting or forbidding the importation of slaves from the Caribbean.[147] As W.E.B.

DuBois pointed out, this same fear doubtless helped to ensure that a national law suppressing the slave trade would be enacted (with Jefferson's support) as soon as permitted by the Constitution, which prohibited legislation on the subject until 1808.[148]

In equally complex and paradoxical ways, the American Revolution both advanced the antislavery cause and set it back. The language of freedom and equality was used in the northern states to advance the cause of slavery's abolition, though in some cases over a rather protracted period, lasting well into the nineteenth century in the case of New York, the largest northern center of slavery.[149] Yet as David Brion Davis, the leading historian of slavery and abolition, has written, it is "impossible to imagine" that the British would have passed the Emancipation Act of 1833 "if the United States had remained part of the empire," since slaveholders in the American South would have combined with the Caribbean planters as a very powerful pro-slavery lobby in Parliament.[150] The separation of the United States reduced by half the number of slaves in the British Empire.[151] "As long as America was our own," the British abolitionist Thomas Clarkson explained, "there was no chance that a minister would have attended to the groans of the sons and daughters of Africa."[152] Yet the new nation not only maintained slavery but was especially supportive of slaveholding classes and regions; the Constitution included a provision that conferred special political advantages for them—the three-fifths clause that counted slaves as three-fifths of a person for purposes of allocating representatives in Congress and the Electoral College.[153] To complete the complex set of relations: once the British ended slavery in the Caribbean, new pressure built up to abolish it in the United States.[154]

One peculiarity of the American Revolution is that it failed to inspire much taste for a revolutionary tradition. American elites were certain that all the necessary revolutionizing had been completed in the eighteenth century. Rufus Choate, a leader in the American bar, made this clear in a lecture at Harvard Law School in 1845. The age of "reform is over; its work is done."[155] Of course, four years later Henry David Thoreau wrote his famous essay "Civil Disobedience," but if Choate and Thoreau represent extremes, most Americans agreed with the former rather than the latter.

And Americans offered only limited support to revolution abroad. To put it differently, and somewhat critically: while they gave at least rhetorical support to various European freedom struggles, from Greece in the 1820s to Hungary and Italy in the 1840s, and they welcomed refugees from the German revolutions of 1848, outside of Europe, and particularly in respect to non-European anticolonial revolutions, they hesitated—and this hesitation has continued even into our own time. It is often said that the radicalism and anticlericalism of the French Revolution soured the Americans on revolution, and there is ample evidence that this is true. But I suggest that the specter of the Haitian Revolution is of at least equal importance. Certainly it was for Jefferson, the most prominent American defender of the violence of the French Revolution.

The Haitian Revolution, writes the Haitian anthropologist Michel-Rolph Trouillot, "entered history with the peculiar characteristics of being unthinkable even as it happened."[156] How could black-skinned slaves make the claims they made, win the victories over European armies they achieved, and enter the family of nations? Haiti haunted the early American republic. Political leaders in the American South did not want to hear of it. Senator Robert Y. Hayne of South Carolina, the nullificationist who debated Daniel Webster on the nature of the Union in 1830, lectured the Senate on the subject of Haiti a few years earlier. "Our policy with regard to Haiti is plain," he declared. "We can never acknowledge her independence."[157] Historians fairly attribute the beginnings of the intellectual blockade—the closing down of freedom of thought—that marked the antebellum South to the need to suppress the unthinkable events of Haiti, which preoccupied the planter elite.[158]

A NEW NATION IN A DANGEROUS WORLD

The peace of 1783 did not in fact pacify. With the departure of Shelburne from active participation in the British government, the Americans were excluded from the benefits of the British navigation system, particularly trade with the West Indies, though the latter was, John Adams said in 1783, "a part of the American system of commerce."[159] Ships of the United States were also excluded from Spanish America, and the nation's borders with Spain's North American territories were neither clear nor enforceable. Ignoring the border, the Spanish promoted Native American resistance in the west and tried to detach western settlements from the confederation, hoping to weaken the United States and to establish small, independent buffers between Spain and the United States. Britain, too, encouraged Indian depredations and, worse, declined to withdraw from their forts in the Ohio Valley and, like the Spanish, dealt directly with the settlements in Ohio and Kentucky. The British minister in charge considered encouraging new governments "distinct" from those of the "Atlantic states" to be developed in the west. (The British were pursuing a similar policy in Southeast Asia, seeking commercial alliances with territories nominally under Dutch control.)[160]

The military victory in the war and the treaty of 1783, the great achievements of the Confederation Congress, also exposed the severe limits of the Articles of Confederation. The Congress evidently lacked both the revenue and the executive authority to conduct an effective foreign policy, and this prompted a coalition of diverse leaders to reform or replace the Articles.[161] "It is no exaggeration," Walter Russell Mead has observed, "to say that we owe the Constitution to the requirements of foreign affairs."[162] Alexander Hamilton made this point in the fourteenth *Federalist* paper. "We have seen the necessity of our union as our bulwark against foreign danger, as the guardian of our commerce."

The new nation was independent, but very limited in its freedom of action. Far from being isolated, it was perhaps more deeply entangled in world affairs, more clearly a participant in histories larger than itself, than at any other time in its history. French, British, and Spanish diplomats expected that the new nation would break up. It was indeed, as John Fiske phrased it in 1888, on the centennial of the Constitution's ratification, a "critical period" in American history.[163] For it was not clear that the thirteen colonies made a natural unit or that they would be willing to sacrifice some of their sovereignty to secure the safety that union promised. Communication over their extensive territory was difficult, and the different regions had distinctive cultures and economic interests. Learned commentators were concerned that two thousand years of political theory—from Aristotle to Montesquieu and Rousseau—taught that republics must be small to maintain their virtue.

Even as they created a polity that was intended to be distinguished from those of Europe, the founders constantly had Europe on their minds: as a military threat, as a potential commercial partner (or obstacle to American commerce), and as a system of relations among sovereign states that might have lessons for their quest for a viable principle of union. They found Europe to be an unavoidable starting point for their thinking.[164] The challenge was to devise a form of governance stronger than a league of sovereign states like the European alliance system of their time, yet not too strong, not like the "despotic" states of Europe. They needed to find, according to Madison, a third way, a middle point between "a perfect separation & a perfect incorporation."[165] To reform the Articles of Confederation, they would have to persuade the states, the locus of the people's sovereignty in the confederation, that a larger, more centralized nation was possible as well as necessary to protect them in a dangerous world.

The movement to replace the confederation government, which assembled, as everyone knows, in Philadelphia in the summer of 1787, intended to remedy this problem. They aimed to form a stronger, more centralized government driven by national, not local, agendas. Again, as is well known, they created a complex federal system, established a revenue base for the national government, and ensured that the presidency would have sufficient executive power to conduct foreign relations.

The authors of the Constitution, all from very elite backgrounds, had domestic concerns as well. They feared that politics was being taken over by men of parochial interests organized in "factions" of limited vision. They believed in a government of statesmen, men of learning and substance like themselves, who could speak for the broadest interests of the nation. The men who went to Philadelphia were also concerned about protecting property from a covetous democracy that seemed rampant in the state legislatures.[166] Madison was direct on this point in the famous tenth *Federalist* paper. He explained that the protection of property was both the object of government and the most important source of factional division and unjust majorities. As he described the new Constitution, it solved this domestic problem and, I would add, established the conceptual foundation for continental expansion.

He began by distinguishing a democracy from a republic. Unlike a democratic assembly of citizens, he understood a republic to be "a government in which a scheme of representation takes place." Power is delegated to men "whose wisdom may best discern the true interest of their country." At this point he brought space to the rescue of the elite leadership he favored. The larger the extent of the republic, he argued, the more likely the election of men of the "most established characters," men of virtue, and the avoidance of "interested and overbearing majorities." "Extend the sphere and you take in a greater variety of parties and interests; you make it less probable that a majority of the whole will have a common motive to invade the rights of other citizens."[167] The structure of the proposed government would, he thought, all at once ensure statesmanship in its leaders and justify a large (and, logically, an ever larger) republic. One need not fear incorporation of the trans-Appalachian west.

Indeed, an important provision of the Constitution was that envisioning the creation of new states. Article IV followed the political logic of the Northwest Ordinance of 1787, another important achievement of the confederation government. Drafted by Thomas Jefferson, the ordinance is celebrated for the survey grid he proposed, the effects of which can still be observed when flying over the Midwest, and for the reservation of every thirty-sixth section for the support of education. Most important, however, was the expansionist logic it rationalized. It defined a new form of empire. It rejected the European model of expansion, which subordinated colonies. The Northwest Ordinance and then the Constitution promised equality among old and new states, producing a uniformity in contrast to the "composite" British nation and empire.

Jefferson's "empire of liberty" promised unlimited expansion to white settlers; they, not Native Americans, would form the new states. Practically, this policy undermined any notion of Native American priority or legitimate presence.[168] The military negotiators who dealt with the Indians in the 1790s treated them neither as sovereigns nor as negotiating partners, but rather as a "subdued people" to whom the United States would dictate the terms of their retreat and the advance of white settlement.[169] This strategy was devastating for the Indians, but it won the allegiance of white settlers in the west to the new government, which was otherwise identified as eastern. The commitment to expansion and the use of military power to protect frontier settlements removed what might have been a serious threat to the integrity of the nation.

FOREIGN AFFAIRS AND PARTISAN POLITICS

It is too seldom noted that George Washington was inaugurated four months *before* the fall of the Bastille, almost to the day. But the French Revolution and its Napoleonic aftermath meant that Washington and his successors would, until 1815, have to "steer . . . between the Scylla of England and the Charybdis of France."[170] The contest between the two powers that had played to the advantage of the Americans in 1776 became a threat to the nation after 1789.

The great question of American politics was not the oft-rehearsed debate between Hamilton and Jefferson on political economy, but rather their views (and the views of the entire political class) on whether the United States should "tilt" toward Britain or France.[171] In fact, their views on the two issues were connected, and their respective positions are not quite as one would expect. Jefferson was the greater internationalist: his nation of farmers would take advantage of the rights of neutral trading nations to reach the markets of the world. More the realist, Hamilton recognized that it would be difficult (as Jefferson later discovered when president) to enforce neutral trading rights. The development of manufacturing, he proposed, would allow Americans to be less dependent on a commerce they could not secure, or could not secure without the protection of Britain.[172]

Political divisions based on attitudes toward the French Revolution began to emerge in late 1791, but the decisive event in the evolving partisanship and in the foundation of the American two-party system (not mentioned or envisioned in the Constitution) was the Jay Treaty (1794).[173] John Jay's mission to Britain was intended to solve various problems remaining after the peace of 1783. For one, the British were maintaining their garrisons in the Ohio Valley, ostensibly on the ground that Americans had not paid various debts to British merchants and to dispossessed Loyalists.

Then, in 1793, British Orders in Council undercut American claims to neutral trading rights and permitted British officers to "impress" American seamen and force them to serve on British ships. The impressments were, in the words of John Quincy Adams, "a national degradation."[174] But the blockage of trade with Britain, the Americans' most important trade partner, was the most serious; the loss of customs duties, the main source of the new government's revenue, threatened the viability of the new nation.

Jay's instructions were to settle the disputes deriving from the treaty of 1783, to win compensation for acts based on Orders in Council, and to obtain a treaty of commerce opening the vital West Indies trade. While he did get the British to agree to evacuate their forts in the west (though they did not then vacate them), to give indemnities for specified spoliations under Orders in Council, and to legalize U.S. trade in the British East Indies, he got no agreement on the impressment of American seamen, no commercial treaty for the West Indies, and no commitment from the British to end their practice of encouraging Indian harassment of Americans, among other grievances. President Washington hesitated to divulge the details of Jay's treaty or to submit it to the Senate for ratification, though in the end he did, for it achieved peace with Britain, a key policy objective.

If it produced peace abroad, the treaty ignited war domestically. Conflict over it institutionalized a quasi-party division, which became what historians call the "first party system." "No-party" voting declined from 42 percent before the treaty to 7 percent afterward—a clear indication that the reason for growing partisanship was not so much Hamilton's financial program as the controversy over foreign affairs in general and the Jay Treaty in particular.[175] British policy and the failure of the Jay Treaty adequately to address it sparked the organization of an opposition party (which became, under the leadership of Jefferson and Madison, the Democratic-Republicans). Federalists, on the other hand, were mobilized by fear of the French Revolution. Ironically, while the French paid little attention to the Americans (they often didn't even answer letters from their own representatives in the United States in the 1790s), their revolution was quite central to domestic American politics.[176]

The leaders of the new nation were intensely aware that American politics was being driven, perhaps disastrously so, by the unavoidable entanglement in the rivalry between France and England. John Quincy Adams, writing to his brother in 1798, expressed his fear that conflict over French and British influences might well produce "a dissolution of the union," leaving the United States broken into "petty tribes at perpetual war with one another, swayed by rival European powers."[177] The artist and staunch Federalist John Trumbull recalled in his autobiography that "the artful intrigue of the French diplomatists, and the blunder of the British government, united to convert the whole American people into violent partisans of one or the other."[178] John Adams and Thomas Jefferson, who stood on opposite sides, had very similar concerns and hopes. As they looked toward the election of 1800, which would pit them against each other in the first presidential campaign organized as a party contest, Adams exploded in a letter to his wife: "I see how the thing is going. At the next election England will set up Jay or Hamilton, and France, Jefferson, and all the corruption of Poland will be introduced; unless the American spirit should rise and say, we will have neither John Bull nor Louis Baboon."[179] Jefferson, two years later, observed that "our countrymen have divided themselves by such strong affections, to the French and the English, that nothing will secure us internally but a divorce from both nations."[180]

Haiti heightened the partisan division.[181] Much of the debate over American policy toward Haiti was framed within the larger debate between France and Britain, as Britain maneuvered to take advantage of troubles on the island. But, as Linda Kerber has observed, the debate about foreign policy "kept sliding into the subject of slavery." When Federalists talked about the profits of trade, southern Republicans— Jefferson's core constituency—saw only the question of American recognition of a black republic. In debating the embargo that Jefferson wanted to impose on Haiti in 1806, a southern legislator was startlingly direct: "We cannot trade with them without acknowledging their independence. If gentlemen are ready to do this, I shall consider it as a sacrifice on the altar of black despotism and usurpation."[182]

The positions of Adams and Jefferson in regard to Haiti were contrasting and in retrospect ironic. Adams, perhaps the most notable American conservative, supported Toussaint L'Ouverture and his revolution. John Marshall, another notable conservative and secretary of state in the Adams administration, assured Toussaint L'Ouverture of the "sincere desire" of the United States "to preserve the most perfect harmony and the most friendly intercourse with St. Domingo."[183] And Adams sent a special consul to St. Domingue, Edward Stevens, a close friend of Alexander Hamilton (who also supported Toussaint L'Ouverture), instructing him to establish a friendly relationship with Toussaint L'Ouverture and his regime. He even authorized Stevens to inform Toussaint L'Ouverture that if Haiti moved toward a declaration of independence, the United States would be supportive. Of course, in the larger geopolitical context the Federalists tended to lean toward British interests and the Republicans toward France.[184] Still, Adams was giving the black revolutionaries essential supplies and matériel. It is quite probable that without this American assistance the French could have put down the revolution.[185]

Jefferson as president recalled Stevens and later embargoed trade with Haiti. Unlike Adams, he was widely recognized for his support of revolutions, even the French one. In defense of its turn to violence, he observed that "the tree of liberty must be refreshed from time to time with the blood of patriots and tyrants."[186] But what was tolerable in Paris was not so in Cap Haitien. The revolution there terrified Jefferson. "I become daily more & more convinced," he wrote to James Monroe on Bastille Day in 1793, "that all the West India Islands will remain in the hands of the people of color; & a total expulsion of the whites sooner or later take place. It is high time we should foresee the bloody scenes which our children certainly and possibly ourselves (south of the Potomac) have to wade through & try to avert them."[187] He feared that trade with St. Domingue would bring that day sooner, for with it "we may expect," he wrote to Madison in 1799, "black crews & supercargoes & missionaries thence into the southern states; & when that leaven begins to work . . . we have to fear it."[188] As he saw it, St. Domingue was the first chapter in a terrible revolution on the horizon. "Unless something is done, and soon done, we shall be the murderers of our own children . . . ; the revolutionary storm, now sweeping the globe will be upon us."[189]

When Haiti achieved independence in 1804, Jefferson refused to recognize the new nation. Indeed, his administration retained the older, colonial name St. Domingue, avoiding any use of the name Haiti.[190] Soon thereafter, over Federalist opposition, he imposed the trade embargo on Haiti. Timothy Pickering, an irascible northern Federalist who had served in the cabinets of Washington and Adams, wrote a long letter to Jefferson from the Senate chambers. How could you, someone who could excuse "blood and slaughter" in the pursuit of "lost liberty" in France, not apply that rule "with ten-fold propriety & force to the . . . Blacks of St. Domingo"? On what grounds could you justify cutting off "necessary supplies"? Is it merely because the "Haytians" are "guilty indeed for their skin not colored like our own"?[191] But the racial objection to recognition held; it was not until 1862, during the Civil War, that the Lincoln administration recognized Haiti.

Another irony: Jefferson's greatest accomplishment as president, the acquisition of the invaluable Louisiana Territory, an act that put the United States on the way to becoming a continental nation, was not his work alone,[192] for it fell into his hands as a gift from Toussaint L'Ouverture, whom Henry Adams was to pair with Napoleon as the two

great men of the era.[193] Toussaint L'Ouverture's brilliant defeat of the
French army in Haiti commanded by General Charles Leclerc, Napoleon's
brother-in-law, persuaded the First Consul to give up his dreams of a
French empire in America with Haiti its center; without Haiti, he no
longer needed Louisiana, which would have fed the rich sugar island.
Thanks to Toussaint L'Ouverture, Napoleon sold Louisiana at a bargain
price.[194] But, again, the link has been all but unthinkable for many Americans. Why? Writing a century ago in his masterpiece, *History of the
United States During the Administrations of Jefferson and Madison*, Henry
Adams, the great-grandson of John Adams, believed that "the prejudice
of race alone blinded the American people to the debt they owed to the
desperate courage of five hundred thousand Haytian negroes who would
not be enslaved."[195] In this observation as in so many others, Adams insisted on embedding his nation's history in the global context.

The Treaty of Amiens in 1802 brought the wars of the French Revolution to an end. But international peace reigned only briefly. In practical
terms the treaty only set the stage for the Napoleonic Wars, which began
the next year, when Britain refused to return Malta to the Knights of
Hospitallers. At first hostilities between France and England enabled
Americans as neutrals to expand their carrying trade vastly. But in 1805
a British judicial ruling (the *Essex* case) declared the Americans in violation of the so-called British Rule of 1756, and the British started to seize
American ships. For the next several years, the Americans were trapped in
a circuit of competing restrictions on trade promulgated by Britain (Orders in Council) and Napoleon (Continental System).

Jefferson, who had great faith in the importance of American commerce, thought that a trade embargo could force the Europeans to the negotiating table, and he instituted one in 1807. It did not work; neither
France nor Britain was sufficiently affected, but American trade fell by
90 percent between 1807 and 1814.[196] Although both the French and the
British were responsible, the British were more offensive, particularly
with their impressment of American seamen, not to mention their efforts
to encourage Indian resistance in the Ohio Valley, which, despite the
treaty of 1783, was still contested territory.

While issues of trade and impressment were important causes of the
War of 1812, much of the impetus came from a group of "war hawks"
from the South and West, the most important of them being Henry Clay

and John C. Calhoun. Should we be surprised that westerners were so worried about maritime issues? In fact, land hunger and ocean commerce were complementary interests, not contradictory or alternative ones. American farmers were commercial farmers, ambitious for foreign markets, and for them to reach those markets, ocean commerce had to be unimpeded. The British seemed to block access both to western land and to global trade. The war hawks not only wanted them to evacuate their forts and stop promoting Indian resistance, but also dreamed of driving them out of Canada and Spain out of Florida. They wanted Britain and Spain out of North America partly because there was continuing talk about a breakaway republic in the Mississippi valley, and Aaron Burr, vice president during Jefferson's first term, was accused of having secured Spanish support for such a scheme. No one knows the truth of the matter, though he was acquitted in a federal court, with John Marshall presiding; but both the reality and the rumor of what he did or did not do kept the concern alive.

President James Madison was not a war hawk, but he understood the material interests and psychology that gave force to the war hawks' campaign. In the end, he brought the United States into war against Britain to insist on its independence, to insist on the nation's right to equal status among the nations of the world. "To have shrunk from resistance, under such circumstances," he recalled, "would have acknowledged that, on the element which forms three-quarters of the globe which we inhabit, and where all independent nations have equal and common rights, the American People are not an independent people, but colonists and vassals. With such an alternative, war was chosen."[197]

The war did not go well for the Americans, and by 1814 matters looked desperate. National finances were troubled, and New England Federalists were proposing secession from the Union at the Hartford Convention. Having checked Napoleon in Europe, Britain was ready to concentrate on the Americans, and, indeed, they marched on Washington and burned the White House and the Capitol. However, an American naval victory on Lake Champlain and a victory at Fort McHenry after the burning of Washington persuaded the British to end the war. Neither side had much to show for its efforts, and the Treaty of Ghent specified only the cessation of hostilities, the restoration of conquered territories, and the establishment of a boundary commission. Neutral rights and impressment were not mentioned. The crucial point, however, is that with the defeat of Napoleon the "Great War" finally ended. And it was ended by events in Europe, not by the messy and inconclusive skirmishes in the United States. Britain's final victory in the Second Hundred Years' War, not the war between Britain and the United States, secured the future of the still fragile new nation.

The dimensions of Britain's victory are hard to grasp, but the island nation achieved dominance over other European powers around the globe. Britain had twenty-six colonies in 1792 and forty-three in 1816, to say nothing of its control over all-important sea-lanes and the most valuable markets. By 1820 it ruled 200 million people, one quarter of the world's population.[198] Oddly enough, that was a victory for the Americans as well, for in the next century the United States depended on British capital for internal development and the British navy's capacity to make the ocean a domain of free movement and trade. The great Anglo-French rivalry of 1776 had become an enormous burden after 1783, but after 1815 Americans were free.

Once again, however, good news for Euro-Americans was bad news for Amerindians. In the peace negotiations in Ghent, the British, no doubt maliciously, proposed to create an Indian republic in the west. Not surprisingly, the Americans refused.[199] There were to be no limits. John Quincy Adams, one of the negotiators, wrote in his diary in 1819: "The United States and North America are identical."[200]

A NEW NATIONALISM

The historian George Dangerfield has written that with the announcement of peace in Washington on February 18, 1815, "the shadow of political Europe withdrew from the scene it had darkened and confused for many years."[201] When Washington in his Farewell Address had articulated his preference for no entangling alliances, he was voicing the common sense of Americans at the time. Perhaps such *alliances* could be avoided, but foreign *entanglements*, it turned out, at first could not, though after the Napoleonic Wars they were of a new sort. European nationalism, industrialization, and the British commitment to free trade together gave Americans the space to define a politics and national agenda for themselves.[202] The change was reflected in coverage of foreign news in the American press: between 1795 and 1835, for example, the percentage of foreign news in Cincinnati newspapers declined from 43 percent to 14 percent.[203]

The early phases of industrialization and nationalism seem to have been mutually reinforcing. In Europe as in the United States, people began to imagine the nation as the means by which their economic development could be carried forward. The nation was not self-contained, of course. We know that labor, capital, and commodities were in motion in the early nineteenth century. Yet claims for an autochthonous nationalism were often sustained. For a brief moment an insular if expansive nationalism had an experiential foundation for Americans, and soon people were having dreams of a grander empire reaching across the Pacific and south into the Caribbean. Industrialism, too, helped to extend both the experience of Americans and their imagination of a grander nation. Well before the end of the nineteenth century, the logic of industrial capitalism could be grasped: it pointed to continuous global interaction, to international patterns of immigration, trade, and financial connections, and to unprecedented interdependence.

Domestic American politics, no longer entangled in the rivalry of the British and French, was calmed, and the Era of Good Feelings commenced. The ideological *passions* stirred by the great contest between Britain and France were replaced by more local or sectional *interests*. Writing in the mid-1800s, John Quincy Adams observed that the end of the war "brought to a close the great struggle between the Federal and Republican Parties."[204] Attention shifted to social and economic issues that geography and the federal system transformed into a spatial politics conducted in the vocabulary of sectional interests: questions of banking and currency, internal improvements, and cheap land for white settlers.[205]

American leaders also associated themselves in a more self-conscious way with "America," using the word to refer not to the continent but to the United States.[206] It was assumed that the whole hemisphere was an extension of this United States–centered America. Americans in the early nineteenth century were intensely interested in the new republics to the south; five of only ten legations worldwide in the State Department's budget for 1824 were in Buenos Aires, Bogotá, Santiago de Chile, Mexico City, and Lima.[207] In the previous year, the United States had enunciated the Monroe Doctrine, claiming hegemony in the Western Hemisphere and warning against any European effort to recolonize it (though we should note that Haiti was excluded from its protection, on account of its having "a government of people of color").[208] Of course, Americans lacked the power to back up the doctrine, but they knew, no doubt, that Britain's navy would enforce a policy of free trade and oppose a European imperium there.

With independence real at last, the American sense of nationalism was refreshed. Albert Gallatin, the great secretary of the Treasury to both Jefferson and Madison, captured the moment and its significance in a letter of 1816:

> The war has renewed and reinstated the national feelings and character which the Revolution had given, and which were daily lessened. The people have now more general objects of attachment with which their pride and political opinions are connected. They are more Americans; they feel and act more as a nation; and I hope that the permanency of the Union is thereby better secured.[209]

Daniel Webster, who had opposed the war and who had been closely associated with the Federalists at the secessionist Hartford Convention, recalled a similar significance for the peace:

> The peace brought about an entirely new and a most interesting state of things; it opened us to other prospects and suggested other duties. We ourselves were changed, and the whole world was changed . . . Other nations would produce for themselves, and carry for themselves, and manufacture for themselves, to the full extent of their abilities. The crops of our plains would no longer sustain European armies, nor our ships longer supply themselves. It was obvious, that, under these circumstances, the country would begin to survey itself, and to estimate its own capacity for improvement.[210]

As Webster's observations suggest, the shift was to what in today's language would be called development and economic opportunity, and this shift, driven partly by the released energy of American individualism, had a nationalist aspect. Gallatin, Henry Clay, and others believed that the development of interregional transportation and trade would weld together the still weakly defined republic. Gallatin had argued this point before the War of 1812 in his great "Report on Roads and Canals," and it was reformulated after the war in Henry Clay's "American System." Clay advocated internal improvements and a tariff to develop manufactures and an internal market that would, he believed, serve the interests of all sections.[211] Nationalism and development became linked. And the international significance of the United States was transformed, over the course of the nineteenth century it evolved from being a political alternative to monarchy to becoming a place of economic opportunity and of startling economic energy.[212]

3

FREEDOM IN AN AGE OF NATION-MAKING

------ ∞∞∞ ------

Historians of the Civil War typically commence their narratives with the war between the United States and Mexico. More specifically, they begin with the Wilmot Proviso that the war prompted. This convention makes sense, for it places slavery at the center of the interpretation of the Civil War, where it should be. The proviso offered by Congressman David Wilmot, a Democrat from Pennsylvania, was attached as an amendment to an administration-sponsored appropriation bill. President James K. Polk was requesting funds to facilitate negotiations with the Mexican government regarding territorial concessions that the United States planned to seek at the war's end.

The wording of Wilmot's proposal closely followed the language of Jefferson's Northwest Ordinance of 1787, reenacted under the Constitution. Its point was clear: "that as an express and fundamental condition to the acquisition of any territory from the Republic of Mexico . . . neither slavery nor involuntary servitude shall ever exist in any part of said territory, except for crime."[1] On the face of it, the proviso is a puzzle. Wilmot was not identified with the antislavery movement and, moreover, was a member of the president's own party. In fact, he was one of several northeastern Democrats associated with the New York Van Buren wing of the Democratic Party; in the 1820s and 1830s Martin Van Buren had put together a powerful electoral alliance between the plantation South and the Northeast, a fragile but effective intersectional arrangement that depended on keeping slavery out of national politics.

These northeastern and middle Atlantic Democrats did not oppose territorial expansion—they had supported Polk when he campaigned on an extravagantly expansionist platform that had called for "the reoccupation of Oregon and the reannexation of Texas." Polk clearly was more interested in the southern part of this agenda, and he settled the Oregon boundary dispute with Britain well short of the expansionist slogan that demanded the whole territory, north to the latitude of 54°40', about four hundred miles north of today's Canadian border. In the eyes of many northern Democrats who imagined farms for northern whites in Oregon, Polk had slighted this interest, favoring instead the South's desire to extend the domain of slavery by annexing Texas and demanding territorial concessions from Mexico. Would the territories where Mexico had abolished slavery be opened to accommodate an expansion of American southern plantation slavery? That put the conventional balance between the sections at risk. The new territories, if slave, would greatly enhance the political clout of the southern planters, who seemed to be pressing for a national ratification of their "peculiar institution."

Moreover, northern constituent politics was as important for Wilmot and his colleagues as intersectional balances of power. They were eager to preserve western lands for white settlers from their districts. Polk's seeming favoritism toward the South threatened access to western lands by free white labor. Wilmot declared this concern to his colleagues in the House of Representatives. His intention, he explained, was to "preserve to free white labor a fair country, a rich inheritance, where the sons of toil, of my own race and color, can live without the disgrace which association with negro slavery brings upon free labor."[2]

The appropriation bill, with the proviso, was passed in the House of Representatives but not in the Senate. No matter: the issue of slavery, which had haunted politics since the Constitution was framed, had now taken a central place on the national stage, and it could not be removed. The controversy produced a principle that was to dominate national politics for a generation: that slavery must not be extended into new territories. It was a principle that within a decade led all but one of the Democrats behind the proviso into the Republican Party.[3]

Reaching too far for too much, the plantation South had undermined the politics of balance that was premised on maintaining an equal number of slave and free states. But the white South continued that pattern of overreaching in the 1850s, talking too much about expansion into Cuba and other parts of the Caribbean basin. Certain northerners, those who would go into the Republican Party in the 1850s, were beginning to re-think the method of balancing difference. A newer notion of nationalism, which envisioned homogeneous states, was circulating in the Atlantic world. Leaders of the new Republican Party, especially William Henry Seward of New York and Abraham Lincoln of Illinois, incorporated this vision of nationhood into their thinking, and that led to a presumption that the future United States would be either all free or all slave—a uni-tary nation rather than a divided and balanced confederation.

When the hypersensitive slavery question was linked to the territory question, which is to say to the land policy of the national government, it found a concrete and unavoidable focus, and the political stakes were vastly increased. The principal wealth of the U.S. government was its possession of thousands of square miles of land, holdings soon to be greatly augmented with the territory taken from Mexico. The sectional competition over access to that land disrupted not only the Democratic Party but all national political institutions—and some cultural ones, most notably the churches. "And," as Lincoln, adopting the passive voice, put it in his second inaugural, "the war came."

The proviso produced a political earthquake. It catalyzed the white South and solidified an always present but unformed sectionalism there. That in turn produced northern worries about what began to be called the "slave power."[4] Sectional tensions were not new, but earlier episodes had not crystallized into a political crisis. Fears of disunion during de-bates surrounding the Missouri Compromise (1820) and nullification (1831) had made political leaders from both the North and the South back off from controversial issues—not only slavery but internal im-provements and central banking as well—and the national government had governed less and less so as not to cause sectional offense. Power had been radically decentralized. Recognizing the sectional divide and the need to create a party that bridged it, Van Buren, the architect of the Jacksonian Democratic Party, had had a very different vision of the nation from that of Gallatin, John Quincy Adams, and Henry Clay. They had wanted to tighten the bonds of nation and empower the national govern-ment, while he denationalized the United States so as to build a national political party on the dual platforms of the white South and the mid-Atlantic cities.

Partisan division thus seemed to shape and to some extent hold together American politics until the 1850s. The political arena was divided between Democrats, a southern party with northern and western allies, and Whigs, a northeastern party with southern and western allies. But increasingly with each passing year after Wilmot, political differences were aligned along a north-south axis. The two-party system could no longer negotiate the sectional divide, and the "second party" system collapsed. The Republican Party, a combination of former Whigs and anti-slavery Democrats, was founded in 1854 on the principle of opposing slavery in the territories. Ironically, in realizing the American nationalist dream of continentalism, Polk, with the uninvited help of Wilmot, had produced a crisis that threatened the nation itself.

In 1848, the Senate ratified the Treaty of Guadalupe Hidalgo, in which the United States took one-half of Mexico's national territory. Save for the purchase of a small amount of land on the Mexico-U.S. border in 1853 (the Gadsden Purchase), this completed the continental expansion of the United States. There were those who wished to take more of Mexico, and various arguments were made for and against more extensive territorial claims. In the end, however, racism and bigotry as much as principle protected the remainder of the neighboring republic. Opposition to having a large nonwhite and Catholic population in the United States was substantial and determining.[5] Americans wanted Mexican land—the more sparsely populated, the better—not Mexican people. And the underlying racism at work here revealed itself in the continuing controversy over slavery. Many who joined the new Republican Party had at best modest commitments to racial justice, if any at all. Most opposed slavery in the territories only so that western lands would be available to white settlement.

The political geography of North America had been transformed by the Mexican War and the treaty that concluded it. A territory including what is today the Southwest of the United States and the North of Mexico had for centuries been a single region; in 1848 it became two. While the new boundary did not end all transnational personal ties or dissolve a partly shared culture, it was still a profoundly important division that marked distinct paths of future development.[6] Even more interesting, atlases published in the United States during the 1850s introduced the then novel concept of the Americas as two continents, not one. The unity of the Western Hemisphere, which Europeans and Latin Americans recognized until at least World War II, was apparently unwelcome to the race-conscious U.S. citizens whose nationalism was heightened after the war with Mexico.[7] The distinction was to be reinforced in the 1860s, when France, seeking to suggest cultural affinities to legitimate its imperial ambitions in Mexico, introduced the rubric "Latin America" to identify the large American domains where Romance languages were spoken.

And the war had profound geopolitical implications within the United States. The historical dissimilarity between North and South became a political division, which was increasingly understood as a conflict between ways of life. Actually, for more than half a century there were enough shared values between North and South to accommodate the differences. But the issue of slavery simplified the distinctions and resulted in a false clarity about difference, which invited an overriding moral absolutism on both sides. During the 1830s and '40s this tension had been resolved by a common psychological trick—keeping one's thoughts about the national union and slavery in separate compartments of the mind. The result had been a politics of avoidance. Yet the practical matter of organizing newly acquired western territories meant that the future had to be decided in real places. The Constitution forbade interference with slavery where it existed in the southern states, but Congress had the power— some said the responsibility—to organize the territories so as either to allow or to prohibit slavery in them.[8] This constitutional circumstance made slavery a national issue, not simply a local or regional one—or so it seemed to those who would become Republicans.

The Compromise of 1850 temporarily resolved the problem. To call it a compromise is a misnomer, however; it was no such thing. Henry Clay, who had managed the Missouri Compromise, proposed an actual compromise which, he hoped, would establish an intersectional middle ground. His resolutions provided for the admission of California as a free state; the territorial organization of the land acquired from Mexico without congressional specification as to slavery; settlement of the Texas–New Mexico boundary and assumption of debt contracted by Texas before annexation; noninterference with the slave trade in the District of Columbia; a more effective fugitive slave law; and a declaration that Congress had no authority to interfere with the interstate slave trade. When Clay submitted these resolutions to the Senate as a package, they were defeated. Though Clay had hoped that their balance would produce a compromising majority, in fact the various components together produced the opposite. Stephen A. Douglas is often credited with saving the "compromise" by seeking separate votes on five slightly repackaged individual components, each of which serially passed Congress. Douglas's insight into the patterning of votes was brilliant, but in itself indicates the failure of compromise. No one changed position or accommodated the other positions. Douglas had instead organized a sequence of distinct coalitions for each measure. The underlying crisis remained.[9]

Douglas reopened and aggravated the political and cultural wound in January 1854 when he introduced a bill to organize the territories of Kansas and Nebraska. He dealt with the difficult issue of slavery by incorporating a principle recently developed within the Democratic Party: "popular sovereignty." The bill he proposed would repeal the Missouri Compromise line that extended across the territory acquired in the Louisiana Purchase and allowed slavery only south of it. The concept of popular sovereignty, seemingly in the spirit of democracy, would allow the settlers in the territory themselves, not Congress, to vote on whether or not to permit slavery. He thought he had removed the slavery question from its troubling position in national politics.

But whether wrapped in the language of democracy or not, his proposal evoked eloquent opposition from Abraham Lincoln and from William Henry Seward, both of whom would become leaders of the soon-to-be-founded Republican Party. Seward declared that there was a "higher law," one that could not be abrogated by a vote. Speaking at Peoria, Illinois, later in the same year, Lincoln objected that Douglas's democracy for the territories was no more than "the liberty of making a slave of other people." Such a "declared indifference" to the "spread of slavery," he exclaimed, "I cannot but hate . . . I hate it because of the monstrous injustice of slavery itself. I hate it because it deprives our republican example of its just influence in the world." The "liberal party throughout the world," he warned, was worried that American slavery might fatally wound "the noblest political system the world ever saw."[10]

Charles Sumner, another Republican leader, made the same point. Slavery, he complained, "degrades our country" and prevents its "example" from leading the world to the "universal restoration of power to the governed."[11] Understanding on this point was not restricted to major Republican leaders. Once the war began, an ordinary soldier, a private from

Massachusetts, wrote to his wife: "I do feel that the liberty of the world is placed in our hands to defend." For another common soldier the stakes of failure were far larger than the future of the United States. Failure, he worried, would mean that "the onward march of Liberty in the Old World, will be retarded at least a century, and Monarchs, Kings, and Aristocrats will be more powerful against their subjects than ever."[12] When Lincoln, Sumner, and ordinary soldiers thus invoke the larger international liberal movement of their time, they draw our attention to a vital and illuminating element of the history of the Civil War not usually captured in the conventions of Civil War historiography but of fundamental importance.[13] Neither the causes, meanings, nor results of the Civil War can be understood adequately outside the international context of liberal ideas of nationality and freedom that were so passionately held—and fought for—in the middle of the nineteenth century. However particular and central slavery and emancipation were to the Civil War and to American history, part of the cause of this central American event came from outside American history, from a larger history of ideas and conflicts over nationalism and freedom and about the proper balance of central and local authority.

1848

If 1848 was the year of the Treaty of Guadalupe Hidalgo, it was remarkable as well for Euro-American liberal and nationalist movements. Lucretia Mott and Elizabeth Cady Stanton, prompted by the sequence of European revolutions that began in February 1848, organized the Seneca Falls Convention that summer. This convention is remembered as one of the initiating events of the modern American and international women's rights movement, and it was recognized at the time by female leaders of the Paris revolution of 1848, one of whom, Jeanne Deroin, a socialist and feminist, wrote to the Americans from a Paris prison to lend her support for subsequent conventions.[14] International movements favoring abolitionism and temperance, among other reforms, were also emerging.

What was called the springtime of nations succeeded the collapse of the French monarchy in February 1848, followed by the proclamation of a republic. Americans watched European developments sympathetically and even organized "monster meetings" in several cities to celebrate them, for they understood that their own republic was an inspiration to the revolutionaries.[15] Europe, it was said, was finally choosing liberty over despotism, and the United States was the first nation to recognize the new French republic. Various other self-identified national peoples claimed entitlement to independent unified states and fundamental civil rights.[16] In Vienna, Prince Metternich, chief architect of post-Napoleonic Europe, and then chancellor of the Habsburg Empire, resigned in the face of liberal nationalist uprisings and fled into exile. The Hungarians under the leadership of Lajos Kossuth claimed administrative independence from Austria and established a parliamentary government. Nationalism and liberal dreams were rampant in Bohemia, Poland, Croatia, and Serbia. Italy became partially united as a liberal constitutional monarchy under the king of Piedmont, and liberals from various German states with visions of a German parliamentary democracy met in Frankfurt as a National Assembly. The established order was shaken; some thought it might crumble, and Marx and Engels were prompted to publish *The Communist Manifesto*.

These European revolutions may have prompted the insurrection against the emperor in 1848 at Pernambuco, Brazil, while opponents of the Rosas dictatorship in Argentina, which fell in 1852, closely followed the ideas and developments of 1848, whether they were at home or in exile.[17] In both Europe and Latin America the U.S. Constitution, *The Federalist Papers*, and other documents of the making of the American republic were often consulted during these heady days.

The results were meager, unfortunately, at least in the short run. But despite the disappointments of the moment, over the course of three decades, from 1848 to 1875, the progress of nationalism, constitutional governments, and new freedoms, as well as the consolidation of capitalism at the center of the international economy, defined the era.[18] It was also an age of emancipation: not only were four million African-Americans liberated from slavery in the United States, but nearly forty million serfs were emancipated in the Habsburg and Russian empires.[19] The American Civil War cannot be separated from these larger movements.

In "The National Idea," a lecture of 1860, Senator Seward identified the Republican Party's nationalism with the contemporary aspirations of

European liberals.[20] And during the Civil War, Richard Cobden, a leader among English liberals, assured the radical Republican Charles Sumner, "You are fighting the battle of liberalism in Europe as well as the battle of freedom in America."[21] The Russian ambassador to the United States recognized these connections when he observed that "the only important difference between the nationality problems in America and in Europe is that in the first case it is complicated by the Negro element."[22]

The liberal Italian Giuseppe Mazzini believed that the long toleration of slavery in the United States limited its significance as a model, but with the Union victory he believed it advanced the liberal cause. He wrote to the American Moncure Conway, a part of the Concord transcendentalist group, that the United States stood "higher and nearer to the ideal than any nation existing." The military hero of Italian unification, Giuseppe Garibaldi, to whom Lincoln had offered a command in the Union army, declined the commission but embraced the northern cause as his own, though he insisted the liberal ideals of "universal freedom" demanded that the war be fought on behalf of the "enfranchisement of the slaves." At the end of the war, Victor Hugo, using a metaphor that suggested endurance, celebrated the United States as "the guide among the nations . . . , the nation pointing out to its sister nations the granite way to liberty." Also after the war, Mazzini wrote that the war and its result is part of "mankind's progress," our "great battle—to which all local battles are episodes—fought on both continents and everywhere, between liberty and tyranny, equality and privilege, . . . justice and arbitrary rule."[23] This close association with European liberal and nationalist aspirations warrants emphasis and elaboration.

The Hungarian Revolution of 1848 was crushed by Russian intervention on behalf of Austria, and in 1850 Kossuth fled to Turkey. When Russia and Austria put pressure on the sultan to turn him over, Americans came to the rescue. In 1851, Secretary of State Daniel Webster offered to extricate Kossuth, a gesture much welcomed both by Kossuth and by the Turks. An American naval vessel took him first to England (where at the American consulate he met Mazzini, his Italian counterpart) and then to the United States. Soon after his arrival in the United States, Abraham Lincoln, as a member of a local committee in Springfield, Illinois, drafted a resolution in support of Kossuth and the Hungarians. The statement affirmed the right of the Hungarians to throw off "their existing form of government" to achieve their "national independence." While the statement did not endorse material assistance, which Kossuth wanted, Lincoln's text praised Kossuth as "the most worthy and distinguished representative of the cause of civil and religious liberty on the continent of Europe." He and his "nation," Lincoln assured the public, were supported by "friends of freedom everywhere." The resolution also lent support to the nationalist struggles of the Irish and Germans.[24]

Like many Americans Lincoln sympathized with these nationalist aspirations, and he affirmed the right to revolution in Congress, a month before the uprisings actually broke out in Europe. In phrasing that strikingly connects the Declaration of Independence to ideas circulating in Europe in 1848, he acknowledged that "any people anywhere have the *right* to rise up, and shake off the existing government." Moreover, "any people that *can*, *may* revolutionize, and make their *own*, of so much of the territory as they inhabit."[25] Here and in other statements he made, the central European analogue might have predicted his support for an independent—revolutionary—South.[26] But Lincoln as president was to reject this way of framing the conflict—as did the white South, which fought a reactionary, not a revolutionary, war.

What was the broader meaning of the revolutions of 1848 for Lincoln and other liberals? The core issue, Lincoln insisted, was "freedom" or "slavery," and he rejected enslavement to either a plantation master or a monarch claiming sovereignty.[27] Stephen A. Douglas accepted the same binary, though with a revealing difference in terminology: "republicanism or absolutism."[28]

Thus nationalism, as understood then, was inherently democratic. The presumption was that sovereignty was possessed by a given national people, not by a monarch or the state as distinct from the people. Freedom and independence were paired, and they were put in contrast with another pair, slavery and dependence. Freedom, equality, and progressive change were associated with republican nations, while hierarchy, despotism, and stasis were associated with monarchies.[29] Liberal nationalism was a progressive movement, with a sense that enlightenment would banish benighted social and political forms. Salmon P. Chase, a member of Lincoln's cabinet and later a Supreme Court justice, understood a liberal nation as one marked by "freedom not serfdom; freeholds not tenancy; democracy not despotism; education not ignorance." For John Stuart

Mill, the American Civil War was central in liberal aspirations. In his *Autobiography*, composed during the war, which he said engaged his "strongest feelings," this paragon of nineteenth-century liberalism wrote that it was "destined to be a turning point, for good or evil, of the course of human affairs for an infinite duration." A southern victory, he was certain, "would give courage to the enemies of progress and damp the spirits of its friends all over the civilized world."[30]

It was easy enough to identify the parallels between the liberal side of the binary and the North American free labor ideology; likewise, the family resemblance of the monarchical-aristocratic side with the pro-slavery, paternalistic claims of the planter class of the American South. Lincoln fully recognized this isomorphic relation, declaring that the American Civil War concerns "more than the fate of these United States"; it addresses the "whole family of man."[31] For Lincoln and those who joined him in the Republican Party, the antislavery crusade was part of a worldwide movement from "absolutism to democracy, aristocracy to equality, backwardness to modernity."[32]

Early-nineteenth-century nationalism was romantic and idealistic, and Americans were particularly susceptible to its appeal.[33] Local difference, the genius of the place, was important to the romantic sensibility, whose concern for distinctiveness fused with notions of national identity. The fame of Walter Scott's novels throughout the Atlantic world, for example, derived in part from his extraordinary capacity to evoke the distinctiveness of Scotland. For romantic nationalists, the cultural nation—whether defined by its way of life or in more formal histories, literature, and music—was properly identical with the political nation.[34] And it was assumed that the nation was the natural "bulwark of freedom."[35] Almost as if everyone accepted a widely dispersed, commonsense version of Hegel's *Lectures on the Philosophy of World History* (1830), it was assumed that a people realized themselves in the establishment of a national state.

At the risk of introducing jargon, I would say that the ambition of the various nationalist movements was that their "space of decision" be identical with their "space of culture."[36] The point was made by contemporary scholars. Writing in 1862, with Hungary in mind, Lord Acton, the widely admired English liberal and historian, made the case with great economy: "The state and nation must be co-extensive." He marshaled additional support from Mill's similar observation in *Considerations on Repre-*

sentative Government (1861) that "boundaries of governments should coincide in the main with those of nationalities."[37]

Liberal nationalism had a second criterion for the nation: it should be constitutional, with representative institutions. "The theory of nationality," Lord Acton insisted, "is involved in the democratic theory of sovereignty."[38] This was one of the great themes of the Frankfurt National Assembly, the other being one that would soon divide Lincoln and Douglas: the balance between "national citizenship" and the right of local self-government.[39] For both questions the men at Frankfurt kept close at hand *The Federalist Papers* and the U.S. Constitution.[40] The constitutional forms proposed varied from place to place, yet everywhere a clear affinity fused liberalism with nationalism, to the point where they seemed to be almost indistinguishable. From a comparative perspective one might fairly argue that Lincoln's fusion of freedom and nation over the course of his presidency strengthened the connection between liberalism and nationalism, while Chancellor Otto von Bismarck's illiberal unification of Germany in 1871 subverted it.[41]

For Americans and for most of the Atlantic world, Lajos Kossuth incarnated the general spirit of 1848, and through him we can further explore the relation of the United States to these broader movements for national unity and freedom. In Kossuth one also discovers important ambiguities and tensions inherent in liberal nationalism that help to explain some of the limits of reform in the United States and elsewhere.

Americans were fascinated with the charismatic and eloquent Kossuth, and press coverage of his time in America was extensive. Between his arrival in December 1851 and his departure six months later, *The New York Times* ran more than six hundred stories about him, along with stenographic reports of his speeches, often extending over several columns, and the menus and toasts at the many banquets in his honor. Kossuth's arrival in New York had been preceded by the publication there of a short book that introduced him, reprinting several speeches he had delivered in England, all of which anticipated his journey to the United States. While interned in Turkey, Kossuth had learned English, and, like Lincoln, he took the Bible and Shakespeare as his teachers. One of the speeches in the little book was obviously directed to Americans, but no less true to his liberal nationalism for that: "Hungary will and wishes to be a free and independent republic; but a republic founded in the rule of law, security to person and property, and the moral development as well as the material welfare of the people—in a word, a republic like that of the United States."[42] These words could have come from Lincoln, Seward, or any number of American liberals.

For Kossuth as for Lincoln and most Americans, the world was divided between "republicanism" and "absolutism," and that distinction shaped his campaign against Austria's domination of Hungary.[43] In the United States, Kossuth won the support of democracy's advocates, but not that of the anti-egalitarian senator John C. Calhoun, who insisted that no good was likely to come of the European revolutions.[44] But the meaning of Kossuth's liberal nationalism was sufficiently complex to invite support from both white southerners and northerners, though for different reasons. When he arrived in Washington in 1852, he was welcomed and celebrated by Daniel Webster, whose oratorical defense of the Union was already legend. Webster toasted Hungarian independence and the Hungarian people's claim "as a distinct nationality among the nations of Europe," while southern nationalists embraced Kossuth and his cause because they identified with the oppressed Hungarians. They thought of their distinctiveness and unease in the Union as part of the larger struggle of the time, akin to Hungary and other central European people's for national recognition and self-rule.[45]

Some northerners embraced the radical potential of the Paris revolution, including Frederick Law Olmsted, the designer of Central Park. His studies of the southern states, written when he was a correspondent for *The New York Times* in the 1850s, offered observational and ideological foundations for the Republican Party's interpretation of the South as a slave society. Prompted by the exciting events in Paris as well as challenges set by both the slave South and the burgeoning northern cities, Olmsted declared himself a "Socialist Democrat." His sympathy with the radical parties in Paris was unusual in the North, but it was entirely absent in the South, where spokesmen made clear their distance from the French radicalism of 1848. Defending southern nationalism, the *Richmond Daily Enquirer* declared that "there is nothing whatever in this movement of a revolutionary or Red Republican character."[46]

Although no new nations emerged from the Habsburg Empire in the wake of the revolutions, the liberal ideas of the time and place, as endorsed and acted upon by the enlightened emperor Joseph II, did bring to an end coerced labor and bondage to the soil across the Habsburg domains.[47] Abolitionists in the United States anticipated that Kossuth would support them; William Lloyd Garrison's *Liberator* had celebrated the Hungarian struggle for freedom. But when New York abolitionists asked Kossuth for a public statement against slavery, he declined to respond for fear that any statement would alienate some part of the American public he was courting. Garrison thereupon condemned his silence as "dishonorable" and vilified him as "demented," like the "renowned Don Quixote," who could not distinguish between giants and windmills.[48] Frederick Douglass and other abolitionists tried without success to dissuade Kossuth from extending his lecture tour to the South, but he made a southern swing.[49]

Kossuth was surprisingly well attuned to the politics of regional difference. Though he gave pretty much the same lecture wherever he went, he made small but important regional adjustments: in the North he emphasized the integrity or autonomy of the nation (complaining of Russian intervention in Hungary), freedom, and progress; in the South he was more likely to accent the evils of centralization (Austrian), the right to determine one's own local institutions, and independence.[50]

The illiberal elements of Kossuth's nationalism were little considered by Americans, who did not attend to the fact that he opposed the nationalist aspirations of Croats, Romanians, Slovaks, and other non-Magyar minorities in Hungary, a position that strengthened his nationalism but weakened his liberalism. When Francis Bowen, editor of Boston's august *North American Review*, attacked him for speaking the language of freedom while suppressing the freedom of linguistic minorities in Hungary, few grasped the significance of his criticism, and on account of it Bowen apparently lost his widely anticipated appointment to the Harvard faculty.[51]

Kossuth's Magyar nationalism was one, indivisible, and intolerant.[52] To Croats the great Hungarian liberal was a tyrant, though he might defend himself, as Lincoln did, by arguing that he was defending his nation against disruptive elements aiming to subvert it.[53] In the United States, too, nationalism had a double edge: it encouraged Republicans to make freedom as extensive as the national territory; but later, after the war and Reconstruction, a racialized nationalism undermined the democratic logic of the liberalism that had sustained the Radical Republicans. This nationalism enabled, even encouraged, the abandonment of the promise

of full citizenship for freedmen, as well as the exclusion and near extermi-
nation of Native Americans in the late nineteenth century.

THE BIRTH OF NEW NATIONS

After the crisis of the American Civil War, the United States became a
distinctly national society, with a national economy headquartered in
New York. New York also became the capital of communications and
cultural production more generally; the art market became concentrated
there, as did the business of publishing books, music, and lithographs.[34]
The Associated Press, established in New York City to take advantage of
the newly invented telegraph, helped to shape a news environment that
operated nationally and simultaneously. Washington became a national
political capital rather than a meeting place of regional leaders, and its
physical expansion between 1860 and 1870 expressed the dimensions of
its growing centrality to American politics and administration.[35] All of
this was part of a larger nineteenth-century global history.[36]

Social scientists argue over many competing explanations for the
emergence of modern, centralized, and development-oriented nation-
states in the third quarter of the nineteenth century. For my purpose here,
a general theory is unnecessary, but it is helpful to consider the cultural
and institutional aspects of nineteenth-century nationalism and nation-
making.

Cultural nationalism refers to the sense of belonging together to an
"imagined community," partly defined by the circulation of a national literature and news among readers in a territorial entity.[37] National affiliations had other sources as well, of course. Increased population (Europe's
population doubled between 1750 and 1900) and new levels of mobility
left people bereft of older forms of identity and social security.[38] Throughout Europe and the Americas the nation became an ever more important
locus of identification and affiliation. In the United States the war itself
had promoted a sense of national belonging: as often happens in war, soldiers meet fellow recruits from other parts of the nation, and since this
war was fought on national territory, they got to know that American national space, giving an experiential dimension to their feelings of national
identity.

The nation-state's offer of citizenship promised new forms of security, even as it made new demands—especially military service. The balance of benefits tended to favor the state rather than the individual in all too many cases, and national state interest frequently compromised the rights promised by liberalism. Still, the institutions of the nation-state and their proffer of a sense of belonging promised welcome security in a world of social turmoil and uncertainty.[59] Indeed, by the time of the Civil War, such attachment seemed a human necessity. It was in the midst of the Civil War that Edward Everett Hale wrote his enormously popular story *The Man Without a Country*, which, he later explained, was intended to show what a "terrible thing it would be if we had not a country."[60]

A second aspect of the new nations was their institutional elaboration: an undeniable historical pattern links the ideology of nationalism to the concentration and centralization of modern state power. This coupling legitimated state capacity and enhanced its effective deployment for economic and other state purposes, including the mobilization of its own citizens for war and development.[61] Industrialization came to have an important connection, though difficult to specify, with nationalism,[62] as the nation-state was increasingly accepted as the "natural unit" in which to promote economic development—and, to a degree, cultural distinction.[63]

In 1848 it was not at all clear that the nation-state—as opposed to empires or confederations—would define the political organization of Europe and the Americas. Over the course of the next decades, however, the globe was reorganized around nation-states, as the many international fairs and exhibitions, beginning with London's Crystal Palace Exhibition in 1851, made clear. The fairs were entertainments, prompts to tourism, and theaters of consumerism, but they also modeled a world of international competition, or competitive nationalism.

The making of these new nation-states was associated with the ideology of freedom, but the process was also marked by unprecedented violence, by civil and interstate wars that achieved new levels of intensity and deadliness. Most of these wars were associated in one way or another with the transformation of eighteenth-century empires or the making or remaking of nations. By one count 177 such wars occurred in the era of the American Civil War.[64]

Although it is commonplace to talk about the extraordinary level of violence and death in the American Civil War, it was not unique. Mili-

tary technologies of the time made high levels of casualties typical rather
than exceptional. The Taiping Rebellion in China (1850–64) resulted in
twenty-three million deaths, equal to about two-thirds of the population
of the United States in 1860. The War of the Triple Alliance (Argentina,
Brazil, Uruguay) against Paraguay (1864–70), which was related to the
national unifications of Brazil and Argentina, was fatal to unimaginable
numbers of Paraguayans and nearly annihilated their nation. Estimates
vary, but this small country, with a population of 525,000 at the onset of
war, may have lost half of its population, leaving as few as 28,000 adult
males.[65]

Consider a very different case, the Paris Commune of 1871. For
seventy-three days Paris was in rebellion against the centralizing policies
of the French government and carried on as an autonomous municipality.
The Communards, including representatives from several other major
French cities, challenged what they considered "arbitrary centralization,"
issuing a "Declaration to the French People" that proposed "absolute autonomy" to localities and a federation of communes on the principle of
"free association." The national government established at Versailles following the fall of Napoleon III sent 130,000 troops to restore national
authority, and these troops killed 20,000–25,000 Parisians and arrested
40,000 more.[66] How does this terrible violence compare with that of the
Civil War, in which 618,000 died? The ratios of deaths to population (of
the city and the nation, respectively) were similar, profoundly affecting
subsequent social and family life. So the Third Republic of France, no less
than the new American nation that emerged from the Civil War, was
born in blood. The oft-repeated American claim that the Civil War has
the dubious honor of being the world's bloodiest before the twentieth
century cannot be sustained, but my point here is that whatever the differences in ratios of victims to survivors, the United States shared with
many other societies the violent process of nation-making.

That the American war and the Haitian Revolution were at heart
struggles to end slavery make them distinctive. While the making of a
modern nation-state often coincided with the emancipation of slaves or
serfs, only in Haiti and the United States did state-sponsored emancipation require a war. In Brazil, by contrast, the planter class eventually ac-
ceded to the inevitability and ultimate rightness of emancipation; one
finds there no literature of justification such as was produced in the

American South.[67] The United States was both a late and a peculiarly hesitant participant in the emancipatory movement. In Latin America emancipation of slaves began in Chile in 1810. By the time of the American Civil War, all republics in the Americas had abolished slavery; Brazil, still an empire, ended slavery in the course of becoming a republic in 1889. Otherwise only European colonies in the Americas continued to rely on enslaved workers: Dutch Guiana, Cuba, and Puerto Rico. Slavery or serfdom had been eliminated in the British Empire in 1833, in the French Empire in 1848, in the Habsburg Empire in 1848, in Portugal in 1858, in the Dutch Empire in 1859–69, and in Russia in 1861.

Nowhere but in the American South did the landlord or planter class seriously resist emancipation in ways that went beyond ordinary political means, let alone resort to violence to prevent it. This resistance not only led to war but gave a distinctive character to the postwar Reconstruction, which imposed reorganization of the American South's social and economic life from the national center. By contrast, the Russian landlords, however unhappy they were about the Tsar's emancipation decree in 1861, did not challenge it, partly because to question his divine authority would generally undermine their own aristocratic rights. As a result, they were prepared to cooperate in (and allowed) the organizing of a new order. They participated—as did the serfs to a lesser degree—in defining the terms of free labor established by emancipation.[68] Lincoln repeatedly invited a constructive response from the southern planters—including compensation, as was the case in Russia—but he found no takers.

THE FEDERATIVE CRISIS

No two sets of precipitating conditions that created modern nation-states were the same, nor were any two resolutions, yet several common themes can be identified. The most important was a desire for more effective administration, for stronger armed forces, and for positive powers of state intervention on behalf of development and modernization (often meaning the advance of industrialism). One might refer to these struggles as contests over degrees and forms of centralization; to describe them as constitutional debates would be correct, too, but it would also obscure the larger interests involved. Both Jefferson Davis, president of the Confederate government, and Alexander H. Stephens, the vice president, tried after the war to justify secession as a high-minded debate over constitutional theory, but slavery was the underlying and fundamental issue in the United States.[69] In all cases one sees various combinations of interest and principle.

One result of 1848 was that the eighteenth-century discussion of constitutions was resumed and reinvigorated. Liberal and nationalist aspirations often foundered on the obdurate difficulty of finding adequate constitutional solutions to the competition between local and central authority. While distinctive, the United States was also typical in how it faced its crisis over the extent of the central state's powers. The trend was toward enhancement of power at the center, but there were important resistances, and not only in the Paris Commune. One of the great themes of Alexis de Tocqueville's political writings, as of nineteenth-century political life generally, concerned this relation between central authority and local autonomy or, in a phrasing common outside France, between unitary states and confederated states.

A "federative crisis" was evident on every continent at mid-century, and it has been identified as a "turning point in modern political history."[70] Certainly it was a protean moment, when new capacities for communication, transportation, and administration became available, industrialization was transforming economies, and the modern nation-state was finding effective form. Together, these revolutionized the sources of national power, shifting the focus from the acquisition of territory from rivals to a concentration on managing internal national resources so as to advance development. Dynamic industrial economies, labor forces as much as armies, technology as much as territory, became sources of national power. And all of this depended on enhanced state capacity, which usually involved a recalibration of central authority.

Several forms of federation and consolidation were pursued and different balances struck. There was an important general shift from the mode of central authority that had been characteristic of Europe's land empires to that of consolidated national states that operated directly on citizens in every part of the national territory. The middle third of the nineteenth century witnessed both the increase of central authority and resistance against it in autonomous entities or breakaway provinces: Egypt under Mehmet Ali's expansionary leadership in the 1830s and '40s, the regional caudillos in South America, the briefly successful Taiping Rebellion whose forces took control of South China in 1850–64, repeated rebellions of the Irish against the English, and the Hungarian demand for autonomy. But more often, as the century advanced, new levels of state centralization and even consolidation were seen all over the globe. Of cases beyond the Atlantic world, Japan is well known, and Thailand (Siam) is another example. Aware of the challenge of Europe's colonizing ambitions in Asia, Siam's absolute monarchy, beginning in 1851 and continuing through two reigns with the assistance of European advisers, centralized its power at the expense of hereditary provincial chieftains. As was common in such cases, the king secured definite borders for his consolidated realm, though at the cost of relinquishing claims to territories in Laos and parts of Cambodia. His strengthened nation was thus able, uniquely in Southeast Asia, to maintain its independence in the age of high imperialism.[71]

At times, centralization and decentralization went on simultaneously. While Mehmet Ali achieved virtual autonomy as Khedive of Egypt in the Ottoman Empire, successive sultans (in part self-consciously emulating his successful modernization) supported a policy of Tanzimat (or reorganization), centralizing the rule of the empire's territorial holdings directly, and they moved toward a modern conception of citizenship rather than relying on negotiations with intermediaries.[72] When, in the 1840s, several Catholic cantons withdrew from the Swiss Confederation to form the Sonderbund, civil war broke out; rather quickly, the breakaway cantons were defeated and brought back into Switzerland on the basis of a confederal constitution modeled in part on the U.S. Constitution of 1787.[73] The Hungarians simultaneously sought autonomy from Austria, a strong state for a Hungarian nation, and the suppression of demands of national minorities within it. Such were the analogous yet varied instances pertinent to the protracted debates Americans had over the degree to which the United States was and was not to be a consolidated nation.

The actual practice of national politics in antebellum America had been highly decentralized. It was not unlike the Ottoman case, in which the center negotiated with provincial elites, the profits from tax farming being the prize. In the United States, of course, there was no sultan and the prize was different. Also, the intense ideological nationalism of the Jacksonian era had no equivalent in the Ottoman Empire, where peoples of various regions recognized the sultan as a focal point of a confidently multicultural and multi-confessional Islamic empire. Rather than negotiating with a central authority like a sultan, American regional elites traveled to Washington to negotiate *with each other*. Such is the portrait of Jacksonian politics Frederick Jackson Turner presents in his great posthumously published book on sectionalism and politics between 1830 and 1850.[74]

We must recall that at the conclusion of the War of 1812 a new sense of national spirit had flourished. Henry Clay and John Quincy Adams, reviving plans developed by Albert Gallatin before the war, wanted to nourish this emergent sense of unity by developing an infrastructure of roads and canals, the connective tissue for a national economy and social imagination. Such public investments, Gallatin had argued, would "tend to strengthen and perpetuate [the] union." This sentiment was echoed by John C. Calhoun, in 1819 the secretary of war and then a strong nationalist. Worried about the dangers of disunity, he urged binding "the republic together with a perfect system of roads and canals."[75]

Henry Clay's "American System" was a precocious formulation of the concept of a national economy. He proposed a balanced, integrated interregional economy, with a tariff to promote manufacturing and to fund an active federal government and internal improvements to move manufactured and agricultural goods, the sale of public lands to encourage settlement and for income, and a bank to manage credit and interregional commercial transactions. His scheme sustained the sense of American nationalism in two ways: it reduced reliance on international trade, and it tied the regions together by making them trading partners.

Historians of economic thought associate the conceptualization of a national economy with the German economist Friedrich List. But List in fact discovered the idea in the United States.[76] As a young professor of economics at the University of Tübingen and liberal activist who spoke out too provocatively, List was imprisoned by the king of Württemberg. His release was conditional, requiring that he leave the country. On the advice of Lafayette, he went to the United States. In Philadelphia he learned about Clay's "American System," the Philadelphia Society for the Promotion of National Industry, and the writings of the local publisher and economist Mathew Carey, whose *Essays on Political Economy; or, the Most Certain Means of Promoting the Wealth, Power, Resources, and Happiness of Nations: Applied Particularly to the United States* (1822) elaborated the idea of a national economy and the means of stimulating it. In a world of nations, List concluded, the "American System" was a superior plan to Adam Smith's. The universalist model of Smith's great work, according to List, ignored "the different states of power, constitutions, and wants and culture of different nations." Despite its title, *Wealth of Nations*, Smith's book was a "mere treatise" on how the economy might work "if the human race were not divided into nations."[77] The understanding of nation and economy that List and Clay shared pointed toward the emerging views held by the leaders both of the modern nation-state and of capitalism: that the nation and economy were territorially coterminous and intertwined, and that the growth of a national economy was an inherent good.

List returned to Germany in 1832, when Andrew Jackson appointed him American consul in Leipzig. It was an odd appointment, considering that List's ideas supported the politics of Henry Clay and the opposition Whig Party. Perhaps it was an example of rewarding one's enemy—and removing him from political debate. List went on to become an important economist who more than any other of the era gave economic content to nationalism. His ideas were influential in Bismarck's plan for German economic development, and the Republican Party in the United States drew upon his and Clay's ideas in its vision of a development-oriented state.[78]

But the ambitious nationalism that followed the War of 1812 had obviously weakened within a decade. John Quincy Adams complained in 1822 that "according to the prevailing doctrine our *national* government" lacks the "power of discharging the first *duty* of a nation, that of bettering our own condition by internal improvement."[79] His vision of an active national economic policy had been blanketed by conflict over the admission of Missouri to the Union as a slave state in 1819, a debate that was, as Thomas Jefferson famously declared, like a "fire-bell in the night." Over the next years assertion of national power was further discouraged. The fight over the tariff of 1828 and the nullification doctrine that emerged from it was—from the southern point of view—ultimately about the powers of the national government over slavery; the danger that a positive state posed for slavery, at least in the minds of southern political leaders, made a national consensus for Washington-led economic policies impossible. As a result, the federal government substantially withdrew from national regulation of the economy.[80] Whigs could not win national elections because of their belief in national power, while Democrats could and mostly did win only by eschewing it.

In the 1830s and '40s, then, the American economy was interconnected but not unified. There was interregional trade, but it was not integrated, a collection of local economies that did business across national space without becoming a national economy. There was not even a national currency. Business was conducted with locally issued banknotes (more than ten thousand different notes were in circulation) discounted on the basis of the reputation (or even mere appearance) of the person presenting the note and the distance from the issuing bank.[81] Nor was the mail service effectively national; southern postmasters did not deliver antislavery materials sent from the North.[82]

Extreme devolution of national power between 1830 and 1860 marked the political system that Frederick Jackson Turner described;[83] there was no positive national authority in Washington. Sections of the United States as large as European countries were "potentially nations in themselves." "Statesmen," Turner explained, went to the "halls of legislation" in Washington to negotiate "adjustments among the sections." With no acknowledged central authority, the capital was the meeting and negotiating place for "regional ambassadors" attached to but not quite representing barely national parties. In this political circumstance, which might be called an associative state, the negotiations had two purposes. One was patronage in the home bases of the statesmen, where local offices were at issue. The other object was national in focus, but not an affirmation of national state power. It was about individual ambition, or a politics of reputation. Regional political leaders wanted to gain reputations—or visibility, as we would say—sufficient to become viable candidates for the presidency. To do that, they had to be able, in Turner's phrasing, "to find adjustments between sections, much in the same way that a skillful European diplomat would form alliances, offensive and defensive—or at least ententes—between different countries."[84] The political parties were essentially interregional alliances requiring constant and careful maintenance, but insofar as they held together, they sustained an American nationalism in spite of the weak state. Indeed, people tended in this era to experience the nation locally, mostly in the festive routine of elections and at post offices, which employed three-quarters of all federal government employees.[85]

Antebellum national politics was premised, then, on only the most limited state structure. No American official had the formal power of the sultan. Perhaps one can draw an analogy with the contemporary "Concert of Europe" managed by Prince Metternich. The Austrian diplomat's system was one of balance: for every shift in power there had to be a balancing compensation, and this was not unlike the American pattern of pairing every admission of a slave state with that of a free one. This kind of arrangement defines a confederative system, not a national, territorial state.[86]

Historians tend to present President Jackson as a strong nationalist, given his stand against Calhoun and nullification. Yet these two rivals were not so far apart as they supposed and as we tend to think. Jackson did not want a consolidated *nation*; he wanted a decentralized *union*, and in fact, Jacksonians tended to refer to the United States as a confederacy. For both Jackson and Calhoun, the relation of the federal government to that of the states was not properly described in terms of a hierarchy, with the federal positions superior to state ones, nor even of an umbrella. Rather, as the contemporary political theorist Frederick Grimké phrased it, they coexisted "side by side." Antebellum politics was about negotiating these parallel boundaries. The difference between Calhoun and Jackson was in a sense stylistic, though Calhoun had a substantive investment in protecting slavery. Calhoun's stance was typically adversarial, while Jackson's was more flexible, willing to let state and federal power touch—gently.[87]

With minimal national structure or guidance, political elites in individual states and regions pursued their own interests, careful, however, to avoid too much contact and thus potential conflict with other states and regions. It was a system of avoidance rather than a collective enterprise. Yet paradoxically, American nationalism as an ideology flourished even as its celebrants were opposed to centralized state power. Such was the state, or semi-state, that Tocqueville found in 1831 and praised for its commitment to decentralized administration, not fully realizing the hollowness at the center.[88]

No wonder romantic nationalism appealed to Americans as to Germans. These national peoples, conscious of having a national culture, were living in pieces of a nation rather than a consolidated whole. Washington hardly felt like the capital of a nineteenth-century nation-state; and neither did Berlin. Washington was more like the headquarters city of an agglomerated league that shared cultural and economic interests, much like the German Confederation, the union of German states that had succeeded the Holy Roman Empire in 1815, with its important centers in Frankfurt, Munich, Hamburg, and Leipzig.

Without having visited the United States but with a theory in mind, Hegel offered a surprisingly apt characterization of the country in 1830. Believing the "destination" of nations was to be formed into states, he was convinced that the United States was not yet a realized state. That would come only, he argued, with cities and industry. Or, one might say, Hegel described a people developing spatially rather than politically:

> As to politics in North America, the universal purpose of the state is not yet firmly established . . . for a real state and a real government only arise when class distinctions are already present, when wealth and poverty are far advanced, and when a situation has arisen in which a large number of people can no longer satisfy their needs in the way to which they have been accustomed. But America has a long way to go . . .
>
> North America cannot yet be regarded as a fully developed and mature state, but merely as one which is still in the process of becoming . . . [It] is still at the stage of cultivating new territories. Only when, as in Europe, it has ceased merely to augment its farming population will the inhabitants press in upon each other to create town-based industries and communications instead of moving outwards in search of new land; only then will they set up a compact system of civil society and feel the need for an organic state.[89]

As this process played itself out in history—as opposed to philosophy—the practical mid-century problem in the United States and elsewhere was how to devise an appropriate and effective balance between unitary and confederative parts of governments, between centralized and decentralized administration. In the United States, the regional geography was increasingly defined by slavery, which greatly complicated the issues Americans shared with others. Speaking with his characteristic southern accent at the time of the Missouri crisis in 1820, Thomas Jefferson had alluded to the dilemma that would not go away and that was to paralyze America's politics and impede its progress to Hegel's modern state. Slavery was the problem that the Union faced, and there was, Jefferson feared, no way out. "We have the wolf by the ears, and we can neither hold him, nor safely let him go."[90]

Jacksonian indefiniteness was challenged, and its equivalent was challenged elsewhere. Empires and dynastic states had been fairly comfortable with a certain vagueness about the location of paramount authority and territorial boundaries. But by mid-century, formal distinctions and categories—whether in law, aesthetics, gender roles, or much more—became more urgent. Governmental definiteness and formal clarity were found in or identified with centralized national states and well-developed state bureaucracies, and the trend of the century, Tocqueville observed in 1855, was for national governments to reduce the "diversities of authority by the unity of a central government."[91] Yet, as Tocqueville knew, the path to the modern nation-state was not direct, nor were the resolutions parallel. And violence was usually a part of the passage.

These issues were present on every continent. All states, whether empires in decline or national states in the making, were addressing similar challenges: nationalist ideologies and increasingly dense and interpenetrating economic relations, both domestic and international. They had to prepare themselves for an emerging world of nations competing not only on the military battlefield but economically, where power was measured by industrial capacity. The second half of the nineteenth century was thus a fertile era of reform in the structure of governments.

For all the distinctions among states and among the various patterns of reorganization, it is possible to establish a crude but useful typology. Imperial reform in Russia, the Ottoman Empire, China, and Japan aimed to strengthen a centralized administration and enhance state capacity. Several imperial powers reconfigured their structures to create a combination of empire and modern nation-state, as in the Dual Monarchy for

Austria-Hungary in 1867 and the Dominion of Canada in 1870. A third pattern consists of confederations becoming centralized nations, sometimes through civil wars (the United States and Argentina) or interstate wars (Germany, Italy, and, again, Argentina). The centralizing strategy often produced regional resistances, as in the quite early case of the Vendée, a part of west-central France that had resisted the Revolution's nationalizing and anticlerical thrust in the 1790s; Argentina (yet again); the southern states of the United States; the Communards in Paris, Lyon, and Marseilles in 1871; and the Canudos rebellion in northeast Brazil at the end of the century.

India exemplifies yet another path. Treated by the East India Company as a colonial economy, with dependent local rulers left in charge, the country saw everything change after the great Sepoy Mutiny of Indian soldiers in the British army (1857). With the abolition of the East India Company in 1858, the British assumed direct imperial administration of the subcontinent, emphasizing the development of infrastructure, the elaboration of administration, and the establishment of unified space and boundaries—all of which provided a foundation and prompt for what by the end of the century had become Indian nationalism.[92] Similar developments can be traced in French North Africa and Indochina.

In Japan, where the shoguns had over the centuries accumulated power that dwarfed that of the emperor at the supposed center, the new Meiji emperor in 1867 reclaimed military and administrative power and located it in Tokyo. The imperial rescript that described the aim of the new policy of centering power was clear: it was the abolition of "the disease of government proceeding from multiform centers." In order to "give protection and tranquility to the people at home and abroad to maintain equality with foreign nations . . . the government of the country must center in a single authority."[93] (This new political hierarchy prompted a new expression among the Japanese. Travel to the capital was described as "going up to Tokyo.") The social sources of this transformation were internal and culture-specific; Western notions of bourgeois revolution do not quite fit. Yet Japan's leaders were aware of global economic and political developments, which they were responding to, adapting to, and circumventing. The results of this new nationalism were similar to the emergence of a modern state elsewhere inasmuch as it produced a state invested in a growth-oriented economy.[94]

Russia, in continuous conflict on its southern borders with Turkey, was shocked by its loss to a coalition of Turkey, England, and France in the Crimean War (1853–56), which ended its presence in southeastern Europe. Worse, from the Russian perspective, Turkey, with British support, was actively undertaking its own modernization project. A worried Russian government determined that it must "become stronger in the center." Political and administrative reforms designed to centralize and enhance national power were combined with the abolition of serfdom, itself signaling a modernizing ambition. Russian concern for centering and focusing its deployment of resources was one reason for the sale of the peripheral territory of Alaska to the United States in 1867.[95] The Russian modernization project had some success, but not enough. When the Communists came to power in 1917, they had the same modernizing agenda and pressed it much harder, often violently so. In the Russian case there was little acknowledgment of the sovereignty of the people, which had been so important to the liberals of 1848.

A succession of Ottoman sultans continued the policy of Tanzimat that Sultan Mahmud II had initiated. They worked to modernize the administration and the armed forces, as well as to promote economic development. Europeans supported this "recentralization" policy because they feared a weak empire that had been losing territories for many decades. Hungarian professionals who fled to Turkey after the failure of 1848—many of whom remained, and some of whom attained high office in the military and state bureaucracies—were important in this modernization program.[96] The reform agenda challenged local elites and extended national power directly into the various provinces of the Ottoman Empire; it extended citizenship to all males, giving them equal rights (meaning access to education and employment) and responsibilities (military conscription). Uniform citizenship was intended to "supercede" the religious, guild, and to some extent ethnic loyalties of various subgroups in the empire.[97] Thus, while it was not until Atatürk's revolution following World War I that a modern Turkish state was established, there was more continuity of aims under the sultan and in the new republican Turkey than is usually acknowledged.[98] But the main point here is that the Ottoman Empire was participating in general efforts to strengthen state capacity, always attentive to European developments, though maintaining its own structure of government.

One sees a certain continuity in the movement from empire to nation in China as well. The Taiping Rebellion was not immediately about modernization; it was mainly a religious movement, even a crusade.[99] It sought to replace a corrupt imperial regime with a virtuous one. China's weakness in the Opium War (1839–42) and in being forced to grant foreign concessions of extraterritoriality doubtless had prepared the ground. Neither was the Taiping Rebellion concerned with centralization or decentralization, though it raised questions about this issue. Its initial success may have afforded an opportunity and example for other regional revolts in China, such as the Muslim separatist revolts in Yunnan Province in the 1860s and '70s. But its significance is less in itself or its goals than in the way it prompted a reinvigoration of the center in China. Local elites were forced to support the imperial authorities in China to protect themselves, and that hastened a long-term process of imperial reforms that were meant to build state capacity. As in the other great land empires, developing nationalist ambition continued and accelerated with the collapse of the imperial structure, becoming the focus of the Republicans (after 1911) and the Communists (after 1949).[100]

If Kossuth and other Hungarian nationalists sought a state that affirmed their identity, Bismarck was more interested in German power. Territorial acquisition held less appeal for him than did a strengthened German capacity for military and economic mobilization. Rather than wanting to include all German-speaking lands—all of those in the German Confederation, including Catholic Austria—he wanted a more limited territory, *Kleindeutschland*, that would extend the powerful, centralized Prussian state.[101] The Austro-Prussian War (1866) was an interstate war, between two nations, but insofar as it was a war for a *Kleindeutschland* it was a civil war. The Prussian army overwhelmed Austria, partly because of the lessons General Helmuth von Moltke had gleaned from the American Civil War—the value of the telegraph and railroads for managing logistical support and moving and massing troops.

Prussia's war with France in 1870, which resulted in the creation of the new German state, was initiated by an old-style dynastic issue, the Hohenzollern candidacy for the Spanish throne in 1868. That claim prompted resistance from Napoleon III, who rightly saw Prussia as the principal challenger to French power on the Continent. The Franco-

Prussian War, begun by France but welcomed by Chancellor Bismarck, brought down Napoleon and prompted the formation of France's Third Republic. Likewise, the Prussian victory provided the occasion for the proclamation of William I as German emperor—at Versailles, to make a point—on January 18, 1871. The imperial trappings spoke to the conservatism of the Prussianized state, but the king of Prussia and German emperor was the ruler of a powerful modern nation-state committed to military power and economic development. When President Ulysses S. Grant congratulated Bismarck on the unification of Germany, he erred in assuming or hoping that the chancellor's aims were democratic. Bismarck's modern nation-state little considered the sovereignty of the people. The constitution that Bismarck put in place had no bill of rights, unlike the 1849 constitution, in which the Frankfurt Assembly had made sure that basic liberties were specified. Though male suffrage was enacted (to dilute the vote of the bourgeoisie), sovereignty in the new Germany resided in the state, not the people. Power was in the hands of the aristocracy and monarchy, to say nothing of the strong hands of the Iron Chancellor himself.[102]

The form of Italy's unification was similar to Prussia's.[103] By means of a series of wars against Austria and France as well as the skillful diplomacy of Camillo Cavour, a conservative, but not so conservative as Bismarck, Piedmont, the most economically advanced of the Italian kingdoms, became the core of a unified Italy. Piedmont's Victor Emmanuel II became king of Italy in 1861, with Venetia (1866) and Rome and the Papal States (1870) added later. As with Bismarck in Prussia, Cavour and Victor Emmanuel both wanted a strong state, as did the more liberal Mazzini, who believed that confederation would preserve an illiberal culture of local elite domination.[104] The French ambassador to Piedmont recognized their success. "Italy," he reported in 1860, "instead of contenting herself with a federative organization, seeks centralization as a powerful state."[105] But unlike Germany, Italy was fairly considered a liberal constitutional monarchy.

Prussia's victory over Austria in 1866 was a boon to the Hungarians. To Austrian officials Prussia was a shocking premonition of future forms of national power. For Austria to remain a dynastic state within a German federation would, they feared, reduce it to being a "second-rate power."[106] They realized, too, that a failure to solve the Magyar problem, as it was called—the perennial Hungarian demand for autonomy—would weaken them. Their solution was the Dual Monarchy, with one monarch but two constitutional monarchies, each with parliamentary governments; the Austrian emperor would also be king of Hungary, with great palaces in Vienna and Budapest. The solution depended on the monarchy, which made possible a continuing connection between the two nations in one empire even as it allowed for Hungarian autonomy. Hungary had complete control over its domestic affairs, while imperial finances, the military, and foreign affairs were managed by the newly named Austro-Hungarian Empire. Two liberal nations emerged from the old empire. Although Kossuth opposed the arrangement, it not only gave the Magyars the freedom and identity they sought but also laid the foundations of a modern nation-state for them.[107] The Dual Monarchy resulted in a half century of Hungarian industrial growth at a rate exceeded in Europe only by Germany's.[108]

The logic of the Dual Monarchy was analogous to the British conception of the Commonwealth, which enabled Britain to maintain its empire but allowed selective colonies (with whiteness a criterion) to become nations. Canada, given dominion status in 1870, was the first example. Within the frame of dominion the Canadians established their own federal system, motivated in part by a fear of U.S. expansion northward, which seemed to demand a stronger, more unified Canada. For both the Habsburgs and the British, then, the crown enabled a distinctive flexibility. One wonders whether something similar might have allowed some kind of dual-state solution in the United States. It seems impossible, but it has been suggested that if the South had won or fought to a more even result, some such dual compromise might have emerged.[109] In fact, at his death in 1850, Senator Calhoun left behind a proposal that there be two presidents, one from each section.

All these variations on the nation-making theme were part of a general movement toward the modern state form. Writing in 1869, John Lothrop Motley, the American historian of the Dutch republic and U.S. minister to Austria (1861–67) and Great Britain (1869–70), as well as a close friend of Bismarck, whom he had known since his studies in Germany in the 1830s, considered both the unification of Germany and the Dual Monarchy to be of a piece with the Union success in the American Civil War.[110]

In Argentina from 1835 until 1852, politics was dominated by a ruthless dictator, Juan Manuel de Rosas. He claimed to speak for the *federales*, and his rhetoric set him against the *unitarios*, but his actions were designed to accumulate power in Buenos Aires, and from his base there he dominated the country. However, his was not a centralized state. Though the comparison is unfair to the Jacksonians, Rosas, like them, promoted negative government; but instead of a politics of avoidance, his was a politics that maintained power through a balance of violence. The decades of his rule were constantly disturbed by civil strife, but he stayed in power by using violent means and by negotiating with provincial caudillos. Rebellion in the provinces finally took him down in 1852, and Argentine liberals, many of whom had earlier been forced into exile, set out to frame a liberal, nationalist constitution.

Just when the U.S. Constitution was breaking under the pressure of conflict over slavery, Juan Bautista Alberdi, the principal author of the Argentine constitution of 1853, turned to North America for his model of a "national government." The constitution drawn up in a convention at Santa Fe included universal male suffrage, separation of executive, judicial, and legislative powers, freedom of religion, and the end of slavery as well. Wanting a strong, centralized Hamiltonian state, as he characterized it, Alberdi and his colleagues included a provision that gave the central government power to intervene in provincial affairs when it deemed this necessary.[111] Probably the heritage of caudillo violence and provincial revolt during the Rosas regime prompted this provision, which went further than Hamilton could have imagined possible during the Philadelphia convention in 1787. In an important way, however, the proviso speaks loudly to the simultaneous constitutional crisis in North America over national and state power to regulate, prohibit, or even abolish slavery.

Ironically, the province of Buenos Aires, the center of Argentina, refused to ratify the constitution, and it remained outside the new government until 1862, when it ratified the constitution and joined the Argentine nation. Alberdi envisioned the new Argentina as a developmental state, and it was a remarkably successful one: a national railroad system was built; a national bank and a national capital market (linked to Britain) were established; the native tribes were violently removed from their territories in the last of the Indian wars, the "Conquest of the Desert" (1879–80) in the southern Pampas and Patagonia; agricultural settlement expanded, and urban industry advanced; and massive immigration was encouraged—to Europeanize and whiten the population. These immigrants prospered, as did Argentina, making Buenos Aires, which was for Argentina a combination of Chicago and New York, one of the richest cities in the world.[112] In Argentina, as in other nation-states formed in this period, economic growth and political unification were "reciprocal and mutually reinforcing."[113]

As with Germany, an interstate war played a part in Argentina's consolidation. The origins of the Paraguayan War (1864–70) are in some ways inexplicable. The events leading to it began in Uruguay, whose constitution was based on the American Articles of Confederation. It defined Uruguay's unity as a "firm league of friendship."[114] This weak nationalism produced ongoing conflict between *unitarios* and *federales* that worried its Brazilian and Argentine neighbors, both of whom were anxious about breakaway provinces of their own. "The question of the provinces," Alberdi explained, "is the sole cause and origin of the Paraguayan war." Given the possibility that a *blancos* (federalist) victory in Uruguay might encourage provincial revolt, Argentina and Brazil both supported the *colorados* (unitarists) in Uruguay's internal conflict. But this agitated Francisco Solano López, the "impetuous *caudillo*" who dominated Paraguay while dreaming of a "South American Empire." He feared the expansion of Brazil's power in the River Plate region and in addition imagined, quite unrealistically, that war might bring Paraguay territorial gains (Matto Grosso) at the expense of Brazil. It was one of the world's great military misjudgments. Brazil, Argentina, and Uruguay (the Triple Alliance) crushed Paraguay. To the victors, however, the war brought unexpected benefits, advancing centralization and national unity.[115]

Something similar might have happened in North America had the regime of Emperor Maximilian, exported to Mexico by France in 1864, survived longer. Enforcing the Monroe Doctrine's insistence that the Americas were for republics only might have affirmed the new, postwar American nation and its liberal principles. In fact, while his troops were still under arms, General Ulysses S. Grant toyed with the idea of a unifying campaign that combined Union and Confederate troops on a mission to return the out-of-place emperor to Europe.[116] The United States did supply arms to Mexican liberals fighting Maximilian and his French sponsors.[117]

The War of the Pacific (1879–83), which arrayed Bolivia and Peru against Chile, was fought over the disputed northern border of Chile, an issue ever since the era of independence. All three nations claimed the Atacama Desert, and in the 1870s the combination of a global economic depression and the rising value (given the new discoveries of scientific agriculture) of the rich guano nitrate deposits there made for tensions among the claimants. When Bolivia unilaterally abrogated a treaty and claimed the territory, Chile declared war, though it was ill prepared for armed action; Bolivia and its ally Peru were even less so. Chile claimed and won the Atacama Desert, extending its national territory by one-third, greatly enhancing its people's sense of nationhood, and strengthening the Chilean state, which, along with the guano nitrate profits, in turn helped to advance Chilean industrialization.[118]

France and the United States refounded their republics after overcoming localized resistance: from the southern states in the American case and, for the French, from the Communards of Paris, Lyon, Marseilles, Toulouse, Narbonne, and other cities. In fact, it has been argued that both the Confederate states and the Paris Commune shared "antique" notions of government and society, the one insisting on the primacy of states, the other of municipalities, in relation to the national government. Both resisted the nineteenth-century movement to centralize, though their underlying interests differed: the South's constitutional challenge was in behalf of a reactionary defense of slavery, while the Communards envisioned a radical people's democracy.[119]

Usually we think of the Third Republic simply as the successor to the Second Empire, but by considering the admittedly short-lived Commune, one realizes, again, the common theme of finding the balance between central and localized political power. The memory of the Communards' challenge in part accounts for the Third Republic's aggressive nationalizing agenda, especially through the schools.[120] The creation of a national identity in politics, schools, newspapers, roads, and more was perhaps the central activity of the republican government.[121]

In Brazil, too, there was resistance to the republic's impulses toward centralization and uniformity. The Canudos rebellion in the northeast—led by Antonio Conselheiro, a charismatic religious leader who, for instance, condemned the liberal state's introduction of civil marriages as a violation of God's law and of the "natural order of things"—gave the leaders of the recently established Republic of Brazil a scare in 1896–97. Euclides da Cunha, a reporter and witness who wrote a classic of Brazilian literature on the siege of Canudos by ten thousand government troops, presented the rebellion as a challenge to the secular normality of the new republic. Because it was still fragile and its capacity to hold Brazil's far-flung states together untested, the new government responded with excessive force. This "war of the end of the world," as the novelist Mario Vargas Llosa has called it in a novel of that title, was only partly about centralization and republicanism. For the rebels, religion was more important, and the government's response may have been shaped by its notions of racial difference as well as by its concern to protect central authority and the liberal state.[122]

The battle against the Canudos resistance has been compared with earlier conflicts between the post–Civil War government of the United States and the Native American tribes.[123] In both cases one can observe the violent work that was all too common in making the modern nation-state. But the general context warrants mention here: the Canudos revolt represents yet another variation on the nineteenth-century struggle to determine and establish the maximum degree of both diversity and central power that a political culture could tolerate.

TERRITORIALITY AND LIBERAL NATIONALISM

The rulers of old dynastic empires tended to be preoccupied with temporality rather than territory—with the survival of the dynasty over time. Uniformity, even contiguity, of territory was less essential. Parcels of imperial or monarchical territory could be linked by extended dynastic families and hierarchical networks of viceroys. No single place or territorial claim was indispensable save the dynastic seat and certain religious sites (such as Mecca for the Muslim Ottomans). The aim was to maintain the center and the dynasty with which it was associated.[124] The center itself could move without disrupting political authority—as in late antiquity the capital of Christian Europe and the Levant was moved from Rome to Constantinople.

Modern nation-states, by contrast, were concerned with territorial integrity, contiguity, and clarity of boundaries. Built as they were on the notion of popular sovereignty and the logic of universal citizenship, they wanted direct or unmediated authority across the whole of the national territory.[125] The nation-state is a spatial framework for the development of power, deployed internally but also projected outward; for the elaboration of the meaning and rights of citizenship; for the development of networks and institutions that ensure the circulation of money and information; and for the institutions of everyday life.[126] Premodern states were marked by a mosaic of different rights and responsibilities, but the logic of the modern nation-state was toward uniformity and homogeneity, with a single national economy, society, culture, and polity.

A nineteenth-century national economy, increasingly industrial, was enclosed; its territory of production was the source of livelihoods and of state power.[127] Yet the industrial economy depended on markets beyond the national boundaries; goods and capital, people and knowledge were expected to flow freely across borders, even as the latter became more important. So the national territorial project, however central to the organization of the world, was inherently international and even transnational.[128] By the end of the century that doubleness had resolved itself into a new state form—the nation-state empires that dominated the political geography of the world until World War II.

The notion of self-contained nations is usually traced to the Treaty of Westphalia, which in 1648 had ended the brutal seventeenth-century wars of religion known as the Thirty Years' War. To avoid such wars in the future, the European monarchies established rules of interstate relations. Borders were to be respected, and no interference with internal affairs was permitted. These principles were carried over into the age of the modern nation-state, which mobilized its population and the resources within its territory (including colonies) for national defense and collective prosperity, and which worked to form citizens and sustain a national culture in the metropole.

An important characteristic of the new nation-state was the consolidation of a once fragmented and highly differentiated society into a uniform public realm.[129] This meant that no point within the national territory could be outside national authority, and this seemed to be connected to the tight linkage of territory and state.[130] Embedded within this new idea of public authority was a critique of the paternalistic authority (or aristocratic authority, as it was commonly phrased at the time) that a slaveholder possessed over slaves.[131] In the United States and Europe, it was believed that this older, aristocratic form of society not only violated the legacy of 1776 but ran against the logic of the emergent nation-state.[132] Abraham Lincoln believed this, and embraced a particularly democratic version of it. In a democratic society, he argued, such mobilization of state power was to be in the interest of expanding individual opportunity and enhancing the material conditions of life. Although Lincoln was often not as inclusive as we might wish, the vision of a democratic America articulated in his message to Congress on July 4, 1861, seems to have included black Americans in a new democracy:

> This is essentially a People's contest. On the side of the Union, it is a struggle for maintaining in the world, that form, and substance of government, whose leading object is, to elevate the condition of men—to lift artificial weights from all shoulders—to clear the paths of laudable pursuit for all—to afford all, an unfettered start, and a fair chance, in the race of life. Yielding to partial and temporary departures from necessity [as existing slavery in the states], this is the leading object of the government for whose existence we contend.[133]

It is important to distinguish America's antebellum nationalism and state capacity from the modern nation-state created after the Civil War. Though the American nation was institutionally underdeveloped in the Jacksonian era, its sense of national distinction had been strikingly ebullient. This nationalism was based not on *patria* or territory, but rather on principles, loudly proclaimed democratic ones.[134] After the consolidation of America's continental space, however, nationalism came to have a territorial cast. Continentalism itself stimulated a national "imaginary," to which remarkable transformations in communication and transportation technologies gave plausibility and even material reality. For example, the Post Office, seldom considered a historical actor, was in fact a vitally important one. If in 1800 most letters were written by merchants and sent abroad, by 1850 domestic mail accounted for a substantial majority of letters, and the Post Office also encouraged the extensive circulation of newspapers by giving them preferential rates. This circulation of books and news, along with a growing awareness of a continent-wide readership, sustained a sense of a distinctly American national literary and political community.[135] These improvements also—and importantly—facilitated an increase in state capacity, allowing administrative structures to operate on a larger, even national scale.[136]

The effect of the telegraph was greater yet. Samuel F.B. Morse's invention in 1844 fundamentally changed the relation of time and space. For the first time in human history a message could travel more rapidly than a messenger. The telegraph enabled people spread across vast spaces to live contemporaneous lives. If Henry David Thoreau famously doubted that Maine had anything to communicate by telegraph to Texas, many thought otherwise. Morse expected the telegraph to make "one neighborhood of the whole country." Another commentator predicted that "we shall become more and more one people, thinking more alike, acting more alike, and having one impulse."[137]

This increase in the means, modes, and volume of communication had opposite effects North and South. For the South, improved and cheaper mails brought closer the threat of northern ideas, particularly those of the abolitionists. Following David Walker's *Appeal to the Colored Citizens of the World* (1829), William Lloyd Garrison's publication of the first issue of *The Liberator* (1831), and Virginia's state convention in 1832 that seriously debated an end to slavery (only to reaffirm it), the South began defending slavery as a permanent institution and a positive good. Had the distance between regions not been shrunk by technology, the South might have been safer for longer from contrary ideas, but now it erected an intellectual blockade; after 1835 abolitionist literature was effectively impounded at southern post offices.[138] At about the same time, southern congressmen established a "gag rule" requiring all petitions to the U.S. Congress dealing with the slavery question to be "tabled" without being read. From the North matters looked different. John Quincy Adams was not alone in his frustration when he declared that these acts were a "violation . . . of the rights and liberties of all the free people of the United States."[139] A growing sense of national, territorial oneness made the "peculiar institution" of the South increasingly anomalous—and southern talk of expansion into the Caribbean, especially Cuba, all the more disturbing to many northerners.

The heightened sense of territoriality, of unified and uniform national territories, was evident throughout the Atlantic world—and beyond. It helps explain the allusions to crisis in the language of Lincoln and other Republicans and the reasons why a historic difference became intolerable to them. The abolition issue was forced in part because they knew of the progress of emancipation elsewhere in the Atlantic world—fueled in part by the liberal ideas of 1848 and by the new understanding of nation and national territory.

The belief that the division of the Union into slave and free states would make for an "irrepressible conflict" was first enunciated by Senator Seward in Rochester, New York, in 1858. The "two systems" of society and politics that characterized the North and the South, he declared, were "incongruous." Indeed, "they are more than incongruous—they are incompatible." If the Union were a "confederation of states," perhaps slavery and freedom might coexist. But if "the United States constitute only one nation," that would not be possible. And the United States, he insisted, was becoming such a consolidated nation:

> Increase of population, which is filling the states out to their very borders, together with a new and extended net-work of railroads and other avenues, and an internal commerce which daily becomes more intimate, is rapidly bringing the states together into a higher and more perfect social unity or consolidation. Thus, these antagonistic systems are continually coming into closer contact, and collision results . . .
>
> The United States must and will, sooner or later, become either entirely a slaveholding nation, or entirely a free-labor nation.

The direction of history, as he saw it, pointed toward the triumph of free labor, on which modern states were built. Even Russia and Turkey, in preparation for joining Europe and "modern times," were making the transition to free labor.[140] Put differently: Seward, like other Republicans, envisioned a modern American state (and perhaps modernity in general) as the North writ large, realizing the European ideals of 1848 and fulfilling American democracy.

The highly commercialized and ever more industrialized North was part of a North Atlantic core of nations that exchanged goods and technologies in all directions. The South, too, had important connections to Europe, especially to England, but it was a semicolonial relationship.

Like India and Egypt, the South provided raw materials for the industrial core, which included the northern states. Again like India and Egypt, the South relied on coerced labor that shared little of the profits, which went to a narrow elite.

The worry about incompatible difference and the threat of disunion was a new one for the United States at mid-century. Its founding generation of political leaders had not been especially alarmed by the possibility of separation, and maintaining territorial integrity on a continental scale was not something they considered essential to republican liberty. The Union was understood as an experiment, which might or might not be perpetual. Washington's Farewell Address included an observation that "experience" would determine the success of the Union. "It is worth a fair and full experiment," he counseled his countrymen. The Federalists at the Hartford Convention who threatened to secede during the War of 1812 also characterized the Union as "experimental." Jefferson, who supported the war that impelled them to Hartford, thought the Union was "a means rather than an end." These comments are all in the language of the eighteenth-century Enlightenment. Only later would romantic nationalism invest the "nation" with emotional power and the assumption of perpetuity.

So union and nation were quite different concepts. Union was a constitutional strategy contrived to bring together and strengthen a vulnerable confederacy, and it was understood to be distinct from a nation. Use of the word "nation" was specifically rejected in Philadelphia in 1787, and Madison described the work of the convention as that of writing a "*federal*, and not a *national* Constitution." Various leaders, including Henry Clay, a strong nationalist, later speculated without panic on the possibility of regional confederacies.[141]

By mid-century, however, liberal nationalism had acquired new emotional and practical power. Since nation was now being identified with unified national space, division was understood as reduction. Without unity, there was no nation; without a nation, there was no liberty. Such thinking was a long way from Jefferson's; a unified nation had become an absolute, an end in itself.

John Marshall, the great chief justice and a staunch nationalist, challenged the Jeffersonian view from the outset. His vision of national consolidation was unusual in its time, and his decisions helped to make the nationalism for which he spoke a reality. *Fletcher v. Peck* (1810), *McCulloch v. Maryland* (1819), and *Gibbons v. Ogden* (1824) established the Constitution as the "supreme law of the land," making the federal government superior to, not merely a partner with, the states. In *Cohens v. Virginia* (1821), a less well known case that was decided in the wake of the controversy over the admission of Missouri to the Union, Marshall outlined his vision of national unity:

> That the United States form, for many, and for most important purposes, a single nation, has not yet been denied. In war, we are one people. In making peace, we are one people. In all commercial regulations, we are one and the same people . . . America has chosen to be, in many respects, and to many purposes, a nation; and for all these purposes, her government is complete; to all these objects, it is competent. The people have declared, that in the exercise of all the powers given for these objects it is supreme . . . The constitution and laws of a State, so far as they are repugnant to the constitution and laws of the United States, are absolutely void. These States are constituent parts of the United States.

In acknowledging the states as constituent parts and a distinct realm of action, he did allow for local difference. He did not describe a consolidated state. Marshall the Virginian here provided space for slavery beyond the power of the federal government. For the sake of slavery, his nationalism had limits. But he allowed no space for a doctrine of secession. He insisted that the Constitution was made by the people and could be unmade only by "the whole body of the people; not in any sub-division of them."[142]

Republicans in the 1850s were more democratic than the conservative Marshall, and they were more comfortable with a consolidated nation-state. Their ideal was one of uniformity and an equal citizenry. Whatever the universalism of rhetoric, before the Civil War the vision of equal citizenship was limited to whites (and males), just as the freedom of linguistic minorities that Kossuth championed was limited to his fellow Magyars and not extended to the smaller linguistic "nations" in Hungary. American Republicans concurred with Mazzini, who believed that "individual liberty and national self-determination" required "a unitary Republic."[143] In Europe and the United States ideas of sovereignty—and thus democracy—became associated with territory. Not that the land was sovereignty incarnate, but rather that the people within a bounded national space were sovereign. Territory defined citizenship and all citizens were formally equal, thus implying (though not always realizing) both democracy and uniformity of standing.

The political theory of the American Civil War was embedded in such an idea of the national state. In his book *The American Republic* (1866), the brilliant, though eccentric, American philosopher Orestes Brownson linked republicanism, territory, and nationalism. Concurring with Lincoln that the war represented a "new start in history," Brownson argued that the struggle "for national unity and integrity" had brought to the nation "a distinct recognition of itself." He insisted that the new democracy was properly associated with the territorial state. A polity such as had existed in the antebellum South relied on personal relations and was thus quasi-feudal. A "people territorially constituted" dissolved this feudal hierarchy; the Civil War established territorial democracy throughout the United States. Slavery was abolished "for reasons of state, in order to save the territorial democracy."[144] Brownson's argument usefully joins Lincoln's expectation of uniformity and his insistence on territorial unity. "The question," Lincoln explained in a special message to Congress soon after the war began, is "whether a constitutional republic, or a democracy—a government of the people, by the same people—can or cannot, maintain its territorial integrity, against its own domestic foes."[145] Or, as he had put it more sharply in 1856, well before the war, "The Union must be preserved in the purity of its principles as well as the integrity of its territorial parts."[146]

If Lincoln's first concern was to preserve the Union, his presidency culminated in a war to emancipate the slaves. His own moral, intellectual, and political journey involved a fundamental transformation in his conception of the United States, which his changing language reveals. The United States became a singular noun. In his first inaugural he used the word "union" twenty times, without mentioning "nation." Then he used the word "union" less and less, while "nation" and "national" became more prominent. The political language in his second inaugural is striking: the South sought to dissolve the "union," while the North was fighting to preserve the "nation."[147] The Gettysburg Address (November 19, 1863) is most telling of all. There Lincoln did not mention the United States once—he was speaking to and for the whole human community—nor did he refer to the Union. Yet five times in this brief speech of only 269 words he used the word "nation." He promised a rebirth of freedom in a *nation*, a democratic nation, and he offered it as a model for all humankind. This new strong and democratic nation was more than a central government. It was founded on a materially unified national territory, not a mystical union. In his second annual message to Congress in December 1862, a month before the Emancipation Proclamation, he had elaborated on this point:

> A nation may be said to consist of its territory, its people, and its laws. The territory is the only part which is of certain durability . . . It is of the first importance to duly consider, and estimate, this enduring part. That portion of the earth's surface which is owned and inhabited by the people of the United States, is well adapted to be the home of one national family; and it is not well adapted for two, or more. Its vast extent, and its variety of climate and productions, are of advantage, in this age, for one people, whatever they might have been in former ages. Steam, telegraphs, and intelligence, have brought these, to be an advantageous combination, for a united people.[148]

During the 1850s the controversy over the territories had prevented the organization and development of the continental domain that constituted the nation as Lincoln described it. It is often said that plans for a continental railroad gave political urgency to the task of resolving the problem of the territories. That is true, yet only part of the story. Land for farmers was more important than Americans might realize today, when farmers are fewer in number than college students. In 1860, 80 percent of the population was rural, and protecting the interest of free, white farmers was a high priority. The Republicans' commitment to homestead legislation was easily as strong as their commitment to a protective tariff for industry and subsidies for railroads.

Whether they were looking for voters in cities or voters on farms, the Republicans' core program and appeal was the ideal of free labor. That ideal was more than a matter of labor relations; it was a vision of individual opportunity. A slave society was incompatible with that national vision, and they considered the extension of slavery into the territories a direct assault on the free labor ideal. If on the other hand slavery were barred from the territories, they would become the destination of new European immigrants. As Seward described the process in a speech in St. Paul, Minnesota, in 1860, these immigrants would submerge their differences into "one nation and one people only." As one reads his speech, however, one cannot but think of the openly acknowledged goals of the immigration policy being developed in Argentina as he spoke. As noted earlier, that nation welcomed massive immigration to populate its agricultural regions so as to Europeanize or whiten the population.[149]

For good constitutional reasons Republicans focused on the territories, not on the existing slavery in the southern states. Republicans believed that Congress had both the power and the obligation to organize the territories. The organization of the Northwest Territory, and the Missouri Compromise, were precedents indicating that prohibition of slavery in the territories was within its power. Jefferson Davis and others since him have declared it would have been easier to respect the Republicans had they proposed ending slavery everywhere in the national territory. But here we must take seriously Lincoln's repeated statements that Republicans were realists and respecters of the constitutional protection of slavery in the states. He, Seward, and other Republican leaders repeatedly said they could live with constitutionally protected slavery in the South so long as they were confident, as they believed the founders had been, that in time slavery, thus contained, would become extinct in the United States.

That confidence was shaken by the Compromise of 1850; by the introduction of the Kansas-Nebraska Bill, with its scheme for popular sovereignty that removed moral censure from slavery (1854); and by the Supreme Court's *Dred Scott* decision (1857), which not only ruled that no Negro could become a citizen or possess "rights which the white man was bound to respect" but also declared—in what Republicans claimed were mere obiter dicta—that Congress had no power to prohibit slavery in the territories.[150] Now Republicans feared, as Lincoln put it in his first debate with Stephen Douglas, that "there is a *tendency*, if not a conspiracy . . . to make slavery perpetual and universal in this nation."[151]

This worrisome prospect reversed the Republicans' reading of American history.[152] To their minds, the preference, tendency, and expectation of right-thinking Americans from the founders on had been of the eventual disappearance of slavery. As Atlantic liberals, they had been cheered to see that slavery was disappearing throughout the Atlantic world, and they did not wish the United States to be an exception. Insofar as they agreed with liberal nationalists everywhere that a modern nation, which the United States was surely becoming, would be uniform, they feared what Lincoln called the "nationalization of slavery." Rather, they sought the nationalization of "free labor, free soil, free men."[153] The issue demanded resolution. In a private letter in 1855, Lincoln asked: "Can we, as a nation, continue together *permanently*—forever—half slave, half free?"[154] Later, when nominated to the Senate in 1858, he made his most famous statement of this Republican worry: "'A house divided against itself cannot stand.' I believe this government cannot endure, permanently half *slave* and half *free*. I do not expect the Union to be *dissolved*—I do not expect the house to *fall*—but I *do* expect it will cease to be divided. It will become *all* one thing or *all* the other."[155]

For the American, or Know-Nothing, Party, a briefly popular nationalist party founded in 1849 that called for the exclusion of immigrants and Catholics from public office and a twenty-one-year residence qualification for citizenship, the question of who was "in" or "out" of the nation was the stuff of politics. But for the Republicans the issue was cast differently; they focused on the question of deviance within the national territory. How far might the nation depart from the promise of freedom and equality in the Declaration of Independence? In their debates, Douglas insisted that Lincoln's House Divided speech envisioned an absolute uniformity across the whole territory of America, and "uniformity" seemed to be "the parent of despotism, the world over." The founders, according to him, recognized diversity in the large nation and accommodated it by leaving to the states the regulation of local institutions.[156] Lincoln responded that he fully recognized the diversities that grew from differences in soil and climate. They were a source of national strength, providing "bonds of Union" and making a "house united." But, he asked, can the "question of slavery be considered as among *these* varieties in the institutions of the country?"[157]

In the 1850s slavery became entangled with another, even more provocative deviation from national uniformity. Polygamy among the Mormons in the Utah Territory was nearly universally condemned—by Lincoln, by Douglas, by the North, and by the South. A local problem became a national embarrassment. The rapid growth of the Mormon population in Utah meant that soon they could seek statehood, which was more than a little worrisome. Marriage, like slavery, was a domestic institution and thus a matter reserved to the states by the Constitution. Utah, which already permitted slavery, could legalize both polygamy and slavery, thus making a mockery of national virtue. The first Republican Party platform in 1856 condemned polygamy and slavery. For Lincoln and the Republicans the issue was clear, and the Republican platform declared it the "right and duty of Congress to prohibit in the territories those twin relics of barbarism—polygamy and slavery." It was less clear for southerners. They wanted to affirm monogamous marriage and the family (which they saw as the foundation of plantation paternalism), but they did not want to endorse congressional power to regulate domestic institutions in territories or, worse, states. Douglas, with his mantra of "popular sovereignty," was in a particularly difficult situation, with little room to maneuver. Lincoln trapped him in the debates by asking whether his policy of popular sovereignty meant that the people of Utah could vote to allow polygamy.[158] Douglas wiggled out by proposing that the boundaries of the Utah Territory be redrawn, attaching half to Nevada, half to Colorado, thus diluting the Mormon vote.[159]

To Republicans, polygamy was a question of freedom or, rather, unfreedom, since they assumed that under the Mormon patriarchal authority the meaningful consent of women was lacking. Justin Morrill, a Republican leader who wrote key legislation, including the Morrill Tariff and the Morrill Act that created the land-grant colleges, also wrote the Morrill Act for the Suppression of Polygamy. Given the political complexity of the issue, the bill, introduced in 1860, was not finally passed until 1862, after the war had begun. But the timing of its introduction is important, for it assumed a supervisory power over the conditions of domestic institutions in the territories, a power that had recently been rejected in the *Dred Scott* decision that Republicans excoriated.[160]

The threat the Mormons posed to the national commitment to monogamous marriages is clear, but here I want to emphasize its challenge to a uniform national state. The Republicans fully understood this. After the war, President Ulysses S. Grant affirmed the national standard by appointing a former Union general as governor of the Utah Territory, and he named as chief justice of the Utah Supreme Court a jurist named

James McKean, who had declared that the Mormons represented an unacceptable "*imperium in imperio.*" "Federal Authority," he worried, was being challenged by a "Polygamic Theodicy."[161]

Grant's successors—Rutherford B. Hayes, James Garfield, and Chester A. Arthur—all thought that the Mormon question was important enough to include in their annual messages to Congress. At the same time, discussion of Mormon marriage was increasingly racialized—which drew an important line between those who were Americans and those who were some kind of "other." Monogamy was identified with European whites, while references to Mormon women likened them to "squaws," "Asiatics," "Africans," or "Mohammadians." This was part of a postwar fusion of Christian civilization, whiteness, and American nationality that paralleled the decline of the Radical Republican vision of justice for those emancipated from slavery. Utah did not gain statehood until 1896, and then only after the Mormon Church in 1890 advised its members "to refrain from contracting any marriages forbidden by the law of the land."[162]

Surviving Native American tribes posed a similar problem. The Constitution gave these tribes quasi-national status and authorized the government to make treaties with them. With the emergence of a modern nation-state, the Indians, always vulnerable because of the whites' nearly unbridled quest for land, became problematic in a new way. The antebellum government had dispossessed the Indians of their land but had accepted the notion of Indian "nations," even if dependent, within the United States, negotiating with and making treaties with them. The postbellum state refused this practice. In 1871 Congress declared that "hereafter no Indian nation or tribe within the territory of the United States shall be acknowledged or recognized as an independent nation, tribe, or power with whom the United States may contract by treaty."[163]

With the end of the treaty system, U.S. Indian policy came under the ordinary statutory process, which meant that Native American tribes were no longer recognized as political communities. But neither were Native Americans granted citizenship; they became "wards of the nation."[164] Current scholarship celebrates the leaders of Radical Reconstruction for using national authority to address issues of race, education, and labor in the South directly and positively, but with respect to Indians they used this new national power in troubling ways. Not only did the Reconstruction Congress deny tribes the status of a polity, but it tried to gather them onto reservations where they were expected to pursue a Euro-American agricultural way of life as individual farmers. It was proposed that individual ownership and monogamous marriage would prepare Native American males for citizenship, which was granted to Indians of both sexes in 1924.[165]

At the same time, the secretary of the interior instructed Indian agents that the reservations were to be "as remote as practicable from any of the leading routes across the plains, or the usual thoroughfares of the people of the different Territories."[166] Indians, save for those living in the Oklahoma and Dakota territories, were dispossessed of their lands, and it was expected that these two territories would receive them. This plan was carefully designed to ensure that Indians did not impede the whites' development, though the objective also meant that the plan to convert Indians into prosperous farmers was compromised from the outset.

Not coincidentally, in the same decades President Domingo Sarmiento of Argentina, who had been Argentine ambassador to the United States during the Civil War, pursued a similar policy after the Paraguayan War.[167] The Indian wars and the relocation policies in the Great Plains of the United States and the Argentine "Conquest of the Desert," south of Buenos Aires, concluded the protracted wars of destruction directed against indigenous peoples and their historical ways of life throughout the Americas. These were the last wars of national consolidation, and they marked the beginning of the great agricultural export economies, which enriched Chicago, New York, and Buenos Aires.

The national consolidation accomplished in 1867 by the Meiji Restoration in Japan also brought destruction to an indigenous "other," the Ainu. These physically distinct, light-skinned aboriginal people were native to the northern frontier island of Hokkaido. Like the American Midwest, this region was well adapted to the cultivation of wheat and to cattle raising, and the government hired an American, Horace Capron, to advise it on development and on the management of the Ainu. The policy he advised and the government pursued was essentially that initiated by the United States in 1871.[168] The Japanese outlawed many of the traditional communal practices of the Ainu, including their language. Henceforth they were to be *heimin*, or "commoners," of the newly centralized Japanese state. A few years later, the government identified them using a remarkable neologism, *kyūdojin*, or "former native." Ainu tribal law was refused recognition, and after 1875 many Ainu were given Japanese names on government registries—for efficiency's sake, the officials sometimes gave a whole Ainu village the same surname.[169] But the parallel extends further: an agricultural and technical college, based on the model of the American land-grant colleges established by the Morrill Act, was established in Sapporo, the capital of Hokkaido, in 1876. In fact, the founder, William Clark, whose statue today faces the American-style brick buildings of the original quadrangle, was the former president of the University of Massachusetts, one of the earliest land-grant colleges. Capron and other American advisers, many of whom learned baseball as Civil War soldiers, also introduced the game to Japan at this time.[170]

THE REPUBLICAN PARTY

In 1854, with the Whig Party dissolving and a series of minor parties emerging, a political realignment was clearly on the horizon. In retrospect, it seems obvious that a third American two-party system was developing, and the new Republican Party would be the successor to the Whigs. At the time, however, it was not so obvious. The Whigs could easily have been replaced by the nativist Know-Nothing Party. Catholics and immigrants might have displaced black slaves as the hot topic of national politics. Certainly hostility to immigrants, especially Catholics, was commonplace. That votes for the antislavery party could have gone to a party of ethnic and religious bigotry is not implausible. After all, antislavery sentiments and racism often resided comfortably in the same mind. Moreover, there was a similarity of outlook among those who condemned slavery and those who condemned immigrants and Catholics: they were strong nationalists who each in his own fashion wanted a more uniform national society. Both plantation slavery and Catholicism evoked worries about family, gender, and sexuality. Although we readily recall that Harriet Beecher Stowe's *Uncle Tom's Cabin* (1852) was a bestseller of the 1850s, we should also take notice of another bestseller: *Awful Disclosures of Maria Monk* (1836, 1855, 1856), a salacious anti-Catholic novel.[171] Tracts of the abolitionists and of the nativists shared a prurient fascination with the sexual power that men, whether slaveholders or priests, held over women in hierarchical social arrangements. The middle-class

Victorian Americans who would in time sustain the Republicans were disturbed about the corruption of families, whether in the largely unknown urban immigrant quarters, or in the equally mysterious world of southern plantations or in the Utah Territory.[172] The regularizing impulse of modernizing nationalism prompted them to pay greater attention and to police more rigorously deviant patterns of sexuality, gender relations, and family arrangements.[173]

Family and gender issues were not central to the political conflicts surrounding slavery, but neither were they irrelevant. Abolitionists and moderate opponents of slavery commonly talked about the dangers that slavery posed for proper family life, a point that was prominent in Stowe's famous novel, whose title character cannot maintain his house, home, or family under slavery.[174]

Promoting marriage among emancipated slaves was a major objective of the Republicans' Reconstruction policy and central to the work of the Freedmen's Bureau, as well as an ambition of the former slaves themselves, who sought the legal marriages that had been denied them in slavery. Republican reformers, working through the Freedmen's Bureau, were also committed to establishing the African-American male as head of the household and the family breadwinner supporting his wife and family. Thus were upstanding, hardworking citizens made. William Kelley, a Republican representative from Pennsylvania and father of the notable Progressive Era reformer Florence Kelley, explained that the "freedman" would become a full participant in American life when he could "feel that he is a man with a home to call his own, and a family around him, a wife to protect, children to nurture and rear, wages to be earned and received, and a right to invest his savings in the land of the country." Republicans understood this as justice for the former slaves, but they also wanted national uniformity in family life. This is one reason why the party's reformers were hesitant to support women's rights, and why suffrage and equal rights for women were not included in the constitutional amendments passed after the Civil War. In fact, an early draft of the Thirteenth Amendment, stating that "all persons are equal before the law," was modified when it was pointed out that such language would mean that "a wife would be equal to her husband and as free as her husband before the law."

Marriage was entangled in a fundamental way with nineteenth-century liberal notions of freedom and government. The republican government celebrated by Americans was, as John Locke insisted and Thomas Jefferson reiterated in the Declaration of Independence, based on consent, and so was a proper marriage. That is why slave marriages were an issue. Only a free person can effectively consent, which is why marriage among slaves was prohibited by planters and championed by abolitionists. Although they recognized that consent made a large difference, still many women's rights activists compared the power of the husband over his wife to that of a master over a slave. The self-possession denied to the slave was also denied to the married woman. Antoinette Brown Blackwell, an abolitionist, made this point in 1853: "The wife owes service and labor to her husband as much and as absolutely as the slave does to his master."[175]

If there was a certain resemblance between the concerns of voters drawn to the American and Republican parties, the American Party, it seems, elicited the worst of American traditions, while the Republican Party—and especially Lincoln—sought association with the best of them, which may in part explain the success of the latter and dissolution of the former. Lincoln despised Know-Nothingism. Writing to the abolitionist Owen Lovejoy in 1855, he expressed a hope to win adherents from among supporters of the American Party, but he would have nothing of their principles. "Of their principles I think little better than I do of those of the slavery extensionists."[176] Similarly to Joshua Speed, with whom in 1841 he had traveled by steamboat from St. Louis to Louisville, where the sight of "ten or a dozen, slaves shackled together in irons" tormented him, he wrote:

> I am not a Know-Nothing. That is certain. How could I be? How can anyone who abhors the oppression of negroes be in favor of degrading classes of white people? Our progress in degeneracy appears to me to be pretty rapid. As a nation, we began by declaring that "*all men are created equal.*" We now practically read it "all men are created equal, *except negroes.*" When the Know-Nothings get control, it will read "all men are created equal, except negroes, *and foreigners and catholics.*"[177]

With unexpected speed, the American Party collapsed after the 1856 election, and the Republican Party absorbed many of its earlier adherents.

But it was a confusing moment, with voters supporting a variety of minor parties and movements in the course of realignment. In the end, Republican affirmations appealed more than Know-Nothing negations.

The Republicans wanted a bigger and better America. Lucy Larcom, a New England writer who in the 1830s had left her poor farm family to work in a Lowell, Massachusetts, textile factory, was one of those Republicans. "What is to become of our country?" she wrote to a friend in 1856. "I do not believe it can remain united long, and I don't know that we *ought* to join hands with wickedness.—*So many* good people are saying now, 'If only the North *could* only withdraw *peacefully* from the Union!' But it is impossible."[178] Apparently, like Seward, Larcom believed that slavery was incompatible with the "greatness of nations."[179]

Audacity appealed more than acquiescence. Republicans believed that the normal condition of life in the United States should be freedom and that this normality would be realized in time, in history. To envision a progressive realization of freedom was ambitious; to work to ensure it was a radical commitment. By embracing a party that condemned slavery without equivocation, the electorate was challenging the antebellum politics of avoidance and radically changing the rules of American party politics. The white South was not wrong to interpret the election of Lincoln as a sort of revolution.

The Republican Party was a sectional party with a nationalist vision. At one level it represented sectional interests and sought national legitimacy and favorable federal policy for those interests. But at another level was the moral grandeur in the Republican condemnation of slavery, even before Lincoln gave his great speeches. When Senator Seward spoke the language of a "higher law," he gave Republican policy a moral meaning that went beyond the conventional politics of maneuver and interest. Some things, he insisted, were beyond procedures and votes. They could imagine the nation without slavery.

More immediately, practically, and determinedly, the Republicans insisted that slavery must not expand beyond its existing borders. Republican antislavery rhetoric was framed around a modern and, they thought, liberating concept of free labor. Their commitment to free labor, as Eric Foner has brilliantly demonstrated, constituted the core of their ideology.[180] In 1860, speaking on "The National Idea," Seward explained the Republican creed to a Chicago audience. It is "based on the principles of free soil, free labor, free speech, equal rights, and universal suffrage," which, he noted, were shared by the liberal and nationalist movements of Europe, and for Republicans were the "great, living, national idea of freedom."[181] The South was the land of the unfree in an era that celebrated liberty. History, as all could see by 1861, was running against the South's "peculiar institution"; the future belonged to free labor and to the indicators of modernization that characterized the North and not the South: literacy, invention, education, urbanization, industrialization, and population growth.[182]

Free labor condemned slavery, but it also had a vision of life that went well beyond the terms of labor. Though after the Civil War it was reduced to an assertion of a worker's freedom to contract for wages, at midcentury—in the United States and elsewhere—free labor principles usually included an expanded sense of individual rights.[183] The ideology included the ideas of self-possession and of not being dependent; it was, especially, a promise of the opportunity to improve one's lot in life. It was a moral vision that found expression in material improvement. Or was it a materialist notion of the meaning of human life expressed in moral terms? In fact, these two perspectives were fused. The pervasive spirit of nationalism had a similar doubleness, at times blending into the spirit of capitalism.[184]

The ideology of free labor suggested the matrix of material incentives to work and, presumably, to rise in society. This ideology of freedom was less about eighteenth-century republican liberty than about nineteenth-century individual opportunity, as Lincoln made clear. "Improvement of condition," he argued, is the "great principle for which this government was really formed." It was a principle that for him included African-Americans: "I want every man to have the chance—and I believe the black man is entitled to it—in which he *can* better his condition."[185] In the slave South, by contrast, as Richard Hildreth—a historian and opponent of slavery—insisted, the "effect of the slaveholding system is to deaden in every class of society that *spirit of industry* essential to the increase of public wealth."[186]

As these Republican spokesmen for economic expansion, modernity, and national progress condemned the South, they declined to acknowledge that its vital economic resources, which accounted for two-thirds of America's exports, fueled the dynamic northern economy that they wished to extend. Without the profits from the slave South, to say nothing of the cotton sent to New England textile factories, northern commercial, financial, and industrial development would have been later and slower.[187]

While Democrats in the North and even more so in the South were uneasy with the idea of a strong national state, with industrialization, and with modernization, Republicans spoke in their favor, and after the war made them the instruments by which the "businessman" became a civic leader, whether a local proprietor or the director of a national corporation.[188] They wanted the newly available positive power of government to be used to reconstruct the South and to build a national and industrial economy. It was a power never before exercised or even known in the United States. No other nation at that time had mobilized such power for internal social transformation and economic development on the scale of Reconstruction and postwar industrialization.

The Republicans' grand vision of the possibilities of economic development was presented in a program fairly characterized as "national economic activism."[189] During and after the war, Congress, dominated by Radical Republicans, invested in transportation, including a transcontinental railroad, symbol both of national unity and of modernity;[190] enacted a protective tariff to help industry and to generate revenue needed for a strong state; created a national bank and a national currency; instituted a homestead policy that made land in the territories available to farmers; and, with the creation of land-grant colleges in every state, established a national system of higher education. Except for the tariff, these were, in the 1860s, Atlantic liberal policies, and by the 1870s the agendas in other Atlantic world nations also turned to protectionism, making the Republicans in the United States no longer outliers.[191]

The Radical Republicans, rightly remembered for their commitment to extending rights to the former slaves, created both a national economy and national (male) citizenship. With the Fourteenth Amendment they established for the first time a constitutional definition of American citizenship. Even with its failures and incompleteness, the work of Reconstruction in the South was a radical deployment of the powers of the national state to reform a society and confer rights on a population previously without legal standing.

It is often and rightly remarked that the failure to provide the former slaves with land reveals the limits of the Radical Republican program. Still, the combination of the Thirteenth, Fourteenth, and Fifteenth amendments, along with the Reconstruction Act of 1867, established the foundation for equal citizenship on which we are still building. Had the national government not later retreated from its commitment to enforce the rights affirmed in these amendments, Reconstruction's full radicalism would be more clearly evident. But that transferring property to freedmen was beyond the reach of Reconstruction still bears noting. Comparison with the emancipation of the serfs in Russia, where the serfs were allowed to gain ownership of the land they had worked, is revealing: by 1900, two-fifths of Russia's agricultural land was owned by former serfs, while in the states of the former Confederacy all but a very small fraction of the land was still owned by white planters.[192] The unhappy consequences were already evident in the economic, political, and indeed personal vulnerabilities of former slaves and their children when Reconstruction came to an end in 1877, when the national government abandoned the freedmen and returned power to the white planter elites of the southern states, the so-called redeemers.

Nation-making, whether in the United States or in France and in other states, combined seemingly antagonistic but in fact complementary tendencies: a centralization of power and administration, concurrent with the individualization of the national citizenry. New state powers and new liberties emerged together.[193] Democracy expanded along with "the birth of the modern American state," including the institutional infrastructure of modern state administration.[194] As the Civil War ended, a writer in *The Nation* grasped the enormity of the accomplishment:

> The issue of the war marks an epoch by the consolidation of nationality under democratic forms . . . This territorial, political, and historical oneness of the nation is now ratified by the blood of thousands of her sons . . . The prime issue of the war was between nationality one and indivisible, and the loose and changeable federation of independent states.[195]

The result was a national government; no longer could one consider that the states were parallel to the national government. Now, as Woodrow Wilson put it in 1889, the state administrations and the federal one were "two parts of one and the same government."[196] But the war meant more; it was to be a government of the people, of citizens, a government "founded upon justice, and recognizing the equal rights of all men," as

Frederick Douglass insisted, "claiming no higher authority for its existence, or sanction for its laws, than nature, reason, and the regularly ascertained will of the people."[197]

In their classic, once widely read history *The Rise of American Civilization* (1927), Charles and Mary Beard underplayed the significance of slavery and overstated the Republicans' economic interests in their interpretation of the Civil War, but they rightly emphasized that the war produced a new social order and a "new power in government."[198] And here they echoed Wilson, who in 1901 wrote: "A government which had been in its spirit federal became, almost of a sudden, national in temper and point of view."[199] Ralph Waldo Emerson, who had closely observed the war and its impact, also remarked on the change: "Before the war, our patriotism was a firework, a salute, a serenade for holidays, and summer evenings . . . Now the deaths of thousands and the determination of millions of men and women show that it is real."[200] Emerson here grasped what geographers have more recently argued: that in the United States patriotic nationalism had preceded state formation.[201] But the crucible of the Civil War fused the nation, which is a "principle" or ethos, with the state, which is a "*réalité concrète.*"[202] Sovereignty, citizenship, central regulation, and capitalism converged in Americans' everyday economic relations. All together it was, as the Beards phrased it, a "Second American Revolution."[203]

Deploying state power unimaginable a generation earlier, Congress, dominated by Radical Republicans, eradicated an institution that had been central to the national economy, a source of enormous private wealth (estimated at $4 billion) in the South, and the cornerstone of southern social life.[204] And they deployed this newly created state to lay the foundations of a powerful industrial economy. One thinks of initiatives ranging from the protective tariff to subsidies for railroads, from homesteads to agricultural experiment stations, but the creation of a national currency may best reveal the government's extension into everyday life. Before the war, ten thousand different bills were printed by hundreds of unregulated private banks and untold numbers of counterfeiters. Could one trust the value of a bill? The question of confidence was, as Herman Melville showed in his novel *The Confidence-Man* (1857), a daily challenge. Now the local uncertainties were removed; a strong national government produced a uniform currency and invited everyone to trust in the nation to ensure its value.[205]

Dollar bills pass so easily and quickly through our hands that we are little inclined to consider their political importance, yet the habitual, unremarkable use of money in fact sustains a "banal nationalism." Establishing a territorially exclusive currency was a fundamental aspect of the making of modern nation-states everywhere.[206] In the United States, antebellum banknotes had been associated with local institutions and were often illustrated with local landmarks, but the new national currency displayed national icons: Washington, Franklin, the flag, and the Capitol. One newspaper commented that every time a citizen "handled" or looked at "a bill bearing the national mark," he or she would be reminded that "the union of these states is verily a personal benefit and blessing to all." No one better understood this than Senator and later Secretary of the Treasury John Sherman, brother of the famous Civil War general William Tecumseh Sherman. A key figure in formulating Republican financial policy, Sherman was attuned to the ways a national currency enhanced a "sentiment of nationality." "If we are dependent on the United States for a currency and medium of exchange," he wrote in 1863, "we shall have a broader and more generous nationality."[207] Holders of notes backed by the Treasury would necessarily be interested in the fate of the national government.

The Civil War marked the transformation of an agricultural society into an industrial nation or, as the Beards famously argued, the triumph of the industrial North over the agricultural South. By 1873, industrial production had increased by 75 percent over its level in 1865, and the United States was second only to Great Britain as a manufacturing nation. Thirty-five thousand miles of new railroad track was laid in the eight years following the surrender at Appomattox. By 1900, the industrial power of the United States was unsurpassed, as would soon be revealed in World War I.

That this development would follow national unification was not unexpected; in fact, it had been a motive of those who worked for that unification. The new nation-states that emerged from the successful resolution of the mid-century "federative crisis" nearly all experienced impressive rates of economic development: this was the case in Germany, while the creation of the Dual Monarchy enabled the creation of the Hungarian nation-state, which produced a burst of entrepreneurial energy. Many people compared rapidly growing Budapest to the example of

American cities. In Japan, too, the consolidation of a modern state underwrote rapid economic development, and with its new liberal constitution and consolidated national government Argentina prospered. Indeed, its massive immigration, agricultural productivity, and rapid industrialzation nearly paralleled those of the United States; by the end of the century Argentina's was the world's sixth-largest economy. And the mid-century pattern of centralization resulted in significant, although not so dramatic, industrialization in the old land empires: Russia, the Ottoman Empire, and China (where it occurred in a complex relation with semi-colonial foreign investment).

The U.S. experience was not unique, but its development was surely among the most striking. In the spirit of the liberal values of 1848, it had undertaken, on behalf of social betterment and economic development, a nationalist program of state-supported initiatives, but the promised benefits were almost immediately compromised by the premature abandonment of Reconstruction. Although slavery was ended, free labor did not flourish in the South—and this setback had everything to do with cotton.

Cotton, as leaders in the South had often claimed, was central to the industrial economies of Europe. They hoped its indispensability made cotton "King" in the Atlantic world. In 1861, they further hoped that the European powers, desperate for cotton to sustain their factories and keep their working classes both employed and clothed, might recognize the Confederacy and perhaps support it in other ways. Certainly, there is ample evidence that the governments in Britain, France, and elsewhere gave this issue much thought. But none came to the aid of the South.

During the war, Europe's industrialized nations (and northern manufacturers in the United States) developed other and sufficient sources of cotton—in Africa, central and South Asia, and South America. In fact, as the historian Sven Beckert has shown, the war's interruption of the flow of American cotton to European factories and then the end of slavery with the northern victory effectively transformed both the geography of raw cotton production and its modes of production.[208] Before 1860, cotton had been produced by slaves, mostly in the American South. After 1865, the proportion of cotton produced in various European empires—especially in British India, Ottoman Egypt, and also parts of Africa—increased significantly. The amount of cotton from India, Brazil, and Egypt in European factories doubled between 1860 and 1865, to 31 percent of the total. These changes did not displace America's preeminence in the world cotton market, once production resumed after 1865, but they did significantly transform cotton agriculture elsewhere in the world. Large numbers of subsistence farmers began to plant cotton and to enter the world market with this cash crop. The agricultural workers were formally not slaves; they were free laborers. But nearly every-where—in India and Mississippi, in Egypt and Pernambuco, Brazil, in Turkmenistan and West Africa—they lived and worked in a condition of peonage, trapped in an unending cycle of indebtedness to local merchants.

Russia, Britain, and other European nations looked to their imperial holdings to replace the interrupted supply of American cotton. This meant they had to establish a legal environment that would encourage and protect merchant investment in the cotton sharecroppers, supplying them with seed, equipment, and marketing services. Slavery was replaced by a particular form of nonindustrial capitalist social relations, in which impoverished farmers were ruled by the merchants' control of credit, and the state protected the credit, not the farmers. Strikingly, this structure of labor discipline evolved all over the world; in the American South poor white farmers but especially former slaves endured this new form of ex-ploitation. In Asia and in North and West Africa, the stakes were very high, and the paradoxical effect of the emancipation of four million slaves in the United States was that Europe's nation-states strengthened and ex-tended their control over the economies and laboring populations of their empires, while they also developed infrastructure to support the cotton economies they were encouraging and depending on. This changed the very nature of the colonial experience throughout North Africa and South Asia especially. The new railroads and communications systems helped to create a sense of national territory that would, in time, be essential to anti-imperialist nationalist movements.[209]

My main point here has been to show that the Civil War in the United States shared in larger nation-making processes, and made broader liberal commitments to free as opposed to unfree labor. But the laborers who benefited most from the Civil War were white, not just in America but in Europe. The new, highly qualified system of free labor was mostly imposed on people of color (except in the American South, where poor whites were incorporated into the new regime of cotton production along with freedmen), and they were everywhere politically marginalized and subject to strict lien laws. Here we begin to see another way of understanding the Civil War as a global event, as a central moment in the "reconstruction of the worldwide web of cotton growing, trade, and manufacturing."

In Egypt, for example, the American Civil War is understood as a turning point in the nation's history. The expanded global demand for cotton in the 1860s enabled the Ottoman viceroy there, Sa'id Pasha, to accelerate the modernizing project begun earlier in the century by Mehmet Ali. Acreage devoted to cotton cultivation was vastly increased after 1861; by 1864 about 40 percent of the fertile land along the lower Nile had been converted to cotton. The resultant fivefold increase in cotton exports fundamentally changed the Egyptian economy.

Major economic transformations such as this one occurred on every continent, and they gave the advantage to financial capital. The banks of Europe supplied local merchants throughout the empires with capital to finance the development of cotton cultivation, and the terms of the loans involved a crop lien to protect the capital. Initially the world price of cotton rose dramatically, but soon it stabilized, especially when the United States resumed production and export after 1865, and the result for farmers was perpetual debt and pressure on the price of cotton. The social relation of master and slave was replaced by law, formally impartial but ultimately an instrument of the differential power of capital over labor. This system of extracting labor turned out to be more effective than slavery; everywhere production increased. In the United States the production of cotton in 1891 was twice what it had been thirty years earlier on the eve of the Civil War. So the war and the abolition of slavery in the American South not only increased productivity in the United States but hugely increased world production. Imperial power was now deployed far more strategically, and it shaped the world cotton market.

REMEMBERING NATIONALISM
AND FORGETTING LIBERALISM

As late as the spring of 1862, Lincoln wrote—rather testily—to Horace Greeley that his "paramount object in this struggle *is* to save the Union, and is *not* either to save or to destroy slavery. If I could save the Union without freeing *any* slave, I would do it, and if I could save it by freeing *all* the slaves, I would do it."[210] But as the celebrated intellectual and political leader Frederick Douglass grasped—better than Greeley and perhaps even more fully than Lincoln in 1862—the war made the fusion of "Liberty and Union" practically unavoidable.[211] As Lincoln invested more and more liberal meaning in what he called the "new nation" (he used this phrase in the Gettysburg Address), the ends of the war expanded. His major speeches, culminating in the one at Gettysburg, gave ever larger significance to the great struggle for freedom, and liberal nationalists in Europe could recognize their aspirations in the success of the Union armies. Giuseppe Mazzini, for example, wrote to the London agent of the U.S. Sanitary Commission, a forerunner of the American Red Cross, that the North's war for freedom and national unity had "done more for us in four years than fifty years of teaching, preaching, and writing from all your European brothers have been able to do."[212]

If Jefferson's language of Enlightenment liberalism was analytical and declarative ("all men are created equal"), the liberal ideals of Lincoln, the romantic nationalist, were expressed in a language of historicism. With active democracy, the ideals of the Declaration of Independence would and must be realized over time. Lincoln's notion of history promised no immanent unfolding or natural progress; he demanded action—vigilance, exertion, even struggle. At Gettysburg, he spoke of "unfinished work" and the "great task remaining." He transformed Jefferson's proposition into a challenge, that "this nation, under God, shall have a new birth of freedom."[213] Liberal nationalism for Lincoln was thus "aspirational," demanding resolute and continuous pursuit.[214]

Like Lincoln, Frederick Douglass looked to a historical dynamic in which the nation was the midwife of human progress. In a remarkable lecture, "Our Composite Nationality" (1869), Douglass affirmed the indispensability of nations, the value of what we would call multicultural nationality, and the inherently progressive work of the world of nations. Modern nations, he wrote, are "the largest and most complete divisions into which society is formed, the grandest aggregations of organized human power." They promote human improvement through "comparison and criticism." The way of nations, he hoped, would be not that of power but rather that of "comparing one nation with another . . . each competing with all." That would expose errors and turn the "wheels of civilization."[215]

Unfortunately, these hopes of Lincoln, Douglass, and Mazzini, as well as the hopes of those for whom they spoke, especially the millions newly freed from slavery, were not wholly realized. Nationalism had other affinities, particularly with the celebration of "constant growth," that undermined the liberal commitment to freedom.[216] To be sure, by 1900 the new nation-state had delivered the economic development it had promised. A "titanic impulse" was given to "all enterprise in America," and the infrastructure of a national high culture was also established: universities, museums, public libraries, symphony halls, and conservatories.[217] There is ample evidence to sustain the claim of the theorist of nationalism Ernest Gellner that there are links between industrialism, nationalism, continuous improvement in material life, and investment in cognitive growth.[218] National consolidation brought military might, too, enough for the United States to become an imperial power itself on a global scale in 1898.

In all too many cases the nationalist feelings and ambitions that had earlier advanced the cause of human freedom and dignity now worked against such aspirations. Sometimes nationalism simply overshadowed liberal commitments; in other cases specific choices favored it over liberalism. The United States was not unique in this regard. While some of the *national* ambitions of 1848 had been realized in Europe by 1900 (though not those of small minorities), *liberal* achievements had been compromised by the quest for power and profit.

The finest historian of Reconstruction calls it the "unfinished revolution."[219] That is what it is from our perspective, perhaps, and the burden is on us to finish it. But the phrase is too generous to describe the actual actions of the 1870s. While it is true that the Radical Republicans were unable to finish the revolution, the reason was not only white resistance in the South but a refusal of support in the North. White Americans, North and South, turned against the project of extending freedom across the color line in the name of the nation.

When blacks in the South demanded their rights in full, and when women and workers in the North did the same, northern leaders pulled back from their ambitious vision of the positive state. And they never even considered rights for Native Americans. Many of the original supporters of the Republican antislavery movement stayed the course, but far more abandoned the radical project of racial justice in the South before it had a fair test, and some of the leaders of the crusade to extend the domain of freedom in 1861 now tried to disenfranchise militant workers in the North.[220] Charles Francis Adams, Jr., the son of Lincoln's ambassador to the Court of St. James's, declared in 1869 that "universal suffrage can only mean in plain English the government of ignorance and vice—it means a European, and especially Celtic proletariat on the Atlantic Coast, an African proletariat on the shores of the Gulf, and a Chinese proletariat on the Pacific." A decade later, as Reconstruction ended, the historian Francis Parkman wrote a long article published in *The North American Review* that announced "the failure of universal suffrage."[221] These were not lone voices; many who had once spoken the principles of 1848 had lost the vision that liberal nationalists had brought into the war.

It is often said that these social and political leaders recognized that the government had overreached its capacity. But that is not entirely clear, and surely is not the whole explanation. More evident was their growing fear of realized democracy, fear of a large number of potential voters whose empowerment and consequent capture of a strong state would substantially alter the distribution of power and social goods in American society. If they could not limit the vote, they would limit the domain of state action, taking social questions out of politics and allocating them to market resolutions.[222]

By contrast with Prussia, indeed with most modern nations to which Americans might compare themselves, the United States in the late nineteenth century was a liberal society and polity. But in comparison with the ideals Lincoln had expressed at Gettysburg, something had been lost. If in the language of 1848 the nation was the expression of the sovereignty of the people, after 1877 it seemed that the "State" had become the "antonym of the People." The liberal ideal of rights-carrying individuals was questioned, and political theorists argued that the state conferred rights on the people, rather than the people conferring legitimacy on the state. Put differently: the state presumed its own sovereignty and indeed became a barrier to the people's claims of rights.[223] Lawyers and academic political scientists articulated a formalist understanding of the state as constituting society, but this obscured the many class, racial, gender, and ethnic aspirations and conflicts in America's actual pluralistic society. The quest for national unity and uniformity, which had once fused with the political quest for abolition and, for Radical Republicans, racial justice, had in some perverse fashion become almost its opposite.

The result is evident in the writings of John W. Burgess, founder of the graduate Faculty of Political Science at Columbia University in 1880, which was organized to train a political elite. Burgess honored Lincoln, but he expounded at some length on Lincoln's limitations as a constitutional theorist. He corrected what he believed was Lincoln's misunderstanding of the constitutional status of secession and sketched the future implications of the new nationalism. The "nationalizing of civil liberty" under the protection of the judiciary (no mention of voters here), Burgess argued, would sustain a nation-state led by "white men, whose mission . . . duty . . . and right" is "to hold the reins of political power in [their] own hands for the civilization of the world and the welfare of mankind." This was necessary, he explained, because of "vast differences in the political capacity of the races." Thus did Burgess justify both the abandonment of Reconstruction and America's imperialist adventure in the war of 1898.[224] Charles Beard and other thinkers of the Progressive Era challenged this theory of the state, but in the 1880s and '90s Burgess's idea of the nation-state's powers and responsibilities seemed to justify a profound weakening of democracy and a racist distortion of citizenship. By the end of the century, Congress and the courts had retreated from the earlier expansive definitions of federal power and individual rights. The Reconstruction amendments and legislation were emasculated. Remarkably, the Fourteenth Amendment was transformed from a basic protection of the political rights of freedmen in the states to the protection of business corporations from government regulation. Yet however limited the domestic powers of the federal government had become, the American state had acquired the capacity to project its power well beyond its territories, joining other North Atlantic nations in establishing a new age of imperialism.

In 1882, the distinguished French historian Ernest Renan asked, in a lecture, "What is a nation?" The essay of this title is a classic, and it continues to be reprinted. Renan had then recently been elected to the French Academy and was soon named president of the Collège de France. His focus, not surprisingly, was on France and Europe, yet one of his main points speaks directly to the American case. In effect, he explained how—even as it was happening—the dynamic of nationalism was undermining the deepest meaning of the Civil War: "The essence of a nation is that all individuals have many things in common, and also that they have forgotten many things . . . Forgetting . . . is a crucial factor in the creation of a nation."[225]

The quest for national restoration and the reconciliation of North and South required forgetting the central meaning of the Civil War—or so writers, editors, and political leaders believed. As David W. Blight has shown in his comprehensive study of "the Civil War in American memory," nationalism displaced the emancipatory meaning of the war, as well as the obvious truth that one side had fought on behalf of freedom and the other to maintain slavery.[226] All were brave; all fought for what they believed. All the old soldiers were heroes.

After Reconstruction, monuments were erected at Gettysburg commemorating both the Confederate armies and the Union ones. There is no obvious indication of their different reasons for fighting. The distortion of the memory of Reconstruction was even greater. Nothing heroic about it was remembered in 1900 or, for that matter, for several decades into the twentieth century. Instead, Reconstruction was thought of as a misbegotten adventure, and this is how D. W. Griffith presented it in his powerful racist film *The Birth of a Nation* (1915). One might call this a failure of memory, but in fact it is an example of the politics of memory: a particular political interest transforming the meaning not only of the Civil War but of the nation itself.

Frederick Douglass tried again and again to recall for Americans the full meaning of the war and Reconstruction, as did W.E.B. DuBois in the next century. Both believed that the emancipation of the slaves had been the central event not only of black history but of U.S. history.[227] Speaking in 1872, Douglass insisted:

> We are sometimes asked in the name of patriotism to forget the merits of this fearful struggle, and to remember with equal admiration those who struck at the nation's life, and those who struck to save it—those who fought for slavery and those who fought for liberty and justice . . . I would not repel the repentant, but . . . may my tongue cleave to the roof of my mouth if I forget the difference between the parties to that . . . bloody conflict . . . I may say if this war is to be forgotten, I ask in the name of all things sacred what shall men remember?[228]

But Douglass's views were little shared, and were shared even less as time passed. E. L. Godkin spoke for the greater part of the nation, North and

South, when in 1877 Reconstruction was ended in a political deal that settled the contested election of 1876. He assured readers in *The Nation*, a magazine that he and other antislavery activists founded in New York in 1865, which became the forum for the intellectual elite of the country, that "the negro will disappear from the field of national politics. Henceforth, the nation as nation, will have nothing more to do with him."[229] The future would be concerned with political reunion and the economic development it would further. Liberal nationalism had become a *Herrenvolk* nationalism.[230]

In truth, the liberal ideals of freedom in 1848 had always been a bit flawed. The minority question continued as a divisive issue in the Austro-Hungarian Empire until its demise, and it was the reason for President Wilson's intense concern for self-determination at Versailles. In a different way, the realization of an Italian state under Cavour compromised Mazzini's liberalism, and the rights of native peoples were no more respected by liberals in Argentina than in the United States. The rights that women claimed were rarely acknowledged. Colonialism was embraced by every state that possessed the power to play the imperial game. One could go on.

In 1898 Americans consolidated their nationalism in another war. This imperial one was hardly emancipatory, and it even voided a significant movement for racial democracy in Cuba.[231] Its justifying rhetoric was infused with racial supremacy—"the White Man's burden," as the British writer Rudyard Kipling helpfully put it for the Americans. John Hay, Lincoln's former secretary and biographer and secretary of state in the McKinley administration, characterized it as a "splendid little war." Americans North and South cheered their soldiers' easy triumph in Cuba and Manila Bay, happily cementing their national reconciliation. Surprisingly, ten thousand blacks enlisted in the American army—but not the son of Frederick Douglass, who understood imperialism differently. To his mind, it was a global extension of "race hate and cruelty."[232]

4

AN EMPIRE AMONG EMPIRES

———∞∞∞———

In 1884–85 representatives of the major European powers met in Berlin. The topic was empire. Great Britain, France, and Germany agreed on ground rules for their great game. They negotiated a blueprint for carving up Africa among themselves, an agreement that, along with new technologies of violence, medicine, and communication, accelerated their imperial expansion and tightened control over their colonies.[1] Between the Berlin meetings and the world war, nearly a quarter million miles were added each year to empires worldwide. By the turn of the century it had become clear to many, including V. I. Lenin, that "the world is completely divided up."[2]

The United States was invited to Berlin (probably because of its interest in Liberia, founded by the American Colonization Society in 1821), and it sent a representative but refused to be a signatory to the final agreement.[3] The reasons derived in part from the legacy of Washington's warning about entangling alliances, and also from a widely held belief, sometimes loudly broadcast, that America's republican institutions were a standing rebuke to Europe's corrupt politics and imperial pretensions. Histories of the United States and Europe have largely accepted this American pretension.

An essential part of American national identity is based on difference, on a tendency to define America as distinct from, even separate from, all that is foreign, whether Europe or those parts of the world Americans unself-consciously called "uncivilized" or "savage."[4] American republicanism and Protestant Christianity, they thought, were the keynotes of their distinctiveness, as was their rejection of imperial ambitions. One could argue—and I will—that here they were indulging in a semantic sleight of hand. They obscured their actual empire by describing it as "the westward movement" or the "westward expansion" of their country. True, the Constitution had a unique provision that seemed anti-imperialist on the face of it: it allowed territories to become states on equal terms with the original states, which is why westward expansion was considered a fair description of the Euro-American settlement of the continent. But it was fair only to the degree that its prior possession by Indians and Mexicans was erased or denied. Empire, as William Appleman Williams long ago argued, has been an American way of life.[5] Dispossession and colonial rule have been central if unacknowledged themes in American history.

It is true and important that with the unhappy exception of the annexation of the Philippines and the somewhat more successful instance of Puerto Rico at the end of the Spanish-American wars of 1898, the United States did not formally colonize any overseas territories. That differentiates it from the European powers and Japan, but it does not close the question. U.S. citizens avidly acquired an entire continent, and they did it through conquest; meanwhile, they developed and militarily defended an overseas empire based on trade and finance. It has been said that the United States was an empire without being imperial.[6] In eschewing territorial control and favoring an empire of commerce and finance, the United States was perhaps prescient. Certainly it helped to shape the global economy and culture that it dominated for most of the twentieth century. The American way of empire raised fewer moral issues than did the European empires—though moral questions there were, and they were revelatory ones.

It has been difficult for Americans to recognize their continental expansion as an empire, especially when ethnocentric assumptions obscure the presence of Native Americans on the supposedly "empty" land. The empire as market power is similarly difficult to grasp, not being visible or tangible. Its abstract character may partly explain the paradox of a nation which is a global power and which does not teach geography in its schools and whose public has little interest in geographical knowledge beyond the borders of the United States.[7] The comparison with Europeans on this point is striking—and it is evident in American mapmaking. World atlases published in the United States typically included more domestic maps than did European ones—and the difference is substantial: up to 80 percent for American atlases, compared with 7–20 percent for those published in Europe.[8]

The participants at the Berlin Conference were not unaware of the rising power across the Atlantic. They had observed closely the military might of the Union armies, and they knew that the United States was on the verge of becoming the world's leading manufacturing nation. They feared that the size alone of the continental nations—the United States and Russia—would confer a worrisome advantage on them in international competition. And they feared that if they themselves could not expand, they would be vulnerable. In 1883, the English historian John Seeley warned,

> If the United States and Russia hold together for another half century, they will at the end of that time completely dwarf such old European states as France and Germany and depress them into a second class. They will do the same to England, if at the end of that time England still sees herself as simply a European state.

German and Japanese leaders made the same point. In France, Jules Ferry told parliamentary critics of his colonial policies that if France abstained from empire, it would "descend from the first rank to the third or fourth."[9] The language of competition was pervasive in this era that relied so often on metaphors of Darwinian struggle. Many leading German academics, including Gustav Schmoller and Adolph Wagner, both liberals who favored the development of social citizenship, were pro-empire. The historian Heinrich von Treitschke told his students at Berlin that "every virile people has established colonial power" and warned that Germany must colonize to preserve the nation, phrasing the issue as a "matter of life and death."[10] The masculinity theme was evident everywhere, including in the United States, and in its decision for war and empire in 1898.[11]

The nineteenth-century system of nations encouraged competition, and it was played out among national empires. Many factors were involved. Economic interests were surely part of the equation, but in a complicated way. The empires were money losers for national treasuries from the beginning, though some individuals made fortunes in them. Yet there were counterbalancing risks in not having an imperial market—being shut out of the markets controlled by rival nations was one. So a defensive economics was as important as visions of new markets.[12] Americans were attuned to this issue in 1898. Prestige and even moral regeneration pressed the newly consolidated nation-states toward empire, and so did fear of internal divisions, which, it was hoped, might be moderated or wholly displaced by a collective imperial pride.[13] Leaders of rapidly industrializing nations, notably Germany and the United States, might see a way to deflect social conflict in imperial adventures, while in other cases empire was pursued in the interest of completing national consolidation, as in Italy's North African colonial efforts or in the United States after the Civil War. The United States entered the race for empire for all these reasons.

There are and have been both imperial and anti-imperial strains in American politics and culture. Often the two battled in the mind and heart of the same person. It is often difficult to predict or even later explain why one or the other is dominant in a given instance. Americans are drawn to both liberty and empire, yet the two political logics have an unstable relation with each other, even if they are often linked. Americans celebrate liberty and sometimes seek to extend it beyond their shores, often by means that others cannot distinguish from imperial ones. To themselves the two are joined by the articulated intention of doing good. An anticolonial logic of empire can be read in Theodore Roosevelt's justification for continuing the control the United States reserved for itself in an "independent" Cuba:

> not only because it is enormously in our interest to control the Cuba market and by every means to foster our supremacy in the tropical lands and waters south of us . . . but also because we should make all our sister nations of the American continent feel that we desire to show ourselves disinterestedly and effectively their friends.[14]

Of course, some Americans saw through talk of disinterested commitments in extending what Jefferson called the "empire of liberty." They recognized that empire put liberty at risk. Abraham Lincoln was one such critic. When those Americans shouting "Manifest Destiny" proposed to extend the blessings of liberty (and slavery, too) by taking half of Mexico's national territory, he objected. The expansionist, he said,

> is a great friend of humanity; and his desire for land is not selfish, but merely an impulse to extend the area of freedom. He is very anxious to fight for the liberation of enslaved nations and colonies, provided always, they *have* land, and have *not* any liking for his interference. As to those who have no land [that is, slaves in the U.S. South], and would be glad for help from any quarter, he considers *they* can afford to wait a few hundred years longer.[15]

It has been argued that American slavery and American freedom were bound together and justified each other, and one might say the same about empire and liberty.[16] Just as a society that depended on slavery formed the basis for republican liberty for white males and even nourished republican statesmen (four out of the first five presidents), so empire has been justified as a means of extending the blessings of American liberty and Protestant Christianity and improving the world.

But another connection between liberty and empire must be addressed, too. The American celebration of the free individual and the release of his (usually his) unbounded ambition implicitly promise access to all the goods of the world (usually by purchase)—and that includes lands of the Native Americans as well as worldly resources beyond the continent, whether or not the possessor desires to sell.

AHAB AND EMPIRE

Few Americans of his time understood the global dimensions of American enterprise better than Herman Melville. Whaling was a global industry, and the United States dominated it, searching out the necessary "raw materials" in the world's oceans and selling to a world market. Melville knew this world, knew the tropical peoples who were being colonized by Europeans and whose cultures were being reformed by evangelical Protestants from the United States. "The same waters," he wrote, "wash . . . the new-built California towns . . . and lave the faded but still gorgeous skirts of Asiatic lands, older than Abraham . . . while all between float milky-ways of coral isles, and low-lying endless, unknown archipelagoes, and impenetrable Japan."[17]

Melville knew his America and Americans well. And in Captain Ahab, who relentlessly pursues the white whale to the farthest reaches of the South Pacific and Asian seas, he created an exemplar of the way Americans lived empire. Having lost a leg to the whale, Ahab has a straightforward reason for his pursuit; American empire was often motivated in part by an unexceptionable concern for security. But if that was all Melville had to tell us, *Moby-Dick* would be no more than an ordinary adventure story, and the story of American empire would be similarly simple. But neither is so.

Moby-Dick is a book of great complexity with innumerable themes, and one of the most obvious concerns Ahab's self-regarding, unbounded ambition. America as opportunity—especially material opportunity—has shaped a culture in the United States that encourages escape from the past, starting over, expanding one's horizons and, ultimately, empire. By naming Ahab's ship the *Pequod*, Melville signals that empire is on his mind, for it was the Pequot War between Puritan settlers and Indians in 1636–37 that established "English hegemony in southern New England" and opened the way for settlement.[18]

Like Ahab, white Americans and especially male Americans were always seeking to expand a temporal and spatial future, repeatedly abandoning the past for newer and wider horizons of ambition. Like the whale, these symbolic and material horizons continually moved out of reach of the sometimes violent quest. Foreign commentators repeatedly noticed this aspect of American culture, none more profoundly than Alexis de Toqueville, who was fascinated by the endless pursuit that never realized itself, that always fell short of satisfaction. It was the product, he thought, of a combination of professed equality and an absence of formal social barriers: the American's "feverish ardor" for his "own welfare" envisions the realization of a "complete felicity" that "forever escapes him."[19] The ambitious Americans were ever sipping Tantalus's cup.

Almost unthinkingly—and to an extraordinary degree—Americans came to associate the meaning of America with an entitlement to unrestricted access to land and markets. Land, freedom, opportunity, abundance, seemed a natural sequence, which nourished something of an

American compulsion to use new lands and opportunities to achieve wealth.[20] The remarkable expansion of America's agricultural frontier, of its cities, and of its markets rested on the premise that people could and should "exploit the wealth of nature to the utmost."[21] This combination of aspiration and abundance reflected and nourished a distinctive way of life, what Richard Hofstadter once called a "democracy of cupidity."[22] The international thrust of this democracy, beginning with the expansion of the United States in the West, constitutes a powerful version of empire.

Melville's remarkable book both elaborated and challenged the expectation that the world should give itself to the ever-aspiring American.[23] He understood, too, that Americans seldom grasped what those on the other side of the territorial or commercial frontier thought or felt about contact and exchange, whether of land or goods. John Quincy Adams, perhaps America's ablest secretary of state and an architect of its empire, was worldly enough to realize that other nations found Americans peculiarly, even graspingly ambitious. Yet even he did not think that required an American adjustment or response. Writing in 1819, he observed that "any effort on our part to reason the world out of a belief that we are ambitious will have no other effect than that we add to our ambition hypocrisy."[24] Twenty years later, attacking China's efforts to restrict its trade with Western countries, he revealed the degree to which he shared this American sense of entitlement and presumption that the world should accommodate itself to American desire and enterprise.[25]

The story of American empire dates from the initial European settlement of the Western Hemisphere. With their utopian dreams and material ambitions, English settlers in North America took possession of lands they alleged to be empty and unused. The American *national* experience thereafter focused on territorial expansion and on developing global markets for agriculture, manufactures, and investment. As we have already seen, the global historical framing requires that we view the American empire in multiple perspectives, and the narrative is as much spatial as linear. We might again take our cue from Melville, who, in his novel *Pierre; or, The Ambiguities* (1852), described a narrative strategy that "goes forward and goes backward, as occasion calls. Nimble center, circumference elastic you must have."[26] The American story also requires a certain nimbleness in respect to ethical matters. Empire, like slavery, sustained Abraham Lincoln's observation that "the philosophy of the human mind" was such that "the love of property and a consciousness of right or wrong have conflicting places in our organization, which often make a man's course seem crooked, his conduct a riddle."[27]

Henry J. Raymond, founding editor of *The New York Times*, writing in 1854—three years after *Moby-Dick* and about the time of Lincoln's reflection on the human capacity for compartmentalization and self-deception—urged Senator William Henry Seward (Lincoln's future secretary of state) to curb his imperial ambitions. "*Empire*," Raymond wrote, "is a grand ambition, but *Freedom* is loftier . . . We are the most ambitious people the world has ever seen: —and I greatly fear we shall sacrifice our liberties to our imperial dream."[28] Raymond was not the first or last to make such a warning. This American worry about its own democracy was far more deeply felt than any concern for those affected by American power. It was almost as if empire were somehow wholly a domestic matter. Anti-imperialists were often no more curious about the experience of empire on the ground than were imperialists.

Historians have been no exception. Most chroniclers of American imperialism, even when highly critical—and perhaps for that reason—limit themselves to questions of intention and morality. But there is more to be examined: a global perspective invites and demands examination of the way American presumptions and policies were understood by those affected by them, and how American empire looked from the outside.[29]

Empire worked in complex and often unpredictable ways; imperial intrusions altered balances of power, allowing, for example, Native Americans to play the European empires against each other in eighteenth-century North America, or the Chinese to do the same when the Americans arrived in their country a century later, advancing the "self-strengthening" policy of chief minister Li Hung-chang.[30] The arrival of imperial authorities could bring new resources but also alter local hierarchies, relations of power, and structures of opportunity. Such was the case in Puerto Rico after 1898. The United States invested in infrastructure, schools, and public health; equally important, the introduction of American law gave support to Puerto Rico's own movements for women's rights, particularly access to divorce, which undercut the ruling elite's paternalistic notions of the island as a harmonious "great national family." Similarly, American consolidation of sugar production there made an island-wide labor movement (the Federación Libre de Trabajadores) both possible and necessary. Empire extracts wealth, but it also creates new opportunities—usually without so intending—that create new possibilities, enabling local groups to make novel claims of political and economic rights.[31] The intrusion of American corporations similarly shook up local power arrangements, and sometimes shifts in patterns of opportunity invited families to adopt novel strategies for advancement, enabling them to rise to positions of greater wealth or power or standing.[32]

In the Philippines and in Cuba, American officials aligned with the conservative local elites, and in the latter case this collaboration tipped the Cuban Revolution's fragile commitment to antiracism ever since 1868 toward a reemphasis on racial difference.[33] In the former, the elite *ilustrados*, as they were called (the educated or "enlightened ones"), were able to limit American colonial authority by raising the specter of popular unrest when the Americans pressed them too hard.[34] These are examples of what Steve J. Stern calls "reverse colonization," whereby the colonized utilize the apparatus of colonial control for their own purposes, a process limited in range of action but nonetheless significant.[35]

Historians writing the history of empire rightly emphasize these complex forms of interaction. It is important to recognize the agency of the colonized, whether in territorial empires or in commercial ones. But one must not overlook the uneven distribution of power. Here I emphasize the structure and power of empire and I do not ignore the circumstances at the "other end." I am especially concerned to challenge the commonplace notion that the United States never or rarely self-consciously deployed its political, economic, and military power to shape the world in the interests of its empire. I challenge, too, the notion that its imperial moment, 1898, was unthinking or accidental.

Americans are always anxious to deny the relevance of empire to their history. They tend to rely on a contrast with Europe to justify this way of understanding their past. They point out that except for an aberration that resulted in the taking possession of Puerto Rico, Guam, the Philippines, and, indirectly, Cuba, Americans did not colonize or rule territories as European powers did. Instead, they used their economic, military, and diplomatic leverage to create a world of free trade available to all. America's activity in the world, according to this account, was primarily that of private actors in the marketplace, not government rule over distant peoples and territories.

The point is true but misleading in two broad ways. First, it is true that the land hunger of individual settlers drove the westward expansion of the United States. Yet the expansion was sustained by national policy and enforced by military means when needed. Taking territory from Native Americans and from Mexico was, except for the Civil War and the emancipation of the slaves, the most important activity of the U.S. government in the nineteenth century. The government also secured, by purchase and treaty from European powers, other land and had little regard for the rights or preferences of those long resident on it. Empire was not wholly the work of private actors.

Second, there was a consistent use of diplomacy and even force to protect Americans' access to global markets and to secure freedom for missionaries abroad. The commercial policy dates at least from the Jefferson administration, which brought the United States into its first foreign war to protect American commerce in the Mediterranean from the Barbary pirates of North Africa. At the same time Jefferson used diplomacy rather than war to secure New Orleans as a shipping point for American agriculture. The Mexican War brought to the United States vast new territory and the great natural harbor of San Francisco. And U.S. government policy was equally evident in the determination to make the Caribbean an "American lake." One sees the twentieth-century formulation of this in Woodrow Wilson's hope, informed by American moral and political precepts, for a postwar world safe for American trade and investment.

The United States, then, entered the twentieth century well experienced in taking territory and in the affairs of empire. It was prepared to seek and protect markets for American agriculture, manufactured goods, and capital, especially in Latin America and Asia.[36] And it competed aggressively with the European powers for market share in the global economy.

The United States was thus part of a larger history of European or Western economic and cultural domination of the planet. If we put it in the provocative formulation of W.E.B. DuBois a century ago, the United States participated in the domination of people of color by the white nations of the North Atlantic. Both as a colony and as a nation, we Americans became part of the larger, ever changing European work of empire that began in the fifteenth century.

BEING THE WHALE

Ahab has lost his leg to the whale, and, as he says, that lessens him as a man. But an apter symbol might have been the loss of his sight, for it was blind ambition that marked Ahab's and the Americans' endless quest. At the core of empire as a way of life is precisely this incapacity to see oneself as a potential enemy.[37] Confident in their ambition and desire, and sure of their own goodwill, Americans were strangers to self-reflection. As Lincoln Steffens acerbically noted, this meant they never learned to do wrong knowingly, but others endured the consequences of the American dispensation. Three brief accounts of interactions with "others" show us the heart of the problem: the Cherokee removal, the taking of half of Mexico's national territory, and an obscure trade mission to Korea.

Two themes unite these disparate cases. First, Americans presumed a position of superiority to the people whose land they coveted or whose trade they sought. Tocqueville made this point with a brutal analogy. Whites, he wrote, consider themselves "to the other races of mankind what man himself is to the lower animals: he makes them subservient to his use, and when he cannot subdue he destroys them."[38] Second, Americans repeatedly misunderstood the culture, ideas, and aspirations of other peoples and nations. Again and again they presumed that their own parochial assumptions were universal and should be controlling in intercultural and international exchanges. Leaving out the guns for a moment, this quality of empire can be partly described as a massive, consistent failure of empathy.

With Native Americans this pattern was especially significant. The terms of interaction—partly contributed by the Indians, it is true—were consistently paternal, marked by a practice of human diminution. Listen to Thomas McKenney, the highly sympathetic superintendent of Indian Trade in the 1820s: "Our Indians stand pretty much in the relation to the Government as do our children to us. They are equally dependent; and need, not unfrequently, the exercise of parental authority to detach them from those ways which might involve both their peace and their lives."[39] That easy presumption of the government's right to "detach" Indians from their inappropriate "ways," their historical culture, made even humanitarian concern frighteningly similar to the frontiersman's greed in its results, if not its intentions.

It did not have to be this way. The first British explorers and adventurers who encountered Native Americans reacted in a far more complex way. They were curious about the Indians and their culture, whom they appreciated as different, novel, perhaps dangerous, and worth some reflection.[40] But by 1776 curiosity had long since been replaced by firm antagonism toward peoples considered anomalous, obstacles fated to disappear through assimilation or death. The well-known story of the Cherokee removal, the tragic "Trail of Tears" (translating the Indian phrase literally, "the trail on which we cried"), is perhaps the most poignant example of this tragic misapprehension, and it reveals the white investment in not understanding. In the hope of preserving their lives, land, and culture, the Cherokees of Georgia accepted the invitation, most famously offered by Jefferson but supported by every president from Washington to John Quincy Adams, to abandon their hunting life, to become "civilized" by adopting Euro-American ways of living, including private property and the pursuit of agriculture, and to live in peace and harmony with whites. "You will mix with us," Jefferson told them, and "your blood will run in our veins and will spread with us over this great land."[41]

To a remarkable degree and in a very short time, the Cherokees did acculturate to Euro-American norms. They took up farming and lived in nuclear family units instead of clans. While they did not accept the Euro-American idea of landownership, they did recognize private ownership of improvements on the land and rights of use of it. This already involved a major change for them: Cherokees had in fact always cultivated the soil; it was an activity of women. But acculturation required that men give up the hunt and do this women's work while women were confined to domestic duties. To put it differently: the line between domesticity and the rest of everyday life shifted, and certain tasks once done by women were now done by men. Also, they began to pass down property along patrilineal lines, weakening, though not wholly abandoning, their earlier matrilineal traditions.

By the 1820s the Cherokees were governing themselves with a written constitution and in 1825 established a capital at New Echota, not far from today's Atlanta. Taking the white world around them as the model of civilization, the more prosperous of them built Greek Revival houses and purchased African-American slaves. A Cherokee named Sequoia invented a Cherokee alphabet and the language became a literate one; they established a printing press and newspaper. They welcomed missionaries from New England, who arranged for some of the most talented Cherokee boys to be sent north to boarding school.[42]

One of those who went north was Galagina ("Buck"), known to history by the name he took for himself in 1818 when he went north to school, Elias Boudinot, after the then president of the American Bible Society. The Native American Boudinot devoted himself to the cause of informing Americans of the successful acculturation of the Cherokees. In "An Address to Whites," a lecture delivered to missionary groups mostly in New England in 1826, he explained that he was born to a "language unknown to learned and polished nations." But now "I am not as my fathers were—broader means and nobler influences have fallen upon me." He believed and meant to inform the white society that "the time has arrived when speculations and conjectures as to the practicability of civilizing the Indians must forever cease."

> A period is fast approaching when the stale remark—"Do what you will, an Indian will still be an Indian," must be placed no more in speech. With whatever plausibility this popular objection may have heretofore been made, every candid mind must now be sensible that it can no longer be uttered, except by those who are uninformed with respect to us, who are strongly prejudiced against us, or who are filled with vindictive feelings towards us; for the present history of the Indians, particularly of that nation to which I belong, most incontrovertibly establishes the fallacy of this remark.[43]

White leaders knew, as Senator John C. Calhoun did, that the Cherokees had made great "progress" in "civilization" and that they were "all cultivators, with a representative government, judicial courts, Lancaster schools [run on the then progressive Lancaster model], and permanent property."[44] But this circumstance produced a "great difficulty," as Calhoun noted. Did civilization protect the Indian lands from those whites who coveted them?

Whites had failed to understand the specific meaning that the work of becoming "civilized" had for the Cherokees, who did not see it as an end in itself. Whites encouraged Cherokees to adopt "civilized" ways because it meant they would need less land. They did not and probably could not have grasped that the Indians valued their land for reasons other than productive or economic, and went along with the acculturation in order to hold on to it. This Native American strategy and commitment disproved an assumption held by Jefferson's generation: that when the Indians, often thought to be a part of nature, left their "natural environment" they would lose their "Indianness." In fact, the Cherokees, like all humans, were adaptable, but land and culture were sufficiently enmeshed for them that they were willing to use the land differently to maintain this connection.[45]

Education and the world around them—including the increasing talk of democracy and nationalism in the Atlantic world—enabled the Cherokees to understand the settlers' concept of territorial sovereignty. In their constitution of 1827 they mixed this idea with their traditional notions of clan loyalties to claim exclusive jurisdiction over the historical lands they held by treaty.[46] But there was a problem. In 1802, when the Jefferson administration had persuaded Georgia to abandon its claims to western lands (in the present states of Alabama and Mississippi), it promised the state that it would "extinguish" the Indians' lands within its borders. Typically, there had been no consultation with the Cherokees, but the agreement indicated the transfer would be done through treaties and mutual consent. Except for a group of fifteen hundred to two thousand Cherokees who moved in 1817, no agreements were made, and fifteen thousand Cherokees remained in Georgia. President Monroe recognized that "the great object to be accomplished" was the removal of the tribes, but he made clear in a message to Congress in 1825 that it could be done only on terms "satisfactory to themselves [the Cherokees] and honorable to the United States."[47]

By 1828 the situation had become critical. With a cotton boom driving up land values, Georgians were impatient with the federal government's inability to secure the Cherokee territory for them. When the Cherokees promulgated a constitution in 1827 that claimed territorial sovereignty within Georgia's borders, the impatience became rage. Even friends of the Indians thought the claim of sovereignty went too far. "They seek to be a People," Thomas McKenney noted, but it was "much to be regretted that the idea of Sovereignty should have taken such a deep hold on these people."[48]

The election to the presidency in 1828 of Andrew Jackson, the famous Indian fighter, emboldened the Georgia legislature to pass a law nullifying the Cherokee constitution. The situation worsened a year later: gold was discovered on Cherokee land, and ten thousand miners flooded into the region. The Cherokees called it the "Great Intrusion," and intrusion it was. With their government abolished, the Cherokees were defenseless and completely exposed to the avarice of the Georgians and others streaming onto their land.[49] John Eaton, Jackson's secretary of war, urged emigration upon them, but they would have none of it. John Ridge, like Boudinot a Cherokee educated by missionaries, embarked on a lecture tour in 1829 to make the Cherokee case at Washington and elsewhere:

> We have noticed the ancient ground of complaint, founded on the ignorance of our ancestors and their fondness for the chase, and for the purpose of agriculture as having in possession too much land for their numbers. What is the language of objection this time?
>
> The case is reversed, and we are now assaulted with menaces of expulsion, because we have unexpectedly become civilized, and because we have formed and organized a constituted government.

In other words, Ridge pointed out, what we have learned has made us "Politicians," and that has made us more strongly attached to our soil. We therefore "set our faces to the rising sun, and turn our backs to its setting." Recalling that "our ancestors revered the sepulchral monuments of the noble dead, we cherish the sacred spots of their repose."[50]

Taking the side of Georgia, as the Georgians had been sure he would, President Jackson pushed through Congress the Indian Removal Act (1830), which empowered him to "extinguish" by treaty the claims of Indians to any lands in existing states and to "forever secure and guaranty to them" land west of the Mississippi in "exchange."[51] Three days after Jackson signed the law, the state of Georgia laid claim to 4.6 million acres of Cherokee land.[52] The Indian Removal Act did not authorize either coercion or intimidation. But obviously Georgia's related actions greatly encouraged the Indians to accept removal. John Ross, principal chief of the Cherokee Nation, described its vulnerability in an address to the Iroquois in 1831:

> Brothers: The tradition of our Fathers . . . tells us that this great and extensive continent was once the sole and exclusive abode of

our race. Ever since [the whites came] we have been made to drink
the bitter cup of humiliation . . . our country and the graves of our
Fathers torn from us . . . [until] we find ourselves fugitives, va-
grants and strangers in our own country.[53]

The Indians challenged Georgia's suspension of their right to governance in the courts, carrying their case to the Supreme Court. In *Worcester
v. Georgia* (1832), Chief Justice John Marshall, in a decision asserting the
supremacy of national authority over that of a state, described the Cherokees as

a distinct community occupying its own territory, with boundaries
accurately described, in which the laws of Georgia can have no
force, and which the citizens of Georgia have no right to enter but
with the assent of the Cherokees themselves, or in conformity with
treaties, and with the act of Congress. The whole intercourse between the United States and this nation, is, by our Constitution
and laws, vested in the government of the United States.[54]

The Cherokee leader Elias Boudinot welcomed this "Glorious news!" But
President Jackson, who believed that the Indians must "yield" to "another and superior race," immediately deflated such celebration. The
Court, he said, "cannot coerce Georgia to yield to its mandate," because
he would not enforce it.[55] Henry Clay, who was more sympathetic to the
Indians than Jackson, nonetheless shared the Indian fighter's sense of
racial hierarchy. The Indians, he declared, "were destined to extinction,"
for they were "inferior to the Anglo-Saxon race which were now taking
their place on this continent."[56]

While some religious leaders and a few politicians from New England
tried to protect the Indians, it was all too clear that American political
culture had no place for them. Politicians had nothing to gain by protecting the Native Americans, while providing land to frontiersmen not only
brought votes but was thought to ensure social stability through geographical expansion.[57] Henry Schoolcraft, an early Indian ethnologist and
somewhat controversial Indian agent, remarked in 1851 that "the whole
Indian race" did not equal in "worth one white man's vote."[58]

In 1835, when John Ross was in a Georgia jail, a small group of
Cherokee leaders, including Elias Boudinot, signed a treaty committing

the Cherokee Nation to remove themselves from Georgia. By Cherokee law this group had no authority to do such a thing, yet the United States negotiated it with full knowledge that the faction was not empowered to bind the nation. An overwhelming majority of Cherokees rejected the treaty; fifteen thousand of them (90 percent) signed a petition to Congress opposing it:

> The land on which we stand we have received as an inheritance from our fathers, who possessed it from time immemorial, as a gift from our common Father in heaven. They bequested it to us as their children, and we have sacredly kept it, as containing the remains of our beloved men. This right of inheritance we have never ceded nor ever forfeited.[59]

Their way of life was founded on this local ecology: their herbs, the minerals they used for healing and divination, their mythologies, were all associated with the place of their historical lands. They believed, moreover, that this homeland was the center of the earth; for them the western territory was associated with death.[60]

Those who signed the treaty did not disagree with the sentiments of those who wished to stay, but they thought it was impossible to survive the assault mounted against them in Georgia. To their minds the best chance for preserving the Cherokee culture was to move west. But they had a further reason. The Indians who signed were among the most acculturated and prosperous, and, equally important, they were darker-skinned than John Ross and other leaders who fought to stay. Elias Boudinot and John Ridge had experienced the racism of white Americans directly, even in the North among the Indians' supposed friends. At boarding school in Cornwall, Connecticut, they met and subsequently married white women, whose relatives disowned these women, saying they had succumbed to "mere lust." The Cornwall townspeople burned pictures of Boudinot and his wife on the village green. In the end, Boudinot argued for removal on racial grounds. With "all the unrelenting prejudices against our language and color," he argued, the Jeffersonian scheme of "amalgamation with our oppressors is too horrid for a serious contemplation . . . Without [Cherokee] law in the States, we are not more favored than the poor African."[61]

After 1836, the Indians who remained in Georgia risked starvation and lived as outlaws in the hills. But permanent resistance was impossible. General Winfield Scott, who a decade later would command the American conquest of Mexico, brought seven thousand troops to Georgia. He concentrated the Cherokees into camps, and then in 1838 marched sixteen thousand of them "at the point of a bayonet" a thousand miles west to Oklahoma; a quarter of them died on the way.[62] The Cherokee experience was not singular. The administration of Andrew Jackson made seventy removal treaties with Indians. In 1890, when the Battle of Wounded Knee marked the end of the Indian wars in the American West, the journalist Theodore Marburg celebrated this final war in the multi-century conquest of the Indians in a way that anticipated the next phase of American imperialism. "We have brushed aside 275,000 Indians," he wrote. "In place of them [we] have this population of 70,000,000 of what we regard as the highest type of modern man . . . [We] have done more than any other race to conquer the world for civilization . . . and we will probably . . . go on with our conquests."[63]

Even as the United States was accumulating Indian lands, there was a developing aspiration to expand American settlement into northern Mexico, beginning with a movement to annex Texas, then a Mexican state. In 1829, when Andrew Jackson proposed to buy Texas from Mexico, Simón Bolívar, the liberator of Spanish America, observed that the United States seems "destined by Providence to plague America with torments in the name of freedom."[64] Advocates for expansion in the United States saw their providential destiny differently, and they tended to be oblivious to the possibility that the beneficent developments they planned could have victims. Taking the lands of the Southwest was simply part of the larger story of their westward expansion, what the Mexican historian Josefina Zoraida Vázquez refers to as North American "spontaneous expansionism."[65] For Mexicans the war was and remains the "central event of Mexico's history and destiny." Not only is it well remembered, but it is remembered as a trauma.[66] The Mexican Nobel laureate in literature Octavio Paz wrote that the U.S. war against Mexico, which "deprived us of over half our national territory," was "one of the most unjust wars in the history of imperialism."[67] In *Memories of the North American Invasion* (1902), José María Bárcena thought the war resulted from a combination of Mexican "inexperience and vanity" and U.S. "ambition unconstrained by concepts of justice."[68]

Admittedly, the war against Mexico was a divisive issue within the

United States. When he wrote his memoirs in 1885, Ulysses S. Grant, who had been a young officer in it, recalled his bitter opposition to the annexation of Texas and his feeling that the war itself was "one of the most unjust ever waged by a stronger against a weaker nation." It was, he added, "an instance of a republic following the bad example of European monarchies, in not considering justice in their desire to acquire additional territory."[69] But North American expansionists, blinded by visions of Manifest Destiny, did not grasp—as most Americans today do not—the perception of the United States as greedy and dangerous, as an enemy. For Stephen A. Douglas and most Americans at the time, expansion concerned only the United States. "You can make as many treaties as you want to contain . . . this great Republic," he declared, but "it will shrug them off and its people will be directed toward a limit I will not dare describe."[70]

We also forget that in the early years of the nineteenth century there were *two* newly independent nations sharing the territory of the North American continent, with equally promising futures. Mexico's constitution of 1824 was a liberal one, significantly influenced by that of the United States.[71] Mexico was 1.7 million square miles, with 6 million people; the United States extended over 1.8 million square miles, with 9.6 million people—so the magnitudes were comparable. (The consequences of the war between them are revealed in the statistics for 1853: Mexico had lost 1 million square miles to the United States; the population in the booming United States grew to 23 million, bolstered by a massive flow of European immigrants, while Mexico stagnated at 8 million.)

Mexicans at the time understood that to have the United States as a neighbor was a challenge, even a trouble. When it was still a Spanish colony, Spanish officials had been apprehensive. Luis de Onís—who on behalf of Spain negotiated the Adams-Onís, or Transcontinental, Treaty (1819), which settled the border between Spanish land and the Louisiana Territory—worried about U.S. expansionism, which he characterized as "presumptuous and frenetic."[72] After their own independence from Spain had been achieved, Mexican leaders continued to feel vulnerable. José María Tornel, minister of war in 1837, observed that the "pronounced desire" of the "Anglo-American people" to "acquire new lands is a dynamic power which is enhanced and nourished by their own industry."[73] Manuel Eduardo de Gorostiza, a distinguished Mexican man of letters and minis-

ter to the United States during the Jackson administration, had an even
harsher view. Writing in 1840, he asked:

> Who is not familiar with that race of migratory adventurers that
> exist in the United States . . . who always live in the unpopulated
> regions, taking land away from the Indians and then assassinating
> them? Far removed from civilization, as they condescendingly call
> it, they are the precursors of immorality and pillage.

Having himself been condescended to in Washington, he was intensely
aware of the negative, openly racist attitudes of North Americans toward
Mexicans. The Americans, he wrote, believed that like the Native Americans, Mexicans should get out of the way of the Anglo-Saxons. He referred to a New Orleans newspaper article that described Mexicans as
"semi-Indian" and "semi-Negro." Even in New Orleans, Anglo-American
anti-Catholicism was palpable: all Mexicans, one newspaper proposed,
"ought to be killed because they are Catholics." And he cited other newspapers that called Mexicans "savage," "barbaric," and "immoral."[74] Luis
Gonzaga Cuevas, the lawyer and diplomat who negotiated the treaty that
ended the war between the United States and Mexico, concluded that the
United States "will never stop bringing about ruin and disaster of entire
peoples in order to add to themselves a span of territory."[75] A great irony
of the U.S. victory over Mexico in a war waged under the slogan of extending freedom is that its effect in Mexico was to discredit the liberals
who had taken the republican United States as a model, and to empower
conservative landowners who leaned toward monarchy, religion, paternalism, and a program of "law and order."[76]

The trouble between the United States and Mexico had begun with
the first Anglo-American settlements in Texas in the 1820s. Mexicans
had initially welcomed this; they even made a specific exception to allow
Americans to bring slaves with them, though the Mexican Republic outlawed slavery in 1829. But the danger to Mexico's territorial integrity
rapidly revealed itself. In that same year President Jackson tried to purchase the territory and in 1836, over the objections of the Mexican government, sent U.S. troops into Texas in support of its revolution.

At the time Mexico's extreme political instability made it difficult to
resist the aggressive Texans and, later, the United States.[77] Between 1829

and 1844, Mexico had fourteen different presidents, with the presidency changing hands twenty times. Many Mexican leaders blamed Joel Poinsett, the first U.S. minister to Mexico, for much of this political division and disorder. Cuevas was convinced that Poinsett, who had arrived in 1825, "worked to foment disorder" and "should be condemned to the execration of history and posterity."[78] Whatever the precise merits of this view, Poinsett, who knew Mexico well and considered himself a friend of Mexico, acknowledged to Secretary of State Martin Van Buren that he was hated in Mexico. But secure in his belief that his interventions would further the cause of republicanism in both Mexico and the United States, he indicated that he "cheerfully encountered all the obloquy and calumny" directed at him.[79]

Mexicans feared the United States because an expansionist spirit and an attitude of ethnocentric superiority were pervasive among the Anglo-Americans with whom they had personal contact. But the Americans' discussion of Texas was especially unnerving. The widespread debates in Washington and elsewhere over whether the United States should annex Texas were mostly arguments about slavery and its extension; rarely did the Americans acknowledge that they were discussing Mexico's national patrimony, its "northern territories." It was no surprise that Mexicans believed the United States was promoting a revolution in Texas. They rightly feared that Texas was the prelude to a larger drama. In 1836 Mexican and Texan troops clashed in San Antonio and then at the San Jacinto River, where the Mexicans were defeated. But Mexico refused to recognize the battlefield Treaty of San Jacinto, signed in Texas by General Santa Anna, at the time held under duress as a prisoner of war, and deemed it invalid because of the circumstances of its execution. Nor did Mexico relinquish its claims to Texas, its official position being that Texas remained a rebellious province. Nonetheless, the United States quickly recognized the new Republic of Texas.[80]

After this, the Mexican press was consistently anti-American. Mexicans were distressed but not surprised when in 1842 Captain Thomas ap Catesby Jones of the U.S. Navy, thinking war had been declared, mistakenly seized the Mexican fortress at Monterey in California. American designs on Texas and California were transparent enough for a Mexican newspaper to declare that the Anglo-Americans believe "themselves destined to occupy [before Americans used the term] the entire continent."[81]

With all these tensions, the Mexicans closely watched the election of 1844, hoping that Henry Clay, who was hesitant about annexation, might, if elected, negotiate a resolution of the conflicts between the two nations. But the winner was James K. Polk, who in Mexican eyes stood for "the South, slavery, and annexation."[82] Using a contrived pretext and slogan ("American blood has been shed on American soil"), Polk sent a war message to Congress, and war was declared May 13, 1846. Representative Abraham Lincoln, elected to the House of Representatives as an opponent of the war, vigorously challenged the justification for war, though most Americans accepted it. Polk's war with Mexico was one of territorial aggrandizement. When the United States triumphed, it took the New Mexico Territory, which became eight states, and California. This treatment of neighbors to its south established a long-standing pattern of U.S. presumption of empire in relation to Central and South America, whether it was repeated Marine landings, shelling of ports, and police actions in Caribbean and South American republics, or wrenching Panama away from Colombia in order to negotiate a Panama Canal Treaty with a government that it had created.

Another war that is largely forgotten by Americans, including historians, is known to Koreans as the "barbarian incursion of 1871."[83] Yet the American public at the time had an intense interest in what a New York newspaper called "The Little War with the Heathens." This was the first time American forces seized Asian territory and raised the flag there, even if only briefly. And it very clearly reveals how Americans unthinkingly dismissed different cultures, especially of nonwhite peoples, while presuming the universal appeal of their own values and national aspirations.

U.S. diplomatic interest in Korea had developed after the Civil War. In 1866 a heavily armed American merchant vessel arrived in Korean waters seeking a trade agreement. The Korean government had recently driven out French Catholic missionaries, and they sent a message to the Americans indicating they wanted neither Christianity nor trade. When the Americans ignored the message and landed at Pyongyang, a crowd formed. The U.S. sailors fired on them, and the Koreans retaliated by killing those whom they presumed guilty and burning the ship. There was war talk in Washington, but nothing was done. Then, in 1870, Hamilton Fish, Grant's secretary of state, sent instructions to Frederick F. Low, the new U.S. minister to China, asking him to open negotiations with Korea to the end of establishing commercial relations and provision for proper treatment of shipwrecked U.S. sailors. He counseled Low that "little is known . . . of the people who inhabit that country."[84]

Lack of knowledge notwithstanding, Americans had strong opinions about all Asians. Low had previously served as governor of California, which had a substantial Chinese population, and he was confident that he knew what was necessary. "I apprehend that all the cunning and sophistry that enter so largely into the oriental character . . . will be brought to bear to defeat the object of our visit," he informed the secretary of state, "and if that fails it is not unlikely that we may be met with a display of force." He also believed that "orientals" were likely to misunderstand Western restraint; a failure to deploy force would only invite a Korean use of force.[85] However wrongheaded his understanding, it produced the predicted results. A sequence of misunderstandings, largely based on racist and cultural presuppositions of superior moral virtue on both sides, produced needless violence.

Korea maintained formal relations with China, and Low now asked Chinese officials to communicate his intentions, which they reluctantly did. Korea's leaders did not respond to the American request. They believed that China and Japan had been corrupted by having regular relations with the Christian West. By contrast, they professed to uphold the true Confucian morality through a policy of self-sufficiency and isolation. Even to establish a dialogue with the Americans would violate their long-standing policy of seclusion and commitment to nonintercourse with the West. Had they received a reply to this effect, the Americans would likely not have had an empathetic understanding of the Korean views. But without a reply, Low determined to visit the emperor anyway, presumably believing that his purposes were obviously benign. However, a flotilla of warships and supporting vessels might have looked other than benign when anchored at the mouth of the Yomha River, a strategic position that led to the Han River and direct water access to Seoul, where the emperor was in residence.

Without making formal contact with Korean authorities, the Americans began to survey the river and coast. Local officials might easily have interpreted these actions as provocative, but the Korean emperor had ordered them to avoid conflict. The Americans misunderstood this restraint, and, finding no resistance, they pressed on, confident of the purity of their motives and rightness of their mission. They believed, moreover, that international treaties and trade relations were central to civilized life, and that they were offering the option of civilization to a people whose commitment to isolation marked them as uncivilized.

Finally, communication of a limited sort commenced. The Americans were asked in writing about their purposes, and in reply they expressed their interest in discussions with a high court official. Lesser bureaucrats met the fleet to begin discussions, but Low refused to talk to them because of their low rank. The emperor then sent a message indicating that he had read Low's initial message, that he desired friendly relations with the United States, but that he had no interest in meeting Low or in negotiating any treaties. The Americans affirmed their peaceful intentions—and indicated their plan to continue the surveys. When survey parties entered the Han River and proceeded upstream toward Seoul, the Koreans opened fire. The American ships landed a contingent of 651 Marines, who defeated the Korean force on shore and then departed.

Low interpreted the Korean attack as "unprovoked and wanton, and without the slightest shadow of excuse." The Koreans, he wrote to the secretary of state, were no more and no less than a "semi-barbarous and hostile race" who resisted the Americans' reasonable aspirations.[86] But the Koreans had understood the withdrawal as an indication of their victory, an example of their moral virtue overcoming the Westerners' superior technology.

The historian Gordon Chang, the principal scholarly analyst of this episode, rightly observes that the American failure to understand the Koreans' point of view or why they might have perceived the U.S. convoy as a hostile one derived largely from their ethnocentric presumptions about Korean barbarism and American superiority. "The very premise of the mission, which aimed to force Korea to join the 'civilized' nations of the world" and to engage in regular intercourse, defined the Koreans as "backward" and "inferior." The United States, by contrast, assumed that its commitment to trade and open markets "represented advanced civilization and a system of international relations in accord with the natural order."[87] Korean resistance to the American pursuit of wealth through global trade was considered unnatural, not just an erroneous policy. Strikingly, the Americans never second-guessed themselves, nor revealed any curiosity about the Korean desire for self-sufficiency and isolation. After the event, reflecting on the loss of life, Low betrayed his real views about Korean racial inferiority and ignorance: for the Koreans, he observed, "human life is considered of little value, and soldiers, educated as they have been, meet death with the same indifference as the Indians of North America."[88]

THE RHETORIC OF EMPIRE

American imperial action, whether on the North American continent or in more distant places, was justified by a cocktail mixed of various rationales—religious mission, theories of social efficiency, and ideas of racial hierarchy and capacity. Happily, or so many Americans thought, self-interest and humanitarianism apparently converged in empire American-style. Richard Olney, secretary of state in the Cleveland administration, gave a lecture at Harvard College in 1898 arguing for greater U.S. engagement in the world, assuring his audience (and readers of *The Atlantic Monthly*) that "our material interests only point in the same direction as considerations of a higher and less selfish character."[89]

Christian missionaries carried these higher considerations throughout the world, and represented the major American cultural influence beyond the borders of the United States. The first generation of them, in the 1830s and '40s, were Christians first and Americans second, having neither a nationalist nor a modernizing agenda. They were propagating God's word. It would be a "mistake," as the secretary of the American Board of Commissioners for Foreign Missions put it, to "reproduce our own religious civilization in heathen lands."[90] But by mid-century, they were carrying specifically American Christianity with them. American culture in its global extension, whether brought by missionaries or by businessmen, increasingly had a similar content, a message of uplift and modernization. Culture and commerce both promised modernity, much as Hollywood culture did a century later. According to a nineteenth-century consular official in the Middle East reporting on missionary activity there: "They are raising the standard of morality, of intelligence, of education . . . Directly or indirectly every phase of their work is rapidly paving the way for American commerce."[91]

The different European empires had particular theories of legitimate possession that governed the way they took land in the Western Hemisphere. From the beginning of settlement in North America the English had framed their justifications in the language of religion and of God's intentions for the world, presuming that effective use—or social efficiency—justified and legitimated their claims to land, whether taken by direct theft or by treaty. The Portuguese believed that discovery itself, or more precisely the technical capacity to discover, conferred dominion, while the Spanish claimed that speech—a ritualized "declaration" of possession—was sufficient to claim actual possession. But for the English, legitimate possession depended on use, on making the land fruitful. Agriculture, fences, and hedges indicated ownership.[92] Unused land, at least as the English would define use, was available for the taking.[93] John Winthrop thus explained the Puritan taking of land in Massachusetts Bay: "[T]he Natives in New England . . . inclose noe land neither have any settled habitation nor any tame cattle to improve the land by . . . soe as if wee leave them sufficient for their use we may lawfully take the rest."[94]

A grander formulation of this logic begins with a presumed right of the world itself to growth, expansion, and the development of resources. This philosophy had religious overtones in the seventeenth century, as the resources were considered God-given. Some centuries later, the justification was a secular social efficiency or economic development. Walter Weyl, a leading American progressive, declared in 1917 that "the resources of the earth must be unlocked."[95] Speaking of the colonization of the Philippines, Alfred Thayer Mahan argued that the right of "an indigenous population" to retain their land "depends not upon natural right" but rather upon their "political fitness," which would be demonstrated in the "political work of governing, administering, and developing [it], in such a manner as to ensure the natural right of the world at large that resources should not be left idle."[96] Local ownership, in other words, was subject to the most productive use.[97]

In the nineteenth century, the taking of land beyond the Mississippi River was thought to be justified by Providence. John L. O'Sullivan, editor of the *Democratic Review* and a leader among the New York intellectuals who called themselves "Young America," declared in 1845 "the right of *our manifest destiny* to overspread and to possess the whole continent which providence has given us for the development of the great experiment of liberty and federated self-government."[98] O'Sullivan here fused liberty, democracy, and the United States. Lincoln made the same connection in his Gettysburg Address. But the implications of these two formulations differed: for Lincoln, the aim and result was an expansion of freedom, while O'Sullivan wanted to justify territorial aggrandizement and empire.

When Jefferson and other founders had spoken of an "empire of liberty," they meant a large and populous nation, not imperial rule, and they did not envision a nation of continental proportions, believing that more than one republic would thrive in North America. William Thornton, first superintendent of the Patent Office (1802–28) and architect of the U.S. Capitol, in 1815 published his "Outlines of a Constitution for United North and South Columbia," which envisioned thirteen confederated states stretching the entire length of the Western Hemisphere, with a capital, to be called America, located on the Isthmus of Panama. Freedom would reign throughout, with mestizos respected and blacks emancipated.[99] In the same year, Simón Bolívar's "Jamaica Letter" hoped a pacific union of nations in the "New World," perhaps led by Mexico, would protect self-rule and freedom.[100]

In only a little more than a decade these mutualist visions of an America of republican freedom beyond the United States gave way to a North American appropriation of "America" to refer to itself and its dreams of hemispheric hegemony. In a private letter of 1843 intended for public disclosure, former President Jackson linked the diffusion of republican government to the open-ended process of incorporating new territories into the United States, slightly but significantly emending Jefferson's phrase to "extending the area of freedom."[101]

Over the next century the religious, social-efficiency, and political arguments associated with the dispossession of the Native Americans were subsumed under the rubric of race. Indeed, throughout the Atlantic world race emerged as a fundamental social category. Partly this was because the romantic movement accented differences among peoples, but it was also the product of so-called racial science, whether identified with the American school of anthropology or the French race theorist Joseph Arthur de Gobineau and his *Essai sur l'inégalité des races humaines* (1853–55).[102] Perceived differences needed explaining, and race was a clarifying option, establishing a literally visible hierarchy. The politics of this race theory carried the implied threat that lower orders of humanity had either to adapt or to become extinct—or both, as the Cherokees had discovered.

"The white race will take the ascendant, elevating what is susceptible of improvement—wearing out what is not," declared Thomas Hart Benton, senator from Missouri, in 1846.[103] Over the next generation, white racial pride became steadily less generous in its expectations of "improvement" of dark-skinned people. In his widely read book *Our Country* (1885), Josiah Strong, a leading Protestant intellectual, observed that "whether the extinction of inferior races before the advancing Anglo-Saxon" seems to be a matter for regret or not, "it certainly appears probable." He proudly noted that Anglo-Saxons represented only "one-fifteenth part of mankind" but ruled "more than one-third of the earth's surface, and more than one-third of its people."[104]

At the top of the nineteenth-century racial hierarchy were the Germanic peoples (meaning whites, or Teutons). In England and the United States special pride was taken in the idea that the Anglo-Saxon line of the Teuton race was, supposedly, the repository of those capacities necessary for self-government. For the historian Francis Parkman, the "Germanic race, and especially the Anglo-Saxon branch of it, . . . is peculiarly fitted for self-government." Senator Benton made the same point: the Anglo-Saxons carried the "Magna Carta and all its privileges" in their "luggage."[105] Ironically, this Anglo-Saxon race pride had been a weapon used against royal absolutism in the seventeenth century,[106] a history that no doubt helped legitimate the ugly work it later performed.

By the late nineteenth century, Manifest Destiny was as much a racial concept as a political one, about the rights (and responsibilities, too, it was believed) of "civilized" nations to rule lesser, uncivilized peoples. For those who accepted it, race offered a comprehensive, if crude, interpretation of global history. At one level, therefore, the spokesmen for Anglo-Saxonism would wholly agree with W.E.B. DuBois that "the Negro problem in America is but a local phase of a world problem," and, as he said, "the problem of the twentieth century is the problem of the color-line—the relation of the darker to the lighter races of men in Asia and Africa, in America and the islands of the sea."[107] But the perspectives and politics differed on either side of the color line. For DuBois the issue was freedom, justice, and dignity for all peoples; those shouldering the "white man's burden" thought they had the task of educating people of color for their (limited) participation in civilized society and of managing them as a labor force for the profits of empire. The principal American scholarly journal addressing global affairs in the first years of the twentieth century was *The Journal of Race Development*, which in 1919 became *The Journal of International Relations* and then, three years later, *Foreign Affairs*, the prestigious journal of the Council on Foreign Relations.[108] The Anglo-Saxons, being a people of the temperate zone, considered themselves called upon to govern and develop the tropics. Franklin Giddings of Columbia University, the first American scholar to hold a university chair in sociology, argued that the "task of governing . . . the inferior races of mankind will be one of great difficulty . . . but it is one that must be faced and overcome." The "civilized world" requires it, he wrote, so that it can continue the "conquest of the natural resources of the globe."[109]

In 1898, when Americans debated the annexation of the Philippines, masculine Anglo-Saxonism was as prominent and probably as influential as the strategic and economic arguments favoring an empire.[110] According to William Allen White, the famous Kansas editor and Progressive, "Only the Anglo-Saxons can govern themselves." It is their "manifest destiny," he continued, "to go forth as world conqueror." Senator Albert Beveridge of Indiana, a leading imperialist, agreed, for Anglo-Saxons and Teutons were made by God to be "the master organizers of the world."[111] As for the Filipinos, he declared, "they are not a self-governing race. They are Orientals, Malays, instructed by Spaniards in the latter's worst estate."[112]

Many imperialists may have come across as bullies, but there was a good deal of anxiety about the challenge of empire in the 1890s. Intellectuals had absorbed the language of Herbert Spencer's "struggle for survival" and Darwin's notion of "natural selection" and transferred them to races and nations. Thus Josiah Strong spoke of "the final competition of the races, for which the Anglo-Saxon is being schooled."[113] Besides a certain energy, aggressiveness, and persistence, the Anglo-Saxon racial capacities supposedly being developed through this evolutionary struggle included a "money-making power—a power of increasing importance in the widening commerce of the world's future"—a "genius for colonizing," and an unmatched excellence "in pushing his way into new countries." But the Anglo-Saxons' virtues went beyond money and power.

Besides being the custodians of liberty and enterprise, they possessed great spiritual resources. The English-speaking peoples of the North Atlantic were, as they saw it, "divinely commissioned" to be their "brother's keeper."[114]

The political theorist John W. Burgess agreed, although his language of justification was racial and political rather than religious. He shared his generation's belief that the Teutonic races had a special capacity for government. In his studies of Reconstruction politics and of international law, Burgess argued against allowing non-Teutons to participate in government, whether at home or abroad. It would result only in "corruption and confusion."[115] The civilized peoples, those organized into nation-states, the political form par excellence, were called upon to govern other peoples, the majority in the world, who "remain in a state of barbarism." The condition of allegedly uncivilized peoples "authorizes" the political nations, as he called them, to "force organization upon them by any means necessary." Such rule, he argued, "violates . . . no rights of these populations which are not petty and trifling in comparison" with the imperial power's "transcendent right and duty to establish political and legal order everywhere."[116] This powerful argument in favor of imperialism on the eve of America's war with Spain, Cuba, and the Philippines contributed to the climate of opinion that accepted the end of Reconstruction, the disenfranchisement and lynching of black Americans, and the Supreme Court decision in *Plessy v. Ferguson* (1896) that gave constitutional approval to Jim Crow America. Racism at home and abroad mutually reinforced each other.

The openly racist rhetoric of empire was eventually supplanted by a vocabulary of "order," "development," "responsible government," "economic efficiency," and "freedom and democracy." It is not clear, however, that the North Atlantic states have wholly abandoned the assumptions that diminished the dignity and even the humanity of those in what is now called the "global South."

A GLOBAL STRATEGY

Historians and journalists often remark on the historical moment when the United States stepped onto the world stage with a new global awareness. Surely there was such a moment, but in my opinion it came earlier than the ones commonly cited—1898, World War I, 1941, 1945, or the beginning of globalization talk in the 1980s. From at least the presidency of Thomas Jefferson, American leaders have been aware of their nation's global position and have sought consistently to expand its commercial and cultural influence. The major cultural influence emanating internationally from the United States was once religion, but in the twentieth century the volume of cultural exports became vastly larger and more diverse. The projection of American culture, whatever its form, is not recent.[117]

Since Jefferson, perhaps even since George Washington, the United States has had a sequence of presidents and secretaries of state who have self-consciously fashioned a global strategy for the nation. "Globalization has been at the heart of American strategic thinking and policy" for the whole of the national history of the United States, the journalist Walter Russell Mead has written.[118] By paying too much attention to President Washington's warning against entangling alliances with the warring European powers of his time, we may have overlooked his encouragement of global trade. We have also underestimated the comprehensive strategies and policies devoted to that end for the next century; the United States was not wholly preoccupied with developing the West and not wholly inward-looking. Charles Francis Adams, writing in 1899 as an anti-imperialist, rightly read Washington's oft-repeated advice as favoring international commerce but with "as little political connection as possible."[119] And American interest in commerce was not limited to residents of its seaport cities. The expansion of the agricultural frontier—and the remarkable productivity it brought—were as important a motive as the development of manufacturing for Americans to want global markets.[120] An Illinois congressman insisted in 1846 that his state "wants a market for her agricultural productions, she wants the market of the world." By the 1850s farm journals were referring to the United States as the "granary of the world."[121] And of course, when the United States acquired vast new continental territories from Mexico by war and entered the China market by treaty, it was acting on behalf of expansive interests and also trying to limit Britain's global influence.[122]

The United States was not reluctant to use its power to negotiate favorable commercial treaties or to use force to protect its commercial interests abroad. Between 1787 and 1920, it intervened abroad 122 times (excluding declared wars); 99 of these interventions occurred in the nineteenth century and involved every continent.[123] Historians and analysts consider that the American state was weak at the time and lacked a military establishment in the nineteenth century, excepting the Civil War era, yet the state effectively supported aggressive territorial expansion and protected American commerce abroad.[124]

As we have already seen, the politics and economy of the early American republic were dominated by the struggle to find markets for agricultural produce and to secure sea-lanes for its merchant marine. This emphasis on international commerce rather than politics was reflected in a preference for establishing "consular" rather than "diplomatic" representation abroad. In 1792, the United States had only two diplomatic missions (in London and Paris) but had established thirty-six consulates.[125] The Louisiana Purchase was a by-product of Jefferson's response to pressure from Ohio Valley farmers wanting free passage to the sea on the Mississippi River and access, by ownership or treaty, to the port of New Orleans. Jefferson not only was sympathetic to their commercial aspirations but characteristically raised their material demands to the level of philosophy. As a matter of natural right, he argued, "the Ocean is free to all men, and the Rivers to all their inhabitants"; that natural right implied a further "right to some spot as an entrepot for our commerce."[126] As Washington's secretary of state, he had declared that since "the ocean" was the "common property of all," it should be "open to the industry of all."[127] National governments should not get in the way of this right, which belonged to private individuals, being a human right. If access to American trade was blocked anywhere on the globe, the United States, Jefferson argued, must be prepared to deploy its resources, including armed force, to protect commerce. Jefferson's—and America's—universalism could be strikingly parochial.

This way of thinking and the policies that followed from it continued to define American foreign relations well into the twentieth century: the global search for markets, initially for agricultural products and later for manufactured goods, too; unrestrained oceanic trade and equal (or "most favored nation") trading rights; support of private entrepreneurs in the global marketplace; a ready deployment of force when need be in support of American business but rarely in advance of it. The United States was thus reenacting abroad the policies at the heart of its westward expansion.[128] The most significant change came when, at the end of the nineteenth century, U.S. investment abroad increased and the United States moved from being a capital importer to being a capital exporter, from being a debtor nation to a creditor.[129]

Each of the two greatest nineteenth-century secretaries of state, John Quincy Adams and William H. Seward, elaborated comprehensive strategies for an American empire that was both continental and global. And the leading imperialists of 1898 built upon their ambitions, ideas, and achievements.[130]

John Quincy Adams came to the offices of secretary of state and president with exceptional preparation in foreign affairs. Before he was twenty, he had studied in France and Holland and served as a secretary to American representatives at the courts of Russia and Great Britain (the latter being his father, John Adams); in his twenties, he was ambassador to the Netherlands and then to Prussia, and he was chairman of the peace commission that negotiated the Treaty of Ghent, ending the War of 1812. He was appointed secretary of state by James Monroe, and he shares credit, perhaps even principal credit, for the doctrine that bears Monroe's name.

The Monroe Doctrine declared that the lands of the Western Hemisphere that Spain was in the process of losing were off-limits to further European colonization. British Foreign Secretary George Canning, worried that European powers might take advantage of Spain's collapse and acquire territory among the former colonies, closing them to British trade, proposed a joint Anglo-American agreement to preserve the independence of the new republics and ensure free trade in the hemisphere. Jefferson and Madison counseled Monroe to agree to this proposal, but Adams had a grander idea. The United States, he argued, could assert itself in world affairs by acting alone to warn European powers away; Britain's interest in commercial access would lead them inevitably to support such a declaration. And in return, the Americans would agree not to meddle in European affairs such as the Greek war for independence against the Ottoman Empire. Adams had envisioned a circular letter to the relevant powers, but President Monroe incorporated the declaration into his annual message to Congress in 1823.[131] Little noticed in European capitals at the time, it became and remains a keystone of American hemispheric policy, and it grew with use, especially as expanded by Theodore Roosevelt's "corollary" to it, which asserted a U.S. right to intervene to bring order to badly managed states in the Western Hemisphere. The doctrine has since been invoked repeatedly to justify American expansion and intervention—to protect against supposed threats of outside colonization or dominion, including that of communism during the Cold War.[132]

Adams also took great pride in his negotiation of the Adams-Onís, or Transcontinental, Treaty (1819). "The achievement of a definite boundary line to the South Sea [Pacific Ocean] forms a great epoch in our history," he wrote in his diary. The world should become familiar with "the idea of considering our proper dominion to be the continent of North America" as a "law of nature," he believed, but he did not support the use of military means to secure this goal.[133] He had faith in treaties and the natural course of events, and, fearful of the expansion of slavery, he openly opposed the annexation of Texas, the Mexican War, and various schemes to acquire Cuba.[134]

In the 1840s, as a congressman from Massachusetts, he shifted his interest to global trade, especially in Asia. Extending his belief in the general freedom of commerce, he was disturbed by China's preference for limited contact with the West and considered trade in China to be of "pre-eminent interest to the People of the North American Union." When China enforced its prohibition against the importation of opium by destroying a large shipment of it owned by British merchants in Guangzhou, and the British retaliated with force, Adams lent his support to the British position with an argument against China's "anti-commercial" stance that was predictably learned but also tendentious. He insisted that "the right of exchange, barter, or, in other words, of commerce, necessarily follows" from the right of property, which was protected by natural law. He went even further: commerce was not only a natural right but one of the "duties of men." And not only men but nations had this duty: "Commercial intercourse between nations is a moral obligation."[135]

This resort to a natural-law argument was prompted, no doubt, by the lack of support for his position in leading theories of international law. The authoritative work on the subject, *The Law of Nations* (1758), by the Swiss jurist Emerich de Vattel, claimed a universal right to buy, but also an "equal right to refuse to sell." Such a position, Adams declared, revealed a "manifest inconsistency."[136] Whether Adams himself was consistent or not, his predisposition became commonplace over the next generation; it had become second nature for Frederick Low in 1871. In the 1840s, however, Adams's argument—or the way he made it—was apparently a hard sell. *The North American Review*, for example, declined to publish it.[137]

But in 1844, after China had ended the Opium War on British terms, the United States negotiated similar terms for itself in its first bilateral trade agreement with China. Over the next generation the principles and the policy orientation for which Adams argued were completely accepted in the United States. And the policies he had adopted as Monroe's secretary of state and then in his own presidency anticipated the nation's later global trade policy—with Navy support for U.S. shipping, trade agreements based on reciprocity, and collaboration with Britain in support of free trade.[138]

William H. Seward, Lincoln's secretary of state, considered Adams his patron, guide, and counselor, and he built on Adams's base.[139] Textbooks often refer to the purchase of Alaska in 1867 as "Seward's folly," but in fact it was a key element in a strategy to establish American presence in the Pacific. If the United States, even before the Civil War but especially after the construction of the Panama Canal, wanted the Caribbean to be an "American lake," Seward grasped the possibility of making the same of the North Pacific.[140]

American dreams of a Pacific or Asian empire were already old in the nineteenth century. The colonization of America had been a product of that ambition, and early on American merchants were familiar with the great arc of the "Pacific Rim"—and with the oceanic islands in the middle, particularly Hawaii, where a substantial American community of missionaries, adventurers, sailors, and planters was well established. The Reverend Samuel Chenery Damon, whose library Melville used, published a newspaper in Honolulu to establish and sustain the American world of the South Pacific.[141] When Melville was writing his novels, American whalers were blanketing the oceans, especially the South Pacific, numbering 722 of the world's 900 whaling vessels.[142]

One of President Polk's major foreign-policy objectives was to obtain a West Coast port, and with the acquisition of Oregon in 1846 and California in 1848, the United States had its place on the Pacific Rim. A decade later President Franklin Pierce commissioned Perry McDonough Collins to explore trade possibilities in Asia. In his report Collins reminded the president that the "problem of the Northwest Passage [which had] occupied the great minds of Europe for centuries" had been "solved by the continuous and onward march of American civilization to the West."[143]

Perhaps it was paradoxical: the great bulk of American trade was with Europe, but talk of the future was all about Asia. Thomas Hart Benton was particularly entranced by the possibilities of escaping from the Atlantic world, where the "European legitimates," as he called them, held "everything American in contempt." The United States would carry "science, liberal principles of government, and the true religion" to China and Japan, while American farms could become Asia's "granary."[144] Like many others, Benton imagined a new, oceanic "silk road,"[145] and he reminded Americans in 1849 that those who have possessed the riches of Asia have "reached the highest pinnacle of wealth and power, and with it the highest attainments of letters, arts, and sciences."[146]

Seward shared these views. In the Senate in 1852, he argued that Europe would "sink" in importance while Asia would rise. The United States would face not the great powers of western Europe but the Slavic empire of Russia in the Pacific. Here was the "new Mediterranean," and its "shores, its islands, and the vast region beyond, will become the chief theatre of events."[147] He had in mind "an empire of the seas," which, he believed, "alone is the real empire."[148] "Commerce," he told his Senate colleagues, is "the empire of the world."[149]

The nation must be liberal and unified to take advantage of its global potential, Seward knew, so it is no surprise that he had a leading position in the Republican Party and the Lincoln administration. Transcontinental transportation was also vital, and the continental railroad and telegraph were major Republican objectives. In addition, Seward as secretary of state secured a transit treaty with Nicaragua so as to connect the Pacific and the Caribbean, and he tried to acquire the Isthmus of Panama (unsuccessfully) and the Danish West Indies (successfully negotiated with Denmark but not ratified by the Senate). He also aimed to make the Pacific accessible from both New York and San Francisco. Just as regular communication was crucial to the Atlantic economy, Seward established regular mail service from San Francisco to Honolulu and Hong Kong. And he worked to establish an international agreement on uniform coinage, based on the dollar if possible.[150]

Seward believed in continentalism, but not colonialism. He imagined in various statements in the 1860s that Canada would someday voluntarily join the United States, and perhaps Mexico would as well. But if so, it would be by "peaceful negotiation."[151] Colonization, he feared, would militarize the United States.[152] (He had opposed the Mexican War.) His ambitious global vision was animated by commerce, "the chief agent of advancement in civilization and enlargement of empire." And his purpose in acquiring Midway Island and Alaska, whose arc of Aleutian Islands reaches nearly to the coasts of Japan and Korea, was to lay the foundation for a network of Pacific coaling stations that would support American commerce with Asia, extending "through the Manilas, and along the Indian coast, and beyond the Persian gulf, to the far-off Mozambique."[153] The war in 1898 aimed to solidify the U.S. commercial presence in the Pacific that he had envisioned and summed up in 1853 in one tight paragraph:

> Open up a highway . . . from New York to San Francisco. Put your domain under cultivation, and your ten thousand wheels of manufacture in motion. Multiply your ships, and send them forth to the East. The nation that draws most materials and provisions from the earth, and fabricates the most, and sells the most of productions and fabrics to foreign nations, must be, and will be, the great power on earth.[154]

One could say that Seward anticipated the famous theories of Alfred Thayer Mahan in recognizing ocean commerce as empire, along with the importance of coaling stations and naval support for that commerce. But while Seward's liberal commercial vision presumed a somewhat conflict-free ocean, Mahan was a realist concerned with power. If in his great book *The Influence of Sea Power upon History* he referred to the ocean as an open "common," Mahan the naval strategist imagined the sea as a domain of power. In a widely read essay titled "Hawaii and Our Future Sea Power," published in 1893, he explained that sea power demands control of "the world's great medium of circulation." For a nation to secure that dominance, "it is imperative to take possession, when it can be done righteously, of such maritime positions as contribute to secure command."[155] When in 1898 the United States secured Puerto Rico, considerable control over Cuba, the Philippines, Hawaii, Guam, and Wake Island, it represented the realization of Mahan's global strategy.

1898

The events of 1898 are often considered an aberration, a departure from American tradition, prompted by a desire to participate in the end-of-the-century European race for empire. Mahan said that American colonization of the Philippines was "but one phase of a sentiment that has swept over the whole civilized European world."[156] It has been estimated that across the globe in 1901 there were 140 colonies, territories, and protectorates, most of them in the tropics.[157] Surely this context is important, but it ought not obscure a key local point: the events of 1898 were also a continuation of America's "westward expansion."

Theodore Roosevelt so understood the matter, as did his fellow imperialist Henry Cabot Lodge. In a new preface for the 1900 edition of his *Winning of the West*, Roosevelt wrote that 1898 "finished the work begun over a century before by the backwoodsman," that "the question of expansion in 1898 was but a variant . . . of the great western movement."[158] Senator Lodge agreed that "to-day we do but continue the same movement." If the anti-imperialists are right, he added, "then our whole past record of expansion is a crime."[159] Buffalo Bill's popular Wild West Show marked both the continuity of western history and its new geography, when in 1899 it replaced its re-creation of Custer's Last Stand with one of the Battle of San Juan Hill in Cuba.[160]

The reason 1898 seems so different from the Indian removal in 1838 or from the taking of Mexico in 1848 is that the earlier work of empire had been "domesticated" as an internal affair—an idea that depended, of course, on ignoring the claims of Indians and Mexicans.[161] Indeed, as we have seen, in 1871 Congress formally transformed relations with Native Americans from a foreign to a domestic issue. At the same time there was continuous American involvement in East Asia: the Charles Wilkes expedition in 1839, the Wanghai Treaty with China in 1844, the so-called opening of Japan in 1854, and a treaty with Hawaii in 1875 that forbade Hawaiians from disposing of any territory to foreign powers. Americans thought of the Pacific and East Asia as extensions of the West, as well as the focal point for their oceanic commercial ambitions.

In fact, the imperial adventures of 1898 were prompted in large part by worry over the closing of the continental frontier, as well as by fears about the overproduction of agricultural and manufactured goods. In that year, the United States for the first time exported more manufactured goods than it imported; with no more than 5 percent of the world's population, it produced 32 percent of the world food supply.[162] Albert Beveridge surely had these developments in mind when he took the Senate floor in 1899 to explain that "American factories are making more than the American people can use; American soil is producing more than they can consume." Under the circumstances, he continued, "fate has written our policy for us; the trade of the world must and shall be ours."[163]

Americans had always looked to expansion as a remedy for social conflict. Free land and opportunity would spare the nation the class conflict that marked Europe. When Frederick Jackson Turner spoke of the closing of the frontier, such a development was clearly on his mind, as it was on the minds of many others. Growing labor strife and turmoil toward the end of the nineteenth century, including the Haymarket Riot of 1886 and the Homestead and Pullman strikes of the 1890s, prompted many to look to American expansion beyond the continent and into the Pacific as a contemporary version of this long-standing mythic solution. Indeed, three years after his famous address of 1893 on "the significance of the frontier," Turner noted—in *The Atlantic Monthly*—that for "three centuries the dominant fact in American life has been expansion"; current "demands for a vigorous foreign policy" seeking to extend American influence to "outlying islands and adjoining countries" suggest that this "movement will continue."[164]

In the nineteenth century United States trade was with Europe, but, as the widely read British sociologist Benjamin Kidd pointed out, in 1898 the North Atlantic economies were converging, becoming more similar in their manufacturing capacities. New markets would thus be necessary. Kidd pointed to the tropical regions, which had not only resources that needed to be unlocked but markets as well. Josiah Strong predicted that in the twentieth century the east-west trade pattern of the nineteenth century would shift to a north-south one, for "commerce, like water, flows only when there is inequality."[165] Kidd advised his American readers that the "relation of the white man to the tropics" must be properly organized, for "these regions must be administered from temperate regions." The low "social efficiency" of the "natural inhabitants" of the tropics could not be permitted to weaken the whole world economy.[166] Making much the same point, but by means of poetry rather than social science, Rudyard Kipling—in a poem specially written to influence President William McKinley and published in *McClure's Magazine*—urged the Americans to take up "the White Man's burden."

McKinley had to make a decision. Given the foregoing, perhaps his decision was predetermined. But still, he had not anticipated such a development, and he went to some lengths to persuade the public that he had deliberated long and seriously. He told the following story, which has been oft quoted, to a group of visiting leaders of the Methodist Church:

> When I realized that the Philippines had dropped into our laps I confess I did not know what to do with them . . . I walked the floor of the White House night after night until midnight; and I am not ashamed to tell you, gentlemen, that I went down on my knees and prayed to Almighty God for light and guidance . . . And one night late it came to me this way—I know not how but it came: (1) that we could not give them back to Spain—that would be cowardly and dishonorable; (2) that we could not turn them over to France or Germany—our commercial rivals in the Orient—that would be bad business and discreditable; (3) that we could not leave them to themselves—they were unfit for self-government . . . ; and (4) that there was nothing left for us to do but to take them . . . and to educate the Filipinos, and uplift and civilize and Christianize them . . . And then I went to bed, and went to sleep, and slept soundly.[167]

Why it would have been "dishonorable" to "give them back to Spain" is unclear, the more so since the United States itself did not in fact possess the Philippines. Nor did it have any right to them, save a claim of military conquest over Spain, but not—and this is important—over the Filipinos, who were still fighting for their independence. As for Christianizing them, the Protestant McKinley speaking to the Methodists seems to have overlooked that the official religion of the Philippines was Roman Catholicism, or he did not consider several centuries of that faith sufficient evidence of Christianity. As for their unfitness for self-rule, the Filipinos, who had been fighting Spain for their independence since well before 1898, had a provisional government and a constitution in place.[168] That leaves avoiding "bad business"—or affirming good business—as the strongest reason for establishing American imperial rule.[169]

The opposition to taking possession of the Philippines was generally based on two considerations, or two sides of the same consideration, one racial and the other constitutional. As 1848 showed, Americans opposed incorporation of and citizenship for peoples they supposed to be racially inferior—Mexicans, Cubans, Puerto Ricans, Filipinos. And this consensus led to the second problem. The United States, it was said, had never taken a territory without the intention of eventually making it a state equal to existing states. To abandon this practice in 1898, it was argued by the anti-imperialists, would compromise republican principles.

There were, in fact, all too many precedents for the United States to become a colonial power. They were bad ones, but the imperialists treated them as good ones. The political scientist and future president of Harvard University A. Lawrence Lowell saw no problem: "The question is not whether we shall enter upon a career of colonization or not, but whether we shall shift into other channels the colonization which has lasted as long as our national existence."[170] As for the question of equal citizenship or political empowerment, he pointed out that the equal-rights tradition did not apply to "tribal Indians, to Chinese, or to negroes."[171] The closest "domestic" analogy was the government's treatment of Native Americans, which provided a model for establishing the legal standing of colonial subjects. They were legally "nationals" owing allegiance to the United States, but not citizens.[172] Harry Pratt Judson, future president of the University of Chicago, argued that Filipinos would hold the "same status precisely as our own Indians . . . They are in fact, 'Indians.' "[173] The Harvard historian Albert Bushnell Hart (who had served as W.E.B. DuBois's dissertation adviser) agreed with these views. The United States was already a "great colonial power," he observed, for "our Indian agents have a situation very like that of British officials in the native states of India."[174]

Thus the constitutional standing of American Indians became a precedent for the rights of peoples in newly annexed territories. In the so-called Insular Cases (1901), the Supreme Court established the legal status of these new territories and their inhabitants. The most important case, *Downes v. Bidwell* (1901), addressed the issue of whether Puerto Ricans were entitled to the "full panoply of constitutional rights." They were not. Overseas possessions, the Supreme Court decided, were "subject to the jurisdiction of the United States," but they were "not of the United States." That meant, according to a narrow majority, that the island and its people were "foreign to the United States in a domestic sense."[175] The exceedingly awkward phrasing is strikingly close to John Marshall's description of the situation of the Cherokees. Indians, he had written, were "domestic dependent nations" in a "state of pupilage."[176] Since racism and paternalism were so prominent in the discussion of the constitutionality of colonial rule, it seems pertinent that the author of the controlling opinions in both *Downes v. Bidwell* and *Plessy v. Ferguson* was the same, Justice Henry B. Brown, and that Justice John Marshall Harlan dissented in both cases. Harlan's second dissent echoed his earlier one:

> Whether a particular race will or will not assimilate with our people, and whether they can or cannot with safety to our institutions be brought within the operation of the constitution, is a matter to be thought of when it is proposed to acquire territory . . . A mistake in the acquisition of territory cannot be made the ground for violating the constitution.[177]

REVOLUTION AND EMPIRE

The Spanish-American War is a misnomer. The misnaming is significant because it masks a central issue and legacy of the war. It was more properly two wars: the Spanish-Cuban-American War and the Spanish-Filipino-American War, each of which was itself two wars. The usual name of the war suggests that the United States went to war with Spain, failing to acknowledge that after two quick victories over Spain, American forces snuffed out long-standing revolutionary wars for national independence in two very different places. In the case of the Philippines, the

United States annexed the islands, and then engaged in several years of brutal warfare against Filipino armies committed to achieving independence. Cuba was not annexed, but the Platt Amendment, which Cuba was forced to accept, recognized a U.S. right to intervene in its affairs to protect "life, property, and individual liberty."

Although both the Filipino and the Cuban armies had long been fighting the Spanish and collaborated with the Americans in the final phase of their war against Spain, neither took part in the surrender ceremonies. In fact, they were both denied access to the cities where the surrenders took place, Santiago de Cuba and Manila. Nor was either consulted on the protocols that established the terms of peace, or a party to the Treaty of Paris (1898) that ended the war. As the American government saw it, it was liberating the Cubans and Filipinos. Certainly the pro-empire faction believed this, but Americans were divided, even in the governing elite, many of whose members, of the same class and status as Roosevelt and Lodge, opposed empire. While the press fanned the flames of imperial nationalism to build popular support for the war, many Americans had particular reasons to favor it. American Jews, thinking of Spain's expulsion of the Jews in 1492, were happy to see it lose an empire that dated from that year. Nationalist feelings in immigrant groups, especially Irishmen and Poles, whose homelands suffered under the rule of empires, made them sympathetic to Cuban independence. Michael Kruszka explained that Poles naturally sympathized with peoples struggling for independence, even if "they be half-savage Malays." In fact, many immigrants were nervous about all the talk coming from American authorities about "civilization" and political rights; they had suffered from such talk both at home and in the United States.[178] Yet W.E.B. DuBois wondered whether imperialism might improve American race relations by increasing the ratio of nonwhites to whites in the population.[179]

But hardly anyone—not imperialists, not anti-imperialists—could get beyond parochial American interests and imagine themselves outside the United States, imagine how the American empire appeared in the eyes of Cubans or Filipinos. Had they been able to do so, they would have had to recognize the different meaning of the war and peace.

The Cuban struggle for independence from Spain began in the mid-nineteenth century, later than in Spain's other possessions in the Americas. And it led to war three different times: the Ten Years' War (1868–78), the Little War (1879–80), and the War of Independence (1895–98). A striking feature of all three is that they were fought by multiracial Cuban armies, officers and soldiers, a novelty in the history of the Americas. The United States was using race as a fundamental, hierarchical category of human difference, but José Martí, the Cuban writer and independence leader exiled in New York, challenged the category. "This is not the century of the struggle of races," he wrote in 1882, "but rather the century of the affirmation of rights."[180] The Cuban revolutionaries were ready, perhaps even eager, to work for a society without a color line. American intervention hijacked their independence movement and subverted their powerful antiracist rhetoric and practice.[181]

By early 1898, the Cubans were clearly on their way to victory over the Spanish, who they believed were demoralized and had "lost the will to fight." The American minister to Spain shared that view; he had reported in late 1897 that Spanish sovereignty in Cuba was "extinct."[182] Americans as far back as John Quincy Adams and Henry Clay had expected that a weakened Spain would lose this island colony, but they were uneasy with the idea of an independent Cuba and deeply opposed the idea of Cuba being attached to another, stronger European power. Americans, especially southern planters before the Civil War, presumed that in due course Cuba would become an American possession, though there was, as with Mexico, the problem of the island's mixed-race or "mongrel" population.

Such was the matrix of concerns when, on professed humanitarian grounds of liberating the oppressed Cubans from the yoke of Spanish tyranny, the United States went to war against Spain in Cuba, alleging that Spain had engineered the explosion of the American battleship *Maine* in Havana harbor on February 15, 1896 (now thought to have been the result of a badly engineered boiler near a powder magazine). The leaders of the Cuban insurrection had explicitly informed President McKinley that they would interpret American intervention as a war against the revolution, but this concern was somewhat allayed by the Teller Amendment to the war resolution, which disclaimed any American intention to acquire sovereignty over Cuba and promised self-rule at the end of hostilities. But the United States found it difficult to let go after victory and soon was opposing the liberation movement there. Its influence on Cuba was substantial, for the thrust of its intervention was to give support and legitimation to the most conservative—and mostly white—Cuban political leaders, who took advantage of their American connections to bolster their position and to reinstall the principle of racial hierarchy.[183]

American participation in this war with Spain was initially brief; seventeen thousand American troops sailed from Tampa, Florida, on June 14, 1898, and the Spanish in Cuba capitulated on July 17. The manner of ending the conflict at Santiago de Cuba raised troubling questions, however, for the Cuban revolutionaries. The Spanish surrendered not to the Cubans, whose war it was and had been since 1895, but to the Americans, who had been in Cuba for only a few weeks. The Spanish commanders acknowledged the centrality of the Cuban army in their own defeat, but the Americans could not take seriously an army made up of people of color.[184] More provocatively, the Americans and Spanish, as they later were to do in Manila, forbade local military leaders from even attending the surrender ceremony, though it was occurring in the city that was the birthplace of Cuban nationalism. Cubans were even forbidden to enter any of the island's cities or towns to celebrate the victory over Spain. Oddly, though Spain was the enemy that had lost the war, Spanish bureaucrats remained in power and Cubans were required to relinquish their weapons.[185]

The bizarre asymmetry of the victory is difficult to grasp. The American expeditionary force was a small one, and casualties had been minimal, while during several years of war the Cubans had lost tens of thousands of soldiers and civilians, some to death in battle or in the detention camps, others to disease, and yet others to exile. Indeed, over the course of the 1895–98 war, the population of Cuba was reduced by as much as 15 percent. The price that the Cubans paid for their ambiguous victory was a "shattered world."[186] Yet the Americans claimed both the victory and the authority to shape Cuba's future.

The Teller Amendment notwithstanding, after the surrender American officials presumed a right to determine the Cubans' capacity for self-rule. The American commanding general, Leonard Wood, sounding like a modern college football coach, declared that he would give the Cubans "every chance to show what is in them, in order that they either demonstrate their fitness or unfitness for self-government."[187]

In making this determination, the North Americans were predisposed to rely on their notions of racial hierarchy. They were skeptical about the capacity of a mixed-race people to rule themselves, and this racist supposition fitted with an important ambiguity in the way upper-class Cubans thought. Even before the American intervention, when Cuban leaders discussed the future, they spoke of "exceptional men" of learning and cultural attainment, men with the marks of high civilization. This was not necessarily a racial concept, but it easily slid into making an elite, white, European-educated Cuban the norm for a leader. This logic undercut the earlier idea of "civilization" articulated by Martí, Juan Gualberto Gómez, and Antonio Maceo, for whom transcendence of race was the mark of civilization. Moreover, in the language of 1898—that of some Cubans as well as Americans—there was an implication that most Cubans did not have the qualities needed for bearing political responsibilities. This notion was well expressed in the circulars that revolutionary leaders distributed after the war urging Cubans to behave in an orderly fashion to show that they deserved to be free and self-governing. The American occupiers unthinkingly but consequentially gave a racial gloss to these Cuban comments. Whiteness and civilization were almost assimilated, one to the other, as in the United States at the time, a racist assumption that prompted Americans to consider most Cubans unfit for self-rule—unless tutored by themselves.[188] And, as was to occur in the Philippines, it meant that Americans formed ties with and supported a Europeanized and conservative elite, often large landholders.[189]

The Cuban constitution was drawn up in 1901 under the watchful eye of General Wood, who also modernized, reorganized, and upgraded the island's public finances and its public-health infrastructure and institutions—all significant gifts to the Cuban people. But the constitution was a different matter. Cuban leaders were told that the withdrawal of the American army was conditional upon their accepting the Platt Amendment and incorporating it into their constitution. This stipulation, which substantially compromised the promise of the Teller Amendment, was predictable, given the historical American fear that a Cuba in hostile hands would threaten American security and commerce in the Caribbean. The provisions imposed on the Cubans prohibited their entering into any treaty with a foreign power that would impair Cuban independence, limited their power to contract public debt, and authorized the United States to intervene to preserve Cuban independence, protect property, and maintain order. (Cuba was released from these terms only in 1934, as part of Franklin D. Roosevelt's Good Neighbor Policy.) In addition, the Cubans were required to lease lands permanently to the United States for coaling and naval stations, including what is now the Guantánamo Bay facility.

U.S. intervention in Cuba had a substantial cultural effect; according to the historian Louis Pérez, it "changed everything," as North American "normative standards and moral hierarchies worked their way into every-day life." Cubans, weakened materially and culturally by their long struggle against Spain, could not project an alternative way of life for a postwar Cuba.[190] There is truth to what Pérez claims, but Ada Ferrer, the best student of the Cuban Revolution, points out that the achievement of even semi-independence made a difference. Cuba's constitution estab-lished universal manhood suffrage, for example; had the people of Cuba lived ninety miles north, in the Jim Crow American South, the substan-tial black majority among them would have been disenfranchised.[191]

Although Theodore Roosevelt and his "Rough Riders" are well re-membered as part of the lore of the American triumph in Cuba, Roo-sevelt played an even more decisive role in the taking of the Philippines. Months before war broke out between the United States and Spain on April 21, 1898, as an assistant secretary of the Navy he had placed Admi-ral George Dewey in command of the Asiatic squadron and ordered him to Hong Kong, only a few days by sail from Manila. And on April 25, the day Congress declared war, Dewey received a telegraphic command from Roosevelt: "War has commenced between the United States and Spain. Proceed at once to Philippine Islands. Commence operations against the Spanish fleet. You must capture vessels or destroy. Use utmost endeavor." At this point, President McKinley like many Americans could not locate the Philippines on a map.[192] Entering Manila Bay in the dark of night, Dewey engaged the Spanish fleet at dawn of May 1, achieving a spectacu-lar naval victory in seven hours.

But here, too, as in Cuba, the Americans were injecting themselves into a complex situation where local opposition to Spain's rule was active and ongoing. The struggle for Philippine independence went back at least a decade. *Noli me tangere* (1886), a novel critical of Spanish rule writ-ten by José Rizal, the Filipino physician, poet, and nationalist, perhaps marked its beginning. In any case, Rizal's execution by the Spanish in

1896 sparked a full-scale anticolonial rebellion. Rizal represented the *ilustrados*, elite Filipinos who initially sought reform within the empire. In 1892 Andres Bonifacio had organized a broader revolutionary society, the Katipunan, devoted to the overthrow of Spanish rule;[193] when hostilities broke out in 1896, Filipinos fought under Emilio Aguinaldo, one of the Katipunan. In December 1897, Aguinaldo and other leaders agreed in the Pact of Biak-na-Bato to end their resistance and leave the Philippines in return for a promise of reforms within five years and a considerable sum of money.

Neither side lived up to the terms of the agreement. Aguinaldo used a portion of the money to purchase arms in Hong Kong, where he also made contact with various American officials and aides to Dewey. A few days before Dewey received Roosevelt's message, Aguinaldo left Hong Kong for Europe, but stopped on the way at Singapore, where he spoke with the American consul, E. Spencer Pratt. Pratt promised him that the United States would support Philippine independence, though later he denied this, and telegraphed Dewey that he had agreed to a "general cooperation" with the "insurgents." Newspaper reports in Singapore at the time indicated that this was indeed the case, and when the press quoted Aguinaldo's claim that he anticipated "independence" for the Philippines with the support of American "friends and liberators," Pratt made no public comment. Nor did he comment when he forwarded the newspaper account to Washington.[194] He reported to Dewey that Aguinaldo was ready to return to Hong Kong, and Dewey replied that the Filipino leader should come "as soon as possible." But by the time Aguinaldo arrived again in Hong Kong, Dewey had received Roosevelt's command and left for Manila. Before departing, however, the American commander arranged for a Navy ship to bring Aguinaldo to Manila Bay, returning the exiled leader of the independence campaign—no small matter.[195]

Although the Americans sank or burned the entire Spanish fleet in Manila, they needed ground troops to take control of Manila and the archipelago, so Admiral Dewey welcomed Filipino support. He gave captured Spanish weapons to Aguinaldo and urged him to recruit an army, clearly and openly expressing sympathy for the rebel cause, whether sincerely or not.[196] Aguinaldo would have been satisfied at this point with independence under the protection of the American Navy, which he thought was agreeable to the Americans.[197] Precisely how much encouragement Dewey gave to Aguinaldo is not clear, but he did not object when Aguinaldo announced that he had returned to his homeland with the support of the "great nation" of North America, the "cradle of liberty."[198] Beyond any dispute, however, was the contribution that Filipino troops under Aguinaldo made to the taking of Manila, which they had surrounded on three sides, with Dewey's fleet on the fourth. Dewey acknowledged this at the time, as did the anti-imperialist Carl Schurz, a former Civil War general, Radical Republican senator, and civil service reformer.[199] The United States quickly forgot this vital contribution of the Filipinos, though it had been appreciated at the time.

Such was the context when on May 24, 1898, Aguinaldo established a provisional Revolutionary Government, followed by a declaration of independence on June 12 and, eleven days later, the establishment of the Philippine Republic. Officials in Washington reprimanded Pratt for his support of Aguinaldo's plans of independence; Dewey, too, was warned against making any political commitments and required to report on all his contacts with the rebels, who were of course his allies. Dewey complied but at the same time commended the Filipinos' capacity for "self-government."[200] From this point on, the more Washington became involved, the more the Filipino nationalist aspirations were challenged.

The American effort to marginalize the Filipinos' military contribution resulted in an elaborate charade that brought the conflict to a close. Working through the Belgian consul in Manila, the Americans and Spanish agreed to stage a pretend fight between themselves, followed by a Spanish surrender on August 13. Late on the evening before, Aguinaldo was informed that he and his army were not invited to the ceremony, denying them a presence at this crucial event in the history of the Filipino independence movement, and denying them as well the fruits of victory.

With the Treaty of Paris in December 1898, the United States gained legal possession of the Philippines, though the Filipino rebels controlled almost the whole of the archipelago. They had, in the words of Renato Constantino, a Filipino nationalist historian, "won their war of liberation."[201] Refusing to acknowledge these facts on the ground, the United States established a military government the next day. Needless to say, the Filipino revolutionaries were disappointed. During the fall of 1898, Felipe Agoncillo, their chief diplomatic officer, had been in Washington and Paris seeking a chance to speak to members of the American administration, but he met with no success. So he put his argument for Philippine independence in a letter to the State Department, hoping to influence the Senate debate over ratification of the peace treaty. Like the Americans a century before, he explained, the Filipinos had struggled to drive out a colonial oppressor, and they had established a constitutional government, based on the right of the people to rule and in a form that was similar in structure to the American government. He also pointed out that Spain, which at the time of the signing of the treaty controlled little more than Manila, had no authority to cede the remainder of the nation, then governed by the Philippine Republic. Renewed war was inevitable, this time between the Philippine Republic and the United States. It broke out on February 4, 1899; two days later the U.S. Senate ratified the Treaty of Paris.

The United States sent seventy thousand troops to fight in what became a guerrilla war that lasted for a decade, though Roosevelt declared it ended in the middle of 1902. As in Vietnam later, in this guerrilla war American troops could not hold territory, and then resorted to unconscionable tactics, including the destruction of whole villages, water torture practiced on captured soldiers, and a policy of forcing Filipinos into overcrowded detention camps. One American general ordered his troops to render a locality into a "howling wilderness."[202] Certainly this brutality was partly enabled by "race antipathy," as John Bass, a correspondent for *Harper's*, phrased it. The soldiers he spoke to associated Filipinos with Indians and African-Americans. "I am in my glory," one told him, "when I can sight some dark skin and pull the trigger." A soldier from Kansas declared that the Philippines would not be pacified "until the niggers are killed off like the Indians."[203] The result was devastation. Mark Twain, a leading anti-imperialist, pondered the sense or lack of it in all this: "There must be two Americas: one that sets the captive free, and one that takes a once-captive's new freedom away from him."[204]

Still, popular resistance in the Philippines had its effect. When the American army used such brutal methods and the same kind of detention camps that the Spanish had used so infamously in Cuba in order to put down the Filipino insurgents, support for the war in the United States eroded. It also gave the Filipino elite leverage to demand a share in governance, accelerating the shift of governing responsibility to Filipinos and

a promise of eventual independence. American leaders also had to appraise the very high price they had paid for territorial colonization, and to
consider alternative forms of empire.

The casualties of the Philippine-American War vastly exceeded those
of the conflict between the United States and Spain in the Philippines,
yet both Americans and Filipinos—for their own reasons—have tended
to forget this war. Memory of it interrupts and confuses the nationalist
narrative in each country. If, as McKinley said to Americans, the United
States knew and acted on behalf of "every aspiration of their [Filipinos']
minds, in every hope of their hearts," then the war simply did not make
sense to them and escaped memory.[205] Filipinos who learned their history
from textbooks written by American colonial authorities could not but
see their own resistance as a foolish rejection of benevolence and enlightenment. Since many of those who had fought the Americans later
assumed public office in the colonial regime, which lasted nearly four
decades, the textbook interpretations seemed to be ratified. From their
perspective, according to Reynaldo Ileto, a Filipino historian, the "war of
resistance was a waste of effort, an event that was best forgotten."[206]

If the war did not find a place in the historical memory or the political culture of the two combatants, it was nonetheless recognized at the
time all over Asia, especially in China, as a political earthquake. Chinese
intellectuals committed to nationalism and modernity saw in the Philippine Revolution, even if crushed by the Americans, an inspiring sign of a
revolutionary future toward which, they hoped, China and other parts of
Asia and Africa might struggle. The Filipinos had given form to revolution "as a modern mode of being in the contemporary world."[207] Although Americans thought it was they who had brought the ideas of
freedom, modernity, and nationhood to Asia, Jujia Ou, a leading Chinese
nationalist, thanked the Filipino resistance, not America, for the "wind of
freedom and independence" that was blowing across Asia.[208]

The United States, the Chinese believed, had betrayed the Filipinos
who had joined them to defeat Spain. When the United States turned
against the independence movement, Chinese opinion toward Aguinaldo
changed, elevating him from a "bandit" creating "disorder" into a
"leader" of a "revolution." The United States, which had been identified
with freedom, became a powerful symbol of hostility to independence, to
nationality, to freedom.[209] Liang Qichao, another Chinese nationalist intellectual, writing in 1901, pointed out that when the Philippine-

American War began, the Philippine Republic controlled almost 170,000 square miles of territory with a population of more than 9 million people, while the Americans held "not more than 143 square miles of territory and not more than 300,000 people." Having relied on Filipino military assistance and encouraged Filipino expectations of independence, the Americans turned on them in a "bloody three-year war in which the number of dead and wounded was enormous." (The usual estimate is 200,000 Filipino deaths, mostly civilians.) Nationhood was destroyed. Liang Qichao warned fellow nationalists against relying on foreigners promising help; they represented a new means "for destroying countries."[210]

The American imperialists had not anticipated the anti-American nationalism that opposed their venture into modern colonization and that brought their aspirations for formal colonies to an end. Theodore Roosevelt, who had been so anxious to enter the race for empire in 1898, was chastened by the Philippine-American War, which as president he officially ended—though skirmishes continued for several years more. The era when American colonies were established abroad by force was quite brief—indeed, concentrated in only one year, 1900—and thereafter the United States backed away from the imperialism associated with the European powers. Experience taught Roosevelt and his generation of imperialists what William Marcy, one of the least notable secretaries of state, had apparently grasped intuitively in 1855: "Remote colonies are not a source of strength to any Government, but of positive weakness, in the cost of their defense, and in the complications of policy they impose."[211]

The Americans took away different lessons for the future from the Philippines and from Cuba. Formal colonial rule, such as they had insisted on in the Philippines, was eventually rejected, but intervention in the domestic affairs of a weaker nation such as Cuba, especially in Latin America, to enforce fiscal responsibility, to protect property, rights of contract, and commerce, and to ensure regional security was developed in various ways over the next decades. This American way of empire was even presented as *anti*-imperialism because it guaranteed openness, in contrast to the exclusivity of the old empires. While the methods of sustaining America's informal empire based on commerce and finance were novel, even technically creative, the fundamental ideas shared much with the earlier ones of Jefferson, Adams, and Seward.

MAKING THE WORLD SAFE FOR EMPIRE

Though in 1898 Woodrow Wilson was less certain of the merits of imperialism than Roosevelt, he did not join the anti-imperialist chorus. The
situation, he thought, demanded serious reflection, which he gave to it.[212]
By 1901, when the brutal war against the Filipino insurgents was becoming a national embarrassment, he was conscious of the complex interplay
of American traditions and world opinion in the work of empire:

> The best guarantee of good government we can give to the Fil-
> ipinos is, that we shall be sensitive to the opinion of the world,
> that we shall be sensitive in what we do to our own standards, so
> often boasted and proclaimed, and shall wish above all things else
> to live up to the character we have established, the standards we
> have professed.[213]

By the time of the First World War, when American power made him a
world leader, he had become a leading opponent of colonization. Less
publicly, Roosevelt and his former imperialist colleagues had also ceased
advocating territorial expansion.[214]

In the midst of the world war, and before America entered it, Wilson became convinced—like DuBois, Jane Addams, Emily Greene Balch,
Crystal Eastman, and others far more radical than he—that imperialism
was the cause of international anarchy, not its cure.[215] Competition among
imperial powers was responsible for the war, he believed. The alternative
he proposed was a world governed by international law that was enforced
by an international institution. Such a structure would be a framework
for national self-determination and would lead to international stability.[216] This view of the world positioned Wilson against the illiberalisms
of the time, against the autocratic imperialist regimes of Europe and
Asia—and after 1917 against international communism.

Notwithstanding these views, Wilson was committed to a vision of
America and the world that amounted to an endorsement of the American way of life as empire. Like many leaders before him, he thought the
United States was at once unique and a universal model. The world
should look like the United States writ large, he thought, and then it
would offer America sufficient space—the globe itself—in which to pur-

sue the felicity that so struck Tocqueville. Jefferson had thought that in the long run the United States would be secure only in a republican world, a world like itself. Wilson offered a similar idea with his Fourteen Points in 1918. Similarly, National Security Council document 68 (1950), the foundation of American policy in the Cold War, sought a particular "order among nations" that would allow "our free society" to "flourish." That society would be not only in the American interest but in the interest of all humankind, of "civilization itself."[217]

While Wilson spoke in universalist terms, he presumed, as Americans always had, that global commodity, goods, and financial markets should always be at the disposal of the United States. Conservatives agreed, but somehow thought an American protective tariff was compatible with this idea. The natural resources, commerce, and investment opportunities of other nations ought to be available whenever and wherever Americans desired and on the terms they preferred. The success of the United States in the global economy would, Wilson and others thought, ratify America's claim to represent a universally desirable future.[218] Whether they realized it or not, Wilson and the America for which and to which he spoke were engaged in their own version of Ahab's restless ambition and tireless pursuit of the whale.

One cannot quite imagine Herbert Hoover as a soul mate of Ahab, but his experiences in his first years out of college offer a good example of the ambition and mobility that circulated American things, money, and knowledge around the globe. In the twelve years after he graduated from Stanford University in 1895, the freshly minted engineer worked in Australia, China, England, France, India, New Zealand, the Hawaiian Islands, Italy, Canada, South Africa, Egypt, and Burma—and few of these were onetime engagements. Talented and ambitious Americans were highly mobile, and more and more often mobile internationally. Note also that he had no work in any of the territories the United States obtained from Spain: Cuba, Puerto Rico, or the Philippines.[219] The letterhead of the New York Life Insurance Company illustrated the general point: "The Oldest International Insurance Company in the World," "Supervised by 82 Governments."[220] Colonies, Americans were realizing, were not necessary to their global ambitions.

At times Wilson insisted that this American commercial drive should not be indulged at the expense of compromising the freedom and political independence of smaller nations. On July 4, 1914, when his views on domestic and foreign policy were at their most radical, he declared that when "American enterprise" abroad has the effect of "exploiting the mass of the people in that country, it ought to be checked and not encouraged," especially in "those foreign countries which are not strong enough to resist us." Two years later, speaking to the Pan-American Scientific Congress, he imagined the United States moving beyond the unilateralism and hierarchical assumptions of the Monroe Doctrine. American republics, he proposed, should unite in "guaranteeing to each other, absolutely, political independence and territorial integrity."[221]

Sometimes Wilson spoke generously; at other times his language was tough. But he always carried a big stick, bigger in fact than Roosevelt's—and he used it more often. Wilson was perfectly comfortable with Roosevelt's "corollary" to the Monroe Doctrine, which justified U.S. intervention to repair "chronic wrongdoing" in the Americas. Roosevelt's standard for a nation's doing right included "efficiency and decency," maintaining "order," and paying "its obligations."[222] Using that standard, Wilson intervened in Haiti in 1915 (where troops remained until 1934), in the Dominican Republic in 1916 (where troops remained until 1924), in Mexico twice (1914, 1916), and in Cuba (1917). He sent troops to Russia in 1918–20 in support of supposed liberal opponents of the Bolsheviks, overestimating the prospects of the literal opposition. He was more cautious, however, in central Asia and the Middle East, showing no interest in discussions at the time of possible U.S. mandates in Armenia, Albania, Turkey, Syria, Iraq, or Palestine.

It could be said that for Wilson the United States as international policeman was an alternative to imperialism as a way of ordering the world. He might even have thought that remaking the world in the image of America was in itself a form of anti-imperialism. But here again one encounters the recurring problem of Americans not being able to see their country as others saw it, to imagine the United States as an enemy. Wilson, and Americans generally, tend to miss the point made several generations later by Sukarno of Indonesia at the Bandung Conference of 1955: "Colonialism does not just exist in the classic form." There is also "a modern dress in the form of economic control . . . [and] intellectual control."[223]

In the end, Wilson, like Theodore Roosevelt, shared the Anglo-

Saxons' assumption that they had the right, even responsibility, to rule and raise up the lesser peoples of the non-European world. Latin Americans, Asians, Slavs, and Africans were, as Roosevelt phrased it, in "the childhood stage of race development." Wilson used almost the same language, saying they were "in the childhood of their political growth."[224] The idea of the civilizing mission and the language of uplift had progressive connotations at the time, and the promise of modernity, efficiency, and open markets also seemed to give a progressive cast to the regulation of the administrative, fiscal, and commercial affairs of smaller nations.

International economic relations had become vastly more complex than they had been in the era of Thomas Jefferson.[225] For Wilson and his generation international economic relations went beyond simple trade or exchange, though most multinational enterprise was still oriented to trade. But America's increased manufacturing capacity and greater investment abroad now gave it an elevated and central position in the global economy. From the periphery the United States was moving unmistakably to the core.[226]

While in the nineteenth century trade diplomacy had mostly concerned access and tariffs, the expanded American economy increasingly depended on a regular supply of raw materials, which meant that matters internal to other nations became important. And as U.S. businesses developed plantations and factories abroad, labor and taxation policies for manufacturing and extractive industries were equally important. The security of investments in foreign public and private sectors was likewise a matter of national interest when direct investment in foreign nations increased significantly.[227] The United States, a debtor nation in the nineteenth century, was a creditor nation by the time it entered World War I, as Wilson noted at the time; by 1918 it was in fact the world's leading creditor nation, with major investments on every continent. Commercial diplomacy now had to be concerned with the internal domestic affairs of other nations.

John Hay, one of the circle of imperialists around Theodore Roosevelt and McKinley's secretary of state, had famously circulated a series of what were called Open Door notes in 1899 and 1900, which outlined policies that he saw as complementary to the U.S. taking of the Philippines. (Admiral Mahan worked with him on them.[228]) Partly prompted by America's new colonial presence in East Asia, the notes recalled the nation's

long tradition of concern for global free trade, not real estate, and they
pointed to the future as well. Wilson, for example, admired and built
upon them, and it has even been claimed—with good reason—that the
World Trade Organization is "a linear heir of the Open Door."[229]

The notes also responded to the then current disorder in China: the
Boxer Rebellion erupting in 1900 aimed to overthrow the Qing dynasty
and threatened the stability of China's imperial government. To boot, the
Chinese authorities as well as the rebellious forces were challenging foreign influence in China, and in the chaos several thousand European military forces arrived, along with a small American contingent dispatched
from the Philippines, to maintain their established trade and other treaty
rights. Hay worried, however, that the European powers might try to
gain yet more control and to partition China into exclusionary markets in
their respective "spheres of influence" previously agreed on. After con-
sulting with the British, but without thinking to consult the Chinese government, he circulated his notes, which stated the principle that
all foreign powers should have equal commercial opportunity in China,
including the freedom to mount financial operations, with no favoritism
given to nations in their spheres of influence.[230] This matter was to be
worked out among the European imperial powers, not by the Chinese. He
also proclaimed a general commitment to preserve China's administrative
integrity—that is to say, to allow no formal colonies. Maintenance of
American access to trade in China was obviously one objective, but Hay
also wanted to prevent rivalry in China among the European powers that
might lead to conflicts disrupting the Atlantic world as well as the Pacific.[231]

The important point here is not the impact of his notes; there was
none. The United States had neither the armies nor the moral authority
to enforce the principles he outlined. In a moment of honest self-
reflection Hay admitted as much, characterizing the excited newspaper
talk about how the United States could now dictate to the world as nothing but "mere flap-doodle."[232] Still, these famous notes express, at the
very moment of its colonizing the Philippines, America's alternative to
formal colonization. Hay defined instead a liberal empire and a liberal
world order, pointing toward Woodrow Wilson's global statement of
principles in the Fourteen Points. Though Wilson didn't call his policy
"dollar diplomacy," for which his predecessor in the White House,

William Howard Taft, became famous, in a technical way the policy of expanding and protecting American export of capital and importation of profits and goods was extraordinarily creative. It made empire almost invisible to Americans and was often welcomed, even solicited, by the leaders of small nations that wanted to grow economically.

Although the United States was still a debtor nation in the time of Taft's presidency, New York City was becoming a tremendously important center of global finance. Declining returns on domestic loans prompted New York's banks and investment houses to look to less developed countries for better interest rates, and they also pursued opportunities in western Europe.[233] Kuhn, Loeb, a New York private investment house, and National City Bank had underwritten German imperial bonds in 1900; with another syndicate they financed Japanese bonds in 1904; J. P. Morgan provided credit to Mexico in 1899. More important, Morgan made substantial loans to Britain to finance the Boer War. While making a large loan to the world's leading creditor nation enhanced the international standing of this bank, the whole cluster of loans brought "global recognition" to American investment banks.[234] There had been no U.S. government involvement in these transactions, but the risks in financing smaller, more volatile nations encouraged bankers eventually to turn to the government.

In 1904 the Dominican Republic, which wanted to divert to itself some of the American capital going to Cuba, approached American banks. Cuba's compromised sovereignty made it attractive to the banks, but the Dominican leaders were unwilling to make concessions, nor did the United States want to take territorial control. President Roosevelt had said, "I have about the same desire to annex it [the Dominican Republic] as a gorged boa-constrictor might have to swallow a porcupine wrong-end to."[235] Still, Kuhn, Loeb hesitated to invest without some form of security. The creative solution that emerged is usually associated with Roosevelt's successor, but it antedated Taft's presidency. It came from two sources: one the British example in Egypt, and the other an extension of a domestic banking practice used in corporate finance. Both involved some form of participation in management and, often, formal financial reorganization.

In 1876 Britain had refinanced Egypt's deficit in an arrangement that placed British "Financial Advisers" in charge of certain revenue sources.

They also controlled borrowing. The British management of Egypt's finances reduced the debt and successfully attracted new investment. It did this without overt colonial control; the expert managers were in the pay of the Egyptian government, not the British. Similar arrangements were subsequently made in Greece and Turkey.[236]

American corporate finance had developed an analogous system. When investment banks made large financial commitments to corporations, they usually demanded a place (or places) on the boards of directors and some power to select managers. Translation of this practice from the corporate sphere to the government raised an important issue that was elided with barely a second thought: in corporations the people whose power was reduced in the arrangement were stockholders, whereas in nations the losers were citizens. But the businessmen in nations seeking and needing capital were not necessarily committed to democratic politics, and they willingly sacrificed the notion of popular sovereignty.

In the case of the Dominican Republic, the United States arranged to have Americans manage the Dominican customs service to ensure its integrity, and 55 percent of the customs revenue was reserved for debt service, which secured the loans.[237] Thus did loans and financial expertise emerge as an alternative to colonization and sometimes, but not always, to military intervention. Britain ended up intervening militarily in Egypt in 1881, and the Americans did the same repeatedly in the Caribbean and South America: in the Dominican Republic and elsewhere, the American loans were followed by interventions ordered by President Wilson to maintain financial obligations. Wilson had an assertive idea of America's place in the world, and he was quicker, perhaps, than Taft would have been to make these interventions. Whatever the merits in each case, intervention was a mark of failure, for the whole point was to avoid formal colonialism and military force.

The system was refined—and protected even more from anti-imperialist critique—in Taft's last year in office. In 1912, his administration negotiated a combination of loans and fiscal reforms for Honduras and Nicaragua, but Congress, in the wake of the Pujo Committee hearings of April 1912 on the "money trust," refused to ratify the convention he had arranged. Taft responded by proposing that the banks write the terms of proper fiscal administration into the contract itself, thus making it a set of obligations between private actors in the marketplace, not a government-to-government agreement.[238] After World War I and until the Great Depression, American financial missionaries were commonplace in the treasury ministries of Latin American nations.[239]

Each case tended to be different, but the important point was that finance, or the establishment of financial dependency, wholly replaced territorial acquisition and partly replaced armed force as a means of bringing order from chaos, responsibility from irresponsibility in the Americas and beyond. Today, finance—in the form of the International Monetary Fund and the World Bank, both vehicles of American interest and fiscal expertise—is an even more powerful instrument of empire. Debt produces dependency and loss of control for the debtor, but the result advances American empire almost imperceptibly, masking power as technique. In the twentieth century, then, American power found a barely visible means to influence, even control, global financial management. It sustained a world responsive to American economic aspirations and moral expectations.

This quasi-invisible American internationalism notwithstanding, Woodrow Wilson, more than any other single person, shaped the way Americans thought about their place in the world.[240] Washington and Lincoln had been greatly admired abroad, but Wilson was the first American to be a world leader (a stature signified, perhaps, by the frequency with which one finds a street named for him in the world's great cities). The now nearly century-long debate between advocates of his internationalist vision and those espousing unilateralism or the unbridled nationalist exercise of power is still a vital one, and consequential to Americans and to the world at large.[241]

For Woodrow Wilson nineteenth-century imperialism carried a large double meaning. It implied outmoded forms of top-down politics of all kinds, and he was not surprised that autocratic rule and conflict among the imperial powers brought forth both a terrible world war and the Russian Revolution. Looking to the future and a world fit and safe for American ideals, he tried to position himself and the United States as a global alternative to both "atavistic imperialism and revolutionary socialism."[242] He repeatedly professed himself thrilled and excited by the idea of the Russian people rising up against autocratic rule. The revolution was part of his justification for American entry into the war, "to make the world safe for democracy."[243]

The United States in 1914 was not what it became after the Second World War: the most powerful and consistent counterrevolutionary force in the world. Wilson invaded revolutionary Mexico twice in the hope of teaching Mexicans a proper politics, but the former professor of politics learned more than he taught. His experience there informed him that sometimes the deep social and economic roots of political issues required more than merely free elections to resolve. He was learning the same from radicals in the United States whom he befriended and with whom he repeatedly spoke and corresponded, from Jane Addams to Max Eastman. It was they who tugged him toward the internationalism that became central to his historical significance.[244]

He could participate in these exchanges because the line between liberalism and socialism was not then so absolute as it became in 1918–20 and then, even more so, in the 1940s.[245] He was open to the ideas of thinkers far more radical than he was or, as president, could be. Wilson opposed Bolshevism, but he never regretted the Russian Revolution, and he hoped a liberal Russia would emerge from the convulsion; he even lent military support to Siberian opponents of Bolshevism who, he hoped, might bring about that result.[246]

Wilson and Lenin shared the world stage by the end of 1917. They both offered the world a new future of social justice at home and peace abroad, and they both directed their vision beyond established leaders to those whom Wilson called "the silent mass of mankind."[247] If in domestic affairs they defended radically different ideas about the proper roles of the state and of private property, their international proposals sounded strikingly similar. They were far more alike than one might expect from the nearly century-long global division that their overall differences first defined.

When Russia left the war in November 1917, Lenin offered the "Petrograd Formula" for ending it: "no annexations, no indemnities, free determination of nationalities."[248] This set of precepts was not far from the precepts in Wilson's great Peace Without Victory address to the Senate in January 1917, nor from his Fourteen Points, which Lenin praised as "a great step toward the peace of the world."[249] In presenting the Fourteen Points to the Senate in January 1918, Wilson in fact specifically associated himself with the "largeness of view" and "universal human sympathy" articulated at Petrograd. He especially commended Lenin's exposure to the public gaze of the secret war agreements that had been found in the Russian archives, and he joined Lenin's plea for open diplomacy.[250] The Petrograd Formula did not, as it turned out, guide Soviet policy, and the Soviet domestic experiments became a nightmare. But in 1918, Wilson and Lenin were in the same conversation. However different the liberal and communist visions of the world order, both proposed to drag the world from an imperialist past to a modern, progressive future.[251]

Wilson's vision was rooted in American tradition and it continued the American way of empire. His astonishingly smooth projection of historical American principles into a global future translated American ideals and interests ever so easily into presumed universal human ideals. Such were the foundations of a century of American liberal internationalism, compromised domestically only by a few recurring episodes not of isolationism but of American unilateralism.[252] Of course, the Soviet Union challenged this world order, and many weaker states caught in the web of empire were not wholly accommodating.

The Fourteen Points were intended to set a global agenda. The first five set out large principles, all of them well grounded in American traditions and practices going back to Thomas Jefferson and John Quincy Adams. Like the Russians, Wilson proposed "open covenants of peace, openly arrived at." He echoed the past in affirming the "absolute freedom of navigation upon the seas," a point logically followed by an endorsement of the removal "so far as possible" of barriers to "an equality of trade conditions among all nations." Arms and imperial rivalry had been the root cause of the war, he believed, so he called for the reduction of "national armaments" and "a free, open-minded, and absolutely impartial adjustment of all colonial claims." Points six through thirteen proposed national self-determination and the right of European nations, including Turkey and Russia, to determine their "own political development." The fourteenth point proposed a "general association of nations."

In the history of American empire two of the fourteen points are of special interest. In the last point, Wilson was proposing that the United States finally reject the advice of Washington's Farewell Address as well as the implication of the Monroe Doctrine. In endorsing a "concert of nations," he accepted the idea of enduring political—not only commercial—relations with the rest of the world. In his Peace Without Victory address he insisted that such an international body would not imply "entangling alliances"; he called it a "community of power" as opposed to a "balance of power."[253] But surely it was the prospect of entanglement that energized the fierce opposition to the League of Nations that killed its prospects in the American political arena.

Even more interesting was the point dealing with colonies. Wilson's concern for self-determination was mostly directed to eastern Europe and the Balkans, where he believed that "unsettled" conditions had been a problem in the past and could be again.[254] He had nothing to offer to the peoples of Asia and Africa. He was thinking of adjustments among the European imperial powers, not between colonized and colonizers. In other words, he did not seriously interfere with the colonies held by European powers or the United States. The system of mandates, where European powers presided over certain areas of the Middle East but did not actually colonize them, was codified in the Treaty of Versailles; it implied a commitment to tutelage but seemed to be little more than a fig leaf to hide the continuous presence of European powers in the areas they had sought to draw into their empires.[255]

The tragedy of Wilson and, as it turned out, the deeply flawed peace that was agreed on at Versailles was that he compromised the hopes of liberals and radicals without winning the support of conservatives. If his goal was, as he said, a "world . . . made fit and safe to live in," it is clear that it would be fitter for some than for others. It was to be a world marked by international law, securing property and contract, thus safe from imperial power politics and the revolutionary socialism of the Bolsheviks. It would be a world where the United States, possessed as it was of the largest economy and the greatest financial resources, would readily acquire "moral and economic pre-eminence."[256] This liberal world would be very fit indeed, a veritable empire tailored to American ambitions and talents.

Even though the League of Nations failed, Wilson's vision was largely realized, reanimated, and developed in the financial and political construction of the "free world" after World War II. Wilson set the course for the twentieth-century iteration of empire as a way of life; he achieved an "ideological fusion of American economic self-interest with American liberal internationalist idealism."[257] This liberal consensus has been dominant. Such debates as have developed from the right have not challenged the premise on which empire as a way of life is founded: the availability of a world to indulge (and suffer) America's passion for the display of moral rectitude and the pursuit of profit. Disagreements within the United States have historically centered on whether the best strategy is unilateralist or internationalist. Ironically, the First World War—and the enhancement of the state it brought as well as the spirit of nationalism it enhanced, partly through repression of dissent—may have reinforced conservative unilateralism. If the multilateral aspect of Wilson's vision is still episodically contested, there has been since Jefferson's presidency near American consensus that the whole globe should be open and available to American enterprise.

5

THE INDUSTRIAL WORLD AND

THE TRANSFORMATION OF LIBERALISM

———— ∞∞∞ ————

In 1848 only two cities in the world, Paris and London, had a population in excess of a million people. By 1900, these were joined by Berlin, Tokyo, Vienna, St. Petersburg, Moscow, New York, Chicago, Philadelphia, Buenos Aires, Rio de Janeiro, Calcutta, and Osaka, and other cities were approaching this urban threshold.[1] The growth of giant cities was a worldwide phenomenon; only Africa did not experience it. A thorough (and still authoritative) statistical study of urbanization undertaken at the end of the nineteenth century began with the statement "The most remarkable social phenomenon of the present century is the concentration of population in cities."[2]

This striking growth of cities, driven by industrial capitalism, was associated with a new level of global integration. Telegraphic communications circled the world, making communication instantaneous across long distances for the first time; steam-powered ocean liners eased intercontinental travel and dramatically increased its speed. Foreign investment rose, reaching higher levels (as a percentage of total investment) than a century later in the 1990s, and industrialism spread with astonishing rapidity. International organizations as well as informal but dense networks of interaction and information exchange developed, too, among political leaders and professionals who discussed political and policy ideas.

If the central experience that held together a shared history of the continents since 1500 had been the oceanic revolution and its military and economic implications, now it was the industrial revolution and its ramifications for political ideas and practices. Charles Beard had it right at the time when he observed that "modern civilization . . . is industrial." And it raised similar challenges in all the industrial regions of the world. Beard, an internationally recognized municipal expert as well as a historian of the United States, discovered this in Japan. He traveled to Tokyo in 1922 and collaborated while there with municipal leaders in establishing a Bureau of Municipal Research modeled on the one he had directed in New York. Beard returned to the United States convinced that the cities of the two nations shared a common history in the era of industrial capitalism and faced similar social policy and administrative issues. Moreover, he realized that his Japanese counterparts in the municipal government and in the academy were working with the same ideas being discussed in Berlin, London, and New York. Everywhere the reform agendas were much the same.[3]

Historians are only now beginning to recognize the degree to which the Progressive movement in the United States was a part of this larger history. The American case has been treated as unique in its moderation or limitations, depending on the point of view. Perhaps this is a legacy of the 1930s; those who regretted the limited challenge to capitalism in the New Deal era felt that the reform impulse in the United States fell short of the welfare states put in place in Europe, while others celebrated the American difference. The historiographical result was to set progressivism in the United States apart from the histories of social democracy and of the welfare states abroad, as well as from fascism and communism.

The brilliant syntheses written a generation ago by Richard Hofstadter in his Pulitzer Prize–winning *Age of Reform* (1955) and by Robert Wiebe in his classic *Search for Order* (1967) are the work of scholars of cosmopolitan intellect, whose minds were formed by deep engagement with major European social theorists. And they were acutely aware of the new global position and responsibilities of the United States as they wrote. Yet their histories of American reform today seem surprisingly, even strangely, parochial, so deeply rooted are they in the analysis of the particularities of American culture—moralism, status anxiety, and the fear of failure among the old middle class in the first, the dissolution of small-town life, the rise of a new middle class, and the emergence of bureaucracy in the second.[4] These snippet summaries do not do justice to two rich, complex, and wonderfully insightful books, but my interest here is not with their specific interpretations. My concern is the confinement of the field of inquiry to the territory of the United States, implying an isolated, autonomous history. Such was the postwar authority of the exceptionalist narrative.[5]

In fact, the American progressive reform they examined was a local version of a nearly global history of intellectual and political responses to industrial capitalism and urbanization. That shared history prompted the development of new academic social-science disciplines that spread from Germany and France to all the industrial societies in the world, offering new capacities for understanding the "social question" that encouraged and made possible a novel political response to the social transformations of the era—a social politics.

More recently, James T. Kloppenberg, Daniel T. Rodgers, and Alan Dawley have begun to tell the story of American progressivism as a North Atlantic one, emphasizing the transatlantic conversations about social policy, reform networks, and regulatory and welfare policies enacted between the 1880s and the 1920s in western Europe and the United States.[6] With varying foci and emphases, they each demonstrate that the United States was a full participant in a transformative rethinking of the role of the state in dealing with the social consequences of industrialism.

Awareness of the common challenge and sharing ideas did not, however, lead to identical results in nation after nation. There was greater similarity in the ideas crossing the Atlantic than in the final political results—which is what one should anticipate. Ideas—whether of a general, even philosophical sort or those concerning specific policies—circulated freely, and they held together the reformers' international networks. But different state forms, distinctive political cultures and political organizations, and individual and historically contingent alignments of political interests made for inevitably varied policy results. Still, there is a family resemblance across the spectrum of political outcomes—at least if one is inclined, as I am, to be a lumper instead of a splitter. The similarity is sufficient to characterize the turn of the century as an era when a new social politics, a politics marked by an infusion of social content, emerged globally—extending well beyond the North Atlantic. By the 1930s that development had spawned quite illiberal as well as liberal outcomes.

European colonies, which in 1900 represented the greater part of the world's landmasses and population, had a distinct place in international reform. Many policies discussed by reformers were implemented in them—notably those that involved public health, management, urban planning, and transportation, as well as other policies that increased the efficiency of the government or economy. In fact, the colonies were often laboratories of reform in these areas.[7] But to the extent that the story I am telling here concerns the expansion of political citizenship as it had been defined in the eighteenth century to include new social dimensions, the colonies were not part of it. Colonial rule was based not on the sovereignty of the governed but ultimately on coercion. Also, their economies were mostly based on mining and agriculture, not urban industry. Only later, after World War I and especially World War II, did popular movements in the colonies press political and social citizenship to the center of relations with the metropole. When they advanced claims to which the imperial authorities could not or would not accede, they led, eventually, to decolonization.[8]

The emergent industrial economies of first England and then the North Atlantic region, South America, and Asia transformed the international environment, affecting all nations and empires. Advanced and less advanced societies were incorporated into this new world and had to address the consequences. Prime Minister Taro Katsura of Japan, a conservative former army minister, made this point in 1908:

> We are now in an age of economic transition. Development of machine industry and intensification of competition widens the gap between rich and poor and creates antagonisms that endanger social order. Judging by Western history this is an inevitable pattern. Socialism is today no more than a wisp of smoke, but if it is ignored it will someday have the force of wildfire and there will be nothing to stop it. Therefore it goes without saying that we must rely on education to nurture the people's values; and we must devise a social policy that will assist their industry, provide them work, help the aged and infirm, and thereby prevent catastrophe.

Leading industrial societies were closely watched, not only for their achievements but for their mistakes. In 1905, Kawakami Hajime, a pioneer Marxist theorist and economist at Kyoto Imperial University until forced out in 1928, noted that "the history of the failures of the advanced countries is the best textbook for the follower nations."[9] Chinese progressives, like Japanese ones, worried about the growing inequality that capitalist industrialism produced in Europe and the United States. Leaders of the Revolutionary Alliance, founded in 1905 by Sun Yat-sen, for example, studied reformers in Japan and reformers in the United States, particularly Henry George and Richard Ely.[10] Every national experience was distinctive, of course, and the reform agenda played out with significant variations. Yet the leading cities and associated "industrial landscapes" or regions were materially quite similar, as photographs of the era and surviving industrial structures from that time reveal.[11]

In 1870, England's was the most advanced industrial economy; its city of Manchester was taken as the symbol of the industrial age. Statesmen and capitalists embraced the apparently successful doctrines of political economy associated with the Manchester school and particularly the theories of David Ricardo, whose *Principles of Political Economy and Taxation* (1817) was a powerful work of deductive reasoning that built upon Adam Smith. Like the liberalism of the Enlightenment, with which they were associated, these ideas emphasized individualism and limited government. The Manchester economists were determined to influence policy, and Ricardo himself was elected to Parliament, having made a fortune in the stock market and retired. Opposed to a tariff that protected the landed classes from the danger of cheaper grain being imported from abroad (the Corn Laws), they argued with great effect against government regulation, which led to overinvestment and diminishing returns in the agricultural sector. Proponents of laissez-faire, they argued that the market, not politics, was the only legitimate and effective way to allocate capital, commodities, and even social goods.

In the wake of global depressions in the 1870s and '90s, however, both ruling classes and working classes around the world were pressed— in different ways—to question this liberal political economy. The rapid, unregulated industrialization that Manchester doctrines promoted had indeed stimulated marked economic development, but the result seemed to be a social crisis as well, and it suggested the limits of liberalism. At the same time, the social experience of life in the modern city challenged the underlying assumption of classical political economy and liberalism that the basic unit of human action was the autonomous individual. A novel sense of social interdependence and collective responsibility now developed there. The industrial city, according to Frederic C. Howe, an American political scientist who devoted his career to reform, was "creating a new moral sense, a new conception of the obligation of political life, obligation which in earlier conditions of society did not and could not exist." Urban social needs, he believed, demanded political actions and policies "which had heretofore lain outside the sphere of government."[12]

"Socialized man" became a premise among social scientists in Europe and the Americas, and in rapidly industrializing Japan.[13] (Indeed, the invention of modern, professional social-science disciplines was itself a response to the growth of industrial capitalism and urbanization. Their claim was to be able to understand and thus manage the new society.[14] New social explanations were invented—in Marxist versions and in more readily assimilated academic disciplines.) Whether the state was construed as a formal (and quite mystical) entity—beyond government, let alone society—as in the political science that American scholars adapted from their German mentors, or believed to be embodied in the emperor (also mystical), as in Japan, new intellectual understandings and political impulses emerged in the 1890s that were entangled with a new "sense of society."[15] This language about society was pervasive, whether in talking about the economy or the novel or education—or sociology. A notable instance is the work of Benjamín Vicuña, a Chilean journalist who wrote a series of articles in Santiago's *El Mercurio* between 1904 and 1907 that were read throughout Latin America. In them, he argued that the "social question" transformed political economy into a *social* science and liberalism into a *social* liberalism.[16]

The heightened awareness of the category of the social enabled sociology to establish itself, especially in the United States and France, as a mediator between the slightly older disciplines of political science and economics. Sociologists claimed to possess a special knowledge, mainly the explanatory power of the idea of social interdependence, which necessarily affected both political science and economics. It was a science that went beyond "traditional ways of interpreting social experience," according to Albion W. Small of the University of Chicago, a founder of the discipline in the United States. It brought intellectual comprehension to the "near-infinity of group relationships and processes" and offered a new and vital "conception of reality."[17]

In a presentation to the American Economic Association in 1895, Small explained that "sociology is not an effort to discredit or supersede economics," but it does claim that economy and society are "interdependent" and need to be understood as such by scholars and citizens.[18] Richard Ely, a founder of the American Economic Association in 1885, did not recognize limiting boundaries between economics, history, and sociology, nor did his colleagues at The Johns Hopkins University.[19] Similarly, Edward A. Ross, who began as an economist, shifted to sociology, a reorientation marked in his classic work *Social Control* (1901). He argued—along the lines of his contemporary Émile Durkheim and Lester Frank Ward, a pioneer American sociologist (and also his father-in-law) who reached these conclusions in the 1880s—that industrialism and urbanism had dissolved the older, "natural" forms of social order and required a self-conscious, purposeful policy of social control.[20]

Today the phrase "social control" connotes a form of elite domination, but Ross and his generation opposed "democratic social control" to the growing danger of "control" by a ruling "parasitic class."[21] Herbert Croly made a related point in his classic work of political theory *The Promise of American Life* (1909): "The solution of the social problem demands the substitution of a conscious social ideal for the earlier instinctive homogeneity of the American nation." This social vision would not be static or fixed, according to Croly. Rather, it was to be the ongoing, never finished work of democracy in successive generations.[22]

An observation that the new social politics or social liberalism was the product of university seminar rooms would not be far off. First in Germany, then rather quickly through a global network, the newly professionalized academic social scientists became prominent in the movement to devise public doctrines based on other than the market values of a laissez-faire philosophy. Dissertations proliferated in the social science faculties of Europe, North America, South America, and Japan. In the United States, Albert Shaw, a notable reform journalist, recalled that when he was a student at Johns Hopkins the atmosphere was that of "an almost passionate international humanitarianism."[23]

The engaged centrality of social science is understandable, given its claim to a particular knowledge of the increased social complexity and interdependence characteristic of modern, industrial life. But another aspect deserves our notice, too. The professionalizing of this academic work was intended to insulate its practitioners from market values and the competition of the chaotic marketplace of ideas, which was filled, they thought, with charlatans. In establishing organized communities whose members could authoritatively validate knowledge claims, they were creating for themselves a system of status, reward, and security outside and even in opposition to dominant market values.[24] There was, therefore, a strong affinity between the pattern of everyday personal experience they desired and the social liberalism they promoted.

In addition, social scientists were coming into key positions in the bureaucracies of newly consolidated nation-states and were helping to develop novel administrative capacities for their governments. Interestingly, there was often a gendered division of labor: males with doctorates in the social sciences tended to be ensconced in the university seminar room, while women with similar training worked in public and private agencies that combined policy research with organized advocacy, supplying expert knowledge to local communities or offering social services directly to various client populations. In the United States one thinks of, among others, Crystal Eastman, Edith Abbott, Mary Kingsbury Simkhovitch, Pauline and Josephine Goldmark, and Florence Kelley.[25]

The development of this new state capacity and bureaucratic leadership was most advanced and influential in Germany and Japan. There is a common assumption that the United States lagged in this development, but its Bureau of Labor Statistics, directed by Carroll D. Wright, was internationally recognized as a pioneer and leader. In 1892 the International Statistical Institute called for the universal adoption of American techniques dealing with social statistics.[26] Wright's correspondence about reforming industrial practices was international; for example, his correspondence with Ernesto Quesada, a sociologist in the Faculty of Philosophy at the University of Buenos Aires, and with the Argentine politician Carlos Pellegrini concerned many issues, including workers' cooperatives and minimum-wage laws.[27] Meanwhile, Josephine Shaw Lowell and the women who created the National Consumers League developed a means by which women as consumers could put pressure on employers to adopt responsible labor practices, and it was emulated in France, Belgium, Germany, and Switzerland.[28]

So the international connections and correspondence among bureaucrats sustained a global discussion of and pattern of response to industrial capitalism. In nation after nation, the home and labor ministries (the names differed from place to place) were constantly collecting information from other countries, and the correspondence files of mayors were filled with policy queries from their counterparts on all continents. Tabulated data in the reports of ministries and reform organizations enabled officials to compare policies in dozens of nations, and the bibliographies supporting proposed new laws—even legal briefs—were impressively international. For example, when Louis D. Brandeis, the reform lawyer later appointed to the Supreme Court by Woodrow Wilson, filed his brief in *Muller v. Oregon* (1908), which successfully defended the constitutionality of regulating the hours and conditions of work for women, he relied as much on historical, economic, and sociological evidence as on traditional legal arguments. This research, mostly done by Josephine Goldmark and Florence Kelley, drew heavily upon international sources; the brief included a substantial appendix titled "The World's Experience upon Which Legislation Limiting the Hours of Labor for Women Is Based," with bibliographical and legislative references to Great Britain, Germany, France, Switzerland, Austria, Holland, and Italy. Similarly, Alejandro Unsain's three-volume compilation *Legislación del trabajo*, published in Buenos Aires in the 1920s, specifically referred to laws and social-policy studies in Italy, New Zealand, Australia, Germany, the Soviet Union, Belgium, England, France, Japan, the United States, Canada, Mexico, Chile, Bolivia, and Guatemala, covering topics ranging from the social question and state intervention, to administration and constitutional organization, to accidents and medical insurance.[29]

This new social politics was also driven by a new and energized public. Extension of the suffrage (and movements demanding it) in Europe and Latin America (less so in Japan), social movements and trade unions helped to press the social question forward from the 1890s until the outbreak of war in 1914.[30] In the United States women's suffrage indirectly but significantly advanced the idea of social citizenship. Many issues the women advocated (under their sometime slogan of "municipal housekeeping") were variations on the central reform themes of social solidarity and social politics.[31] Many civic activists also were motivated by the Protestant Social Gospel (in Anglo-America) or Catholic Social Teachings (in Latin America, France, and central Europe).

Social liberals in general wanted to offer a compelling alternative to socialism. That said, many of them were drawn to the ethical aspirations of socialism, which they were willing to incorporate into their own politics. The new liberal reformers, no less than socialists, insisted on the importance of social facts and social ethics.[32] For them as well as for socialists, socialism was not a fixed state form to be taken or rejected, but rather, as Ramsay MacDonald of Britain's Labour Party put it in 1909, "a tendency, a mode of thought, a guiding idea."[33] The American progressive Walter Weyl echoed this sentiment. "Socialization of industry," he wrote in *The New Democracy* (1912), is a "point of view, . . . less a definite industrial program than the animating ideal of a whole industrial policy."[34]

The threat of socialism compelled the reform of liberalism. Not only conservatives but many social liberals recoiled from the prospect of actual socialism. Everywhere socialism was a danger to be avoided. Still there were modest, mostly symbolic socialist victories that had their own importance. And contrary to the exceptionalist claim (or regret), socialism showed its face in the United States with considerable force during the Progressive Era, with the Socialist candidate Eugene V. Debs winning 6 percent of the national vote in the 1912 presidential election, a race that included two, perhaps even three, other progressive choices—Woodrow Wilson, Theodore Roosevelt, and William Howard Taft.

By then, the "labor question," the contentious and often violent relations between capital and labor, had evolved into the broader "social question," filling the press from Tokyo to Lima, from Buenos Aires to Glasgow, from Chicago to Mexico City, from São Paulo to St. Petersburg, from Santiago, Chile, to Milan, from New York to Budapest. There was, as the historian Alan Dawley observes, a worldwide "reaction against the unwanted consequences of the unregulated market."[35] Advocates of a new liberalism (or in the United States progressivism) rejected socialism and communism, and they accepted capitalism, but they had lost faith in the capacity of the market to create social justice.[36] In his book *Social Organization* (1909), Charles H. Cooley insisted that it "would be fatuous to assume that the market process expresses the *good* of society."[37]

In Birmingham, England, Joseph Chamberlain, who as Liberal mayor had advocated municipal socialism and successfully established municipal ownership of utilities, proposed as early as 1883 that the "politics of the future are social politics." Later, in 1907, the American Jane Addams, who had established the Hull-House settlement in Chicago in 1889 and who by now had earned an international reputation as a reformer, explained that contemporary life was marked by the passage "from an age of individualism to one of association." "A large body of people," she was convinced, had come to a conclusion that the "industrial system is in a state of profound disorder" and that it was unlikely that "the pursuit of individual ethics will ever right it." In the same year, Winston Churchill observed that if political parties were to survive into the future, they must address "in some effective form or another" the issues of "wages and comfort—and insurance for sickness, unemployment, and old age." The "tendency of civilization" was in the direction of multiplying the "collective functions of society."[38]

Seki Hajime, a reform-oriented university economist who challenged laissez-faire policies and became mayor of Osaka, Japan, believed in 1914 that industrialization meant that "people became more interdependent." The task of "social democracy" was to achieve a "social economy" that would shift from the stress on "competition" to a "cooperative basis."[39] Again, this fell far short of socialism; the aim was to ward off the threats of class conflict by establishing a balance between individualism (or laissez-faire) and collective goods (or socialism). In *The Meaning of Liberalism* (1912), J. M. Robertson, a British New Liberal, explained that "laissez faire . . . is not done with as a principle of rational limitation of state interference, but it is quite done with it as a pretext for leaving uncured deadly social evils which admit of curative treatment by state action."[40]

Within a decade on either side of 1900, politics in every industrial nation on the globe had been transformed. Liberalism was "fundamentally reformulated" in industrial societies and the political culture deepened, reaching into society.[41] The shift in the United States was striking. National electoral politics during the Gilded Age (roughly 1877 until the beginnings of progressivism in the 1890s) had avoided anything resembling the social question. The issues of the very lively national quadrennial contests—beyond simple patronage—focused on race, the currency, and tariffs. But as the twentieth century began, politics could no longer be separated or isolated from social issues, which moved to the center and thereby changed the meaning and work of politics. In a lecture to Wisconsin teachers in 1891, the historian Frederick Jackson Turner explained that the "questions that are uppermost" today "are not so much political as economic questions"—and, he added, they would become increasingly important. "The age of machinery, of the factory system, is also the age of socialistic inquiry." Similarly, Walter Weyl, who with Herbert Croly and Walter Lippmann became a founding editor of *The New Republic* in 1914, wrote in *The New Democracy* that in the emergent democracy of the twentieth century, "ideals from the political" will be carried into "the industrial and social fields."[42]

The stakes were higher than a mere challenge to Manchester liberalism. The inherited meaning of politics—whether of the ancient polis or of the eighteenth-century revolutions—was being either vastly expanded or displaced. One could interpret it either way. The latter view was held by the renowned political theorist Hannah Arendt. Looking back from the mid-twentieth century, with her eye largely but not exclusively fixed on the ideas of Karl Marx, she lamented the change. For her it meant the end of the pure politics of the classical republican tradition, categorically distinct from society, economy, and administration. As she saw it, the change marked the fall of political man, of a long-enduring definition of politics and citizenship. But from another point of view—for example, that of the British sociologist T. H. Marshall, writing at about the same time—it marked the welcome emergence of a social conception of citizenship that built on its political antecedents.[43] Either way, industrialism effectively brought an end to the practical utility of the republican tradition and of laissez-faire political economy. Any "pure" notions of *homo politikon* and *homo economicus* were challenged by the new social facts of industrialism and urbanism.

THE TWO REVOLUTIONS AND SOCIAL CITIZENSHIP

In 1887, Woodrow Wilson read a book titled *The Labor Movement in America* (1886), written by Richard Ely, his former teacher at Johns Hopkins. The book troubled him, and he took notes on it, which he saved but never turned into a published article. In the past, he noted, there was a "recognized difference between social and political questions," and, he continued, such a view was still affirmed by the "best thought" of the present. Yet, he mused, perhaps, as the socialists were saying, the economic and social circumstances of the time were so radically different that the state might have to engage the problems posed by the concentration of corporate power and growing inequality.[44]

Two years later at the Universal Exposition in Paris that marked the centennial of the French Revolution, a French exhibit on "social economy" suggested that the eighteenth-century political citizen might properly be succeeded by some form of social citizen. Visitors no doubt understood the exhibit to suggest that the Revolution remained "unfinished." Like Wilson, the organizers were not ready to move away from conventional thinking, but they were troubled, and they were thinking new thoughts.[45] Somehow the inherited political vocabulary was inadequate to the industrial transformations of the time. If 1776, like 1789, was a landmark in the history of political rights, the implications of Adam Smith's great book of that year seemed to require something more, some form of socioeconomic rights, a social citizenship.[46]

The social question that became so widely discussed throughout the Atlantic world was not an utterly novel one. At the end of the Napoleonic Wars, no European or American law regulated the conditions of labor for ordinary workers, yet, as Carroll Wright pointed out, "minute and incessant" regulations were made concerning contracts relating to property; soon thereafter, however, Jean-Charles-Léonard Simonde de Sismondi in France and Thomas Chalmers in Scotland raised the issue of social economy.[47] Though Wright did not mention him, so did Mike Walsh, a radical labor journalist in New York, who in 1843 explicitly linked the political legacy of the eighteenth century to the social challenges of the nineteenth: "No man can be a good political democrat without he's a good social democrat."[48] By the Progressive Era, Herbert Croly was making the same point—though in different language—about democracy, reform, and socialism in *The Promise of American Life*. Democracy, he argued, might be called "socialistic" if by that one considers "democracy inseparable from a candid, patient, and courageous attempt to advance the social problem towards a satisfactory solution."[49]

In the 1880s, when industrial capitalism showed its expansive force and labor-capital strife was regularly in the headlines, the economist John Bates Clark expressed his sympathy for the social rights of workers. Clark—a decade later a leader in the transatlantic "marginalist" revolution that created a core theory of modern neoclassical economics—

believed in the universality of economic theory (or the scientific laws of classical economics) and the efficacy of markets. Yet for him economics was a means to social ends. Social betterment was for him a continuation and fulfillment in some form of the eighteenth-century political revolutions as well as a completion of Ricardo's theory. In that spirit he deployed the oxymoronic phrase "economic republicanism."[50]

Over time Clark's language changed, but his commitment to the social dimensions of the economy remained. In 1914, he wrote a pamphlet making this point, *Social Justice Without Socialism*. Since political democracy did not alone elevate the condition of labor, a failure evident even before the Civil War, he argued that it was "necessary to carry democracy into a social sphere in order to improve the conditions of the poorer classes." Socialists might substitute public for private capital, but reformers aimed "to use the power of the state to correct and improve our system of industry." He made this idea axiomatic: "A democracy carried into industrial life is the dominating principle of every political body that can hope for success."[51]

An ambitious agenda of specifics followed these general statements. First, more democracy was required, and he endorsed progressive measures that aimed to achieve it: the ballot initiative, the referendum, direct primaries, and proportional representation. Like Woodrow Wilson, he favored competition and antitrust legislation as antimonopoly strategies, and he advocated tariff reform and supported the conservation movement. What would a reformed democracy and economy offer society, especially its vulnerable members? The list was long: shorter work hours without lower wages (relying on productivity increase through technology); laws restricting or prohibiting child labor; factory safety legislation; worker accident insurance; pure food and drug laws; money and banking reform; emergency public employment; high quality and accessible postal, telegraph, and telephone services; mass transit in cities; city planning and land-use regulation; improvement in the status of working women; better access to the courts, including some form of legal aid services; control of monopolies; and protection for small investors so that labor could "acquire a modest share of capital" and "invest it securely."[52]

Until social citizenship was understood as a concept and practice, the heart of liberal citizenship had been protection of the individual from hindrances that originated in state power. The expansion of private power, with the advent of the factory system and corporate capitalism, raised new questions about the individual's autonomy, rights, and security. Worry that they might be threatened in turn placed new demands on the state, prompting notions of a positive state that would reject the *cordon sanitaire* which, under a laissez-faire regime, had surrounded the individual. The state would be invited into society.[53] While one might see this as a surrender of eighteenth-century revolutionary principles to the novel claims of the industrial age, that would be a mistake, obscuring the importance of the earlier revolution in rights to the securing of—indeed the sustaining of the very aspiration for—the second. In fact, the transformation of liberalism in the late nineteenth century joined the two in many locally determined balances, producing many social liberalisms along a spectrum that combined respect for individual rights with support for positive state intervention on behalf of those rights and of society as a whole.

The legacy of the French and American revolutions, as Ira Katznelson has argued, was an affirmation of the potential for "all members of civil society" to become "actual or potential citizens." Of course, the eighteenth-century political elites who made those revolutions could not easily imagine a worker citizen. Certainly Jefferson, whom Alexis de Tocqueville considered the greatest eighteenth-century voice on behalf of democracy, could not. But a century later sheer numbers made such republican fastidiousness impossible. The needs, interests, and access to the vote that marked claimants to effective citizenship challenged the inherited notions both of citizenship and of the proper work of the state. The relationship between market and citizenship had to be reexamined and the tensions between them understood and resolved. Might the "political relations of citizens modify the operations of markets"? That was the question.[54]

As the suffrage (and the logic of suffrage) became more inclusive, nation-states were pressed—for reasons of maintaining social order as well as for considerations of justice—to bring politics and the state into the work of regulating markets. Why? In the interest of mitigating the social risks and inequities that unregulated markets had produced. Walter Weyl, writing just before World War I, witnessed and approved of the shift. The "inner soul of the new democracy," he explained, was no longer the protection of "unalienable rights, negatively and individualistically interpreted." Rather, the rights to "life, liberty, and the pursuit of happiness" were "extended and given a social interpretation."[55]

One wonders what Woodrow Wilson, still in 1901 a professor of politics at Princeton, might have thought of Ely's address to the American Economic Association at the economists' first meeting in the new century. (We do not even know whether he heard his former teacher's presentation or read it. This time no notes have survived.) The meeting was oriented to the challenges of the new century, and Ely engaged the topic of "industrial liberty" directly. Characteristically, he placed it in a historical context. He began with 1776 and the Declaration of Independence ("among the greatest and grandest documents in the world's history"), then moved to Adam Smith's secondary but still very important book *The Wealth of Nations*. He pointed out that in 1776, for both Jefferson and Smith, there was a "simplicity" to the "problem of liberty." Liberty was understood in its "negative" aspects, and it was conceived as a "unity, and not as a complex . . . bundle of rights." All that liberty required was to be released from constraints that government imposed. Liberty was thus a political challenge, not a social or economic one.

Ely explored the meaning of liberty in the work of various thinkers, most notably Herbert Spencer, John Stuart Mill, and Thomas H. Green. The last of these English philosophers, he pointed out, recognized that liberty involved positive capacities, often in common with others, not simply the individual's freedom from government constraint. And there were reasons, Ely argued, for this shift in liberty's meaning. The "economic ties uniting men in society were relatively few and simple in 1776," but they had multiplied in the industrial age. As a result, the threat to political liberty seemed less urgent than did the novel "restrictions on our positive liberty . . . due to the coercion of economic forces." Without doubting that Smith's and Jefferson's "philosophy of liberty" was an invaluable legacy, Ely pressed his fellow economists to recognize that Green's was "an expression of the philosophy of liberty with which the twentieth century begins." The two revolutions—political and industrial—were sequential, the second building upon the first, yet they also came into tension with each other. For example, the state prevents the employer from hiring "little children." This restricts his liberty, "but the liberty of the children is increased." That second liberty needed to be protected in new ways that used state power.

Ely was sure that neither anarchism (the unlimited extension of individual liberty) nor socialism, which radically extended positive liberty in the collective interest, could rise to the challenge of the new century. How were the negative rights enshrined in the eighteenth-century revolutions to be balanced against and related to the positive capacities required by the new century's interdependence and industrialism? For Ely the answer was clear. Positive liberty on behalf of the collective good must secure and supplement the negative liberty won in the eighteenth-century political revolutions. In the end, using the language of the apostle Paul, he concluded, "We are members of one another." For the sake of liberty and equality, he urged his audience, the twentieth century required "fraternity," which he affirmed as the most important of the revolutionary triad of 1789.[56]

Woodrow Wilson may not have heard or read Ely's paper, but when he delivered his inaugural address in 1912, this connection between the promise of equality and personal autonomy in 1776 and the issue of modern collective responsibility was very much on his mind. "There can be no equality of opportunity," he insisted, "if men and women and children are not shielded in their lives . . . from the consequence of great industrial and social processes which they cannot alter, control, or singly cope with."[57] A few years later Wilson's Argentine counterpart, President Hipólito Yrigoyen, sent a similar message to his Congress. The recent rapid industrialization of Argentina raised serious questions about its "social constitution." He warned his fellow Argentines that the promise of their country, to which so many immigrants were then flocking, "will be unobtainable until governments realize their inescapable duty to promote the means for justice to extend its benefits to every social rank." Echoing Ely and Wilson (and many other scholars and political leaders, including the Argentine *reformista* Alfredo L. Palacios, author of *El nuevo derecho*), he insisted that "democracy does not simply consist in the guarantee of personal liberty: it also involves the opportunity of everyone to enjoy a minimum level of welfare."[58] In Japan, Seki Hajime rejected the "production-vision" of economic development that Japan shared especially with Germany but to some degree with most other industrializing nations. He conceived of a "citizen-centered" economy that pointed toward social democracy or what he called a "people's national economy."[59]

In Italy, Giovanni Giolitti, five times prime minister between 1892 and 1921, sought a middle ground between reaction and revolution. He rejected the strategy of repression that had been deployed in the 1890s, arguing the necessity of "social pacification" and trying to define a new "social liberalism."[60] His third way included working with "parliamentary socialists" who supported liberal social reform as "a sensible short-term goal." What Giolitti offered was a vision of a modern capitalist state that was an "impartial" but active, not passive, "mediator of class relations."[61] At the same time in England, David Lloyd George, representing the radical wing of the Liberal Party, defended its "People's Budget" of 1909 in a similar way:

> I shall be little troubled at being called a socialist if I be given that title because I take measures to make the majority of the nation happy. As a matter of fact there is no way to check the swelling tide of the people's power, and my social policy is intended as a palliative, and may serve in the end the purpose of preventing a revolutionary movement. Therefore this policy is, on one side, in accordance with the interests of capitalists.

Most of the international leaders of the new liberalism would concur, including Franklin D. Roosevelt, a generation later. In fact, a Japanese liberal party leader, Katō Takaaki, who was Japanese ambassador in London in 1909, specifically singled out Lloyd George's speech in pressing a reform agenda in Japan.[62]

PATHS AWAY FROM LAISSEZ-FAIRE

The most widely discussed path away from laissez-faire was associated with the German historical economists who organized the Verein für Sozialpolitik (Association for Social Policy), founded in 1872 as a platform from which to project academic knowledge into public discussion and to influence policy. Though founded by scholars, its membership was broad, including civil servants, journalists, and even a few industrialists. It was an opportune moment. Germany's quick and decisive victory in the Franco-Prussian War in 1871 and the subsequent unification of the nation under Chancellor Otto von Bismarck's leadership created a strong state, and this group hoped to affect its development. In this moment of high nationalism the reforming economists looked to challenge the laissez-faire economics identified with Great Britain, a rival on the world stage where Germany wanted a prominent place. The Manchester school's claim that there were absolute and universal laws of economics was the focus of their criticism.[63] These laws, treating the economy as autonomous and thus self-justified, were largely deductive, abstract, and formal, with scant empirical foundation. The German historical economists insisted that such theories had to be submitted to the empirical test of history. The depression of 1873 strengthened their critique and gave their new organization a hearing.

Though sometimes called *Kathedersozialisten*, or "socialists of the chair," these men were not socialists. While they recognized competing class interests, they were ameliorators who believed in neither class struggle nor revolution. Still, the social question was at the center of their concerns, and they insisted that social policy was a legitimate and necessary activity of the modern state. In the founding call for the Verein für Sozialpolitik they explained: "We are convinced that the unchecked reign of partially antagonistic and unequal individual interests cannot guarantee the common welfare." Many among them even appreciated the conservative welfare state promoted by Bismarck's government. Their message was that industrial capitalism brought in its wake radically new conditions and social needs requiring state action that laissez-faire doctrines did not recognize. Addressing these problems, they proposed, was one of the "highest tasks of our time and nation."[64]

Within the frame of these fairly general statements, there was a great deal of diversity among the economists advocating reform, ranging from liberals (Lujo Brentano) to conservatives (Adolph Wagner), but the central figure both in Germany and for many of the foreign students who flocked to the German universities was perhaps Gustav von Schmoller, as both the American Richard Ely and the Japanese Seki Hajime thought. In Latin America, too, Schmoller's name showed up on syllabi.[65]

Schmoller's legendary speech at the founding of the Verein für Sozialpolitik in 1872—insisting that state intervention in the economy for social good was of fundamental importance in the industrial age— echoed far and wide. American and other foreign students did not have to study directly with Schmoller to feel his influence. Richard Ely, for example, studied with Karl Knies, while the most radical American historical economists—Edmund J. James and Simon Patten—studied with Johannes Conrad at Halle. It was Conrad who most pressed the Americans to establish an organization along the lines of the Verein für Sozialpolitik, a suggestion to which they responded positively.[66] In fact, the Americans had an almost worshipful regard for their German mentors as the very models of intellectual integrity and responsibility. Consequently, when several of their teachers, including Schmoller, Conrad, and even the liberal Brentano, later signed a public letter justifying the German invasion of Belgium in the opening days of the war in 1914, the Americans felt betrayed.[67]

The specific interventions that Schmoller and his colleagues in the Verein für Sozialpolitik as well as their students in Germany and abroad supported as legitimate included regulation of hours of labor, especially for women and children; factory safety regulations; accident, sickness, and old-age insurance; and legalization of trade unions. Some went farther, advocating tax reform, including income taxes; city planning and public housing; and municipal socialism, which entailed the municipalization of primary social services.

Their research method was as important as the various policies they advocated. Rejecting the deductive method of Ricardo and abstract laws of economics characteristic of the Manchester school, they insisted on considering historical practice in particular times and places. One might say theirs was a pragmatic method, suspicious of universal and absolute theories or laws. They asked a question that presumed historical contingency: In this time and place, marked by complex social interdependencies in city life, by industrial labor, and by substantial inequalities between worker and employer, is some kind of state intervention for the collective good warranted?[68] This shifted the debate from one over abstract moral absolutes to historical facts, with all the contingency and variability this implied. Empirical investigations of actual conditions were used to justify intervention on a case-by-case basis. The British economist L. T. Hobhouse (a critic of Manchester liberalism) arrived at the same understanding: "The social ideal is not to be reached in logical processes alone, but must stand in close relation to human experience."[69]

Edmund James and Simon Patten initiated the American movement for an equivalent of the Verein für Sozialpolitik. They had in mind an organization with a strong program and commitments to specific policies. Ely, who was sympathetic, worried nonetheless that their approach might have only limited appeal to most American economists. E.R.A. Seligman, a Columbia economist and scion of a leading German-Jewish banking family in New York, was skeptical, but, more important, he was firmly committed to an inclusive organization that, being comprehensive, would become influential. He used his considerable diplomatic skills to move the plans in this direction, with the result that the American Economic Association was designed "to attract as many members as possible."[70]

Instead of being organized around a program or "creed," as was the Society for the Study of National Economy proposed by James and Patten, the American Economic Association stressed research.[71] It still had as a central principle that intervention in the economy to achieve social goods was an appropriate and necessary activity of the state. This was less than James and Patten had hoped for, but it was substantial and in line with the work and objectives of the Verein für Sozialpolitik. James and Patten were realists who accepted Seligman's strategy and supported the AEA. But they advanced their more radical program at the newly established Wharton School at the University of Pennsylvania, then a center for the critical study of American business.

The AEA stressed two main points: "the encouragement of economic research" and "the encouragement of perfect freedom in all economic discussion." The committee of five who developed its "platform" included not only the economists Henry C. Adams, Alexander Johnson, John Bates Clark, and Ely but also the Social Gospel minister Washington Gladden, and they emphasized the social concerns of the economists, some of whom, including Ely, were closely associated with the Social Gospel movement.[72] The first of its four statements began, "We regard the state as an education and ethical agency whose positive aid is an indispensable condition of human progress," and continued: "The doctrine of laissez faire is unsafe in politics and unsound in morals; and . . . it suggests an inadequate explanation of the relations between the state and citizens." The other three statements rejected claims to absolute truth of the deductive economics of the "past generation" and insisted on "an impartial study of actual conditions of economic life," a study that would rely on statistics and history. They explicitly declined "to take a partisan attitude" toward the then inflammatory political issue of tariffs. They also declared that the "vast number of social problems" would be resolved only through the "united efforts of church, state and science." They ended by saying that they believed in "a progressive development of economic conditions which must be met by corresponding changes of policy."[73]

The site chosen for the AEA's organizing meeting suggests the permeability of boundaries between academic disciplines at the time and the centrality of history. Because "nearly all economists belonged" to the American Historical Association, they met at the AHA's second annual meeting in 1885 at Saratoga, New York.[74] Andrew Dickson White, a leading historian and founding president of Cornell University, was pleased, and assured Ely that he agreed "entirely that the laissez faire theory is entirely inadequate to the needs of modern states." He also endorsed the moderate plan of emphasizing research over deductive theories and ideology: "I agree, too, entirely, with the idea that we must not look so much to speculation, as to an impartial study of the actual conditions of economic life, etc."[75]

The "past generation" of economists mentioned in the AEA's statement of principles was not entirely past, and men of it were highly critical of this new historical school of economists. But note should also be taken of two leading critics of laissez-faire economists from an in-between generation, a generation that had not had European training in the new social sciences. Francis A. Walker and Carroll Wright were brilliant collectors and analysts of social statistics. Wright, a pioneer in the field of labor statistics, was the first commissioner of labor statistics in Massachusetts and, as we have seen, of the United States; he later served as U.S. commissioner of labor. Walker was the director of the 1870 and 1880 U.S. censuses, and he became president of the Massachusetts Institute of Technology. Both believed that trade unions were a necessary part of industrial society (Walker as early as 1876), but they thought more was required. They called for regulation of work conditions, arguing that without state intervention workers would still be at the mercy of employers.[76]

E. L. Godkin, the founding editor of *The Nation*, and William Graham Sumner, an old-style political economist teaching at Yale, were the leading critics of this position and of the historical-school economists. Both were not only notably intelligent and learned but also highly skilled polemicists. Their basic argument was that economics was a "science" and social policy was not. The idea of a social economy is "a political or social measure," Godkin argued, "not an economic one." It was not, he asserted, "a conclusion of economic science." Sumner could not have agreed more. A shift from economic science to social policy, he declared, amounted to moving from a science of the possible to one of the impossible.[77]

To their credit Godkin and Sumner were consistent. They also thought the state ought not assist capital in the marketplace any more than it did labor. Both, therefore, damned tariffs and other schemes that manufacturers favored to enlist government assistance. It was a profound distrust of democratic politics that made them so absolute in their defense of economic science. Godkin worried that the historical school had "extravagant expectations about the powers of the state"; he professed himself "lost in amazement" that the "young lions of the historical school" could imagine that such a "glorious future" would follow state intervention when one considered that in New York government meant, largely, Tammany Hall, the corrupt Democratic Party machine, and the Albany legislature it dominated.[78] Sumner, who had been on the special commission that decided the contested election of 1876, was equally sensitive to political corruption. For him, the defect of democracy in Gilded Age America "compels all sober men to insist upon laissez faire as an absolute principle of safety."[79] Neither man changed his position on laissez-faire, though Godkin came to accept mass democracy (at least its inevitability). And Sumner's great anthropological work *Folkways* (1907) indirectly made a good case against the individualism that lay behind laissez-faire doctrines.

Tokutomi Sohō, a Japanese journalist and admirer of Godkin, played a similar but less consistent role in Japan. He founded Japan's first modern political magazine (*Kokumin no tomo*), explicitly modeled on Godkin's *Nation*. In the 1880s, also like Godkin, he was a good British liberal. In the 1890s, however, he left that old liberal camp, having concluded that modern industrial life required more state interventionist and collectivist practices. He saw this not as an emulation of the West (as perhaps his earlier position had been), but rather as a recognition of a modern global condition—that of industrialization and urbanization. By the turn of the century he differed from Godkin in another important way: while Godkin was a leading anti-imperialist, Tokutomi's advocacy of social politics was attached to his support of Japan's imperialistic ambitions, much as was the case for many scholars and journalists in Bismarck's Germany.[80] (Social reform and imperialism were often linked, as in the cases of Joseph Chamberlain in Britain and Theodore Roosevelt in the United States.)

Generally, however, nineteenth-century liberals became twentieth-century liberals by moving to the variously characterized new liberalisms. Tokutomi's route to social politics was not typical, though neither was it unique. For some, particular national circumstances seemed, as we shall see, to have paved a path from laissez-faire through the new liberalism to various forms of illiberal or authoritarian politics.

Resistance to social politics tended to come from conservatives, often landed ones, as in Latin America, or from corporate conservatives, as was clearest in the United States and Japan. (Japanese conservatives were emboldened by the example of their corporate counterparts in the United States, whose antilabor behavior and rhetoric they observed quite closely.[81]) But not all conservatives resisted social politics. Some, most notably Bismarck, embraced state responsibility for the social protection of workers (though he combined this with a brutal suppression of his political opposition: the Social Democratic Party). His aim was social stability, and his plan was to beat the socialists at their own game, so to speak. Bismarck's fairly liberal commerce minister accepted this logic, writing soon after the unification of Germany in 1872 that "state power as it exists today appears to be the only means of halting the socialist movement in its path of error; to steer it in a more beneficial direction it is necessary to acknowledge that which is justified in the socialist demands and can be realized in the framework of the state and social order."[82] The liberal Lujo Brentano, though highly critical, discerned an even subtler strategy in Bismarck's embrace of social insurance. "It is simple to summarize" Bismarck's aim, he observed in 1881: "Every individual will be inexorably caught up in the life and development of the state."[83] For similar reasons Bismarck challenged the Catholic Church's control over schools, marriages, and ecclesiastical appointments in Germany in the *Kulturkampf* (1871–87), attacking the ultramontane influence of the Vatican.

In the past historians have drawn a sharp dividing line between socialists and liberals. More recent accounts, whether in the United States or elsewhere, see a good deal of border crossing and even collaboration. What Eduardo Zimmermann says of the "liberal reformistas" in Argentina holds for the United States and other places: they accepted the socialist description of the consequences of industrialization for the working classes and were drawn to socialism's ethical commitments, but they resisted the ideology of revolution and state ownership.[84] Fear of the socialist movement and revolution motivated them as much as the ideal of socialist ethics. The same balancing—so characteristic of progressivism in the United States—was evident in Japan. Reform economists in the Shakai Seisaku Gakkai (Association for Social Policy), founded by Tokyo University professors in 1896 (again modeled on the Verein für Sozialpolitik), declared their opposition to laissez-faire because "it creates extreme profit consciousness and unbridled competition, and aggravates the differences between rich and poor." That said, they also opposed "socialism because it would destroy the present economic organization, obliterate capitalists, and therefore impede national progress."[85]

Social liberals wanted a politics that embraced the humanistic aspirations of socialism or, better, socialisms—not only Marxian socialism but the many other movements from social Christianity to cooperatives to communitarianism. For Sun Yat-sen, leader of the republican movement in China, the best ideals of socialism were associated not so much with Marx as with the collectivist vision in Edward Bellamy's novel *Looking Backward* (1888), Henry George's land-reform ideas, including the "Single Tax," and Richard Ely's Christian Socialist reformism. Writing in the *People's Journal*, Sun Yat-sen argued that Chinese socialism must think "of a way to reform social and economic organization [so as to] forestall a social revolution at a later time. This is our greatest responsibility."[86] Writing about the Mexican Revolution—which was after all contemporary with the American Progressive Era—the American sociologist Edward A. Ross commented that for the revolutionary leaders "socialism" was a broad term that translated into support for improved conditions for workers, with most socialists supporting "constructive legislation."[87] That was not atypical. Perhaps Walter Weyl caught the spirit of social liberalism best with his phrase "conditional socialism," which he embraced and contrasted with "absolute socialism."[88]

Before the onset of what might be called the first Cold War, after the triumph of the Bolshevik Revolution in 1917, the line dividing "new" or "social" liberals from socialists was not clear.[89] In the United States and elsewhere the "open border" between them was exceedingly difficult to define, but it allowed cooperation.[90] Even anarchists had their pragmatic side, and often worked with liberals on behalf of various forms of worker protection. Pragmatic anarchism was evident in several Latin American nations—Mexico, Brazil, Argentina, and especially Chile, which had weaker ties with the European anarchist movement.[91] I would not call this pattern an actual collaboration; it was less formal, and better described as a confluence, an acceptance of an informal practice of "pragmatic pluralism."[92]

The international development of social liberalism and the idea of social citizenship in the years before World War I merged, confused, and sometimes obliterated inherited political and ideological categories.[93] Even more striking, then, was the postwar sharpening of these categories, which became more rigid and firmly bounded. The reason for this change was mainly the transformation of Russia because of the Bolshevik Revolution of 1917. The actual existence of a socialist state in the territories of what became the Soviet Union transformed vague, inclusive commitments to the ideals of socialism into concrete policies that seemed to demand either support or rejection. What was imaginary and thus accommodating became specific and controversial. Commitments were invited and often demanded—of socialists and liberals, in the United States especially, where Wilson and other progressives promoted the new liberalism as an American alternative to the Soviet utopia.[94] The same erosion of the middle and obstacles to collaboration were strongly marked in Japan. The Association for Social Policy stopped meeting in 1924, riven by unbridgeable differences in an increasingly divided political culture.[95]

At the same time, religion was a larger influence in the international response to the crises of modern industrialism than is usually recognized—not only the Social Gospel strains in American progressivism, but the policies of the Roman Catholic Church. Pope Leo XIII's encyclical *Rerum novarum* (1891) commanded recognition in its time and warrants attention from historians. It was not a radical document: its aim was to combat socialism, but it was also suspicious of liberal individualism, as was Bishop Wilhelm E. Ketteler of Mainz, for example, who opposed the "limitless" freedom of the market, which he thought produced a society marked by an amoral Darwinian struggle for "survival of the fittest."[96] Social Catholicism and *Rerum novarum* were paternalist in spirit, favoring social hierarchy and rejecting individualism, often characterizing it as an ethic of selfishness. But if this position justified rule from the top, it accepted that established authority had obligations, including improvement in the wages and welfare of workers. Though Bismarck and the Vatican were often at odds, they shared a conservative appreciation of the need for those with power to incorporate the powerless.

To the American reformer Monsignor John A. Ryan, the pope's position justified "all reasonable measures of protective legislation," including protection for child and female labor, reduced hours, minimum wages, and insurance against sickness, old age, and unemployment. *Rerum novarum* did not advocate specific policies, but at a philosophical level it was quite clear and pointed: "Whenever the general interest, or any particular class, suffers or is threatened with injury which can in no other way be met or prevented, it is the duty of the public authority to intervene."[97] For Catholic elites, even conservatives, particularly in Latin America, this encyclical transformed the "social question" into an ethical one demanding resolution. And it gave great encouragement to working-class Catholic leaders in the United States as well as in Catholic nations.

Not only were social scientists in American Catholic colleges and universities inspired by *Rerum novarum*, but several of them studied, like their Protestant counterparts, in Germany, taking courses from Schmoller and Wagner.[98] During the Progressive Era and into the 1930s Ryan was the most important and influential Catholic social scientist and activist. He elaborated on the social implications of the logic of the Catholic philosophy of natural law and paternalist responsibility. For him and for his Catholic colleagues, economics was an ethical practice: "Economic inquiry is intended to serve solely as a basis for ethical conclusions." It was probably not surprising that Ryan taught moral theology as well as economics at the Catholic University of America.[99] He wanted to strike a balance between private property and social justice in his teaching, and in his books, *A Living Wage: Its Ethical and Economic Aspects* (1906) and *Distributive Justice: The Right and Wrong of Our Present Distribution of Wealth* (1916).

The Vatican's social teachings inspired social scientists in Catholic countries to examine anew the social problems emerging from industrial capitalism. For example, at the turn of the century legal and social-science dissertations on various social issues at the University of Chile were prompted by and written within the frame of Leo's encyclical. Juan

Enrique Concha, who was one of the dissertation writers, later helped to compose Chile's first comprehensive labor bill, passed in 1919 by a conservative government whose leadership was also influenced by the encyclical.[100]

Protestant contributions to social liberalism in Catholic nations have been almost completely overlooked, most notably in France. But Protestant social reformers there had close ties not only with American Social Gospel leaders but also with Jane Addams of Chicago's Hull-House, other American settlement houses, and the YMCA, as well as with Toynbee Hall, the first settlement house in Britain, located in the slums of London's East End.[101] They were important in helping to create the Musée Social in Paris in 1894 and in developing the idea of a social economy there. (The career of Max Lazard, of the Lazard Frères banking family, who had similar transatlantic reform connections, underlines the Jewish social liberalism that paralleled that of the Protestants in this network.)[102] The Musée Social, as we shall see, was enormously influential as a national and international headquarters for reform. Its reports were central to the development of social liberalism in France and focal points for international discussion and research.[103]

The religious impulses behind this social liberalism in France and elsewhere in Europe depended for their expression on voluntary associations, which are often celebrated as uniquely American. But France and the United States were surprisingly similar in this respect at the turn of the century. And in Italy a minimalist program of state intervention was supplemented by substantial private charitable programs. These were not up to the task of addressing the entirety of the "social question," however, and the challenge for new liberals was to find a workable combination of charity and state provision.[104] In all three cases nongovernmental social-service agencies gave a variety of supports to vulnerable members of the working classes and in turn received program-related support from the state for their provision of these services. American charities that became social-service organizations as the nineteenth turned into the twentieth century, similarly, were incorporated or licensed by the state and also often received state funds.

In the 1890s, France's Third Republic stressed solidarism, which was something like a "cooperative republic." The ideas of the philosopher Alfred Fouillée, who combined Rousseau's idea of the social contract with the social organicism of Herbert Spencer to argue for a notion of interdependence, influenced Prime Minister Léon Bourgeois. Bourgeois's book *Solidarité* (1896) proposed collective solutions to the social question.[105] Without a republican feeling of "moral duty of solidarity," he argued, the "glorious" French Revolution "will not be fully realized."[106] Various forms of mutual-aid societies were encouraged, many of them organized by workers and even given state funding.[107] Jeanne Weill, one of the planners of the Musée Social, established the École des Hautes Études Sociales in 1901, infused with the philosophy of "solidarity." Weill (who went by the pen name Dick May) envisioned an institution dedicated to applied sociology, in which professors could and would articulate the policy implications of their social research.[108]

In the United States similar aspirations were apparent. As Jane Addams remarked in 1907, the sense of worker "brotherhood" and of growing collective responsibility was part of a "sweep of world-wide moral impulse" that encouraged "associated effort."[109] And some of the founders of the New School for Social Research in New York in 1919, most notably Herbert Croly, had hoped that like its counterpart in Paris, it would advance a liberal social agenda.[110] While Americans like to stress the distinctiveness of their voluntarist tradition, we can see that at the turn of the century voluntarism's relation to the state was being examined and tested in many nations in Europe. French labor unions had already shown in the 1880s that they were wary of the state, preferring to use their associated power rather than relying on the state to protect workers, which might weaken the relation of workers to the unions.[111] The American Federation of Labor, an organization of craft unions founded in 1886, operated on the same principle under the leadership of Samuel Gompers, the immigrant cigar maker who was its president and the acknowledged spokesman for American labor until his death in 1924.

In France and Latin America these influences of the Vatican, of international voluntarist groups, and of labor unions were felt in an intellectual context set by the powerful cluster of ideas called positivism. Positivism had developed in France under the influence of Auguste Comte's "positive philosophy." Comte's *Cours de philosophie positive* (1830–42), written in the spirit of the Enlightenment, was committed to empiricism and to the evidence of experience. Moreover, like the *philosophes* of the French Enlightenment, he wanted to bring all knowledge together in one system, producing a unified social and natural science. He sought to found a discipline of social physics, a positive science of society that would enable humans to manage the development of their society. Positivism did not specifically address politics or the state; rather, it concerned itself with the whole of social life and its improvement.

The specific contribution of positivism to the international movement away from laissez-faire and toward the idea of a social economy derives from its rejection of the autonomous individual. It directed attention to the social organism and to theories construing the individual as a part of and shaped by history and society. The hope was for a self-conscious social reconstruction done scientifically. The method of positivism, like that of the German historical economists, eschewed abstract theories and laws. Grounded on facts, it relied on "observation, patient investigation, and experience."

Positivism did not cross the English Channel, though it did cross the Atlantic. The English radical Harriet Martineau translated Comte's great work into English, but, save for its empiricism, which owed much to David Hume in any case, it did not have a great impact in Britain. There was, however, a small but significant Comtean circle in the United States that included Herbert Croly's father, David Croly, and to some degree positivism influenced Lester Frank Ward, Edward Ross, and Herbert Croly himself.[112] But the major impact of positivism was in Latin America. The educational systems there—and in Mexico especially—became infused with the spirit of positivism, and it replaced the idealist humanist notions of what education should be. Though there was a tendency toward technocratic or authoritarian management that compromised classic liberal principles, many positivist reformers in Latin America considered themselves new liberals, committed to equality under the law, constitutionalism, private property, and civil freedoms. Their positivism framed the thinking of Latin American scholars and the educated elite in general, and it directed them away from the old laissez-faire economy to the ideals of a social economy.[113]

PROFESSIONAL RISK AND THE MORAL IMAGINATION

In societies as distant and different as France and Japan, the 1880s saw a revolution in the moral imagination that pointed toward what might be called a recognition of *objective* social rights and obligations. The risks and misfortunes that made the working classes vulnerable and insecure in everyday life were understood in a new, modern way—as "professional risks." People detached these risks from the old-fashioned moralism that assigned individual responsibility and blame. Industrial accidents were thought of not as moral failures or carelessness, but rather as a condition of modernity that should be addressed in an objective way that acknowledged the rights of victims. From nation to nation the local, particular formulations differed, but a new understanding of responsibility emerged that shifted the focus from the individual to the collective, with a crucial—though not judgmental—role for the state. And it effectively created a right to security for industrial workers. For example, the many and wide discussions in Japan of the "social question" were striking for the degree to which poverty was seen less as a "consequence of individual moral deficiency" than as the product of modern conditions, and the poor "as victims of impersonal structural forces in modern economies."

Yet it was not the poor who first benefited from this new understanding, for it had been nursed into being by the recent decline of the ancient samurai class. The first acknowledgment in public policy of a social cause for misfortune came in response to the samurai's loss of power and privilege as a consequence of the Meiji Restoration in 1867, which moved Japanese political and economic institutions out of the feudal past toward modernity. The samurai, the traditional military aristocracy, lost their property and their livelihoods. Their decline—and the threat of their resistance to change—was recognized to be the product of social and political change, not the result of personal qualities. Accepting that the individual hardship of the class had a social cause, the government, beginning in 1871, pursued a samurai rehabilitation policy that was intended to give them new opportunities, enabling them to contribute to the modernization of Japan's economy.

However unexpected and unusual the occasion, this shift in thinking about misfortune and responsibility had general ramifications. In 1885, Ueki Emori wrote that "the poor are not selected by heaven [that is, not for sin]; they tumble into that state as a result of social conditions." This reorganization of the moral imagination worked in favor of reformers, and it was pressed by the Japanese scholars and bureaucrats of the Japanese Association for Social Policy.[114]

In France and Belgium, the "social question" was seen differently, but the answers were not dissimilar. There was an early, perhaps counterintuitive awareness that modernity brought more rather than less physical insecurity, especially in cities, but above all in the workplace, particularly in factories. And a new moral understanding arose about workplace risks, for which the modern science of statistics was the midwife. Industrial accidents were statistically predictable: social scientists had studied the number of accidents at the same factory over time, with different personnel, and discovered that changing the workers did not affect the rate of accidents. Individual carelessness was ruled out; the accidents were not the fault of any individual actor.[115]

Whatever the methodological merits of such research, it encouraged the idea that industrial accidents were a modern phenomenon, not the result of individual carelessness, nor blameworthy. They were an objective problem to which the old notions of individual responsibility and morality were irrelevant. This new objective understanding was the basis of the French Workers' Compensation Law, enacted in 1898. While the employer was expected to bear the cost of the compensation, that did not mean that he was blameworthy. He paid the cost because statistical analysis showed that an industrial organization, even when run properly, would produce industrial accidents. That was an objective, statistical fact, not a moral one.[116] The worker was compensated not out of charity or on the basis of litigation, but rather on the grounds of an implied, state-backed contract that acknowledged professional risk and established his right to benefits.

Workers had already devised a method to deal with the risk of modern industrial society: insurance organized by their mutual-aid societies. Insurance socializes risk; the larger the pool of insured, the more secure the insurance. Gradually the government itself—in France and elsewhere—assumed responsibility for insuring against risk, and state-sponsored insurance minimized not only risk but in a certain way inequality. Every person in the category of worker would be eligible, without any individual inquiry, for protection against risk. So the conflict between capital and labor in the laissez-faire economy shifted from one of blame, responsibility, and litigation to one that was resolved by an objective social practice lifting from both sides the burden of guilt and the need to find fault.[117]

One can argue that the logic of this insurance recognized social inter-

dependence and was thus a de facto model for social solidarity. In fact, the
French socialist leader Jean Jaurès made just this point in the Chamber of
Deputies in 1905.[118] At about the same time, Léon Bourgeois proclaimed:

> The organization of *assurance solidaire* of all citizens against the en-
> semble of risks of everyday life—sickness, accidents, unemploy-
> ment, old age—appears now, at the beginning of the twentieth
> century—the necessary condition for peaceful development of any
> society, indeed the necessary realization of social duties.[119]

In short, then, the emergent social welfare state was really a social insurance state. In the first two decades of the twentieth century, as this
pattern spread around the world, the technical management of "professional risk" gradually replaced the older "social question," particularly
the ideological response to it that blamed workers' carelessness and irresponsibility for their misfortunes.[120]

The United States, however, was slow to move national policy in this
direction. It was not until the passage of the Social Security Act in 1935
that the United States accepted the idea of social insurance, and state-
sponsored medical insurance is still not an accepted idea in the United
States, uniquely among industrialized nations. The American government was also late in putting the authority of the state behind the right
of workers to organize labor unions, which was part of nineteenth-century
solidarity policy in most industrialized countries. The right to unionize
was not recognized and protected by the national government until the
passage of the National Labor Relations Act, or Wagner Act, in 1935.
Many of the most important New Deal social policies were, in effect,
forms of insurance against the risks of modern society—from old-age
pensions, to mortgage insurance, to the insurance of savings accounts, to
unemployment insurance—that had been in place elsewhere for decades.

The language of professional risk was much less evident in the United
States than elsewhere. When American reformers recognized the importance of social and environmental causes of individual misfortune, their
focus was on the home and domestic life rather than on the workplace
and industrial labor. The most famous example of this approach is provided by Jacob Riis and his remarkable book of photographs *How the
Other Half Lives* (1890), which prompted important environmental re-

form in American cities, notably the creation of parks and playgrounds and the enactment of effective regulation of housing conditions of the poor that would ameliorate the unhealthy, even dangerous circumstances of their lives. These reforms intervened in the marketplace but fell short of positive state action. They prohibited certain practices (as in the famous New York Tenement House Law of 1901), but did not require that landlords provide adequate environmental conditions and did not furnish public funds for that end. Once again, the United States adopted a positive housing policy much later than other industrial nations, only with the Wagner Housing Act of 1937.

Was this lag merely a matter of timing, however consequential, or does it suggest that Americans had a different way of thinking about the issues? Is it enough to say simply that Americans were slow to develop and act on the new moral imagination that recognized the link between modernity and risk, that made industrial circumstances an objective condition to be remedied, not an opportunity to debate blameworthiness? The relative absence of the language of professional risk in American discussions of the social question and the American tendency to focus on the domestic environment rather than on the workplace are two symptoms that suggest the answer.

Except for instances where the home was also the workplace, Riis took no notice of industrial conditions. But when Upton Sinclair wrote his novel *The Jungle* (1906), an early exposé of the working conditions of the meatpacking industry in Chicago, his intention was to show the objective dangers of industrial work and the insecurity of city life. His title asserted that urban industrial society offered no more security for the worker than life in the jungle. Sinclair's novel is noteworthy more for its sentiment than for its literary quality, but it paints a powerful portrait of the industrial workplace and its risks. Yet readers, let alone the U.S. government, seem not to have registered these hundreds of pages. Instead, they responded with alacrity to the few pages in the book devoted to contamination of food. Instead of the industrial legislation for which Sinclair was an advocate, the result was the passage of a consumer-protection law, the Pure Food and Drug Act (1906). It was and remains an important law, but it also marks a failure to acknowledge the larger social question surrounding industrial capitalism at the time.

The focus on consumption moved that larger question into the domain of consumer protection and domestic risk. This American way of thinking made the working-class and middle-class home, not the factory, the focus, even the issue itself. In 1900 the home was the domain of women, and by the conventions of the time that made it the terrain of morality, where the language of morality prevailed.[121] Such a framing exaggerated the importance of "traditional family values" and the traditional gender roles of the time in resolving the social problems and insecurities of modern industrial life. The effect was that the market was regulated— but only in domains relating to domesticity and women's work in securing their families' domestic safety. It made for what some have called a maternal bias in forming American welfare, but it also hindered the capacity of Americans to imagine the larger ethical implications of the new social world.[122] That, I suspect, is why the United States lagged. Other nations earlier and more fully understood and responded to modern industrial conditions—and their risks—with laws securing protection against those risks.

Americans, then, had different notions—guided, as we have seen, by gender considerations—of the domains the market served well and those it did not, where there were rights that went beyond the market. Business was allowed full play in the factory, but the market was highly regulated when it touched the home. These distinctions were quite firm, and because of them the United States relied on a charitable idea about protecting the vulnerable in industrial society rather than acknowledging general rights to protection and security. The crisis of the Great Depression forced a rethinking of these moral assumptions about home, work, and the insecurities of industrial society, however, and the U.S. government engaged in a wider consideration of workers' rights, the value of state intervention in the workplace, and the importance of social insurance. Still, when the state accepted responsibility for the security of workers, policy continued to be compromised by gender assumptions and racial distinction.[123] The United States, considered by outsiders and by itself as peculiarly modern, was trapped here in older assumptions about morality and blameworthiness, and slower to grasp the objectivity of social rights.

THE REFORM INTERNATIONAL AND
THE WORLD WIDE WEB

In his autobiography, *Myself*, John R. Commons, a leading progressive labor reformer, recalled taking on the challenge of drafting the Industrial Commission Law for Wisconsin in 1910. He was at the time a professor at the University of Wisconsin, and the first thing he did to prepare himself was to hire fifty undergraduates who together spoke an array of languages to search out labor legislation from all over the world. He then mounted "large sheets" in his seminar room with "the labor laws of all countries."[124] His behavior confirms the two points already noted: that scholars were deeply involved in the reconstruction of liberalism, and that it was understood as a challenge of global scope. Commissioning a multilingual company of students was one way to internationalize reform agendas and move information around the globe. There were many others—some institutionalized, others informal.

Examining communications among reformers—whether academics or bureaucrats, elected officials or philanthropists—sustains the notion of a "reforming international."[125] After closely studying the archives of the city of Lyon, a French historian of urban reform, Pierre-Yves Saunier, became convinced that the network of urbanists and reformers was sufficiently dense to be considered an international movement. The files of the mayor's office and those of various urban agencies in Lyon revealed a virtually global pattern of correspondence, in which the writers shared social-science findings and identified model policies of the emerging social liberalism. The correspondence files of the mayors of New York show similar evidence of international communication and consultation.[126] The volume of information in circulation was immense. (It was, as one might expect, uneven in distribution. At least one commentator, a British authority on European industrial reform, Arthur Shadwell, believed that the United States and Germany seemed to have more information than other nations, surely more, he thought, than Britain.)[127]

Much of this sharing of knowledge was admittedly "haphazard and fortuitous," the result of travel, of study tours and junkets, of accidental contacts at innumerable conferences on industrial and urban issues.[128] But it also included highly focused inquiries, often by the growing numbers of state bureaucrats and, especially, by social-scientific doctoral theses. At every modern research university in Europe, the Americas, and Japan, seeming armies of graduate students were examining social issues in research projects framed by international bibliographies.

Legislatures and government agencies also developed the equivalent of international bibliographies. The report of the Tenement House Committee of the New York State Legislature in 1894, for example, included summaries of housing policies in different nations and compared density, health indicators, and rents for New York City and big cities around the world—not only in western Europe but also in India, Japan, Russia, and the Austro-Hungarian Empire.[129] The National Conference on Industrial Conciliation cast its survey nearly as wide for its investigation of labor-management issues in 1902, including data from England, Canada, France, Germany, Belgium, Italy, and Turkey.[130] After World War I the Argentine National Labor Department compiled information on policies concerning labor and management in the new Soviet Union, Italy, New Zealand, Australia, Germany, Norway, Sweden, Belgium, England, France, Japan, the United States, Canada, Mexico, Chile, Bolivia, and Guatemala.[131] Edward Ross, who visited Argentina in 1914, noticed that "anything that worked well in advanced countries now obtains an attentive hearing in Argentina."[132] And we have seen that when Charles Beard went to Japan in 1922, he found that reformers and urban experts there all read the same studies and knew the same policy initiatives as his colleagues back in New York's Bureau of Municipal Research. Viscount Gotō, mayor of Tokyo, who had invited Beard (he became home minister in 1923), was "more deeply interested in important municipal events in New York City than any American mayor west of the Alleghenies."[133] Similarly, Seki Hajime, both as a university professor in Tokyo and later as mayor of Osaka, closely watched housing developments in Europe, following legislation, such as the British Town Planning Act of 1909, and attending conferences, including the International Planning Conference in Brussels in 1913. His correspondents included most of the major urban reformers in the world: Patrick Geddes, Peter Kropotkin, William Bennett Munro, John Nolen, A. C. Pigou, B. Seebohm Rowntree, Lawrence Veiller, and Raymond Unwin.[134] Like John Commons in the United States, José Aguirre, Alejandro Unsain, Cosme Sánchez Antelo, and Joaquín V. González—social scientists at the University of Buenos Aires who were deeply involved in industrial reform—were eager to be abreast of international thinking and policies. They traveled, went to conferences, and read the work of reformers in Belgium, Denmark, Spain, France, Germany, Great Britain, Hungary, Holland, Luxembourg, Portugal, Italy, Switzerland, New Zealand, and Australia.[135] Mexico's constitution of 1917 provided, in its Article 123, the strongest commitment to the rights and protection of workers anywhere in the Americas at the time, and established an important claim to social citizenship in Mexico.[136] It was self-consciously representative of international thinking about this subject. José Macías, who wrote it, was a close associate of President Venustiano Carranza, and before the constitutional convention met at Querétaro, Carranza sent him to the United States to interview labor and management in New York, Chicago, Baltimore, and Philadelphia. He also studied the labor laws of European nations and in a speech on industrial issues at the convention specifically mentioned Belgium, France, Germany, and the United States.[137]

Labor leaders were also engaged in international discussions and networks. The first labor union established in Japan, for example, was founded by Takano Fusatarō in 1890, who, though a university graduate in Japan, had worked as a laborer on the West Coast of the United States; when he returned to Japan, he had the support of Samuel Gompers of the American Federation of Labor for the organizing work he did there. He also had the backing of Japanese Christian Socialists, a group with international ties, and with their cooperation created the Association for the Promotion of Labor Unions in Japan (1897).[138] We might also note that the global aspect in the name of the controversial Industrial Workers of the World was significant: the IWW had chapters in Europe and Australia and places in between. The labor movement in Mexico, wanting to consolidate the gains of the Mexican Revolution, in the aftermath of World War I closely observed developments in Russia, Barcelona, and the United States.[139]

At Versailles in 1919, where the former belligerents were meeting to work out the terms of the peace treaty after the end of four horrific years of world war, David Lloyd George, pressed by the trade unions that were so powerful in the British Labour Party, put labor questions on the agenda. Robert Owen had put them on the agenda after the Napoleonic Wars at the Congress of Vienna in 1814–15; but such a proposal was probably incomprehensible to Prince Metternich, and nothing came of it. A century later, however, in 1919, with the support of Wilson and Gompers, Title XIII of the Versailles Treaty created the International Labor Organization, and made it a requirement that all signatories to the treaty grant workers the right to organize.[140] One of the many ironies of Wilson's failure to gain U.S. ratification for the peace treaty he did so much to shape was that this proviso was not binding in the United States, and American labor had to wait until the New Deal before the government affirmed its right to organize.

The ILO was supposed to inquire into "the conditions of employment from an international aspect" and then discuss these concerns at an annual meeting, the first of which was held in Washington, with the support of Wilson and Gompers.[141] The ILO is little noticed by American labor historians, but it was taken seriously in other industrialized and industrializing nations, and it positively affected the development of the idea of social citizenship. The Japanese, for example, were stung by international criticism at the Paris Peace Conference, where their labor policies were characterized as "antiquated." The possibility of censure or, worse, exclusion from international debate worried them—and aided the cause of reform. International opinion encouraged Japanese conservatives to be more flexible and helped to bring about recognition of unions.[142] Japan was not alone in its concern to avoid being labeled backward. Chile and Argentina, wanting to identify themselves with international progress in respect to social legislation, were also eager to meet international labor standards. South American workers saw an opportunity and organized a hemispheric conference in Buenos Aires in 1919 to discuss proposed labor laws; most national labor movements also sent representatives to an international labor congress in Washington.

When Arturo Alessandri Palma was elected president of Chile in 1920, he wanted to establish a labor policy that met the criteria of the ILO. In the name of a "Liberal Alliance" and speaking the language of "social liberalism," he proposed an ambitious labor code that had been drafted by Moisés Poblete Troncoso, a prominent Chilean social scientist influenced by French critics of laissez-faire. Conservative opposition to this social policy created a crisis that in turn prompted a military coup. Yet in an odd alliance with liberals, the Chilean army secured the passage of Palma's progressive legislation in 1924.[143]

Just before war broke out in 1914, the National Civic Federation in the United States sent a committee to England and Germany to study health insurance; they were still in England when hostilities began, so they abandoned the plans to go on to Germany and returned home. Also just before the war, the Institute of Educational Travel, which regularly arranged sometimes quite extensive tours, had organized a Civic and Social Tour that lasted more than two months, examining social insurance in Frankfurt, housing in London, and the Musée Social in Paris.[144] After the war, as we have seen, curiosity as well as a well-timed invitation brought Beard to Japan. In 1919 John Dewey, Beard's former Columbia University colleague, made a similar trip to Japan and China. Beard was more impressed with what he saw in Asia than was Dewey, but the point here is less their findings than the curiosity that prompted these two prominent American progressives to embark on arduous transpacific journeys. Both assumed that social liberalism as a condition of modernity was global in its reach, whatever its local variation and degree of success, and they both found evidence of that condition.[145]

A subscription to the *Annals of the American Academy of Political and Social Science*, published in Philadelphia beginning in 1896, enabled the reader to take a similar world tour while sitting at home. The tables of contents for the first two decades of its publication suggest its sense of the world's geography. Admittedly most stops on this armchair tour were in Europe, but the tour included Persia, China, Russia, and Latin America—as well as various European colonial sites of policy innovation. In fact, many European social and urban reform ideas were tested in the colonies, which often served as laboratories for new policies (French urban policies were perhaps the most important and the most widely observed).[146]

The Musée Social in Paris, for many the headquarters of the international reform network, had regular contacts with like-minded researchers and activists in the United States, Russia, Germany, Italy, Belgium, Spain, New Zealand, Argentina, Morocco, Algeria, Tunisia, and the Netherlands. Being a place where university social scientists, politicians, philanthropists, and state administrators could meet, it created a "mélange" of reforms and reformers that allowed and promoted "social experimentation."[147] Its library contained publications from all over the world and from a variety of reform groups—ranging from socialists to anarchists, English Fabians to the American Knights of Labor.[148] And there were im-

itators of the Paris institution: following the centennial celebration of the
Argentine republic in 1910, El Museo Social de Buenos Aires was established, its purpose, as its founder, Tomás Amadeo, wrote in *Economía Social*, to "promote justice in the production and distribution of riches."[149]
A year later Amadeo established the Museo Social Argentino in Buenos
Aires—national rather than urban in concern, as the name indicates. In
1913 it hosted the former president Theodore Roosevelt. He discussed
state action to resolve the social question, though the major reason for the
invitation was to query him rather aggressively about the Monroe Doctrine and the Roosevelt "corollary."[150] José M. Salaverría observed that
these institutions demonstrated "that here, as throughout the world," the
social question existed, and so did the answers. The Argentines were extremely proud to win the Grand Prize at San Francisco's Panama-Pacific
International Exposition (1915) for their exhibit on "social economy."[151]
In New York a short-lived Social Economy Museum was considered a version of the Musée Social, and in Milan a longer-lasting institution (more
closely related to the labor movement than the Musée Social) was founded
in 1911 but closed down by the fascists in 1925.[152]

The Italian international network links were not limited to a French
connection. Italian social scientists also looked to the example of the
Verein für Sozialpolitik in Germany. Under the leadership of Achille Loria and Luigi Einaudi, they organized, as American economists had, an association modeled on the German one, which they called the Laboratorio
di Economia Politica.[153] Perhaps not surprisingly, Argentine social scientists maintained important ties with Italian scholars. José Ingenieros, a
leading Argentine sociologist and himself the child of Italian immigrants,
turned to the work of Loria and introduced it to Argentina. (Loria, incidentally, was a major influence on Frederick Jackson Turner.) In 1913, Ingenieros articulated a powerful and influential vision for Argentina of a
"progressive socialization" that could, with increasing state intervention,
develop a social economy.[154] Although German ideas on city planning and
municipal socialism were the most closely followed and the most influential in the United States, the Italians also published an important journal
dealing with urban reform. And the French journal *Annales de la régie di-
recte* (renamed in 1925 *Annales de l'économie collective*) eventually had sub-
scribers in North America, South Africa, Ceylon and India, Palestine,
New Zealand, and Australia.[155]

Everywhere these reformers worked hard to communicate their ideas to the public, and their methods of presentation, as well as the policy issues being promoted, also traveled. The techniques used ranged from mere newspaper articles to innovative exhibits that graphically displayed statistical data on health, housing, public expenditures, and the like, photographic exhibits, slide shows, and even cinema presentations. New York pioneered posters and public exhibits on social issues; Beard remarked that similar exhibits mounted in Ueno Park in Tokyo, a rough equivalent of New York's Central Park, "compared favorably with similar exhibits in American cities."[156]

How might one best describe the circulation of these reform ideas? In an important study of the international dimensions of American progressivism, Daniel Rodgers tended to presume a North Atlantic channel, as is shown in the title of his book *Atlantic Crossings*. He makes a crucial point about Americans eagerly learning from Europeans, but he makes the equally important point that traffic in ideas also went in the opposite direction, particularly ideas about education. The two-way traffic was also observed by James Kloppenberg for philosophical ideas.[157] Americans may have been more eager for European ideas than the other way around, but they gave as well as received.

But the reform international was not confined to the Atlantic world. As I have tried to make clear, it was only one theater of activity for the reform international. Concern about the social question arose in response to the globalization of industrial capitalism and massive urbanization the world over. How might we map this global circulation of reform ideas and policies? Do we simply multiply the channels, adding shipping lines to more destinations? Of course we can do that, but to leave it there would, I believe, mask a fascinating dynamic in the movements of ideas and policies. We need a completely different metaphor to suggest the very different, open pattern of international exchange of ideas and policies.

Instead of sea-lanes, imagine a World Wide Web—a non-place that gives open access to information located everywhere in the world. In fact, no metaphor or analogy better describes the circulation of information among the international reform community than computer file sharing of the sort we are familiar with in the exchange of music files on the Internet today. There was a vast store of information available more or less for the asking. Social scientists, philanthropists, labor leaders, and bureaucrats actively exchanged the available files. One could surf this network for potentially useful policy ideas or models. There was no fixed pattern of buyers and sellers, or "importers" and "exporters" of ideas and policies.[158] More ideas and policies came from Germany than from Argentina or the United States, but files moved in every direction. There was enough European interest in South American social legislation between 1910 and 1925 to prompt many governments there (Chile, Argentina, Uruguay, and Cuba) to publish compilations of labor and social legislation.[159] Some countries, given their size, population, and levels of industrialization, drew more browsers than one might expect: reformers were eager for information from Denmark, Belgium, and New Zealand. New Zealand, generally conceded to be the most advanced in social policy, was of especial interest to Americans because there, too, the commitment to individualism was high. Among cities, Glasgow was, perhaps surprisingly today, the "holy grail" between 1890 and 1920 for those drawn to the municipalization of city services.[160] Of course not every file turned into a policy. But ideas and policies never adopted often initiated important discussions. And the simple volume of activity gave weight and force to the movement. Every reformer, every city, every nation, knew they were part of something much larger when they looked at their pile of files from all around the world.

This global sharing of information points to a global social and political issue, and the simultaneity suggests common and global causes. It is clear that intellectuals and politicians, reformers and bureaucrats, industrialists and workers were facing the challenges posed by industrial capitalism on a global scale. Few ideas flowed from South America to North America, or from Asia to Europe—that is true and significant. But the heart of the matter is that the search for solutions to the social problems caused by industrialization was an intense international effort involving many countries all over the world.

COMMON CHALLENGES AND LOCAL POLITICS

This does not mean that each nation entering the twentieth century devised the same solutions as the others. The outcomes were varied, sometimes extreme. It is crucial to recognize that one should not expect common ideas or converging policies to develop similarly in very different political environments.

In the twentieth century the responses to the "social question" spanned the political spectrum—from communism to fascism. Most outcomes, however, were some version of the new liberalism, with balance struck variously between the individualistic values of the old liberalism and the collective responsibility inherent in the new. The United States actually entered two world wars on behalf of its version—and engaged in a prolonged Cold War from 1917 until 1989 to both defend and extend it. The interventionist methods that the U.S. government advocated to extend its model produced a good deal of resentment toward the United States, especially in Latin America, as Theodore Roosevelt's visit in Argentina had shown him.

To recognize national difference within a common history of capitalist industrial development and the liberal response to it is important. To take a global perspective is not to ignore or banish distinctive national histories. Rather, it is to recognize each nation as a province, a singular case of a larger history. But distinction notwithstanding, no nation can be understood outside that larger history. Even those countries that consider themselves "exceptionalist"—and here the United States is joined by, at least, Japan, Germany, and Argentina—were provinces. Yasui Eiji, a labor expert in the Social Bureau of the Japanese Home Ministry, was quite familiar with the labor policies of France, Germany, and England. He recognized the common issues, and he learned from them. But he also insisted—drawing upon the English Fabian G.D.H. Cole—that there is everywhere a national particularity within the general development: "the labor movements today run through all contemporary civilized nations," yet a "comprehensive solution" to the labor problem in Japan "must be closely based on our nation's special conditions."[161]

The academics and policy experts who devoted so much time to the study of industrial policy did not think that what they found in the transferred files were templates to be adopted mechanically; rather, they creatively adapted the ideas and policies. Examples were available as loose analogies that could focus thought and as important sources of technique and technical information. It is astonishing to consider how quickly electric streetcars spread around the world, for example, and, later, public restrooms and baths, later yet traffic signals. Not only did different local circumstances produce different solutions to common problems, but the same solution might emerge from radically different political and ideological circumstances. Unemployment insurance was pioneered by the conservative government of Otto von Bismarck, but it was a socialist congressman from New York's Lower East Side, Meyer London, who in 1916 forced America's first congressional hearing on a national program of unemployment, sickness, and old-age insurance.[162]

There was constant comparison among nations, especially among bureaucrats in the relevant ministries eager to keep up with the newest social legislation.[163] Italy, for example, regularly reviewed the social-insurance programs of other nations, not wanting to fall too far below the European standard.[164] They were not unique in this concern; competition among home ministries on social policy was not unlike that waged among war ministries.

Coming late to the reform agenda was interpreted as either an advantage or an embarrassment. For many Japanese policy bureaucrats, it seemed an advantage to learn from the mistakes as well as from the achievements of others. Kaneko Kentarō observed in 1896, "It is the advantage of the backward country that it can reflect on the history of the advanced countries and avoid their mistakes."[165] But others were prodded into action by their sense of arriving late to the reforms of the age. Benjamin DeWitt, an American progressive, for example, was eager "to bring the United States abreast of Germany and other European countries in the matter of remedial legislation." Theodore Roosevelt worried about the reputation of the United States in his 1908 annual message to Congress: "It is humiliating that at European international congresses on accidents the United States should be singled out as the most belated among the nations in respect to employer liability legislation."[166] Nothing had changed by 1912, and Jane Addams made the same point at the Progressive Party convention that year, complaining that the United States has been "lagging behind other great nations [and] has been unaccountably slow."[167]

The degree of labor integration into the state or polity greatly varied from country to country. Prewar France and England probably had the optimal degree of integration, but prerevolutionary Russia and Japan had little. The record in Germany was mixed, since the context was a policy of co-optation, yet residual social democratic opposition was on the increase. Although Mexico and Argentina had strong labor laws and trade unions were welcomed into the ruling populist parties, their governments were prone to authoritarianism, and the labor movement lost autonomy. As for the United States, labor's unfavorable position was largely the result, as we have seen, of a fairly consistent pattern of the government's favoring business. During 1916–18 government, business, and labor were forced into a degree of cooperation by the War Industries Board, but after the war, when labor tried to hold on to some of its wartime gains and went on strikes to insist on them, the government made clear its affiliation: federal troops were deployed to protect strike-breakers—as many as were sent to Europe in 1916–18 it has been estimated.[168]

Noting that business interests were the greatest obstacle to a legislative program of social liberalism in the United States, Luis Cabrera, the finance minister in Carranza's government, made an interesting observation in 1922: in the United States, "capital is native, while labor is largely foreign," with the result that "labor is weakened"; in Mexico, by contrast, "labor is native, while capital is largely foreign, the result being that capital is weakened."[169]

The political contest over social liberalism was not limited to industrial capital and the urban working class; just as often the lines of conflict were drawn between the cities and the countryside. Landed oligarchs, who often retained considerable political power as the nineteenth turned into the twentieth century, resisted reform. In Russia, for example, academic experts, labor leaders, and industrial leaders were all sympathetic to the reform ideas and policies being enacted abroad, but Russia's imperial government, trapped in an antique paternalistic model that gave privilege to the aristocrats who owned most of Russia's agricultural land, would not support the international reform agenda.[170] In South America again and again landowners with a commitment to an aristocratic, paternalistic society and politics blocked industrial reform, and when reform came, the political price for it undercut the idea of social citizenship.[171] The scenario was the same for a good part of Latin America: positive industrial laws would be passed, typical of the era, but they would demand the co-optation of labor and ensure that labor unions would have no or little political independence. Too often, as in Brazil under Getúlio Vargas (president in 1930–45) and Argentina under Juan Perón, the soldier who held the presidency from 1946 to 1955, this relationship was managed by right-wing, populist, sometimes quite repressive governments—hence the phrase "co-optation and repression" used by a historian of labor in Brazil.[172]

In Mexico the situation was more complex and subtle. There the PRI (Institutional Revolutionary Party), which for decades after the revolution ruled the country, "reconciled class interests through the mediation of the state," but the price was labor's loss of independence and voice.[173] The milestone Article 123 was more a symbolic than a real victory, for under the PRI the state controlled labor relations through many mediating institutions.[174] In practice, according to the historian Alan Knight, the result was a kind of unequal alliance between government and the unions, which produced both "moderation" and "clientelism."[175]

In Japan, too, industrial protections were not paired with working-class empowerment or social citizenship. Despite the brief episode of democratization during the reign of Emperor Taishō (1912–26), which suffered some of the same debilitating problems that confronted the Weimar democracy in Germany, social reform devolved into "technocratic authoritarianism" in the 1920s. By the 1930s war and depression pushed Japanese labor policy in a strong statist direction that led, ultimately, to fascism.[176] If before the war conservatives in Japan had pointed to the United States as a model (with its dynamic economy and few worker rights), they later turned to the Germany of Hitler and the Italy of Mussolini.

We might turn at this point to the famous question posed in 1905 by the German economist Werner Sombart: "Why is there no socialism in the United States?"[177] The question has been implicit in many exceptionalist approaches to American history. Yet at the time he wrote, it was hard to point to governing socialism anywhere. And the communist socialism that a decade later emerged in the Soviet Union, later still in the Eastern bloc and China, was so deeply flawed that it is not much of a standard of comparison. Perhaps these outcomes are not relevant to the century-old question. More pertinent is how the question is conceptualized or framed. It presumed a norm against which the United States was being measured, but, as should be apparent, the responses to industrialism and the social question could be found along a wide spectrum, where the United States was probably somewhere to the center right but certainly not in an exceptional position. I have already referred to the surprising similarity in actual practices in France and the United States during the 1890–1914 period, and neither of them was socialist, though both had socialist parties that were important components of the social liberal landscape. So we can see that in the large frame of the global history of industrialism, it is hard to talk about the binary that Sombart's famous but badly formed question suggests and that a century-long debate has been devoted to. In a global perspective, the U.S. response to industrial capitalism was clearly closer to the western European one (if less developed) than to other instances outside Europe.

In any case, the speculative question about socialism is less important than the specific nature of the American response to industrial and urban issues in the 1850–1950 century. After World War I the balance between individualism/private property and governmental social intervention tilted toward the former more than in any other industrial society of the time. The New Deal was both later and less complete a response to the social question posed by industrial capitalism than in other nations. Yet Americans' strong commitment to individual rights helped to protect them from the authoritarian, even repressive, governments that emerged in Europe, Asia, and Latin America. And they were more sensitive to consumer issues, if not to workers in the workplace and to social security in general.

This observation prompts a larger, perhaps more controversial speculation. The 1930s and '40s saw the rise of various illiberal regimes, whether short- or long-lived, on every continent but the North American one. This fact reflects positively on New Deal liberalism, but there is a larger pattern to be noted. The global network of British-derived settler societies, which is to say white societies granted parliamentary institutions as colonies, escaped the illiberalisms that marred so much of the century's international history. This was true whether the colonial origins were in the eighteenth century, as for the United States and Canada, or later, as for the antipodean nations, Australia and New Zealand, celebrated in the early twentieth century for their combination of strong individualism and advanced social provision. Most of the world then was still under colonial rule, but in Europe, Asia, and Latin America the number of countries that escaped the installation of illiberal governments

was very small. One cannot but ask whether England's legal and constitutional traditions and long-standing tradition of philosophical liberalism,
both of which emphasize rights, might have been at work. (South Africa,
where the Afrikaner Nationalist Party formalized apartheid in 1948, may
seem to undercut such an interpretation, yet as its name suggests, that
party was largely devoted to opposing the remnants of British liberalism
and took South Africa out of the British Commonwealth in 1961.) The
United States was not without its illiberal extremists in the interwar
years—the Ku Klux Klan and American Legion in the 1920s, and Father
Coughlin's National Union for Social Justice and Huey Long's Silver
Shirts in the 1930s—but they all ended up being marginalized. After the
war, the McCarthy period's ugly and damaging illiberalism was nearer
the center. Yet one cannot fairly call the Truman and Eisenhower administrations illiberal regimes.

It is the race-based denial of rights in the southern states that raises
the issue of illiberalism more forcefully. (One could mention the twentieth-
century treatment of indigenous peoples in Canada and Australia, to say
nothing of the United States, but bad as those cases are, the racial
system in the American South, because of its scale and centrality, is a significantly greater challenge to the notion of a liberal society.) Yet it is important that at the same time Americans initiated a social movement
(ultimately successful) that rejected racial exclusion and demanded rights
across the color line—and that the courts began enforcing that claim.

We may now have witnessed the end of the age of industrialism that
began in the mid-nineteenth century and the end of the liberalism that
responded to its structural transformations of our societies. Again, a
global history is unfolding. We are too close to grasp its dimensions or
direction, but it does seem that the United States is largely defining it—
both structurally and in terms of policy responses. Economics seminars at
the University of Chicago and other American universities may be play-
ing the role once played by the German universities. More than the inhabitants of any other country, Americans accept capitalism and the
market as a public philosophy, and they marginalize political interventions premised on social considerations; these attitudes have been more or
less adopted on all continents, sometimes under pressure from global financial institutions largely controlled by the United States. Developing
nations in need of capital are often made to accept the fiscal theories and

practices demanded by lenders, whether they are private American banking institutions or international financial institutions, notably the International Monetary Fund and the World Bank, in which the United States, among other supporting nations, has a preponderance of influence. Like the social liberalism or social politics of a century ago, these neoliberal politics and economics are carried by an international reform network.[178] And social scientists and businessmen in the United States are at the center, this time as generators of ideas and policies. The process looks familiar, but these neoclassical ideas of political economy point in a very different direction. Indeed, they seem to promote patterns of inequality very like those that, a century ago, prompted the new, social liberalism.

6

GLOBAL HISTORY AND AMERICA TODAY

————— ∞∞∞ —————

This book has made clear, I hope, that the history of the United States is bound up with the beginnings of global history; that global history and American history are products of the same conjuncture of historical events; that American history has been significantly shaped by its global context. The United States is not unique in this respect: since the discovery of the ocean world around 1500 A.D., all peoples have shared in a global history, and many new worlds were discovered by every people on every continent. Being in and of the world is the condition of modern history for all societies. Americans ought not be surprised, annoyed, or angry when the "world" seems to "intrude" on their lives. The very notion of intrusion confuses the issue. The United States is not outside of or apart from the common history of humanity, as some proponents of American exceptionalism would have us believe.

When I began work on this book, the idea of American exceptionalism was not of particular interest to me. My initial concern was with the question of how context affects historical narratives. I also wanted better to understand the way the bounded units of historical narratives related to their public constituencies. But as I worked, a discourse of exceptionalism and policies based on it became omnipresent in American public life. The framing of American history that I have offered here will give little comfort to its proponents, for I believe the facts make it clear that there is both a common global history *and* a history that reveals many national differences. On the spectrum of difference the United States is one of many, and there is no single norm from which it deviates—or that it establishes.

The question of a norm makes for the most troubling difficulty with exceptionalist claims about America, which tend to obscure national differences and, for that matter, internal differentiation within any given nation-state. They have as a premise the idea of a uniform nation, and imply that beyond its territorial borders all is simply "not-U.S.," with no significant differences among peoples and nations elsewhere. (This is not unlike the category "non-Christian," which makes all Muslims, Jews, Hindus, Buddhists, and Confucians—and nonbelievers, too—the same.)

As I mentioned at the opening of this book, world or global history has become a required subject in our schools, since we proclaim our interest in educating worldly citizens. The civic impulse behind these requirements is heartening, but if world history is taught separately from that of the United States, then world history leaves out the United States and American history leaves out the world. Is it because of this disconnect that American leaders can so regularly invoke the idea of American exceptionalism even as they propose our country as the model toward which all other nations are or should be tending?

On one narrative scale the whole world is one, with a broad spectrum of local differences, with many unique local resolutions of social, political, and cultural preferences and constraints, accumulations of power, and accidents of circumstance, with multiple perspectives (still mostly national: a legacy of the nineteenth century). We need to consider other histories: after all, transnational social solidarities (regions, movements, diasporas) are carriers of history, and so are subnational local, regional, and ethnic affiliations. Historical synthesis, like lived experience, should relate and at least contingently sum up a multiplicity of narratives of varying time frames (from *la longue durée* to events of the moment) and geographical scales (from the village to the globe).

The history most of us have been taught carries an old, nineteenth-century ideology about the nation being the natural, sometimes the only carrier of historical meaning. But experience belies that presumption, the persistence of which makes it difficult to understand the world we live in. There are those who say the time has come to abandon national narratives; post-national history beckons. But not to me. I believe such a move would be a mistake. We need, rather, a better form of national narrative.

The nation is simply too important in modern history, in the past, in the present, and for the foreseeable future to stop studying it. It is the most effective structure for mobilizing human societies for economic development—as well as war, tragically—yet devised. If we regret the violence nations wreak on each other and sometimes on their own citizens, we must acknowledge that at present we have no more effective or alternative institution to defend and protect citizens and human rights.

In this book I have examined five major events or themes in American history in order to suggest a historical narrative that better connects our past with our internal diversity and our global interconnection and interdependence. I have argued that history is above all a contextualizing discipline, and I have tried to fulfill that historiographical assignment, making the globe itself the context. I have not covered all the important themes and events, people and places; my concern was to offer examples, to demonstrate both the value and the practicality of synthetic history composed in this fashion. No one is more aware than I that the themes discussed in the previous five chapters deserve greater development— with book-length, even multivolume examination. Nor do I need to be reminded of the many important topics I did not address. But comprehensiveness was not my aim. Rather, I have tried to show, by concrete example, that a national history cannot properly be written as if it were self-contained.

I must, however, also point out the danger in the narrative form I adopted and am advocating. Just as nineteenth-century narratives legitimated the nation and sustained a narrow patriotism, so the global approach might be used as an ideological defense of American global hegemony. The simple story line is all too predictable: small colonies on the "periphery of the periphery" of European empires grow into the United States, the predominant world power; the United States *in* global history might all too easily morph into U.S. history *as* global history. My aim has been quite to the contrary: not to write an apologia for empire but to present a cosmopolitan appreciation of American participation in a history larger than itself. There is indeed a civic purpose behind this book, but it is not to encourage hubris. Rather, it is to imbue our national history and civic discourse with appropriate humility, accepting the country's condition of being one among many in an interdependent world.

I have tried to make this point by insisting that circa 1500 there was a "New World" for every people on the planet. And I have tried to get beyond our usual perspective and to see how the projection of America beyond our national territory appears to others. Americans have always found it difficult to imagine themselves as an enemy, as a problem for other people. But our history should teach us that every contact beyond our borders has an impact somewhere—and what other people experience as America and think of America counts in our history as well as in theirs. Such shared histories need to be recognized and appreciated, not appropriated. This means recovering the historiographical and civic worldliness that was so evident more than a century ago among historians as diverse as Henry Adams and W.E.B. DuBois, and the sense of interconnection that Frederick Jackson Turner emphasized.

Jane Addams, with the imperial adventure in the Philippines on her mind, had it right in 1901. Though a staunch critic of war and imperialism, she was no isolationist. The United States, she understood, had important work to do in the world, and the essential question for her was "How shall we go out?" As an urban reformer in Chicago, she had challenged the "charitable relation" between the established classes and the needy, insisting on a spirit of mutuality, on working together. She extended that approach to the world: "Shall we go out with the narrow notion of national life, which would claim democracy for itself alone, or shall we be really and truly inter-national in that we throw our energy into other lands, mingling in an absolute equality and only knowing that progress belongs to us together?"[1]

The time has long since come for a more cosmopolitan vision to inform civic work in the humanities. Early in the twentieth century, J. Franklin Jameson, a leader in the professionalization of history, proposed ideas about the "future uses of history" that warrant recovery. "The nation," he wrote in 1912, "is ceasing to be the leading form of the world's structure; organizations transcending national boundaries are becoming more and more numerous and effective . . . We are moving into a new world which will be marked by cosmopolitan thought and sentiment."[2] So the humanities, whether in the classroom or in public debate, must move beyond the North Atlantic nations once categorized as "civilized" and for that reason worthy of historical and literary study. They must extend to humanity as a whole, recognizing thereby the vast enrichment of the archives of the human experience. Like the humanities generally, history must do this, too, even as historians examine in detail the many provincial manifestations of being human in distinct communities, including national ones.

Notions of American exceptionalism cut us off from this larger understanding of ourselves and our place in the world, as a nation among nations, a people among peoples. They produce an odd combination of parochialism and arrogance. They encourage intellectual and moral isolation and discourage the concern for the "decent respect to the Opinions of Mankind" that was so important to the writers of the Declaration of Independence.

In recent years, this disregard has been evident in the American government's approach to foreign affairs, in respect not only to war but also to the environment, trade, nuclear, and other policies. A striking example comes from a recent public disagreement between two justices of the U.S. Supreme Court. It followed a Court finding, in *Roper* v. *Simmons* (2005), that executing convicts for crimes committed as juveniles was "cruel and unusual" punishment and thus prohibited by the Constitution. The majority opinion noted that "the United States now stands alone in a world that has turned its face against the juvenile death penalty." That is, it looked to the "Opinions of Mankind" in determining whether such executions were indeed cruel and unusual. Justice Antonin Scalia, dissenting, complained that "foreigners" should not have any role in interpreting the Constitution—and he did not acknowledge, by the way, that the Constitution itself drew heavily on "foreign" opinions and histories, ancient and modern. In an unusual public response, Justice Ruth Bader Ginsburg urged American judges to devote more rather than less attention to foreign jurisprudence. Fear of foreign opinion "should not lead us to abandon the effort to learn what we can from the experience and good thinking foreign sources may convey." Echoing Jefferson's phrasing in the Declaration of Independence, she argued that especially today, when the United States "is subject to the scrutiny of a candid world," it should attend to the views of the "international community" and those "concerned with the advancement of the rule of law and respect for human dignity." This blending of national concern with a global human-rights perspective exemplifies the cosmopolitan citizenship that being in the world invites and demands.

I have tried to exemplify this cosmopolitan approach to our national history, for I believe it will enable us better to negotiate the relationship between our own national traditions and the larger human experience. Equally important, the global context I propose here has the virtue of verisimilitude. History and humanity are not in fact enclosed in boxes, whether national, ethnic, local, or continental. Good empirical history ought to reflect this truth; it then proffers, as well, a fundamental ethical principle.

NOTES

INTRODUCTION

1. Lester H. Cohen, "Creating a Usable Future: The Revolutionary Historians and the National Past," in Jack P. Greene, ed., *The American Revolution: Its Character and Limits* (New York, 1987), p. 315.

2. Joyce Appleby, "The Power of History," *American Historical Review* 103, no. 1 (1998), p. 10.

3. Twenty years ago, however, I did controversially enter that debate with a related but distinct worry that the newer social history was fragmenting American history, losing the whole in the parts. See Thomas Bender, "Making History Whole Again," *New York Times Book Review*, Oct. 6, 1985, pp. 1, 42–43; Thomas Bender, "Wholes and Parts: The Need for Synthesis in American History," *Journal of American History* 73, no. 1 (1986), pp. 120–36.

4. Thomas Bender, *The La Pietra Report* (Bloomington, IN, 2000); Thomas Bender, ed., *Rethinking American History in a Global Age* (Berkeley, CA, 2002).

5. Clifford Geertz, *Local Knowledge: Further Essays in Interpretive Anthropology* (New York, 1983), p. 16.

6. See Akira Iriye, *Global Community: The Role of International Organizations in the Making of the Contemporary World* (Berkeley, CA, 2002), intro. and ch. 1. See also Thomas Peyser, *Utopia and Cosmopolis: Globalization in the Era of American Literary Realism* (Durham, NC, 1998).

7. See Ian Tyrrell, "Making Nations/Making States: American Historians in the Context of Empire," *Journal of American History* 86, no. 3 (1999), pp. 1015–44; Daniel T. Rodgers, "Exceptionalism," in Anthony Molho and Gordon Wood, eds., *Imagined Histories: American Historians Interpret the Past* (Princeton, NJ, 1998), pp. 21–40.

8. Frederick Jackson Turner, "The Significance of the Frontier in American History," in Ray Allen Billington, ed., *Frontier and Section: Selected Essays of Frederick Jackson Turner* (Englewood Cliffs, NJ, 1961), p. 38.

9. Frederick Jackson Turner, "The Significance of History," in *Frontier and Section*, pp. 20–21.

10. W.E.B. DuBois, "Careers Open to College-Bred Negroes," in Nathan Huggins, ed., *DuBois: Writings* (New York, 1986), p. 831.

11. Herbert E. Bolton, "The Epic of Greater America," *American Historical Review* 38, no. 3 (1933), pp. 448–49.

1. THE OCEAN WORLD AND THE BEGINNINGS OF AMERICAN HISTORY

1. Edmundo O'Gorman, *The Invention of America: An Inquiry into the Historical Nature of the New World and the Meaning of Its History* (1958; Bloomington, IN, 1961), pp. 54–57; Felipe Fernández-Armesto, *Before Columbus: Exploration and Colonization from the Mediterranean to the Atlantic* (Philadelphia, 1987), p. 248. My notion of the "new world" as interactional and mutual, here vastly expanded to the globe, is derived from James H. Merrell, *The Indians' New World: Catawbas and Their Neighbors from European Contact Through the Era of Removal* (Chapel Hill, NC, 1989).

2. This map is reprinted in Peter Whitfield, *The Image of the World* (San Francisco, 1994), p. 33.

3. Excerpted in George Kish, ed., *A Source Book in Geography* (Cambridge, MA, 1978), p. 229.

4. See Denis Cosgrove, *Apollo's Eye: A Cartographic Genealogy of the Earth in the Western Imagination* (Baltimore, 2001), p. 63. An example of a map with such a monstrous border is at p. 23.

5. O'Gorman, *Invention of America*, p. 131.

6. Quoted in Jesús Carrillo Castillo, " 'The World Is Only One and Not Many': Representation of the Natural World in Imperial Spain," in Chiyo Ishikawa, ed., *Spain in the Age of Exploration* (Lincoln, NE, 2004), pp. 140–42, quote p. 140.

7. Greg Dening, *Islands and Beaches: Discourse on a Silent Land, Marquesas, 1774–1880* (Honolulu, 1980), p. 23.

8. Alfred Thayer Mahan, *The Influence of Sea Power upon History, 1660–1783* (Boston, 1890), p. 25.

9. J. H. Parry, *The Discovery of the Sea* (Berkeley, CA, 1981), p. 212.

10. O'Gorman, *Invention of America*, p. 157.

11. The relation of the original letter to the surviving printed versions has been contested. Parry, *Discovery of the Sea*, p. 219.

12. Quoted in O'Gorman, *Invention of America*, p. 120.

13. Quoted in John M. Archer, *Old Worlds: Egypt, Southwest Asia, India, and Russia in Early Modern English Writing* (Stanford, CA, 2001), p. 1.

14. M. N. Pearson, *The Portuguese in India* (Cambridge, UK, 1987), p. 12.

15. Sanjay Subrahmanyam, *The Portuguese Empire in Asia, 1500–1700: A Political and Economic History* (London, 1993), p. 59.

16. Quoted in David R. Ringrose, *Expansion and Global Interaction, 1200–1700* (New York, 2001), p. 147.

17. See K. N. Chaudhuri, *Trade and Civilisation in the Indian Ocean: An Economic History from the Rise of Islam to 1750* (Cambridge, UK, 1985), pp 14–15, 63–79; Pearson, *Portuguese in India*, pp. 29–32.

18. Philip E. Steinberg, *The Social Construction of the Ocean* (Cambridge, UK, 2001), pp. 45, 46, 75.

19. Adam Smith, *An Inquiry into the Nature and Causes of the Wealth of Nations*, eds. R. H. Campbell and A. S. Skinner (Indianapolis, 1981), vol. 2, pp. 626, 448, 626. Smith's cel-

ebration of the importance of discovery echoes the contemporary French writer Abbé Raynal, *Philosophical and Political History of the Settlement and Trade of Europeans in the East and West Indies* (1772).

20. Felipe Fernández-Armesto, *Millennium: A History of the Last Thousand Years* (New York, 1995), p. 364; Bernard Lewis, *Cultures in Conflict: Christians, Muslims, and Jews in the Age of Discovery* (New York, 1995), pp. 13–14.

21. David S. Landes credits European culture in *The Wealth and Poverty of Nations* (New York, 1998) for its distinctive economic development, while Kenneth Pomeranz argues that slavery and its profits produced the cultural achievements in *The Great Divergence: Europe, China, and the Making of the World Economy* (Princeton, NJ, 2000).

22. Fernández-Armesto, *Before Columbus*, p. 276.

23. On the biological aspects, see Alfred W. Crosby, *The Columbian Exchange: Biological and Cultural Consequences of 1492* (Westport, CT, 1972). I thank Kathleen Brown for bringing to my attention the gender dimensions of this exchange.

24. Philip D. Curtin, "Africa in World History," in Isaac James Mowoe and Richard Bjornson, eds., *Africa and the West* (New York, 1986), p. 24.

25. For the curiosity in North America, see Karen Ordahl Kupperman, *Indians and English: Facing Off in Early America* (Ithaca, NY, 2000).

26. See Anthony Pagden, *The Fall of Natural Man: The American Indian and the Origins of Comparative Ethnology*, 2nd ed. (Cambridge, UK, 1986).

27. Whitfield, *Image of the World*, p. 8.

28. Cited in Kish, *Source Book in Geography*, p. 26.

29. Martin Lewis and Kären Wigen, *The Myth of Continents: A Critique of Metageography* (Berkeley, CA, 1997), p. 26; Cosgrove, *Apollo's Eye*, p. 43. Of course, Afro-Eurasia is a world island, with its three divisions connected.

30. For these linguistic connections, I am indebted to David Bender.

31. Matthew H. Edney, *Mapping an Empire: The Geographical Construction of British India, 1765–1843* (Chicago, 1997), p. 3.

32. Barry Cunliffe, *Facing the Ocean: The Atlantic and Its Peoples, 8000 BC–AD 1500* (Oxford, 2001), p. 4.

33. Quoted in Cosgrove, *Apollo's Eye*, p. 29.

34. Jerry H. Bentley, *Old World Encounters: Cross-Cultural Contacts and Exchanges in Premodern Times* (New York, 1993), p. 35.

35. This general point is made by Peter Brown, *The World of Late Antiquity* (New York, 1989).

36. Fernand Braudel, *Civilization and Capitalism: 15th–18th Century*, trans. Siân Reynolds, 3 vols. (New York, 1981–84), vol. 3, p. 137; quotation in Ronald Segal, *Islam's Black Slaves: The Other Black Diaspora* (New York, 2001), p. 104.

37. This book was on display at the Library of Congress, with translation of its title and main themes, in June 2003.

38. Fernand Braudel, *The Mediterranean and the Mediterranean World in the Age of Philip II*, trans. Siân Reynolds, 2 vols. (New York, 1972), vol. 1, pp. 224, 187. See also Braudel, *Civilization and Capitalism*, vol. 3, p. 467.

39. Lewis, *Cultures in Conflict*, p. 22.

40. Richard Eaton, "Islamic History as Global History," in Michael Adas, ed., *Islamic and European Expansion* (Philadelphia, 1993), p. 12.

41. Lewis, *Cultures in Conflict*, p. 10; John Voll, "Islam as a Special World System," *Journal of World History* 5, no. 2 (1994), p. 217; Lewis and Wigen, *Myth of Continents*, p. 148.

42. Ibn Battuta, *Travels in Asia and Africa, 1325–54*, trans. and sel. H.A.R. Gibb (New York, 1969), p. 47.

43. This point is made by Eaton, "Islamic History as Global History," pp. 31–32; Voll, "Islam as a Special World System," p. 219.

44. Braudel, *Civilization and Capitalism*, vol. 3, pp. 467, 475–76.

45. Kenneth Pomeranz and Steven Topik, *The World That Trade Created: Society, Culture, and the World Economy, 1400 to the Present* (Armonk, NY, 1999), p. 151.

46. See James M. Blaut, *The Colonizer's Model of the World: Geographical Diffusionism and Eurocentric History* (New York, 1993), p. 2 and passim; and Pomeranz, *Great Divergence*.

47. The Victorian comparison comes from Lewis, *Cultures in Conflict*, pp. 13–14.

48. Reproduced in Whitfield, *Image of the World*, pp. 40–41.

49. Sidney W. Mintz, *Sweetness and Power: The Place of Sugar in Modern History* (New York, 1985), ch. 2; Cedric J. Robinson, *Black Marxism: The Making of the Black Radical Tradition* (1983; Chapel Hill, NC, 2000), pp. 104–105, 110; Robin Blackburn, *The Making of New World Slavery: From the Baroque to the Modern, 1492–1800* (New York, 1997), p. 77.

50. Philip D. Curtin, *The Rise and Fall of the Plantation Complex*, 2nd ed. (New York, 1998).

51. Eric Hobsbawm, *The Age of Capital, 1848–1875* (London, 1975); Pomeranz, *Great Divergence*; Robinson, *Black Marxism*, p. 110; Blackburn, *Making of New World Slavery*, p. 9. On the link between slavery and industrial capitalism, see Eric Williams, *Capitalism and Slavery* (1944; Chapel Hill, NC, 1994). The Williams thesis remains controversial, but it is hard not to accept its broad outlines, especially in respect to the question of the accumulation of investment capital for industrialization. See the appraisal by Stanley Engerman and Barbara Solow, eds., *British Capitalism and Caribbean Slavery* (Cambridge, UK, 1987). Williams does not address the consumer side of the economy, a subject increasingly the focus of studies of the Atlantic world, which I think complements rather than displaces his concern.

52. So, too, the Jewish trading networks to the east, though they were never so secure or highly developed. See Braudel, *Civilization and Capitalism*, vol. 2, p. 157. One of the key routes to which the Mediterranean connected was not a land route, but rather the Muslim-controlled Red Sea route to the Indian Ocean.

53. Fernández-Armesto, *Millennium*, p. 241.

54. Perhaps the Soviet Empire, which can be said to have lasted until 1989 and beyond, is an exception, but the price of its persistence has been high.

55. Ringrose, *Expansion and Global Interaction*, p. 14; see also Bentley, *Old World Encounters*, p. 165.

56. See John Noble Wilford, "A New Theory Puts the Chinese Fleet Ahead of Columbus," *New York Times*, March 17, 2002. Neither the evidence cited in this article nor the book to which it refers is compelling, though the possibility of such a voyage cannot be ignored. Magellan was killed in the Philippines before completing his voyage around the world, but his crew did complete it.

57. Pomeranz and Topik, *World That Trade Created*, pp. 51–53.

58. Richard Von Glahn, *Fountain of Fortune: Money and Monetary Policy in China, 1000–1700* (Berkeley, CA, 1996), pp. 76, 83; Pomeranz, *Great Divergence*, pp. 159–62; Dennis O. Flynn and Arturo Giráldez, "Born with a Silver Spoon: The Origin of World Trade in 1571," *Journal of World History* 6, no. 2 (1995), p. 395; Braudel, *Civilization and Capitalism*, vol. 2, p. 198; William S. Atwell, "International Bullion Flows and the Chinese

Economy Circa 1530–1650," in Dennis O. Flynn and Arturo Giráldez, eds., *Metals and Monies in an Emerging Global Economy* (Aldershot, UK, 1997), p. 159.

59. See Braudel, *Civilization and Capitalism*; Pomeranz, *Great Divergence.*

60. Pomeranz, *Great Divergence*, p. 43; Flynn and Giráldez, "Born with a Silver Spoon." See also John E. Wills, *1688: A Global History* (New York, 2001), p. 29.

61. Ringrose, *Expansion and Global Interaction*, p. 195.

62. Atwell, "International Bullion Flows and the Chinese Economy," pp. 160–63.

63. Braudel, *Civilization and Capitalism*, vol. 3, p. 138.

64. For an account of the Portuguese pursuit of that goal, see Pearson's fine *Portuguese in India.*

65. Quoted in Braudel, *Civilization and Capitalism*, vol. 3, p. 493.

66. John Thornton, *Africa and the Africans in Making the Atlantic World* (New York, 1992), p. 35. The ventures were almost wholly privately funded.

67. Basil Davidson, *Africa in History*, rev. ed. (New York, 1974), p. 172.

68. Quoted in Eric Wolf, *Europe and the People Without History* (Berkeley, CA, 1997), p. 58.

69. Pearson, *Portuguese in India*, p. 35.

70. Pomeranz and Topik, *World That Trade Created*, pp. 16–18; C. A. Bayly, *Imperial Meridian: The British Empire and the World, 1780–1830* (London, 1989), pp. 16–19. Later, when the English and Dutch succeeded the Portuguese in dominating trade in the Indian Ocean, their policies were "more restrictive and damaging [to local regimes]." Bayly, *Imperial Meridian*, p. 18.

71. For this speculation, see Mintz, *Sweetness and Power*, p. 29. On Islamic slavery in the Mediterranean, which was usually urban, not agricultural, see Segal, *Islam's Black Slaves*, p. 115.

72. Robert C. Davis, *Christian Slaves, Muslim Masters: White Slavery in the Mediterranean, the Barbary Coast, and Italy, 1500–1800* (New York, 2003), p. 23.

73. See Blackburn, *Making of New World Slavery*, p. 79.

74. Quoted in Michael H. Hunt, *The Making of a Special Relationship: The United States and China to 1914* (New York, 1983), p. 42.

75. Excerpted in Miguel León-Portilla, ed., *The Broken Spears: The Aztec Account of the Conquest of Mexico*, expanded ed. (Boston, 1992), p. 16.

76. See Michael N. Pearson, *Port Cities and Intruders: The Swahili Coast, India, and the Portuguese in the Early Modern Era* (Baltimore, 1998).

77. Curtin, "Africa in World History," p. 21.

78. Wolf, *Europe and the People Without History*, pp. 31–33, 40.

79. Braudel, *Civilization and Capitalism*, vol. 3, p. 434; Thornton, *Africa and the Africans*, pp. 13–14 and passim.

80. William Dalrymple, "The Truth About the Muslims," *New York Review of Books*, Nov. 4, 2004, p. 34.

81. Wyatt MacGaffey, "Dialogues of the Deaf: Europeans on the Atlantic Coast of Africa," in Stuart Schwartz, ed., *Implicit Understandings: Observing, Reporting, and Reflecting on the Encounters Between Europeans and Other Peoples in the Early Modern Era* (Cambridge, UK, 1994), pp. 251, 257. See also John Thornton, *The Kingdom of Kongo* (Madison, WI, 1983), pp. xiv–xvi. Inland, in Timbuktu, Arabs were identified as "white men" from abroad.

82. James Lockhart, "Sightings: Initial Nahua Reaction to Spanish Culture," in Schwartz, ed., *Implicit Understandings*, p. 219.

83. Richard White, *The Middle Ground: Indians, Empires, and Republics in the Great Lakes Region, 1650–1815* (New York, 1991).

84. Quoted in Davidson, *Africa in History*, p. 158.

85. Thornton, *Kingdom of Kongo*, p. 25.

86. John Thornton, "Sexual Demography: The Impact of the Slave Trade on Family Structure," in Claire Robertson and Herbert Klein, eds., *Women and Slavery in Africa* (Portsmouth, NH, 1997), p. 41.

87. Davidson, *Africa in History*, p. 221.

88. On the strength of the institutions, see Curtin, "Africa in World History," p. 22. No primitive society, he argues, could possibly have organized the capture, sale, and export of 100,000 people, as Africans did in the peak years of the eighteenth-century slave trade.

89. Segal, *Islam's Black Slaves*, pp. 55–57.

90. Patrick Manning, *Slavery and African Life* (Cambridge, UK, 1990), p. 30.

91. See the illustration in Ringrose, *Expansion and Global Interaction*, p. 65.

92. Fernández-Armesto, *Millennium*, pp. 191–97. See also Braudel, *Mediterranean*, vol. 1, pp. 468–70.

93. Robinson, *Black Marxism*, pp. 81, 82, 119.

94. Wills, *1688*, p. 44; Thornton, *Africa and the Africans*.

95. See Thornton, *Africa and the Africans*, p. 5.

96. Pomeranz, *Great Divergence*, p. 81. See also M. N. Pearson, *Merchants and Rulers in Gujarat: The Response to the Portuguese in the Sixteenth Century* (Berkeley, CA, 1976).

97. Braudel, *Civilization and Capitalism*, vol. 3, pp. 142–43, 149.

98. Ibid., p. 175.

99. E. A. Wrigley, *People, Cities, and Wealth* (Oxford, 1988), ch. 6.

100. Ringrose, *Expansion and Global Interaction*, p. 153.

101. Alan Taylor, *American Colonies* (New York, 2001), p. 452.

102. This point is made by Germán Arciniegas, *America in Europe: History of the New World in Reverse*, trans. Gabriela Arciniegas and R. Victoria Arana (1975; San Diego, 1986), ch. 1.

103. Anthony Pagden, *Lords of All the World: Ideologies of Empire in Spain, Britain, and France, c. 1500–c. 1850* (New Haven, CT, 1995); Patricia Seed, *Ceremonies of Possession in Europe's Conquest of the New World, 1492–1640* (New York, 1995).

104. Curtin, *Rise and Fall of the Plantation Complex*, p. 98; David Eltis, *The Rise of African Slavery in the Americas* (Cambridge, UK, 2000), p. 97.

105. See Archer, *Old Worlds*.

106. Blaut, *Colonizer's Model of the World*, p. 170.

107. See Jorge Cañizares-Esguerra, "The Devil in the New World: A Comparative Perspective"; and Kenneth Mills and Allan Greer, "A Catholic Atlantic," in Jorge Cañizares-Esguerra and Erik Seeman, eds., *Beyond the Line: The North and South Atlantics and Global History, 1500–2000* (forthcoming).

108. Mills and Greer, "Catholic Atlantic."

109. Richard H. Grove, *Green Imperialism: Colonial Expansion, Tropical Island Edens, and the Origins of Environmentalism, 1600–1860* (Cambridge, UK, 1995), pp. 313, 315, 486.

110. On Cook and Pacific explorations, see Taylor, *American Colonies*, ch. 19.

111. James A. Field, Jr., "All Economists, All Diplomats," in William H. Becker and Samuel F. Wells, Jr., eds., *Economics and World Power* (New York, 1984), p. 48.

112. Gary Okihiro, *Common Ground: Reimagining American History* (Princeton, NJ, 2001), p. 21.

113. For a critique of this narrative, see Thomas Bender, "The Geography of Historical Memory and the Making of Public Culture," in Anna Maria Martellone, ed., *Towards a New American Nation? Redefinitions and Reconstruction* (Staffordshire, UK, 1995), pp. 174–87.

114. Karen Ordahl Kupperman, "International at the Creation: Early Modern American History," in Thomas Bender, ed., *Rethinking American History in a Global Age* (Berkeley, CA, 2002), p. 110.

115. At the time of contact, Europe and North America were *both* divided into about five hundred mostly very small polities. See Charles Tilly, "Reflections on the History of European State Making," in Charles Tilly, ed., *The Formation of National States in Western Europe* (Princeton, NJ, 1975), p. 15; Alvin Josephy, Jr., *500 Nations: An Illustrated History of North American Indians* (New York, 1994). My guess is that the number of African polities is roughly similar.

116. Kupperman, *Indians and English*, pp. 11, 14.

117. Braudel, *Mediterranean*, vol. 1, p. 445.

118. See Pomeranz and Topik, *World That Trade Created*, p. 7.

119. Fernández-Armesto, *Millennium*, pp. 245, 251.

120. For an example of this highly romanticized view not sustained by the evidence, see Peter Linebaugh and Marcus Rediker, *The Many-Headed Hydra* (Boston, 2001).

121. See the rich analysis in Greg Dening, *Mr. Bligh's Bad Language: Passion, Powers, and Theatre on the Bounty* (Cambridge, UK, 1992), esp. pp. 81, 89, 121, 123, 154.

122. Braudel, *Civilization and Capitalism*, vol. 3, pp. 437–38; Blackburn, *Making of New World Slavery*, p. 113; Ira Berlin, *Many Thousands Gone: The First Two Centuries of Slavery in North America* (Cambridge, MA, 1998), p. 25; Colin Palmer, *Slaves of the White God: Blacks in Mexico, 1570–1650* (Cambridge, MA, 1976), p. 229 (variety of occupations, pp. 44–45).

123. For accounts of Paquiquineo, as well as two other Native Americans who ventured into the Atlantic world (Namontack and Uttamatomakkin), see Donald K. Richter, "Voyagers to the East: Virginia Algonquians and the Atlantic World, 1560–1622" (paper presented to the Atlantic History Workshop, New York University, Feb. 24, 2004).

124. On the nonagricultural and urban slavery in the Mediterranean, see Segal, *Islam's Black Slaves*.

125. See Blackburn, *Making of New World Slavery*.

126. Susan M. Socolow, "Spanish Captives in Indian Societies: Culture Contact Along the Argentine Frontier, 1600–1835," *Hispanic American Historical Review* 72, no. 1 (1992), pp. 73–99.

127. See James F. Brooks, *Captives & Cousins: Slavery, Kinship, and Community in the Southwest Borderlands* (Chapel Hill, NC, 2002).

128. Philip D. Curtin, *The Tropical Atlantic in the Age of the Slave Trade* (Washington, DC, 1991), p. 31. On Portuguese and "racial interbreeding," see J. D. Roberts, *History of the World*, 3rd ed. (London, 1997), p. 621.

129. Berlin, *Many Thousands Gone*, p. 20; Blackburn, *Making of New World Slavery*, p. 121.

130. See Berlin's beautifully crafted account in *Many Thousands Gone*, esp. chs. 1–2.

131. For this final point, I am indebted to Jorge Cañizares-Esguerra.

132. See James H. Merrell, *Into the American Woods: Negotiators on the Pennsylvania Frontier* (New York, 1999), 56; Merrell, *Indians' New World*; John Kessell, "The Ways and

Words of the Other: Diego de Vargas and Cultural Brokers in Late Seventeenth-Century New Mexico," in Margaret Szasz, ed., *Between Indian and White Worlds: The Cultural Broker* (Norman, OK, 1994), pp. 25–43; Alan Taylor, "Captain Hendrick Aupaumut: The Dilemmas of an Intercultural Broker," *Ethnohistory* 43, no. 3 (1996), pp. 431–57; Daniel K. Richter, "Cultural Brokers and Intercultural Politics: New York–Iroquois Relations, 1664–1701," *Journal of American History* 75, no. 1 (1988), pp. 40–67; Daniel K. Richter, *Facing East from Indian Country: A Native History of Early America* (Cambridge, MA, 2001), esp. chs. 3 and 5; and Nancy L. Hagedorn, " 'A Friend to Go Between Them': The Interpreter as Cultural Broker During the Anglo-Iroquois Councils, 1740–1770," *Ethnohistory* 35, no. 1 (1988), pp. 60–80.

133. Nancy Shoemaker, "Kateri Tekakwitha's Tortuous Path to Sainthood," in Nancy Shoemaker, ed., *Negotiators of Change: Historical Perspectives on Native American Women* (New York, 1995), pp. 49–71; Natalie Zemon Davis, "Iroquois Women, European Women," in Margo Hendricks and Patricia Parker, eds., *Women, "Race," and Writing in the Early Modern Period* (New York, 1994), pp. 243–58.

134. See Rolena Adorno, "Images of *Indio Ladinos* in Early Colonial Peru," in Kenneth J. Andrien and Rolena Adorno, eds., *Transatlantic Encounters: Europeans and Andeans in the Sixteenth Century* (Berkeley, CA, 1991), pp. 223–70.

135. Gary Nash, *Red, White, and Black: The People of Early America* (Englewood Cliffs, NJ, 1974), pp. 104–105.

136. Merrell, *Into the American Woods.*

137. Ibid., p. 77.

138. Berlin, *Many Thousands Gone*, ch. 1. The next two paragraphs depend heavily on this brilliant chapter. For the specific details on Anthony Johnson, see pp. 29–32; for Mary Johnson and gender issues raised here, see Kathleen M. Brown, *Good Wives, Nasty Wenches, and Anxious Patriarchs: Gender, Race, and Power in Colonial Virginia* (Chapel Hill, NC, 1996), pp. 107–108, 119.

139. Berlin, *Many Thousands Gone*, p. 41.

140. Curtin, "Africa in World History," p. 25.

141. Pomeranz, *Great Divergence*; Segal, *Islam's Black Slaves*, p. 106.

142. The relation of slavery and capitalism has long been debated. The work initiating the modern debate is Williams, *Capitalism and Slavery*, and recently support for his interpretation can be found in Pomeranz, *Great Divergence*. On the other side, one should take account of the skepticism of two major economic historians: Curtin, "Africa in World History," p. 26; and Braudel, *Civilization and Capitalism*, vol. 3, p. 429. My sense is that Williams over-argues the case, and any claim for a sole role for slavery would not hold, but it seems undeniable that this central sector of the sixteenth-, seventeenth-, and eighteenth-century Atlantic economy was a source of both organizational methods and capital essential (if perhaps not sufficient) to the development of industrial capitalism in Europe and America—and thereby the "rise of the West." The growth of consumerism is a dimension of this discussion that both Williams and the critics do not address, but I think it supports a broadened formulation of Williams's position. See Blackburn, *Making of New World Slavery.*

143. Curtin, *Rise and Fall of the Plantation Complex.*

144. For the development of slavery in Asia by Europeans, see Wolf, *Europe and the People Without History*, p. 195.

145. Blackburn, *Making of New World Slavery*, pp. 332–43.

146. Curtin, *Tropical Atlantic*, p. 25.

147. Curtin, *Rise and Fall of the Plantation Complex*, p. xiii.

148. Edmund S. Morgan, *American Slavery, American Freedom: The Ordeal of Colonial Virginia* (New York, 1975), chs. 1–2. (Quoted phrases from p. 30.)

149. Kwame Anthony Appiah and Henry Louis Gates, Jr., eds., *Africana: The Encyclopedia of the African and African American Experience* (New York: Basic, 1999), pp. 1724, 1726.

150. Mintz, *Sweetness and Power*, pp. 32–38.

151. Frederick Cooper, "What Is the Concept of Globalization Good For: An African Historian's Perspective," *African Affairs* 100 (2001), p. 198.

152. Pomeranz, *Great Divergence*, p. 4. See also pp. 13, 20, 21, 25.

153. Mintz, *Sweetness and Power*, pp. 47–48.

154. Curtin, *Rise and Fall of the Plantation Complex*, p. 108.

155. Berlin, *Many Thousands Gone*, p. 95. This paragraph and the next two rely on Berlin, pp. 95–108.

156. Mary Waters, *Black Identities: West Indian Immigrant Dreams and American Realities* (Cambridge, MA, 2001), p. 31.

157. Ibid.; Curtin, *Rise and Fall of the Plantation Complex*, p. 108.

158. Waters, *Black Identities*, pp. 33, 42.

159. Howard Temperly, "Wealth of a Nation," *TLS*, April 9, 2004, p. 7.

160. Arciniegas, *America in Europe*, p. 97.

2. THE "GREAT WAR" AND THE AMERICAN REVOLUTION

1. On the novelty of the word in the lexicon of European diplomacy, see Richard B. Morris, *The Peacemakers: The Great Powers and American Independence* (New York, 1965), p. 147.

2. Carl Becker, *History of Political Parties in the Province of New York, 1760–1776* (Madison, WI, 1909).

3. Max Farrand, ed., *The Records of the Federal Convention of 1787*, rev. ed., 4 vols. (New Haven, CT, 1966), June 28, 1787, vol. 1, p. 448. Emphasis mine.

4. Robert J. Allison, *The Crescent Obscured: The United States and the Muslim World, 1776–1815* (New York, 1995), pp. xv, 17.

5. Edmund S. Morgan, *The Birth of the Republic* (Chicago, 1992), pp. 1–3; Gordon Wood, *The American Revolution* (New York, 2002), p. 3.

6. See R. Ernest Dupuy, Gay Hammerman, and Grace P. Hayes, *The American Revolution: A Global War* (New York, 1977), p. 18. See also T. H. Breen, "Ideology and Nationalism on the Eve of the American Revolution," *Journal of American History* 84, no. 1 (1997), pp. 13–39, where he shows that a vigorous English nationalism also weakened colonial claims of the "rights of Englishmen." Of course, these putatively universal rights were denied to women, to black slaves, to Indians.

7. Octavius Pickering, *The Life of Timothy Pickering, by His Son*, ed. Charles Upham, 4 vols. (Boston, 1867–73), vol. 4, p. 464.

8. Jacques Godechot, *France and the Atlantic Revolution of the Eighteenth Century, 1770–1799*, trans. Herbert H. Rowen (New York, 1965), p. 3; Morris, *Peacemakers*, p. 386.

9. See Robert Morris to John Jay, Sept. 23, 1776. Henry P. Johnston, ed., *The Correspon-*

dence and Public Papers of John Jay, 4 vols. (New York, 1890–93), vol.1, p. 85. I am indebted to Stacy Schiff for bringing this letter to my attention.

10. Louis Gottschalk, "The Place of the American Revolution in the Causal Pattern of the French Revolution," in Esmond Wright, ed., *Causes and Consequences of the American Revolution* (Chicago, 1966), p. 296. For another measure of the place of the American Revolution in European politics, see Paul W. Schroeder, *The Transformation of European Politics, 1763–1848* (Oxford, 1994), an excellent international history of the era from 1763 to 1848 from a European perspective. There are twenty times more references in the index to the Ottoman Empire (eighty) than to the United States (four), and four times more to India (fifteen).

11. Stacy Schiff, *The Great Improvisation: Franklin, France, and the Birth of America* (New York, 2005), p. 4.

12. Gottschalk, "Place of the American Revolution," p. 294.

13. Richard Morris describes it as "hobbled not alone by senescent leadership but by inept civilian direction as well." Morris, *Peacemakers*, p. 29.

14. Gottschalk, "Place of the American Revolution," pp. 294, 296–97. See also Alexander Deconde, "The French Alliance in Historical Speculation," in Ronald Hoffman and Peter Albert, eds., *Diplomacy and Revolution: The Franco-American Alliance of 1778* (Charlottesville, VA, 1981), pp. 1–37.

15. The best accounts of the peace are Morris, *Peacemakers*; and Vincent T. Harlow, *The Founding of the Second British Empire*, 2 vols. (London, 1952–64).

16. J. M. Roberts, *History of the World*, 3rd ed. (London, 1997), pp. 634, 636, 637. See also Felix Gilbert, *To the Farewell Address: Ideas of Early American Foreign Policy* (Princeton, NJ, 1961), p. 104.

17. Quoted in Gilbert, *To the Farewell Address*, p. 57.

18. Quoted in ibid., p. 106.

19. Quoted in Lawrence Stone, introduction to Lawrence Stone, ed., *An Imperial State at War: Britain from 1689 to 1815* (New York, 1994), p. 25.

20. John Robert McNeill, *Atlantic Empires of France and Spain: Louisbourg and Havana, 1700–1763* (Chapel Hill, NC, 1985), pp. 76–78.

21. John Brewer, "The Eighteenth-Century British State," in Stone, ed., *Imperial State at War*, pp. 57–61. See also John Brewer, *The Sinews of Power: War, Money, and the English State, 1688–1783* (London, 1989).

22. Molly Green, "The Ottoman Experience," *Daedalus* 134 (Spring 2005), p. 96; Jack A. Goldstone, *Revolution and Rebellion in the Early Modern World* (Berkeley, CA, 1991), pp. 324–93; C. A. Bayly, *The Birth of the Modern World, 1780–1914: Global Connections and Comparisons* (Oxford, 2004), p. 90; William H. McNeill, "The Ottoman Empire in World History," in Kemal H. Karpat, ed., *The Ottoman State and Its Place in World History* (Leiden, 1974), p. 44.

23. P. J. Marshall, introduction to P. J. Marshall, ed., *The Eighteenth Century*, vol. 2 of *The Oxford History of the British Empire* (Oxford, 1998), p. 3.

24. Quoted in ibid., p. 8.

25. P. J. Marshall, "Britain and the World in the Eighteenth Century: I, Reshaping the Empire," *Transactions of the Royal Historical Society*, 6th ser., 8 (1998), pp. 10–11.

26. Quoted in ibid., p. 11.

27. Here, as in the following paragraph, for the cases of Spain and Portugal, I rely on Jeremy Adelman, *Empire and Revolution in the Iberian Empire* (Princeton, NJ, forthcoming).

28. Khaled Fahmy, *All the Pasha's Men: Mehmet Ali, His Army, and the Making of Modern Egypt* (Cambridge, UK, 1997).

29. See Breen, "Ideology and Nationalism," pp. 13–39.

30. Bayly, *Birth of the Modern World*, pp. 88–89.

31. For Britain, see the following articles by P. J. Marshall: "Britain and the World in the Eighteenth Century: I, Reshaping the Empire," pp. 1–18; "Britain and the World in the Eighteenth Century: II, Britain and the Americans," *Transactions of the Royal Historical Society*, 6th ser., 9 (1999), pp. 1–16; "Britain and the World in the Eighteenth Century: III, Britain and India," *Transactions of the Royal Historical Society*, 6th ser., 10 (2000), pp. 1–16; "Britain and the World in the Eighteenth Century: IV, The Turning Outwards of Britain," *Transactions of the Royal Historical Society*, 6th ser., 11 (2001), pp. 1–15. For Spain and Portugal, I rely on Adelman, *Empire and Revolution in the Iberian Empire*.

32. Jacques Bernard, *The Acts and Negotiations, Together with the Particular Articles at Large of the General Peace, Concluded at Ryswick* (London, 1798), pref.

33. T. H. Breen, " 'An Empire of Goods': The Anglicanization of Colonial America," *Journal of British Studies* 25, no. 4 (1986), pp. 467–99; T. H. Breen, " 'Baubles of Britain': The American and British Consumer Revolutions of the Eighteenth Century," in Cary Carson, Ronald Hoffman, and Peter Albert, eds., *Of Consuming Interest: The Style of Life in the Eighteenth Century* (Charlottesville, VA, 1994), pp. 444–82; and T. H. Breen, *The Marketplace of Revolution: How Consumer Politics Shaped American Independence* (New York, 2004).

34. On consumption and colonial identity in Boston, see Phyllis Hunter, *Purchasing Identity in the Atlantic World: Massachusetts Merchants, 1670–1780* (Ithaca, NY, 2001), pp. 163–65.

35. Jack P. Greene, *The Quest for Power: The Lower Houses of Assembly in the Southern Colonies* (Chapel Hill, NC, 1963), pp. 451–52.

36. The range within the empire was remarkable, from Ireland to British Honduras, from Gibraltar to the British Raj in India, from Canada (after 1763) to trading posts in West Africa. For some sense of this range, see Lawrence H. Gipson, *The Triumphant Empire: The Empire Beyond the Storm*, vol. 13 of *The British Empire Before the American Revolution* (New York, 1967).

37. Brewer, "Eighteenth-Century British State," p. 68; Nicholas Canny, "Irish Resistance to Empire?" in Stone, ed., *Imperial State at War*, pp. 288–321; Breen, "Ideology and Nationalism."

38. The Irish rebellion, according to Harlow, was "sparked off" by the American revolt, but it would probably have emerged at any event, and the French sympathy and, later, direct aid were unrelated to the American revolt. See Harlow, *Founding of the Second British Empire*, vol. 2, p. 787. See also Canny, "Irish Resistance to Empire?"

39. Gipson, *Triumphant Empire*, pp. 3, 29–31.

40. Marshall, *Eighteenth Century*. There have been recent changes. See Marshall's remarkable sequence of presidential addresses (1998–2001) published in the *Transactions of the Royal Historical Society* and C. A. Bayly, *Imperial Meridian: The British Empire and the World, 1780–1830* (New York, 1989), and "The British and Indigenous Peoples, 1760–1860: Power, Perception, and Identity," in Martin Daunton and Rick Halper, eds., *Encounters with Indigenous Peoples, 1600–1850* (Philadelphia, 1999), pp. 19–41. This criticism does not hold for an earlier generation, particularly the classic work of Harlow, *Founding*

of the Second British Empire. A similar case describes the historiography of the British Caribbean in relation to the mainland colonies. In the interwar years, discussions of Britain's Atlantic empire embraced the Caribbean and mainland, and then after World War II the focus narrowed. See the prefatory comments in Andrew Jackson O'Shaughnessy, *An Empire Divided: The American Revolution and the British Caribbean* (Philadelphia, 2000).

41. Julius S. Scott III, "The Common Wind: Currents of Afro-American Communication in the Era of the Haitian Revolution" (Ph.D. diss., Duke University, 1986).

42. Bayly, *Birth of the Modern World*, p. 86.

43. Bayly, *Imperial Meridian*, pp. 334–44; Roberts, *History of the World*, pp. 543–45.

44. See Robert R. Palmer, *The Age of the Democratic Revolution: A Political History of Europe and America*, 2 vols. (Princeton, NJ, 1959–64).

45. Henry F. May, *The Enlightenment in America* (New York, 1976), pp. 90, 155–56.

46. For general comments on these themes in the Atlantic world, see Roberts, *History of the World*, pp. 549–75; Alexis de Tocqueville, *Democracy in America*, ed. Thomas Bender (New York, 1981); Alexis de Tocqueville, *The Old Regime and the French Revolution*, trans. Stuart Gilbert (Garden City, NY, 1955); Jacob Burckhardt, *The Civilization of the Renaissance in Italy* (New York, 1929).

47. Roberts, *History of the World*, pp. 549–75; Stone, introduction to *Imperial State at War*, p. 30; Philip D. Curtin, *The Rise and Fall of the Plantation Complex*, 2nd ed. (New York, 1998), p. 151; Fernand Braudel, *Civilization and Capitalism: 15th–18th Century*, trans. Siân Reynolds, 3 vols. (New York, 1981–84), vol. 3, p. 418.

48. D. A. Brading, *The First America: The Spanish Monarchy, Creole Patriots, and the Liberal State, 1492–1867* (Cambridge, UK, 1991), p. 485.

49. I have based this paragraph on Adelman, *Empire and Revolution in the Iberian Empire*; and Steve J. Stern, "Andean Insurrection: Time and Space," in John Lynch, ed., *Latin American Revolutions, 1808–1826* (Norman, OK, 1994), pp. 212–13.

50. See Sinclair Thomson, *We Alone Will Rule: Native Andean Politics in the Age of Insurgency* (Madison, WI, 2002).

51. Brading, *First America*, p. 489.

52. Ibid., pp. 477, 481.

53. Ibid., pp. 484–85.

54. Quoted in ibid., pp. 478–79.

55. Quoted in Adelman, *Empire and Revolution in the Iberian Empire*.

56. Bayly, *Imperial Meridian*, p. 60; C. A. Bayly, "The British Military-Fiscal State and Indigenous Resistance: India, 1750–1820," in Stone, ed., *Imperial State at War*, p. 339.

57. This paragraph and the following two are based on Bayly, *Imperial Meridian*, pp. 96–98; Bayly, "British Military-Fiscal State and Indigenous Resistance," p. 339. See also Marshall, "Britain and the World in the Eighteenth Century: III, Britain and India," pp. 8, 12–16, with Clive quotations on pp. 13 and 14.

58. Richard B. Sheridan, "The British Credit Crisis of 1772 and the American Colonies," *Journal of Economic History*, no. 20 (1960), pp. 161–86.

59. For two outstanding studies of the Indians in this large region, see Richard White, *The Middle Ground: Indians, Empires, and Republics in the Great Lakes Region, 1650–1815* (New York, 1991); and Daniel K. Richter, *Facing East from Indian Country: A Native History of Early America* (Cambridge, MA, 2001).

60. Alan Taylor, *American Colonies* (New York, 2001), p. 424.

61. On the centrality of the Ohio Country, see Fred Anderson, *Crucible of War: The Seven Years' War and the Fate of Empire in British North America* (New York, 2000), p. 18.

62. Daniel A. Baugh, "Maritime Strength and Atlantic Commerce," in Stone, ed., *Imperial State at War*, p. 211.

63. See Breen, " 'Empire of Goods.' "

64. Thomas Pownall, *The Administration of the Colonies* (London, 1765); Harlow, *Founding of the Second British Empire*, vol. 1, passim.

65. See D. W. Meinig, *Atlantic America, 1492–1800*, vol. 1 of *The Shaping of America* (New Haven, CT, 1986), pp. 267–69. Anderson promises a global history of the war in *Crucible of War*, but he offers a rather conventional Anglo-American framework.

66. Anderson, *Crucible of War*, p. xvi.

67. Harlow, *Founding of the Second British Empire*, vol. 1, pp. 20, 60.

68. Ibid., p. 3.

69. Jacques Godechot, *Histoire de l'Atlantique* (Paris, 1947), pp. 183, 185–86.

70. Richter, *Facing East from Indian Country*, p. 191.

71. See Linda Colley, *The Britons: Forging the Nation, 1707–1837* (New Haven, CT, 1992); Richard L. Merritt, *Symbols of American Community, 1735–1775* (New Haven, CT, 1966); Breen, "Ideology and Nationalism."

72. Lawrence S. Kaplan, *Colonies into Nation: American Diplomacy, 1763–1801* (New York, 1972), p. 3.

73. See Jay Gitlin, "On Boundaries of Empire: Connecting the West to Its Imperial Past," in William Cronon, George Miles, and Jay Gitlin, eds., *Under an Open Sky: Rethinking America's Western Past* (New York, 1992), pp. 81–82.

74. On libertarian political thought, see Bernard Bailyn, *The Ideological Origins of the American Revolution* (Cambridge, MA, 1967); for the rise of the legislatures, see Greene, *Quest for Power*.

75. The literature on the intellectual origins of the Constitution is enormous, but in the past generation it has been built around the work of Bailyn, *Ideological Origins*; Gordon Wood, *The Creation of the American Republic, 1776–1787* (Chapel Hill, NC, 1969); and J.G.A. Pocock, *The Machiavellian Moment: Florentine Political Thought and the Atlantic Republican Tradition* (Princeton, NJ, 1975), and commentators on that work. The best conclusion to that debate is offered by James T. Kloppenberg, "The Virtues of Liberalism: Christianity, Republicanism, and Ethics in Early American Political Discourse," *Journal of American History* 74, no. 1 (1987), pp. 9–33.

76. This is the implication of two exceptionally perceptive articles by Bernard Bailyn, both less celebrated than much of his other work: "Political Experience and Enlightenment Ideas in Eighteenth-Century America," *American Historical Review* 67, no. 2 (1962), pp. 339–51; and John Clive and Bernard Bailyn, "England's Cultural Provinces: Scotland and America," *William and Mary Quarterly* 11, no. 2 (1954), pp. 200–213.

77. Robert A. Kann, *The Multinational Empire: Nationalism and National Reform in the Habsburg Monarchy, 1848–1918*, 2 vols. (New York, 1950–64), vol. 1, pp. 53–54.

78. See Georges Lefebvre, "The French Revolution in the Context of World History," in Lawrence S. Kaplan, ed., *Revolutions: A Comparative Study* (New York, 1973), p. 159.

79. On the impact of the new American nation, see Bernard Bailyn, *To Begin the World Anew: The Genius and Ambiguities of the American Founders* (New York, 2003), p. 143; David Armitage, "The Declaration of Independence in World Context," *OAH Magazine of History* 18, no. 3 (2004), pp. 61–66.

80. See Gary B. Nash, *The Urban Crucible: Social Change, Political Consciousness, and the Origins of the American Revolution* (Cambridge, MA, 1979).

81. Harlow, *Founding of the Second British Empire*, vol. 1, pp. 313, 315–16, 333.

82. Esmond Wright, "The British Objectives, 1780–1783: 'If Not Dominion Then Trade,' " in Ronald Hoffman and Peter Albert, eds., *Peace and Peacemakers: The Treaty of 1783* (Charlottesville, VA, 1986), p. 25.

83. Francis Piggott and G.W.T. Omond, eds., *Documentary History of the Armed Neutralities, 1780–1800* (London, 1919), pp. 334–44. For a thorough, very able account of the complexity of the peace negotiations, see Morris, *Peacemakers*.

84. On the importance of St. Eustatius, see J. Franklin Jameson, "St. Eustatius in the American Revolution," *American Historical Review* 8, no. 4 (1903), pp. 683–708. See also Piggott and Omond, eds., *Documentary History*, pp. 357–60.

85. Harlow, *Founding of the Second British Empire*, vol. 1, p. 406; Lawrence H. Gipson, *The Great War for the Empire*, vol. 8 of *The British Empire Before the American Revolution* (New York, 1953), p. vii.

86. Robert O. Keohane, "International Commitments and American Political Institutions in the Nineteenth Century," in Ira Katznelson and Martin Shefter, eds., *Shaped by War and Trade: International Influences on American Political Development* (Princeton, NJ, 2002), p. 61.

87. This is the argument of Schroeder, *Transformation of European Politics*, p. 38.

88. Jonathan R. Dull, *The French Navy and American Independence: A Study in Arms and Diplomacy, 1774–1787* (Princeton, NJ, 1975), pp. 62, 297–304. I owe this reference to Stacy Schiff.

89. The most thorough study of the American peace commission, its dramatis personae, and its work is Morris, *Peacemakers*.

90. Edmund S. Morgan, *Benjamin Franklin* (New Haven, CT, 2002), p. 295. For a very positive account of the assets Franklin brought and his skill in their deployment, see Schiff, *Great Improvisation*; and Durand Echeverria, *Mirage in the West: A History of the French Image of American Society to 1815* (Princeton, NJ, 1957), pp. 22–31, 45–66.

91. Quoted in Morgan, *Benjamin Franklin*, p. 286.

92. Quoted in Harlow, *Founding of the Second British Empire*, vol. 1, p. 6.

93. Ibid., p. 299. His view of trade and empire was not generally shared, but neither was it unique to him. Like Adam Smith earlier, Josiah Tucker in 1783 articulated such a theory of empire specifically in reference to the Americans, as did Richard Price, a friend of Americans and an adviser of Shelburne. Ibid., pp. 210, 150. On trying to create space between France and the United States by being generous, see Wright, "British Objectives," p. 18.

94. Harlow, *Founding of the Second British Empire*, vol. 2, p. 792; Morris, *Peacemakers*, p. 433.

95. Morris, *Peacemakers*, p. 409.

96. The question of the role of the American war in producing this debt was raised by Turgot, minister of finance and a rival of Vergennes. Historians have generally accepted Turgot's judgment. But there is dispute. Among many supporting Turgot's position, see Dull, *The French Navy and American Independence*, p. 344. Challenging Turgot is Robert D. Harris, "French Finances and the American War, 1777–1783," *Journal of Modern History* 48, no. 2 (1976), pp. 233–58.

97. Frederick E. Hoxie, introduction to Frederick E. Hoxie, Ronald Hoffman, and Peter Albert, eds., *Native Americans and the Early Republic* (Charlottesville, VA, 1999), pp. ix–x.

98. Eric Hinderacker, *Elusive Empires: Constructing Colonialism in the Ohio Valley, 1673–1800* (New York, 1997), p. 224.

99. Quotations from Colin Calloway, "The Continuing Revolution in Indian Country," in Hoxie, Hoffman, and Albert, eds., *Native Americans and the Early Republic*, pp. 23, 25. See also Edward Countryman, "Indians, the Colonial Order, and the Social Significance of the American Revolution," *William and Mary Quarterly* 53, no. 2 (1996), pp. 342–62; and Colin Calloway, *The American Revolution in Indian Country* (New York, 1995), p. 281.

100. James H. Merrell, "Declarations of Independence: Indian-White Relations in the New Nation," in Jack P. Greene, ed., *The American Revolution: Its Character and Limits* (New York, 1987), pp. 202, 216, 217.

101. Quoted in Meinig, *Atlantic America*, p. 408.

102. James H. Merrell, "American Nations, Old and New," in Hoxie, Hoffman, and Albert, eds., *Native Americans and the Early Republic*, p. 338. Even the "progressive" Indian policy of Henry Knox, which aimed for reasonably fair treaties and imagined assimilation, was locked into the notion of a line of white progress, and after the War of 1812, when America turned with new energy to interior lands, the aim became simply removal. See Reginald Horsman, "The Indian Policy of an 'Empire for Liberty,' " in ibid., pp. 37–61.

103. Quoted in Richter, *Facing East from Indian Country*, pp. 235–36.

104. For this insight, see Kathleen Wilson, *The Sense of the People: Politics, Culture, and Imperialism in England, 1715–1785* (Cambridge, UK, 1998), ch. 5. For the evidence, though without the argument as here elaborated, see the impressive volumes of Harlow, *Founding of the Second British Empire*.

105. Bayly, *Birth of the Modern World*, p. 94, and *Imperial Meridian*, pp. 7–8.

106. J. H. Parry, *Trade and Dominion: The European Overseas Empires in the Eighteenth Century* (New York, 1971), p. 178.

107. Eric Williams, *Capitalism and Slavery* (1944; Chapel Hill, NC, 1994), p. 123.

108. Bayly, *Imperial Meridian*, p. 98.

109. Quoted in John C. Rainbolt, "Americans' Initial View of Their Revolution's Significance for Other Peoples, 1776–1788," *Historian* 35 (1973), p. 428.

110. See Palmer, *Age of the Democratic Revolution*; Godechot, *France and the Atlantic Revolution*; George Rudé, *Revolutionary Europe, 1783–1815*, 2nd ed. (Oxford, 2000); and Franco Venturi, *Utopia and Reform in the Enlightenment* (Cambridge, UK, 1971), ch. 5.

111. Eric Hobsbawm, *The Age of Revolution, 1789–1848* (New York, 1996), p. 54.

112. Quoted in Horst Dippel, "The American Revolution and the Modern Concept of 'Revolution,' " in Erich Angermann, ed., *New Wine in Old Skins: A Comparative View of Socio-Political Structures and Values Affecting the American Revolution* (Stuttgart, 1976), pp. 117–18.

113. Ibid., pp. 134, 136.

114. Peggy Liss, "Atlantic Network," in Lynch, ed., *Latin American Revolutions*, p. 267.

115. John Lynch, "The Origins of Spanish American Independence," in Leslie Bethell, ed., *Independence of Latin America* (Cambridge, UK, 1987), pp. 43–44.

116. Ibid., p. 44.

117. Quoted in ibid.

118. Horst Dippel, *Germany and the American Revolution, 1770–1800* (Chapel Hill, NC, 1977), pp. 259–62; Henry Steele Commager, *The Empire of Reason: How Europe Imagined and America Realized the Enlightenment* (Garden City, NY, 1977).

119. Quoted in Stuart Andrews, *The Rediscovery of America: Transatlantic Crosscurrents in an Age of Revolution* (New York, 1998), p. 59.

120. Chris Dixon, *African Americans and Haiti: Emigration and Black Nationalism* (Westport, CT, 2000), p. 25; David Geggus, "The Haitian Revolution," in Franklin W. Knight and Colin Palmer, eds., *The Modern Caribbean* (Chapel Hill, NC, 1989), p. 25.

121. See Scott, "Common Wind."

122. Sylvia Frey, *Water from a Rock: Black Resistance in a Revolutionary Age* (Princeton, NJ, 1991), pp. 226–32.

123. David Walker, *Appeal to the Colored Citizens of the World* (1829; New York, 1965), p. 21. On celebrations, see Lester D. Langley, *The Americas in the Age of Revolution, 1750–1850* (New Haven, CT, 1996), p. 142. On press coverage, see Craig S. Wilder, *In the Company of Black Men* (New York, 2001), p. 147.

124. Alfred N. Hunt, *Haiti's Influence on Antebellum America* (Baton Rouge, LA, 1988), p. 124.

125. David Patrick Geggus, "Slavery, War, and Revolution in the Greater Caribbean, 1789–1815," in David Barry Gaspar and David Patrick Geggus, eds., *A Turbulent Time: The French Revolution and the Greater Caribbean* (Bloomington, IN, 1997), p. 13. The number of slave conspiracies "discovered" in the South increased dramatically. See, for example, Robert L. Paquette, "Revolutionary Saint Domingue in the Making of Territorial Louisiana," in ibid., p. 216.

126. Anthony Maingot, "Haiti and the Terrified Consciousness of the Caribbean," in Gert Oostindie, ed., *Ethnicity in the Caribbean* (London, 1996), p. 62.

127. Quoted in Lynch, "Origins of Spanish American Independence," p. 46.

128. See Scott, "Common Wind"; James Sidbury, *Ploughshares into Swords: Race, Rebellion, and Identity in Gabriel's Virginia, 1730–1810* (New York, 1997), pp. 11–12, 39. On awareness of a possible world turned upside down after Haiti, see Ira Berlin, *Many Thousands Gone: The First Two Centuries of Slavery in North America* (Cambridge, MA, 1998), p. 222.

129. Geggus, "Haitian Revolution"; Berlin, *Many Thousands Gone*, p. 362.

130. Bernard Bailyn, "The Transforming Radicalism of the American Revolution," in Bernard Bailyn, ed., *Pamphlets of the American Revolution, 1750–1776* (Cambridge, MA, 1965), pp. 3–202.

131. See Dippel, *Germany and the American Revolution*, p. xv.

132. Edmund S. Morgan, *Inventing the People: The Rise of Popular Sovereignty in England and America* (New York, 1988).

133. John Adams, *Diary and Autobiography of John Adams* (New York, 1964), vol. 3, p. 352.

134. On the fictive quality of sovereignty, see Morgan, *Inventing the People*.

135. Hinderacker, *Elusive Empires*, p. 261.

136. Countryman, "Indians, the Colonial Order, and the Social Significance of the American Revolution," p. 355.

137. See James Kettner, *The Development of American Citizenship* (Chapel Hill, NC, 1978).

138. J. Franklin Jameson, *The American Revolution Considered as a Social Movement* (1926; Boston, 1966); Gordon Wood, *The Radicalism of the American Revolution* (New York, 1992).

139. Wood, *Radicalism of the American Revolution*, p. 126.

140. For an insightful comparison, see Langley, *Americas in the Age of Revolution*. On the ways the logic of democratization played itself out in the United States, see, among others, David Hackett Fischer, *The Revolution in American Conservatism: The Federalist Party in the Era of Jeffersonian Democracy* (New York, 1965); Wood, *Radicalism of the American Revolution*; and Robert Wiebe, *The Opening of American Society: From the Adoption of the Constitu-*

tion to the Eve of Disunion (New York, 1984). This logic was already becoming apparent in middle colony cities before the Revolution. See Patricia Bonomi, "The Middle Colonies: Embryo of the New Political Order," in Alden Vaughn and George A. Bilias, eds., *Perspectives on Early American History* (New York, 1973), pp. 63–92; Gary Nash, "The Transformation of Urban Politics, 1700–1765," *Journal of American History* 60, no. 3 (1974), pp. 605–32.

141. The classic account is that of C.L.R. James, *The Black Jacobins: Toussaint L'Ouverture and the San Domingo Revolution* (1938; New York, 1963).

142. Eugene D. Genovese, *From Rebellion to Revolution: Afro-American Slave Revolts in the Making of the Modern World* (Baton Rouge, LA, 1979), pp. xvii–xx, 85.

143. See Frederick Cooper, "What Is the Concept of Globalization Good For? An African Historian's Perspective," *African Affairs* 100 (2001), p. 199.

144. David Brion Davis, *The Problem of Slavery in the Age of Revolution, 1770–1823* (Ithaca, NY, 1975), p. 329.

145. Frederick Douglass, "Haiti and the Haitian People" (1893), in John W. Blassingame and John R. McKivigan, eds., *The Frederick Douglass Papers, Series 1*, 5 vols. (New Haven, CT, 1979–92), vol. 5, p. 523.

146. Franklin Knight, "The American Revolution and the Caribbean," in Ira Berlin and Ronald Hoffman, eds., *Slavery and Freedom in the Age of Revolution* (Charlottesville, VA, 1983), p. 255.

147. Hunt, *Haiti's Influence on Antebellum America*, pp. 108–109.

148. W.E.B. DuBois, *The Suppression of the African Slave Trade to the United States of America, 1638–1870* (New York, 1896), p. 97.

149. See Shane White, *Somewhat More Independent: The End of Slavery in New York City, 1770–1810* (Athens, GA, 1991).

150. David Brion Davis, "American Slavery and Revolution," in Berlin and Hoffman, eds., *Slavery and Freedom*, p. 279; Williams, *Capitalism and Slavery*, pp. 123–24; Knight, "American Revolution and the Caribbean," p. 256.

151. O'Shaughnessy, *Empire Divided*, p. xii.

152. Quoted in Williams, *Capitalism and Slavery*, p. 124.

153. See Garry Wills, *"Negro President": Jefferson and the Slave Power* (Boston, 2003).

154. Harlow, *Founding of the Second British Empire*, vol. 2, p. 795.

155. Rufus Choate, "The Position and Functions of the American Bar, as an Element of Conservatism in the State," repr. in Laurence Veysey, ed., *Law and Resistance: American Attitudes Toward Authority* (New York, 1970), p. 60.

156. Michel-Rolph Trouillot, *Silencing the Past: Power and the Production of History* (Boston, 1995), p. 73.

157. Quoted in Charles C. Tansill, *The United States and Santo Domingo* (Baltimore, 1938), pp. 121–22.

158. Hunt, *Haiti's Influence on Antebellum America*, p. 111; Winthrop D. Jordan, *White Over Black: American Attitudes Toward the Negro, 1550–1812* (Chapel Hill, NC, 1968), p. 384. See, more generally, Clement Eaton, *Freedom of Thought in the Old South* (Durham, NC, 1940).

159. Quoted in Knight, "American Revolution and the Caribbean," p. 242.

160. Harlow, *Founding of the Second British Empire*, vol. 2, pp. 596, 601–602.

161. Kaplan, *Colonies into Nation*, p. 148; Wood, *Radicalism of the American Revolution*, p. 150.

162. Walter Russell Mead, *Special Providence: American Foreign Policy and How It Changed the World* (New York, 2002), p. 26.

163. John Fiske, *The Critical Period of American History, 1783–1789*, 6th ed. (New York, 1890).

164. See David C. Hendrickson, *Peace Pact: The Lost World of the American Founding* (Lawrence, KS, 2003).

165. Quoted in ibid., p. 5.

166. Wood, *Creation of the American Republic*.

167. All quotations are from *The Federalist Papers* (1787–88; New York, 1961), no. 10, pp. 77–84.

168. Hinderacker, *Elusive Empires*, pp. 269, 236.

169. Ibid., p. 233.

170. Bradford Perkins, *The First Rapprochement: England and the United States* (Philadelphia, 1955), p. 24.

171. Mead, *Special Providence*, p. 26; Kaplan, *Colonies into Nation*, p. 186.

172. Stanley Elkins and Eric McKitrick, *The Age of Federalism: The Early American Republic, 1788–1800* (New York, 1993), pp. 259–61. For an insightful analysis of Hamilton's position, see Gilbert, *To the Farewell Address*, pp. 112–14.

173. See Joseph Charles, "The Jay Treaty: The Origins of the American Party System," *William and Mary Quarterly* 12, no. 4 (1955), pp. 581–630.

174. Adrienne Koch and William Peden, eds., *The Selected Writings of John and John Quincy Adams* (New York, 1946), p. 330.

175. Charles, "Jay Treaty," pp. 583, 586. See also Joseph Charles, *The Origins of the American Party System* (Williamsburg, VA, 1956).

176. Elkins and McKitrick, *Age of Federalism*, pp. 366, 824n, 355.

177. John Quincy Adams to Charles Adams, June 9, 1798, in Koch and Peden, eds., *Selected Writings*, pp. 248–49.

178. John Trumbull, *Autobiography, Reminiscences, and Letters* (New York, 1841), p. 168.

179. John Adams to Abigail Adams, March 17, 1797, in Koch and Peden, eds., *Selected Writings*, p. 144.

180. Quoted in Walter LaFeber, "Jefferson and an American Foreign Policy," in Peter Onuf, ed., *Jeffersonian Legacies* (Charlottesville, VA, 1993), p. 375.

181. Donald R. Hickey, "America's Response to the Slave Revolt in Haiti, 1791–1806," *Journal of the Early Republic* 2, no. 4 (1982), p. 362; Hunt, *Haiti's Influence on Antebellum America*, pp. 84–85.

182. Cited in Linda Kerber, *Federalists in Dissent: Imagery and Ideology in Jeffersonian America* (Ithaca, NY, 1970), pp. 47, 48.

183. John Marshall to Toussaint L'Ouverture, Nov. 26, 1800, in Charles Hobson, ed., *The Papers of John Marshall* (Chapel Hill, NC, 1990), vol. 6, p. 22.

184. On Federalist support for Toussaint L'Ouverture, see Michael Zuckerman, *Almost Chosen People* (Berkeley, CA, 1993), pp. 186–95.

185. Davis, *Problem of Slavery in the Age of Revolution*, p. 152.

186. Quoted in ibid., p. 45.

187. Thomas Jefferson to James Monroe, July 14, 1793, in Paul L. Ford, ed., *The Writings of Thomas Jefferson*, 10 vols. (New York, 1895), vol. 6, pp. 349–50.

188. Quoted in Tansill, *The United States and Santo Domingo*, p. 17.

189. Quoted in Jordan, *White Over Black*, p. 386.

190. Tim Matthewson, "Jefferson and Haiti," *Journal of Southern History* 61, no. 2 (1995), p. 237.

191. Timothy Pickering to Thomas Jefferson, Feb. 24, 1806, in Thomas Jefferson Papers, American Memory Web site, Library of Congress.

192. Henry Adams ranks the Louisiana Purchase "in historical importance" with the Declaration of Independence and the adoption of the Constitution. See Adams, *History of the United States During the Administrations of Jefferson and Madison*, 2 vols. (1889–91; New York, 1986), vol. 1, pp. 334–35.

193. Ibid., vol. 1, pp. 255, 259.

194. Ibid., vol. 1, p. 311–12. See also DuBois, *Suppression of the African Slave Trade*.

195. Adams, *History*, vol. 1, p. 311. It is intriguing that the significance of Haiti in Napoleon's thinking according to Henry Adams was dismissed a few years later by William M. Sloan, an early leader of the American Historical Association. See William M. Sloan, "The World Aspects of the Louisiana Purchase," *American Historical Review* 9, no. 3 (1904), pp. 507–21.

196. Mead, *Special Providence*, p. 17.

197. Quoted in Alfred Thayer Mahan, *Sea Power in Its Relations to the War of 1812*, 2 vols. (Boston, 1905), vol. 1, p. 41.

198. Parry, *Trade and Dominion*, p. 197; Bayly, *Imperial Meridian*, p. 2.

199. Walter LaFeber, ed., *John Quincy Adams and American Continental Empire* (Chicago, 1965), p. 61.

200. Quoted in ibid., p. 37.

201. George Dangerfield, *The Awakening of American Nationalism, 1815–1828* (New York, 1965), p. 1.

202. Gilbert, *To the Farewell Address*, p. 135.

203. Michael Schudson, *The Good Citizen: A History of American Civic Life* (New York, 1998), p. 116.

204. John Quincy Adams, "Parties in the United States" (1822–1825?), in Koch and Peden, eds., *Selected Writings*, p. 333.

205. Frederick Jackson Turner, *The Rise of the New West, 1819–1829* (New York, 1906); Frederick Jackson Turner, *The United States, 1830–1850: The Nation and Its Sections* (New York, 1935).

206. Langley, *Americas in the Age of Revolution*, pp. xv–xvi.

207. Arthur Preston Whitaker, *The United States and the Independence of Latin America, 1800–1830* (Baltimore, 1941), pp. xi, xii.

208. Langley, *Americas in the Age of Revolution*, p. 141.

209. Albert Gallatin to Matthew Lyon, May 7, 1816, in Henry Adams, ed., *The Writings of Albert Gallatin*, 3 vols. (New York, 1879), vol. 1, p. 700.

210. Quoted in Turner, *Rise of the New West*, p. 5.

211. E. James Ferguson, ed., *Selected Writings of Albert Gallatin* (Indianapolis, 1967), esp. p. 232; on Clay, see Clement Eaton, *Henry Clay and the Art of American Politics* (Boston, 1957). More generally, see Carter Goodrich, *Government Promotion of Canals and Railroads, 1800–1890* (New York, 1960).

212. Eric Hobsbawm, *The Age of Capital, 1848–1875* (London, 1975), p. 137.

3. FREEDOM IN AN AGE OF NATION-MAKING

1. Quoted in David M. Potter, *The Impending Crisis, 1848–1861*, completed and edited by Don E. Fehrenbacher (New York, 1976), p. 21.

2. *Congressional Globe*, 29th Cong., 2nd sess., app., p. 317, Feb. 8, 1847. I owe this reference to my colleague Martha Hodes.

3. Eric Foner, "The Wilmot Proviso Revisited," *Journal of American History* 56, no. 2 (1969), pp. 269–71, 273, 277.

4. Leonard Richards, *The Slave Power: The Free North and Southern Domination, 1780–1860* (Baton Rouge, LA, 2000).

5. Reginald Horsman, *Race and Manifest Destiny: The Origins of American Racial Anglo-Saxonism* (Cambridge, MA, 1981).

6. Juan Mora-Torres, *The Making of the Mexican Border* (Austin, TX, 2001), p. 11.

7. Martin Lewis and Kären Wigen, *The Myth of Continents: A Critique of Metageography* (Berkeley, CA, 1997), pp. 219–20.

8. Potter, *Impending Crisis*, p. 43.

9. *Ibid.*, p. 113.

10. Abraham Lincoln, *Speeches and Writings*, ed. Don E. Fehrenbacher, 2 vols. (New York, 1989), vol. 1, pp. 309, 315. He repeats these words in the first debate with Douglas in 1858 at p. 510.

11. Quoted in William Earl Weeks, *Building the Continental Empire* (Chicago, 1996), p. 163.

12. Quoted in James McPherson, *Drawn with the Sword* (New York, 1996), pp. 211–12.

13. There are, to my knowledge, only five efforts by American historians to explore this dimension of the war, none of them developed: David M. Potter, "Civil War," in C. Vann Woodward, ed., *The Comparative Approach to American History* (New York, 1968), pp. 135–45; Carl Degler, *One Among Many: The Civil War in Comparative Perspective* (Gettysburg, PA, 1990); James A. Rawley, "The American Civil War and the Atlantic Community," *Georgia Review* 21 (1967), pp. 185–94; Harold Hyman, ed., *Heard Round the World: The Impact Abroad of the Civil War* (New York, 1969); and McPherson, *Drawn with the Sword*, ch. 14. In European historiography, the exception is the remarkable book on the middle decades of the nineteenth century by Robert C. Binkley, *Realism and Nationalism* (New York, 1935).

14. Margaret H. McFadden, *Golden Cables of Sympathy: The Transatlantic Sources of Nineteenth-Century Feminism* (Lexington, KY, 1999), p. 144.

15. Merle Curti, "The Impact of the Revolutions of 1848 on American Thought," *Proceedings of the American Philosophical Society* 93, no. 3 (1949), p. 209.

16. Eric Hobsbawm, *The Age of Capital, 1848–1875* (London, 1975), pp. 83, 86. Small nations, the ones Woodrow Wilson would empower decades later at Versailles, were not then acknowledged. Giuseppe Mazzini, the most generous of the mid-century nationalists, could imagine only eleven sovereign nations in Europe's future; Wilson's notion of national self-determination promised nationhood to twenty-six. A certain scale was required, and the ideal of uniformity could absorb some diversity, including groups that would later resist incorporation—Catalans and Basques in Spain, various minorities in Hungary, Bretons in France.

17. *Ibid.*, p. 10. Domingo Faustino Sarmiento and Juan Bautista Alberdi, the leading intellectuals and politicians in opposition to Rosas and leaders in the new Argentine republic, closely followed the international movement of liberal ideas. See Nicolas Shumway, *The Invention of Argentina* (Berkeley, CA, 1991).

18. Hobsbawm characterizes the era as "the age of capital," and surely capitalism belongs on this list, though I have incorporated it into my discussion of the modernizing agenda of nationalism.

19. Stanley Engerman, "Emancipation in Comparative Perspective: A Long and Wide View," in Gert Oostindie, ed., *Fifty Years Later: Antislavery, Capitalism, and Modernity in the Dutch Orbit* (Pittsburgh, 1996), p. 226.

20. William H. Seward, "The National Idea: Its Perils and Triumphs," in *The Works of William H. Seward*, 5 vols. (New York and Boston, 1853–84), vol. 4, p. 349.

21. Quoted in H. C. Allen, "Civil War, Reconstruction, and Great Britain," in Hyman, ed., *Heard Round the World*, p. 65.

22. Quoted in Rawley, "American Civil War," p. 192.

23. Statements of Garibaldi and Hugo are excerpted in Belle Becker Sideman and Lillian Friedman, eds., *Europe Looks at the Civil War* (New York, 1960), pp. 73, 307. For Mazzini, see Howard Marraro, "Mazzini on American Intervention in European Affairs," *Journal of Modern History* 21, no. 2 (1949), pp. 109, 111.

24. Abraham Lincoln, *The Collected Works of Abraham Lincoln*, ed. Roy P. Basler, 9 vols. (New Brunswick, NJ, 1953–59), vol. 2, pp. 112–116.

25. Lincoln, *Speeches and Writings*, vol. 1, p. 167. Kossuth used almost identical language in making the Hungarian case at a congressional dinner in his honor soon after his arrival in the United States. *New York Times*, Jan. 6, 1852.

26. For another such statement, see Lincoln, *Collected Works*, vol. 1, p. 438.

27. Lincoln, *Speeches and Writings*, vol. 2, p. 140.

28. *New York Times*, Jan. 6, 1852.

29. Potter, *Impending Crisis*, p. 138.

30. Chase quoted in Weeks, *Building the Continental Empire*, p. 163; John Stuart Mill, *Autobiography*, ed. John M. Robson (1873; London, 1989), p. 198.

31. Quoted in Potter, *Impending Crisis*, p. 141.

32. Eric Foner, *Free Soil, Free Labor, Free Men: The Ideology of the Republican Party Before the Civil War* (New York, 1970), p. 72.

33. Potter, *Impending Crisis*, p. 343.

34. Binkley, *Realism and Nationalism*, p. 124.

35. Potter, *Impending Crisis*, p. 343.

36. I adapt this from Charles Maier's distinction between "identity" and "decision" spaces. See his "Consigning the Twentieth Century to History: Alternative Narratives for the Modern Era," *American Historical Review* 105, no. 3 (2000), p. 827.

37. J.E.E. Dalberg Acton, "Nationality," in John Neville Figgis and Reginald Vere Laurence, eds., *The History of Freedom and Other Essays* (London, 1922), p. 285.

38. Ibid., p. 287.

39. Gordon Craig, *Germany, 1866–1945* (Oxford, 1978), p. 685.

40. Bernard Bailyn, *To Begin the World Anew: The Genius and Ambiguities of the American Founders* (New York, 2003), p. 148.

41. Potter, "Civil War"; Craig, *Germany*, pp. 38–39.

42. Henry Gibbs, ed., *Kossuth: His Life and Career* (New York, 1851), p. 30.

43. Ibid., p. 23.

44. Charles M. Wiltse, "A Critical Southerner: John C. Calhoun on the Revolutions of 1848," *Journal of Southern History* 15, no. 3 (1949), pp. 299–310.

45. For Webster's toast, see John Bach McMaster, *A History of the People of the United States*, 8 vols. (New York, 1926), vol. 8, p. 152; for white southerners and European nationalist movements, see Edward Ayres, "What We Talk About When We Talk About the South," in Edward Ayres et al., eds., *All Over the Map: Rethinking American Regions* (Baltimore, 1997), p. 76.

46. Olmsted quoted in Thomas Bender, *New York Intellect* (New York, 1987), p. 200; *Richmond Daily Enquirer* in Drew Faust, *The Creation of Confederate Nationalism* (Baton Rouge, LA, 1988), p. 13.

47. Robert A. Kann, *The Multinational Empire: Nationalism and National Reform in the Habsburg Monarchy, 1848–1918*, 2 vols. (New York, 1950–64), vol. 1, pp. 53–54.

48. Donald S. Spencer, *Louis Kossuth and Young America: A Study of Sectionalism and Foreign Policy, 1848–1852* (Columbia, MO, 1977), pp. 23, 76–78. Later Kossuth referred to constitutional limitations on interfering with slavery in the United States.

49. *New York Times*, May 1, 1852.

50. I cannot claim conclusiveness for these observations. Of the more than six hundred indexed reports in *The New York Times* on Kossuth's visit to the United States, I read thirty-five closely, covering all regions. It is a small sample, so the generalizations are tentative.

51. Curti, "Impact of the Revolutions of 1848 on American Thought," p. 213.

52. See Kann, *Multinational Empire*, vol. 1, pp. 112–13; István Deák, *The Lawful Revolution: Louis Kossuth and the Hungarians, 1848–1852* (New York, 1979), pp. xv–xvi.

53. David M. Potter, *History and American Society: The Essays of David M. Potter*, ed. Don E. Fehrenbacher (New York, 1973), p. 71.

54. On the relation of the Civil War to the concentration and expansion of publishing in New York, see Alice Fahs, *The Imagined Civil War: Popular Literature of the North and South, 1861–1865* (Chapel Hill, NC, 2001). On New York more generally as a cultural center after the war, see Bender, *New York Intellect*.

55. See Constance M. Green, *Washington: Village and Capital, 1800–1878* (Princeton, NJ, 1962).

56. C. A. Bayly, *The Birth of the Modern World, 1780–1914: Global Connections and Comparisons* (Oxford, 2004).

57. See Benedict Anderson, *Imagined Communities: Reflections on the Spread of Nationalism* (London, 1983).

58. Robert Wiebe, "Framing U.S. History: Democracy, Nationalism, and Socialism," in Thomas Bender, ed., *Rethinking American History in a Global Age* (Berkeley, CA, 2002), p. 236; William H. McNeill, *Polyethnicity and National Unity in World History* (Toronto, 1986), pp. 32–45; Maier, "Consigning the Twentieth Century," p. 815.

59. See Robert Wiebe, *Who We Are: A History of Popular Nationalism* (Princeton, NJ, 2002); Wiebe, "Framing U.S. History"; Ernest Gellner, *Nations and Nationalism* (Ithaca, NY, 1983); Eric Hobsbawm, *Nations and Nationalism Since 1870* (Cambridge, UK, 1990).

60. Edward Everett Hale, *The Man Without a Country* (1863; Boston, 1906), p. iv.

61. Wiebe, "Framing U.S. History"; Wiebe, *Who We Are*, p. 48. See also Richard Bensel, *Yankee Leviathan: The Origins of Central State Authority in America, 1859–1877* (New York, 1999). Liah Greenfeld's work is highly questionable in its logic and much of its historical generalization, yet better than any other scholar she captures the developmental aspect of nationalism, especially in her most recent book, *The Spirit of Capitalism: Nationalism and Economic Growth* (Cambridge, MA, 2001), but see also her *Nationalism: Five Roads to Modernity* (Cambridge, MA, 1992).

62. See Gellner, *Nations and Nationalism*.

63. See Hobsbawm, *Age of Capital*, pp. 69–97 (quotation at p. 86).

64. These wars occurred between 1840 and 1880. See Michael Geyer and Charles Bright, "Global Violence and Nationalizing Wars in Eurasia and America: The Geopolitics of War in the Mid-Nineteenth Century," *Comparative Studies in Society and History* 38, no. 4 (1996), pp. 619–57.

65. Shumway, *Invention of Argentina*, p. 237; Paul Lewis, "Paraguay from the War of the Triple Alliance to the Chaco War, 1870–1930," in Leslie Bethell, ed., *The Cambridge*

History of Latin America (Cambridge, UK, 1986), vol. 5, p. 476. On the controversy over estimates, see Geyer and Bright, "Global Violence," p. 628.

66. See Theodore Zeldin, *France, 1848–1945*, 2 vols. (Oxford, 1973), vol. 1, pp. 737–44. Quotations from Philip M. Katz, *From Appomattox to Montmartre: Americans and the Paris Commune* (Cambridge, MA, 1998), p. 22, and Louis Greenberg, *Sisters of Liberty: Marseille, Lyon, Paris, and the Reaction to a Centralized State, 1868–1871* (Cambridge, MA, 1971), p. 128. See also Manuel Castells, *The City and the Grassroots* (Berkeley, CA, 1983), pp. 19–22.

67. Barbara Weinstein, "Constructing National Identity in a Slave Society: Brazil and the United States Compared" (paper presented at the conference "Nationalism in the New World," Vanderbilt University, Oct. 10, 2003); Thomas Skidmore, "Racial Ideas and Social Policy in Brazil, 1870–1940," in Richard Graham, ed., *The Idea of Race in Latin America, 1870–1940* (Austin, TX, 1990), pp. 8–10.

68. See Peter Kolchin, "After Serfdom: Russian Emancipation in Comparative Perspective," in Stanley Engerman, ed., *Terms of Labor: Slavery, Serfdom, and Free Labor* (Stanford, CA, 1999), pp. 87–115; Peter Kolchin, *Unfree Labor: American Slavery and Russian Serfdom* (Cambridge, MA, 1987).

69. Jefferson Davis, *The Rise and Fall of the Confederate Government* (New York, 1881); Alexander H. Stephens, *A Constitutional View of the Late War Between the States*, 2 vols. (New York, 1868–70).

70. Binkley, *Realism and Nationalism*, p. 259.

71. For helpful observations on the Thailand case, see Lewis and Wigen, *Myth of Continents*, p. 212.

72. See Donald Quataert, "The Age of Reform, 1812–1914," in Halil Inalcik and Donald Quataert, eds., *An Economic and Social History of the Ottoman Empire, 1300–1914* (Cambridge, UK, 1994), pp. 759–943.

73. Degler, *One Among Many*, pp. 23–25.

74. Frederick Jackson Turner, *The United States, 1830–1850: The Nation and Its Sections* (New York, 1935).

75. Both quoted in D. W. Meinig, *Continental America, 1800–1867*, vol. 2 of *The Shaping of America* (New Haven, CT, 1993), p. 347.

76. On the importance of his seldom discussed sojourn in the United States, see William Notz, "Frederick List in America," *American Economic Review* 16, no. 2 (1926), pp. 249–65.

77. Friedrich List, *Outlines of American Political Economy* (Philadelphia, 1827), pp. 5, 7.

78. On List's infusion of economics into nationalism, see Greenfeld, *Spirit of Capitalism*, pp. 200–214.

79. John Quincy Adams to James Lloyd, Oct. 1, 1822, in Adrienne Koch and William Peden, eds., *The Selected Writings of John and John Quincy Adams* (New York, 1946), p. 342.

80. William Freehling, *Prelude to Civil War: The Nullification Controversy in South Carolina, 1816–1836* (New York, 1966).

81. Robert Wiebe, *The Opening of American Society: From the Adoption of the Constitution to the Eve of Disunion* (New York, 1984), p. 260; Stephen A. Mihm, "Making Money, Creating Confidence: Counterfeiting and Capitalism in the United States, 1789–1877" (Ph.D. diss., New York University, 2003).

82. See Richard John, *Spreading the News: The American Postal System from Franklin to Morse* (Cambridge, MA, 1995), ch. 7.

83. Charles Bright, "The State in the United States During the Nineteenth Century," in Charles Bright and Susan Harding, eds., *Statemaking and Social Movements* (Ann Arbor, MI, 1984), p. 121.

84. All quotations from Turner, *United States*, pp. 1, 381, except "regional ambassadors," which is from Bright, "State," p. 131. The notion of an associative state is my adaptation of William Novak, *The People's Welfare* (Chapel Hill, NC, 1996), p. 240.

85. Thomas Bender, *Community and Social Change in America* (New Brunswick, NJ, 1978), pp. 87–93. On post offices, see John, *Spreading the News*, ch. 1.

86. On this analogy, see Binkley, *Realism and Nationalism*, p. 162.

87. Wiebe, *Opening of American Society*, pp. 247–48. Quotation from Grimké on p. 248.

88. See Alexis de Tocqueville, *Democracy in America*, ed. Thomas Bender (New York, 1981), pp. xxxv–xxxvii, 55–67, 556–69. On the political incompleteness of the United States and the degree to which Tocqueville doubted it was a nation-state in 1831, see Sheldon Wolin, *Tocqueville Between Two Worlds* (Princeton, NJ, 2001), pp. 34, 75.

89. G.W.F. Hegel, *Lectures on the Philosophy of World History* (1830), trans. H. B. Nisbet (Cambridge, UK, 1975), pp. 134, 168–70.

90. Thomas Jefferson to John Holmes, April 22, 1820, in Adrienne Koch, ed., *The American Enlightenment* (New York, 1965), pp. 366–67.

91. Quoted in Binkley, *Realism and Nationalism*, p. 141.

92. Manu Goswami, *Producing India: From Colonial Economy to National Space* (Chicago, 2004), p. 45.

93. Quoted in James C. Baxter, *The Meiji: Unification Through the Lens of Ishikawa Prefecture* (Cambridge, MA, 1994), pp. 5–6.

94. Binkley, *Realism and Nationalism*, p. 250; Greenfeld, *Nationalism*, pp. 227–28.

95. Binkley, *Realism and Nationalism*, pp. 172–73; Meinig, *Continental America*, p. 543.

96. Kemal H. Karpat, *Studies on Ottoman Social and Political History* (Leiden, 2002), pp. 170–71, 181.

97. Ibid., p. 49; Donald Quataert, *The Ottoman Empire, 1700–1922* (Cambridge, UK, 2000), pp. 65–66.

98. Bernard Lewis, *The Emergence of Modern Turkey* (Oxford, UK, 1961).

99. See Yu-wen Jen, *The Taiping Revolutionary Movement* (New Haven, CT, 1973); Michael Franz, *The Taiping Rebellion*, 3 vols. (Seattle, 1966). On the religious mystic who led it, see Jonathan Spence, *God's Chinese Son* (New York, 1996).

100. Frederic Wakeman, Jr., *Strangers at the Gate: Social Disorder in South China, 1839–1861* (Berkeley, CA, 1966).

101. See James J. Sheehan, *German History, 1770–1866* (Oxford, 1989), ch. 14.

102. Craig, *Germany*, pp. 38–39, 41, 44–45.

103. See Denis Mack Smith, *Italy: A Modern History* (Ann Arbor, MI, 1959), p. 21.

104. Adrian Lyttelton, "The National Question in Italy," in Mikuláš Teich and Roy Porter, eds., *The National Question in Europe in Historical Context* (Cambridge, UK, 1993), p. 81.

105. Quoted in Binkley, *Realism and Nationalism*, pp. 215–16.

106. Quoted in ibid., p. 233.

107. Deák, *Lawful Revolution*, pp. xiv, 62.

108. Kann, *Multinational Empire*, vol. 1, pp. 331–35.

109. John Hawgood, "The Civil War and Central Europe," in Hyman, ed., *Heard Round the World*, p. 175.

110. John Lothrop Motley, *Historic Progress and American Democracy* (New York, 1869), pp. 44–51.

111. Cited in Robert J. Kolesar, "North American Constitutionalism and Spanish America," in George A. Billias, ed., *American Constitutionalism Abroad* (New York, 1990), p. 53. See also Bailyn, *To Begin the World Anew*, p. 147.

112. Kolesar, "North American Constitutionalism," pp. 53–55; David Bushnell and Neill Macaulay, *The Emergence of Latin America in the Nineteenth Century*, 2nd ed. (New York, 1994), pp. 221–31; Jeremy Adelman, *Republic of Capital: Buenos Aires and the Legal Transformation of the Atlantic World* (Stanford, CA, 1999), pp. 282–83; Aline Helg, "Race in Argentina and Cuba, 1880–1930," in Graham, ed., *Idea of Race in Latin America*, ch. 3, esp. pp. 43–44. On Alberdi and the developmental state, see Tulio Donghi Halperín, *Proyecto y construcción de una nación (Argentina, 1846–1880)* (Caracas, 1980), p. xxxi. On Buenos Aires at the turn of the century, see Margarita Gutman, *Buenos Aires, 1910: Memoria del porvenir* (Buenos Aires, 1999).

113. David Rock, *Argentina, 1516–1982* (Berkeley, CA, 1985), p. 118.

114. Bailyn, *To Begin the World Anew*, pp. 146–47.

115. The best account of this war in relation to nationalism is Shumway, *Invention of Argentina*, ch. 9. The quoted material is ibid., pp. 237, 231, and Lewis, "Paraguay," p. 476. See also Rock, *Argentina*, p. 127.

116. William McFeely, *Grant: A Biography* (New York, 1981), pp. 198, 206.

117. John Mason Hart, *Empire and Revolution: The Americans in Mexico Since the Civil War* (Berkeley, CA, 2002), p. 9.

118. Harold Blakemore, "Chile from the War of the Pacific to the World Depression, 1880–1930," in Bethell, ed., *Cambridge History of Latin America*, vol. 5, pp. 501–505.

119. Wolfgang Schivelbusch, *The Culture of Defeat: On National Trauma, Mourning, and Recovery* (New York, 2001), p. 334.

120. On the importance of education, see Zeldin, *France*, vol. 2, p. 4; Gordon Wright, *France in Modern Times*, 3rd ed. (New York, 1981), p. 239.

121. See Eugen Weber, *Peasants into Frenchmen: The Modernization of Rural France, 1870–1914* (Stanford, CA, 1976).

122. Euclides da Cunha, *Rebellion in the Backlands* (1902), trans. Samuel Putnam (Chicago, 1944), pp. 162–64, 277. See also Mario Vargas Llosa, *The War of the End of the World*, trans. Helen Lane (New York, 1984), which makes the question of centralization and decentralization more central than does da Cunha.

123. Samuel Putnam, introduction to da Cunha, *Rebellion in the Backlands*, p. v.

124. Peter J. Taylor, "The State as Container: Territoriality in the Modern State System," *Progress in Human Geography* 18, no. 2 (1994), pp. 152–53.

125. Ibid., p. 156; Wiebe, *Who We Are*, p. 20.

126. Goswami, *Producing India*, p. 45, who builds on the ideas about the production of space developed by Henri Lefebvre.

127. Maier, "Consigning the Twentieth Century," p. 818.

128. See Charles Bright and Michael Geyer, "Where in the World Is America? The History of the United States in the Global Age," in Bender, ed., *Rethinking American History in a Global Age*, p. 76.

129. Taylor, "State as Container," pp. 153, 156. See also Gellner, *Nations and Nationalism*, pp. 24–25, 32, 35, 39. Tocqueville makes this point again and again in *Democracy in America*.

130. Maier, "Consigning the Twentieth Century," p. 820.
131. John Ruggie, "Territoriality and Beyond: Problematizing Modernity in International Relations," *International Organization* 47, no. 1 (1993), p. 151.
132. See Anne-Marie Thiesse, *La création des identités nationales: Europe XVIIIe–XXe siècle* (Paris, 1999), p. 229.
133. Lincoln, *Speeches and Writings*, vol. 2, p. 259.
134. See Wilbur Zelinsky, *Nation into State: The Shifting Symbolic Foundations of American Nationalism* (Chapel Hill, NC, 1988), p. 18.
135. John, *Spreading the News*, pp. 157–68; Ronald J. Zboray, *A Fictive People: Antebellum Economic Development and the American Reading Public* (New York, 1993).
136. Maier, "Consigning the Twentieth Century," p. 816.
137. Quoted in Jill Lepore, *A Is for American* (New York, 2002), p. 154.
138. On the intellectual blockade, see Clement Eaton, *Freedom of Thought in the Old South*, rev. and enl. ed. (New York, 1964); on the mails, see John, *Spreading the News*, ch. 7.
139. Quoted in John, *Spreading the News*, p. 279.
140. William H. Seward, "The Irrepressible Conflict," in Seward, *Works*, vol. 4, pp. 289, 291, 292.
141. Quotations in Kenneth M. Stampp, "The Concept of a Perpetual Union," *Journal of American History* 65, no. 1 (1978), pp. 21, 22, 23; for rejection of the use of the word "nation" see Davis, *Rise and Fall of the Confederate Government*, vol. 1, p. 97.
142. Quoted in Stampp, "Concept of a Perpetual Union," p. 27. Marshall's accommodation to slavery is specifically noted by Wiebe, *Opening of American Society*, p. 227.
143. Lucy Riall, *The Italian Risorgimento: State, Society, and National Unification* (London, 1994), p. 67.
144. Orestes Brownson, *The American Republic* (New York, 1866), pp. 6, 2, 348, 356.
145. Lincoln, *Speeches and Writings*, vol. 2, p. 250.
146. Ibid., vol. 1, p. 365.
147. See Meinig, *Continental America*, pp. 523–24.
148. Lincoln, *Speeches and Writings*, vol. 2, p. 403.
149. Seward, *Works*, vol. 4, pp. 334, 338–39.
150. Dred Scott decision quoted in Potter, *Impending Crisis*, p. 275; the Republican claim about obiter dicta noted at p. 284.
151. Lincoln, *Speeches and Writings*, vol. 1, p. 516.
152. Potter, *Impending Crisis*, p. 351; Richards, *Slave Power*.
153. Lincoln, *Speeches and Writings*, vol. 2, p. 21. The second quotation is the source for the title of Foner's outstanding study of Republican ideology, *Free Soil, Free Labor, Free Men*.
154. Lincoln to George Robertson, Aug. 15, 1855, in Lincoln, *Speeches and Writings*, vol. 1, p. 360.
155. Ibid., vol. 1, p. 426.
156. Quoted in Harry V. Jaffa, *Crisis of the House Divided: An Interpretation of the Issues in the Lincoln-Douglas Debates* (1959; Chicago, 1982), p. 333. Douglas introduced this issue in the first debate in 1858; see Lincoln, *Speeches and Writings*, vol. 1, pp. 503–504, 507.
157. Lincoln, *Speeches and Writings*, vol. 1, pp. 513–14.
158. Ibid., pp. 390–91.
159. Bensel, *Yankee Leviathan*, pp. 89–90, 91. See also Nancy Cott, *Public Vows: A History of Marriage and the Nation* (Cambridge, MA, 2000), pp. 72–76.

160. Susan Barringer Gordon, *The Mormon Question: Polygamy and Constitutional Conflict in Nineteenth-Century America* (Chapel Hill, NC, 2002), pp. 63, 81.

161. Quoted in Cott, *Public Vows*, p. 111.

162. Ibid., ch. 5, quotations on pp. 111, 120.

163. Reprinted in Francis Paul Prucha, ed., *Documents of United States Indian Policy*, 2nd ed. (Lincoln, NE, 1990), p. 136.

164. T. Alexander Aleinikoff, *Semblances of Sovereignty: The Constitution, the State, and American Citizenship* (Cambridge, MA, 2002), p. 19.

165. Cott, *Public Vows*, p. 123.

166. Quoted in Annie H. Abel, *The American Indian Under Reconstruction* (Cleveland, 1925), p. 225.

167. Shumway, *Invention of Argentina*, p. 225.

168. See Brett L. Walker, *The Conquest of Ainu Lands* (Berkeley, CA, 2001), p. 233.

169. See Richard Siddle, *Race, Resistance, and the Ainu* (London, 1996), p. 62.

170. Sayuri Guthrie-Shimizu, "For the Love of the Game: Baseball in Early US-Japanese Encounters and the Rise of a Transnational Sporting Fraternity," *Diplomatic History* 28 (2004), pp. 637–62.

171. Initially published in 1836, it was then a bestseller, and its various reprints in the 1850s (with various titles, but always including the "Awful Disclosures" phrase used here) found a responsive audience and again it was a bestseller. Maria Monk, who—with the "collaboration" of various anti-Catholic writers—authored the book, reportedly died in 1849. At least one major abolitionist, Arthur Tappan, was deeply involved with making her a celebrity.

172. See Potter, *Impending Crisis*, pp. 250–65.

173. See Ida Blom, Karen Hagemann, and Catherine Hall, eds., *Gendered Nations: Nationalism and Gender Order in the Long Nineteenth Century* (Oxford, 2000).

174. For a general argument along this line, see John Ashworth, "The Relationship Between Capitalism and Humanitarianism," in Thomas Bender, ed., *The Antislavery Debate: Capitalism and Abolitionism as a Problem in Historical Interpretation* (Berkeley, CA, 1992), pp. 180–99.

175. See generally Cott, *Public Vows*, chs. 3–4, quotations from pp. 82, 80, 64.

176. Lincoln, *Speeches and Writings*, vol. 1, pp. 357–58.

177. Ibid., pp. 360, 363.

178. Lucy Larcom to Harriet Hanson Robinson, Boston, July 9, 1856, Harriet H. Robinson Collection, Schlesinger Library, Harvard University, folder 67.

179. Seward quoted in Foner, *Free Soil, Free Labor, Free Men*, p. 51.

180. Ibid.

181. Seward, *Works*, vol. 4, pp. 348, 349, 362.

182. In 1859, Lincoln strongly articulated a vision of modernization marked by high levels of education, inventions and new technologies, and cultural institutions. See Lincoln, "Lecture on Discoveries and Inventions," and "Address to Wisconsin State Agricultural Society," in his *Speeches and Writings*, vol. 2, pp. 3–11, 90–100.

183. See Leon Fink, "From Autonomy to Abundance: Changing Belief About Free Labor Systems in Nineteenth-Century America," in Engerman, ed., *Terms of Labor*, pp. 116–36; Engerman, introduction, ibid., p. 3.

184. See Greenfeld, *Spirit of Capitalism*.

185. Lincoln, *Speeches and Writings*, vol. 2, pp. 85, 144.

186. Quoted in Foner, *Free Soil, Free Labor, Free Men*, p. 51.

187. Carl Degler, "Thesis, Antithesis, Synthesis: The South, the North, and the Nation," *Journal of Southern History* 53, no. 1 (1991), p. 8.

188. On these Democratic worries, see Thomas R. Hietala, *Manifest Design: Anxious Aggrandizement in Late Jacksonian America* (Ithaca, NY, 1985), ch. 4. The triumph of business is the theme of much progressive historiography, most notably that of Charles Beard and Mary Beard in *The Rise of American Civilization*, 2 vols. in one (New York, 1933), vol. 2. For an account of the emergence of national business leaders, see Sven Beckert, *The Monied Metropolis: New York City and the Consolidation of the American Bourgeoisie, 1850–1896* (New York, 2001).

189. Eric Foner, *Reconstruction: America's Unfinished Revolution* (New York, 1988), p. 21. See also Bensel, *Yankee Leviathan*, p. 66.

190. Nearly everywhere, nationalists held this view of railroads. For Italy, see Lyttelton, "National Question in Italy," pp. 87–88.

191. See Binkley, *Realism and Nationalism*, p. 101.

192. Kolchin, "After Serfdom," p. 100.

193. For a characterization of this change, see Novak, *People's Welfare*, pp. 240–41.

194. Foner, *Reconstruction*, p. 23. See also Rogan Kersh, *Dreams of a More Perfect Union* (Ithaca, NY, 2001), p. 196.

195. *The Nation*, July 13, 1865, quoted in Foner, *Reconstruction*, pp. 24–25.

196. Woodrow Wilson, *The State* (1889; Boston, 1904), p. 467.

197. Frederick Douglass, "Our Composite Nationality," in John W. Blassingame and John R. McKivigan, eds., *The Frederick Douglass Papers, Series 1*, 5 vols. (New Haven, CT, 1979–92), vol. 4, pp. 242–43.

198. Beard and Beard, *Rise of American Civilization*, vol. 2, p. 53.

199. Woodrow Wilson, "The Reconstruction of the Southern States," *Atlantic Monthly* 87 (1901), p. 14.

200. Quoted in Merle Curti, *The Roots of American Loyalty* (New York, 1946), p. 169.

201. Zelinsky, *Nation into State*.

202. Thiesse, *La création des identités nationales*, p. 227.

203. Beard and Beard, *Rise of American Civilization*, vol. 2, p. 53.

204. Eric Foner, *The Story of American Freedom* (New York, 1998), p. 99.

205. See Mihm, "Making Money, Creating Confidence," pp. 297, 324–28, 365, 370.

206. Cited in Eric Helleiner, *The Making of National Money* (Ithaca, NY, 2003), p. 107. For the importance of territorial exclusivity, see Emily Gilbert and Eric Helleiner, eds., *Nation-States and Money* (London, 1999), pp. 4–5.

207. Quoted in Helleiner, *Making of National Money*, pp. 111, 101, 113.

208. I base these paragraphs on the excellent article by Sven Beckert, "Emancipation and Empire: Reconstructing the Worldwide Web of Cotton Production in the Age of the American Civil War," *American Historical Review* 109, no. 5 (2004), pp. 1405–38.

209. Goswami, *Producing India*.

210. Abraham Lincoln to Horace Greeley, Aug. 22, 1862, in Lincoln, *Speeches and Writings*, vol. 2, p. 358.

211. Quoted in Foner, *Story of American Freedom*, p. 99.

212. Quoted in Rawley, "American Civil War," p. 194. For context, see Allan Nevins, *The War for the Union: The Organized War to Victory*, 4 vols. (New York, 1959–71), vol. 4, p. 404.

213. More generally on this point, see Garry Wills, *Lincoln at Gettysburg* (New York, 1992).

214. For the quoted phrase, see James T. Kloppenberg, "Aspirational Nationalism in American Intellectual History," *Intellectual History Newsletter* 24 (2002), pp. 60–71; for the notion, see Lincoln, *Speeches and Writings*, vol. 1, pp. 398–400.

215. Douglass, "Our Composite Nationality," pp. 240–41.

216. Greenfeld, *Spirit of Capitalism*, p. 23; the book emphasizes the connection of nationalism and growth.

217. Nevins, *War for the Union*, vol. 4, p. 393.

218. Gellner, *Nations and Nationalism*, p. 40.

219. Foner, *Reconstruction*.

220. See David Quigley, "Reconstructing Democracy: Politics and Ideas in New York City, 1865–1880" (Ph.D. diss., New York University, 1997), and David Quigley, *Second Founding: New York City, Reconstruction, and the Making of American Democracy* (New York, 2004).

221. Adams quoted in Foner, *Reconstruction*, p. 497; Francis Parkman, "The Failure of Universal Suffrage," *North American Review* 127 (July–Aug. 1878), pp. 1–20.

222. Foner, *Reconstruction*, p. 489.

223. Daniel Rodgers, *Contested Truths: Key Words in American Politics Since Independence* (New York, 1987), pp. 146, 153, 159–62, 169.

224. John W. Burgess, *Reconstruction and the Constitution* (New York, 1902), pp. ix, viii.

225. Ernest Renan, "What Is a Nation?" repr. in Homi Bhabha, ed., *Nation and Narration* (London, 1990), p. 11.

226. David W. Blight, *Race and Reunion: The Civil War in American Memory* (Cambridge, MA, 2001).

227. David W. Blight, " 'For Something Beyond the Battlefield': Frederick Douglass and the Struggle for the Memory of the Civil War," *Journal of American History* 75, no. 4 (1989), pp. 1156–78. For DuBois, see his *The Souls of Black Folk* (1903; New York, 1961), esp. chs. 1–2, and *Black Reconstruction: An Essay Toward a History of the Part Which Black Folk Played in the Attempt to Reconstruct Democracy in America, 1860–1880* (New York, 1935).

228. Quoted in Blight, " 'For Something Beyond the Battlefield,' " p. 1160.

229. Quoted in Blight, *Race and Reunion*, p. 138.

230. Meaning master-race democracy, the term was adapted to southern history by George Fredrickson in his *Black Image in the White Mind* (New York, 1971).

231. See Ada Ferrer, *Insurgent Cuba: Race, Nation, and Revolution, 1868–1898* (Chapel Hill, NC, 1999).

232. Quoted in Blight, *Race and Reunion*, p. 350.

4. AN EMPIRE AMONG EMPIRES

1. C. A. Bayly, *The Birth of the Modern World, 1780–1914: Global Connections and Comparisons* (Oxford, 2004), pp. 228–30.

2. Quoted in Neil Smith, *American Empire: Roosevelt's Geographer and the Prelude to Globalization* (Berkeley, CA, 2003), p. 14.

3. Richard Olney, "International Isolation of the United States," *Atlantic Monthly* 81 (May 1898), pp. 577–88.

4. David Reynolds, "American Globalization: Mass, Motion, and the Multiplier Effect," in A. G. Hopkins, ed., *Globalization in World History* (New York, 2002), p. 250.

5. William Appleman Williams, *Empire as a Way of Life* (New York, 1980).

6. Gareth Stedman-Jones, "The History of U.S. Imperialism," in Robin Blackburn, ed., *Ideology in Social Science* (New York, 1973), pp. 207–37.

7. Smith, *American Empire*, p. 19.

8. Susan Schulten, *The Geographical Imagination in America, 1880–1950* (Chicago, 2001), p. 29.

9. Seeley and Ferry cited in Harry G. Gelber, *Nations Out of Empires: European Nationalism and the Transformation of Asia* (New York, 2001), p. 117.

10. Ibid., p. 127; Gordon Craig, *Germany, 1866–1945* (Oxford, 1978), p. 119.

11. Kristin L. Hoganson, *Fighting for American Manhood: How Gender Politics Provoked the Spanish-American and Philippine-American Wars* (New Haven, CT, 1998).

12. Eric Hobsbawm, *The Age of Empire, 1875–1914* (New York, 1989), p. 67.

13. Gelber, *Nations Out of Empires*, pp. 122–24.

14. Quoted in Bayly, *Birth of the Modern World*, p. 461.

15. Quoted in Richard White, "The Geography of American Empire," *Raritan* 23, no. 3 (2004), p. 19.

16. Edmund S. Morgan, *American Slavery, American Freedom: The Ordeal of Colonial Virginia* (New York, 1975).

17. Quoted in Christopher Benfey, *The Great Wave: Gilded Age Misfits, Japanese Eccentrics, and the Opening of Old Japan* (New York, 2003), p. xi.

18. Albert A. Cave, *The Pequot War* (Amherst, MA, 1996), p. 1.

19. Alexis de Tocqueville, *Democracy in America*, ed. Thomas Bender (New York, 1981), pp. 430–31.

20. David Potter, *People of Plenty: Economic Abundance and the American Character* (Chicago, 1954), pp. 92, 93, 96, 165.

21. William Cronon, *Nature's Metropolis: Chicago and the Great West* (New York, 1991), p. 150.

22. Richard Hofstadter, *The American Political Tradition and the Men Who Made It* (New York, 1948), p. viii.

23. Michael Paul Rogin, *Subversive Genealogy: The Politics and Art of Herman Melville* (Berkeley, CA, 1983), p. 109.

24. Quoted in Williams, *Empire as a Way of Life*, p. 67.

25. John Quincy Adams, "On the Opium War," *Proceedings of the Massachusetts Historical Society* 43 (1910), pp. 303–26. Originally published in a missionary magazine, *The Chinese Repository*.

26. Herman Melville, *Pierre; or, The Ambiguities* (1852; New York, 1964), p. 79.

27. Abraham Lincoln, *Complete Works*, eds. John G. Nicholay and John Hay, 2 vols. (New York, 1922), vol. 1, p. 613.

28. Quoted in Richard W. Van Alstyne, "Empire in Midpassage, 1845–1867," in William Appleman Williams, ed., *From Colony to Empire: Essays in the History of American Foreign Relations* (New York, 1972), p. 120.

29. See Louis A. Pérez, Jr., *The War of 1898: The United States and Cuba in History and Historiography* (Chapel Hill, NC, 1998).

30. See Michael H. Hunt, *The Making of a Special Relationship: The United States and China to 1914* (New York, 1983), pp. 115–42.

31. See Julian Go, "American Empire: The Limit of Power's Reach," *Items and Issues* 4, no. 4 (2003–2004), pp. 18–23; Eileen Suárez Findlay, *Imposing Decency: The Politics of Sexuality*

and Race in Puerto Rico, 1870–1920 (Durham, NC, 1999), esp. chs. 4–5. Quotation from p. 16.

32. For an essay making this point—rather too generously—see Catherine C. LeGrand, "Living in Macondo: Economy and Culture in a United Fruit Company Banana Enclave in Colombia," in Gilbert Joseph, Catherine C. LeGrand, and Ricardo Salvatore, eds., *Close Encounters of Empire: Writing the Cultural History of U.S.–Latin American Relations* (Durham, NC, 1998), pp. 333–68.

33. See Ada Ferrer, *Insurgent Cuba: Race, Nation, and Revolution, 1868–1898* (Chapel Hill, NC, 1999).

34. Go, "American Empire," p. 22; Julian Go, "Colonial Reception and Cultural Reproduction: Filipino Elite Response to U.S. Colonial Rule," *Journal of Historical Sociology* 12, no. 1 (1999), p. 341.

35. Steve J. Stern, "The Decentered Center and the Expansionist Periphery: The Paradoxes of Foreign-Local Encounter," in Joseph, LeGrand, and Salvatore, *Close Encounters of Empire*, p. 53.

36. See Walter Russell Mead, *Special Providence: American Foreign Policy and How It Changed the World* (New York, 2002), ch. 1.

37. "Unfortunately, the United States has never learned to listen to itself as if it were the enemy speaking." Thomas Franck and Edward Weisband, *Word Politics: Verbal Strategy Among the Superpowers* (New York, 1971), p. 8.

38. Tocqueville, *Democracy in America*, ed. Bender, p. 201. See also Josiah Strong, *Our Country* (New York, 1885), a book that sold 175,000 copies, filled with the ideas pervasive in American political rhetoric of the time.

39. Quoted in Bernard W. Sheehan, *Seeds of Extinction: Jeffersonian Philanthropy and the American Indian* (New York, 1974), p. 153.

40. See Karen Ordahl Kupperman, *Indians and English: Facing Off in Early America* (Ithaca, NY, 2000), p. 11.

41. Quoted in Priscilla Wald, *Constituting Americans: Cultural Anxiety and Narrative Form* (Durham, NC, 1995), p. 26.

42. For a brief but careful and thorough account of the civilization of the Cherokees, see Mary Young, "The Cherokee Nation: Mirror of the Republic," *American Quarterly* 33, no. 5 (1981), pp. 502–24.

43. Reprinted in Theda Perdue, ed., *Cherokee Editor: The Writings of Elias Boudinot* (Knoxville, TN, 1983), p. 69.

44. Quoted in Reginald Horsman, *Race and Manifest Destiny: The Origins of American Racial Anglo-Saxonism* (Cambridge, MA, 1981), pp. 196–97.

45. See Emily Greenwald, *Reconfiguring the Reservation: The Nez Perces, Jicarilla Apaches, and the Dawes Act* (Albuquerque, NM, 2002), pp. 5–6.

46. William L. Anderson, ed., *Cherokee Removal: Before and After* (Athens, GA, 1991), pp. vii–ix.

47. Francis Paul Prucha, ed., *Documents of United States Indian Policy*, 3rd ed. (Lincoln, NE, 2000), p. 39.

48. Quoted in Wald, *Constituting Americans*, p. 27.

49. Robert V. Hine and John Mack Faragher, *The American West* (New Haven, CT, 2000), p. 175.

50. Quoted in Thurman Wilkins, *Cherokee Tragedy: The Ridge Family and the Decimation of a People* (Norman, OK, 1986), p. 201.

51. Prucha, *Documents*, 3rd ed., 52–53.
52. William McLoughlin, *Cherokee Renascence in the New Republic* (Princeton, NJ, 1986), p. 438.
53. Quoted in Ronald Wright, *Stolen Continents: The Americas Through Indian Eyes* (Boston, 1992), p. 219.
54. Prucha, *Documents*, 3rd ed., p. 61.
55. First quotation from McLoughlin, *Cherokee Renascence*, p. 449; second quotation from Hine and Faragher, *American West*, p. 178.
56. Quoted in McLoughlin, *Cherokee Renascence*, p. 449.
57. See Thomas R. Hietala, *Manifest Design: Anxious Aggrandizement in Late Jacksonian America* (Ithaca, NY, 1985).
58. Quoted in Ronald N. Satz, "Rhetoric Versus Reality: The Indian Policy of Andrew Jackson," in Anderson, *Cherokee Removal*, p. 30.
59. Quoted in Tocqueville, *Democracy in America*, ed. Bender, p. 219.
60. Perdue, *Cherokee Editor*, pp. 25–53.
61. Quoted in Young, "Cherokee Nation," p. 522.
62. Ibid., p. 519.
63. Quoted in Emily S. Rosenberg, *Spreading the American Dream: American Economic and Cultural Expansion, 1890–1945* (New York, 1982), p. 41.
64. Quoted in Lester D. Langley, "The Two Americas," in Virginia M. Bouvier, ed., *Whose America?* (Westport, CT, 2001), p. 25.
65. Cecil Robinson, ed., *The View from Chapultepec: Mexican Writers on the Mexican-American War* (Tucson, AZ, 1989), p. 200.
66. Quoted in ibid., p. x.
67. Octavio Paz, *The Labyrinth of Solitude* (New York, 1985), p. 124.
68. Robinson, ed., *View from Chapultepec*, p. 44.
69. Ulysses S. Grant, *Memoirs and Selected Letters* (New York, 1990), p. 41.
70. Quoted in ibid., p. xxxiv.
71. Gene M. Brack, *Mexico Views Manifest Destiny, 1821–1846* (Albuquerque, NM, 1975), p. 25.
72. Quoted in ibid., p. 41.
73. Quoted in Frank A. Knapp, "The Mexican Fear of Manifest Destiny in California," in Thomas Cotner and Carlos Castañeda, eds., *Essays in Mexican History* (Austin, TX, 1958), p. 196.
74. Quoted in Brack, *Mexico Views Manifest Destiny*, pp. 96–97, 99, 120, 121.
75. Robinson, ed., *View from Chapultepec*, p. 82.
76. Brack, *Mexico Views Manifest Destiny*, pp. xx–xxii, xxviii.
77. Ibid., pp. 75–79.
78. Robinson, ed., *View from Chapultepec*, pp. 85, 82.
79. Quoted in Brack, *Mexico Views Manifest Destiny*, p. 35.
80. Ibid., pp. 65, 54.
81. Ibid., p. 56; Mexican paper quoted on p. 103.
82. Ibid., p. 129.
83. I draw here heavily on Bruce Cumings, *Korea's Place in the Sun: A Modern History* (New York, 1997); and Gordon H. Chang, "Whose 'Barbarism'? Whose 'Treachery'? Race and Civilization in the Unknown United States—Korea War of 1871," *Journal of American History* 89, no. 4 (2003), pp. 1331–64.

84. Quoted in Chang, "Whose 'Barbarism'? Whose 'Treachery'?" p. 1335.
85. Quoted in ibid., p. 1337.
86. Quoted in ibid., pp. 1346–47.
87. Ibid., p. 1353.
88. Quoted in ibid., p. 1356.
89. Olney, "International Isolation of the United States," p. 588.
90. Quoted in Jean Heffer, *The United States and the Pacific: History of a Frontier* (Notre Dame, IN, 2002), pp. 113–14.
91. Quoted in Williams, *Empire as a Way of Life*, p. 125.
92. Patricia Seed, *Ceremonies of Possession in Europe's Conquest of the New World, 1492–1640* (New York, 1995), pp. 9–14.
93. Ibid., pp. 19, 25, 31, 39.
94. Quoted in Albert K. Weinberg, *Manifest Destiny: A Study of Nationalist Expansionism in American History* (1935; Chicago, 1963), p. 74.
95. Walter Weyl, *American World Policies* (New York, 1917), p. 93.
96. Alfred Thayer Mahan, *The Problem of Asia and Its Effect upon International Policies* (Boston, 1900), p. 98, quoted in Weinberg, *Manifest Destiny*, p. 93.
97. Weinberg, *Manifest Destiny*, p. 98.
98. *New York Morning News*, Dec. 27, 1845, quoted in Frederick Merk, *Manifest Destiny and Mission in American History* (New York, 1963), pp. 31–32.
99. N. Andrew N. Cleven, ed., "Thornton's Outlines of a Constitution for the United North and South Columbia," *American Historical Review* 12 (1932), pp. 198–215. Thornton inherited a plantation in the West Indies, lived off that income, and never freed his slaves. Greg Grandin called my attention to this document.
100. David Bushnell, ed., *El Liberator: Writings of Simón Bolívar*, trans. Frederick Fornoff (New York, 2003), pp. 12–30. Camilla Fojas called my attention to this statement.
101. Weinberg, *Manifest Destiny*, p. 109. Jackson was supporting the annexation of Texas when he used this phrase. Without using it, John Quincy Adams by 1811 had begun imagining a single continental republic, as in a letter he wrote to his father, John Adams, quoted in Horsman, *Race and Manifest Destiny*, p. 87.
102. On the American school of anthropology, see William R. Stanton, *The Leopard's Spots: Scientific Attitudes Toward Race in America* (Chicago, 1960); Thomas F. Gossett, *Race: The History of an Idea in America* (Dallas, 1963); and, more generally, George W. Stocking, *Race, Culture, and Evolution* (New York, 1968).
103. Quoted in Hietala, *Manifest Design*, p. 134.
104. Strong, *Our Country*, pp. 177, 161–62.
105. Quotations from Horsman, *Race and Manifest Destiny*, pp. 184, 213.
106. Ibid., pp. 62, 77.
107. First quotation is from David Engerman, "Thinking Locally, Acting Globally," *Reviews in American History* 30, no. 3 (2002), p. 463; second from W.E.B. DuBois, *The Souls of Black Folk* (1903; New York, 1961), p. 23. Engerman points out that Warren G. Harding in 1921 almost precisely repeated DuBois's phrasing of the first quotation: the U.S. "race problem . . . is only a phase of a race issue the whole world confronts."
108. This connection can be traced in the catalog of the New York Public Library. It was first brought to my attention by Robert Vitalis.
109. Franklin H. Giddings, *Democracy and Empire* (New York, 1900), pp. 284–85. He cites and heavily relies on the enormously influential work of the British social theorist Ben-

jamin Kidd, *The Control of the Tropics* (New York, 1898), which made the same argument on grounds of what Kidd called "social efficiency."

110. Julius W. Pratt, "The Ideology of American Expansionism," in Avery Craven, ed., *Essays in Honor of William E. Dodd* (Chicago, 1935), pp. 351–52.

111. Quoted in ibid.

112. Quoted in Weinberg, *Manifest Destiny*, p. 307.

113. Strong, *Our Country*, p. 175.

114. Ibid., pp. 173, 159–61.

115. John W. Burgess, *Political Science and Comparative Constitutional Law*, 2 vols. (Boston, 1890), vol. 1, p. 45; John W. Burgess, *Reconstruction and the Constitution* (New York, 1902).

116. Burgess, *Political Science and Comparative Constitutional Law*, vol. 1, pp. 45–46, 37. Burgess was writing in 1890, before the Spanish-American War, and he claimed later in his autobiography that he opposed that war, for it created "subjects," not citizens. Whatever he did in 1898, and he took no public stand against imperialism, he made a powerful and influential argument for empire in 1890. For the autobiographical statement, see John W. Burgess, *Reminiscences of an American Scholar* (New York, 1934), p. 316.

117. On the changing relations of religion and Americanism, see Heffer, *The United States and the Pacific*, pp. 113–14.

118. Mead, *Special Providence*, p. 80, but the whole book makes this argument.

119. Charles Francis Adams, *Imperialism* (Boston, 1899), p. 12.

120. See Morton Rothstein, "The American West and Foreign Markets, 1850–1900," in David M. Ellis, ed., *The Frontier in American Development* (Ithaca, NY, 1969), esp. p. 394.

121. Quoted in ibid., pp. 386, 381n.

122. Hietala, *Manifest Design*, p. 59.

123. This data is taken from a sequence of tables in Williams, *Empire as a Way of Life*, pp. 73–76, 102–10, 136–42.

124. See Robert O. Keohane, "International Commitments and American Political Institutions in the Nineteenth Century," in Ira Katznelson and Martin Shefter, eds., *Shaped by War and Trade: International Influences on American Political Development* (Princeton, NJ, 2002), p. 60.

125. James A. Field, Jr., "All Economists, All Diplomats," in William H. Becker and Samuel F. Wells, Jr., eds., *Economics and World Power* (New York, 1984), pp. 2, 4, 7.

126. Quoted in Weinberg, *Manifest Destiny*, pp. 26–27.

127. Quoted in Field, "All Economists, All Diplomats," p. 2.

128. See Gregory H. Nobles, *American Frontiers: Cultural Encounters and Continental Conquest* (New York, 1997), p. 131; Kingsley J. Brauer, "Economics and the Diplomacy of American Expansionism," in Becker and Wells, eds., *Economics and World Power*, pp. 84, 87, 92. On American protection of the interests of missionaries, see Hunt, *Making of a Special Relationship*, pp. 165–68.

129. See Mira Wilkins, *The Emergence of Multinational Enterprise: American Businesses Abroad from the Colonial Era to 1914* (Cambridge, MA, 1970); Emily S. Rosenberg, *Financial Missionaries to the World: The Politics and Culture of Dollar Diplomacy, 1900–1930* (Cambridge, MA, 1999).

130. See Warren Zimmermann, *First Great Triumph: How Five Americans Made Their Country a World Power* (New York, 2002).

131. For key documents, see Walter LaFeber, ed., *John Quincy Adams and American Continental Empire* (Chicago, 1965), pp. 96-116.

132. See Zimmermann, *First Great Triumph*, pp. 31-32.

133. LaFeber, ed., *John Quincy Adams and American Continental Empire*, pp. 88, 36-37.

134. William Earl Weeks, *John Quincy Adams and American Global Empire* (Lexington, KY, 1992), pp. 194-96.

135. Excerpted in LaFeber, *John Quincy Adams and American Continental Empire*, p. 116.

136. Adams, "On the Opium War," pp. 307-308, 313.

137. On his difficulty in finding a publisher, see Hunt, *Making of a Special Relationship*, p. 34.

138. Weeks, *John Quincy Adams and American Global Empire*, p. 47.

139. See his speech in the Senate "Continental Rights and Relations" (1853), in William H. Seward, *The Works of William H. Seward*, 5 vols. (New York and Boston, 1853-84), vol. 3, pp. 605-18.

140. On the development of this notion of the Pacific after 1850, see Arthur P. Dudden, *The American Pacific* (New York, 1992), p. 17. On Seward, see *Works*, vol. 3, p. 618.

141. Benfey, *Great Wave*, p. 16.

142. Dudden, *American Pacific*, p. 14.

143. Quoted in Charles Vevier, "American Continentalism: An Idea of Expansion, 1845-1910," *American Historical Review* 65, no. 2 (1960), p. 329.

144. Quoted in Dudden, *American Pacific*, p. 13.

145. Heffer, *The United States and the Pacific*, p. 13.

146. Quoted in Henry Nash Smith, *Virgin Land* (Cambridge, MA, 1950), p. 31.

147. Quoted in Josiah Strong, *Expansion Under New World-Conditions* (New York, 1900), pp. 184-85.

148. Quoted in Ernest N. Paolino, *The Foundations of the American Empire: William Henry Seward and U.S. Foreign Policy* (Ithaca, NY, 1973), p. 27.

149. Seward, *Works*, vol. 3, p. 618.

150. D. W. Meinig, *Continental America, 1800-1867*, vol. 2 of *The Shaping of America* (New Haven, CT, 1993), p. 555; Paolino, *Foundations of the American Empire*, p. x.

151. See Paolino, *Foundations of the American Empire*, pp. 9-12, quotation on p. 12.

152. Walter LaFeber, *The New Empire: An Interpretation of American Expansion, 1860-1898* (Ithaca, NY, 1963), p. 27.

153. Quoted in Paolino, *Foundations of the American Empire*, pp. 26, 29, 32.

154. Seward, *Works*, vol. 3, p. 616.

155. Quoted in Weinberg, *Manifest Destiny*, p. 259.

156. Quoted in Paul A. Kramer, "Empires, Exceptions, and Anglo-Saxons: Race and Rule Between the British and United States Empires, 1880-1910," *Journal of American History* 88, no. 4 (2002), p. 1315. See also Julius W. Pratt, *The Expansionists of 1898* (Baltimore, 1936), p. 2 (quoting Henry Cabot Lodge).

157. Gervasio Luis García, "I Am the Other: Puerto Rico in the Eyes of the North Americans, 1898," *Journal of American History* 87, no. 1 (2000), p. 43.

158. Quoted in Kramer, "Empires, Exceptions, and Anglo-Saxons," pp. 1331, 1332.

159. Quoted in Walter L. Williams, "United States Indian Policy and the Debate over Philippine Annexation: Implications for the Origins of American Imperialism," *Journal of American History* 66, no. 4 (1980), pp. 817, 820.

160. Shelly Streeby, *American Sensations: Class, Empire, and the Production of Popular Culture* (Berkeley, CA, 2002), p. 3.

161. See Michael H. Hunt, *Ideology and U.S. Foreign Policy* (New Haven, CT, 1987), p. 55.

162. Strong, *Expansion*, pp. 48, 44.

163. Quoted in Merk, *Manifest Destiny and Mission*, p. 232.

164. Frederick Jackson Turner, "The Problem of the West," in Ray Allen Billington, ed., *Frontier and Section: Selected Essays of Frederick Jackson Turner* (Englewood Cliffs, NJ, 1961), p. 74.

165. See Strong, *Expansion*, p. 34; and Kidd, *Control of the Tropics*.

166. Kidd, *Control of the Tropics*, pp. 32, 86, 83–84.

167. Quoted in Grayson Kirk, *Philippine Independence* (New York, 1936), p. 17.

168. In 1898 most European journalists and authorities on the Philippines believed that an independent Philippines would fail. See Ernest R. May, *American Imperialism* (New York, 1968), p. 254. However, the Filipino leaders had hoped that the establishment of a U.S. naval protectorate might secure their independence.

169. Elsewhere, to a different audience, he referred to the markets the Philippines would make available, not to moral or other uplift. See Kirk, *Philippine Independence*, p. 15.

170. Quoted in Williams, "United States Indian Policy and the Debate over Philippine Annexation," p. 817. The distinguished Harvard historian Albert Bushnell Hart concurred: "for more than a hundred years" the U.S. has been "a great colonial power." The year 1898 represents only an "enlargement" of the policy long adopted in relation to the Indians. Ibid., p. 831.

171. Quoted in Brook Thomas, "A Constitution Led by the Flag: The *Insular Cases* and the Metaphor of Incorporation," in Christine Duffy Burnett and Burke Marshall, eds., *Foreign in a Domestic Sense: Puerto Rico, American Expansion, and the Constitution* (Durham, NC, 2001), p. 95.

172. Williams, "United States Indian Policy and the Debate over Philippine Annexation," p. 811.

173. Quoted in ibid., p. 819.

174. Quoted in Hine and Faragher, *American West*, p. 376.

175. Quotations from T. Alexander Aleinikoff, *Semblances of Sovereignty: The Constitution, the State, and American Citizenship* (Cambridge, MA, 2002), p. 23, and Winfred Lee Thompson, *The Introduction of American Law into the Philippines and Puerto Rico, 1898–1905* (Fayetteville, AR, 1989), pp. 101–104, quotation from case on p. 102.

176. Quoted in Williams, "United States Indian Policy and the Debate over Philippine Annexation," p. 811.

177. Ibid., p. 817.

178. Matthew Frye Jacobson, *Special Sorrows: The Diasporic Imagination of Irish, Polish, and Jewish Immigrants in the United States* (Cambridge, MA, 1995), pp. 141–58, 177–216. Quotation from p. 180.

179. W.E.B. DuBois, "The Present Outlook for the Dark Races of Mankind," *AME Church Review* 17, no. 2 (Oct. 1900) pp. 102–103.

180. Quoted in Ferrer, *Insurgent Cuba*, p. 195.

181. Ibid., pp. 3–5. Race and antiracism were not fixed categories over the long course of the Cuban struggle, and Ferrer's subtle examination reveals the ebbing and flowing of antiracism and its various forms, but she is clear that U.S. intervention was a powerful blow to the vision of a race-free Cuba.

182. Pérez, *War of 1898*, p. 11.

183. Ada Ferrer, "Cuba, 1898: Rethinking Race, Nation, and Empire," *Radical History Review* 73 (Jan. 1999), pp. 22–46.

184. Ibid., pp. 94–95.
185. Ferrer, *Insurgent Cuba*, pp. 187–89.
186. Pérez, *War of 1898*, p. 150.
187. Quoted in Ferrer, *Insurgent Cuba*, p. 188.
188. Ibid., pp. 171, 188–92.
189. See Pérez, *War of 1898*; Ferrer, *Insurgent Cuba*; Renato Constantino, *Insight and Foresight* (Quezon City, Philippines, 1977), pp. 24–37.
190. Pérez, *War of 1898*; Luis A. Pérez, Jr., "1898 and the Legacies of Intervention," in Bouvier, ed., *Whose America?* p. 151.
191. Ferrer, *Insurgent Cuba*, p. 199.
192. See Dudden, *American Pacific*, p. 82.
193. Renato Constantino with Letizia R. Constantino, *A History of the Philippines* (New York, 1975), pp. 162–63.
194. Maximo Kalaw, *The Development of Philippine Politics, 1872–1920* (Manila, 1926), p. 101. In addition, the American consul in Hong Kong—in a letter to Aguinaldo—indicated an expectation of Philippine independence. Ibid., p. 102.
195. Dewey quoted in Zimmermann, *First Great Triumph*, p. 303.
196. Kalaw, *Development of Philippine Politics*, p. 106.
197. Kirk, *Philippine Independence*, p. 10. Since an independent Philippines was vulnerable to other powers, a protectorate made sense. On vulnerability, see H. W. Brands, *Bound to Empire: The United States and the Philippines* (New York, 1992), p. 25.
198. Quoted in Kalaw, *Development of Philippine Politics*, pp. 106–107. There seems to be no doubt that many U.S. consular and military officials gave vague but positive assurances of independence. See Constantino, *History of the Philippines*, pp. 207–208.
199. Constantino, *History of the Philippines*, pp. 207–208; Carl Schurz, *The Policy of Imperialism* (Chicago, 1899).
200. See Zimmermann, *First Great Triumph*, p. 306.
201. Constantino, *History of the Philippines*, p. 213.
202. Renato Constantino, *Identity and Consciousness: The Philippine Experience* (Quezon City, Philippines, 1974), pp. 33–34.
203. Quoted in Stanley Karnow, *In Our Image: America's Empire in the Philippines* (New York, 1989), p. 154.
204. Quoted in Alan Dawley, *Changing the World: American Progressives in War and Revolution* (Princeton, NJ, 2003), p. 18.
205. Quotation from Weinberg, *Manifest Destiny*, p. 294, who uses it to make a different point: whether permission was needed from the Filipinos to colonize them.
206. Reynaldo C. Ileto, "The Philippine-American War: Friendship and Forgetting," in Angel Velasco Shaw and Luis H. Francia, eds., *Vestiges of War: The Philippine-American War and the Aftermath of an Imperial Dream, 1899–1999* (New York, 2002), p. 4.
207. Rebecca Karl, *Staging the World: Chinese Nationalism at the Turn of the Twentieth Century* (Durham, NC, 2002), p. 86.
208. Quoted in ibid., p. 93.
209. Ibid., p. 87.
210. Liang Qichao, "On the New Rules for Destroying Countries" [*Mieguo xinfa lun*], *Journal of Pure Critique* [*Zingyiu bao*], July 16–Aug. 24, 1901, repr. in Liang Qichao, *Yinbingshi wenji*, vol. 6, pp. 32–47. I am indebted to my colleagues Marilyn Young, for bringing this to my attention, and Rebecca Karl, for sharing her translation of it.

211. Quoted in Brauer, "Economics and the Diplomacy of American Expansionism," p. 64.

212. See the memorandum he wrote to himself in Aug. 1898, "What Ought We Do?" in *The Papers of Woodrow Wilson*, ed. Arthur S. Link, 69 vols. (Princeton, NJ, 1966–94), vol. 10, pp. 574–76.

213. Woodrow Wilson, "Democracy and Efficiency," *Atlantic Monthly*, March 1901, p. 298.

214. May, *American Imperialism*, p. 222. The messy Boer War also soured Roosevelt on colonies.

215. See Thomas J. Knock, *To End All Wars: Woodrow Wilson and the Quest for a New World Order* (New York, 1992).

216. This point was made recently and strongly (perhaps too strongly) by John Judis, "History Lesson," *New Republic*, June 9, 2003, pp. 19–23.

217. On Jefferson, see William Earl Weeks, "American Nationalism, American Imperialism: An Interpretation of American Political Economy, 1789–1861," *Journal of the Early Republic* 14, no. 4 (1994), p. 492; on NSC-68, see Williams, *Empire as a Way of Life*, p. x.

218. Williams, *Empire as a Way of Life*, p. 127.

219. These travels are gleaned from Herbert Hoover, *The Memoirs of Herbert Hoover: Years of Adventure, 1874–1920*, 2 vols. (New York, 1952), vol. 1, chs. 5–8.

220. Quoted in Wilkins, *Emergence of Multinational Enterprise*, p. 71.

221. Quoted in Knock, *To End All Wars*, pp. 28, 71.

222. Quoted in Anders Stephanson, *Manifest Destiny: American Expansion and the Empire of Right* (New York, 1995), p. 107.

223. Quoted in Michael Doyle, *Empires* (Ithaca, NY, 1986), p. 32.

224. Quoted in Dawley, *Changing the World*, p. 82.

225. See Alexander Hamilton, *The Federalist Papers*, no. 11. See also Mead, *Special Providence*, pp. 79–80.

226. Wilkins, *Emergence of Multinational Enterprise*, pp. 36, 70–71; David Pletcher, "Economic Growth and Diplomatic Adjustment," in Becker and Wells, eds., *Economics and World Power*, p. 122; John Agnew, *The United States in the World Economy: A Regional Geography* (Cambridge, UK, 1987), p. 21.

227. Wilkins, *Emergence of Multinational Enterprise*, p. 203.

228. On Mahan's role, see LaFeber, *New Empire*, p. 92.

229. Alfred E. Eckes, Jr., and Thomas W. Zeiler, *Globalization and the American Century* (Cambridge, UK, 2003), p. 14.

230. On overlooking the Chinese, see Hunt, *Making of a Special Relationship*, p. 197.

231. See Frank Ninkovich, *The United States and Imperialism* (Oxford, 2001), p. 206.

232. Zimmermann, *First Great Triumph*, p. 447.

233. On declining returns, see Rosenberg, *Financial Missionaries to the World*, p. 15.

234. Ibid., p. 48.

235. Quoted in Niall Ferguson, *Colossus: The Price of America's Empire* (New York, 2004), p. 56.

236. Ibid., p. 54. For an excellent account by Lord Cromer, the British official who was instrumental in shaping this form of imperialism, which may have directly influenced the Americans, see Evelyn Baring Cromer, *Modern Egypt*, 2 vols. (New York, 1908), vol. 2, pp. 280–87.

237. Rosenberg, *Financial Missionaries to the World*, p. 50; Ferguson, *Colossus*, p. 56.

238. Ferguson, *Colossus*, p. 71.

239. Barry Eichengreen, "House Calls of the Money Doctor: The Kemmer Mission to Latin America, 1917–1931," in Paul W. Drake, ed., *Money Doctors, Foreign Debts, and Economic Reforms in Latin America from the 1890s to the Present* (Wilmington, DE, 1994), pp. 111–32, esp. p. 111.

240. On the significance of Wilson as a world leader, see N. Gordon Levin, *Woodrow Wilson and World Politics* (New York, 1968); Knock, *To End All Wars*; Dawley, *Changing the World*.

241. On the continuing perceived relevance of Wilson, see, for example, Judis, "History Lesson."

242. Levin, *Woodrow Wilson and World Politics*, p. 182.

243. One finds this language in his address on the Fourteen Points and in his War Message to Congress. See *Papers of Woodrow Wilson*, vol. 41, pp. 535–36. The famous passage on making the world safe for democracy is at p. 524.

244. Such is the principal argument of Knock, *To End All Wars*.

245. Ibid.

246. See Woodrow Wilson, *The Road Away from Revolution* (Boston, 1923), originally published in *The Atlantic Monthly* (1923).

247. See *Papers of Woodrow Wilson*, vol. 40, p. 538.

248. Quoted in Dawley, *Changing the World*, p. 173.

249. Quoted in Knock, *To End All Wars*, p. 145.

250. See *Papers of Woodrow Wilson*, vol. 45, pp. 535–36.

251. Levin, *Woodrow Wilson and World Politics*, p. 7.

252. Knock, *To End All Wars*, makes this point strongly.

253. See *Papers of Woodrow Wilson*, vol. 40, p. 539.

254. Quoted in Arno J. Mayer, *Politics and Diplomacy of Peacemaking: Containment and Counterrevolution at Versailles, 1918–1919* (New York, 1967), p. 364.

255. The fig leaf image comes from Dawley, *Changing the World*, p. 251.

256. Levin, *Woodrow Wilson and World Politics*, p. vii.

257. Ibid., p. 237.

5. THE INDUSTRIAL WORLD AND THE TRANSFORMATION OF LIBERALISM

1. Geoffrey Barraclough, *An Introduction to Contemporary History* (London, 1964), p. 46.

2. Adna F. Weber, *The Growth of Cities in the Nineteenth Century* (1899; repr., Ithaca, NY, 1963), p. 1.

3. Charles A. Beard, *The Administration and Politics of Tokyo* (New York, 1923), pp. 163, 15.

4. Richard Hofstadter, *The Age of Reform* (New York, 1955); Robert Wiebe, *The Search for Order* (New York, 1967).

5. On the flowering of postwar exceptionalism, see Daniel T. Rodgers, "Exceptionalism," in Anthony Molho and Gordon Wood, eds., *Imagined Histories: American Historians Interpret the Past* (Princeton, NJ, 1998), pp. 21–40.

6. See James T. Kloppenberg, *Uncertain Victory: Social Democracy and Progressivism in European and American Thought, 1870–1920* (New York, 1986); Daniel T. Rodgers, *Atlantic Crossings: Social Politics in a Progressive Age* (Cambridge, MA, 1998); Alan Dawley, *Strug-*

gles for Justice: Social Responsibility and the Liberal State (Cambridge, MA, 1991); Alan Dawley, *Changing the World: American Progressives in War and Revolution* (Princeton, NJ, 2003).

7. See Gwendolyn Wright, *The Politics of Design in French Colonial Urbanism* (Chicago, 1991); and Alice L. Conklin, *A Mission to Civilize: The Republican Idea of Empire in France and West Africa, 1895–1930* (Stanford, CA, 1997).

8. Frederick Cooper, *Decolonization and African Society: The Labor Question in French and British Africa* (Cambridge, UK, 1996).

9. Quoted in Kenneth P. Pyle, "Advantages of Followership: German Economics and Japanese Bureaucrats, 1890–1925," in Peter Kornicki, ed., *Meiji Japan: Political, Economic, and Social History*, 4 vols. (London, 1998), vol. 4, pp. 233, 212.

10. Arif Dirlik, "Socialism and Capitalism in Chinese Socialist Thinking: The Origins," *Studies in Comparative Communism* 21, no. 2 (1988), pp. 136–37.

11. For the phrase "industrial landscapes" as well as the point being made, see Rodgers, *Atlantic Crossings*, p. 44.

12. Frederic C. Howe, *The City: The Hope of Democracy* (New York, 1905), pp. 27–28, 30.

13. Anson Rabinbach, "Social Knowledge, Social Risk, and the Politics of Industrial Accidents in Germany and France," in Dietrich Rueschemeyer and Theda Skocpol, eds., *States, Social Knowledge, and the Origins of Modern Social Policies* (Princeton, NJ, 1996), pp. 48–49.

14. See Thomas L. Haskell, *The Emergence of Professional Social Science* (Urbana, IL, 1977); Nathan Glazer, "The Rise of Social Research in Europe," in Daniel Lerner, ed., *The Human Meaning of the Social Sciences* (New York, 1959), pp. 43–72; and Thomas Bender, *Intellect and Public Life* (Baltimore, 1993), chs. 3–4.

15. Daniel T. Rodgers, *Contested Truths: Keywords in American Politics Since Independence* (New York, 1987), ch. 5; Carol Gluck, *Japan's Modern Myths: Ideology in the Late Meiji Period* (Princeton, NJ, 1985), p. 27.

16. Benjamín Vicuña, *El socialismo revolucionario y la cuestión social en Europa y en Chile* (Santiago de Chile, 1908), pp. 9–23.

17. Albion W. Small, *The Origins of Sociology* (Chicago, 1924), pp. 335–37.

18. Albion W. Small, "The Relation of Sociology to Economics," *Publications of the American Economic Association* 10, no. 3, supp. (1895), p. 106.

19. Richard T. Ely, *Ground Under Our Feet: An Autobiography* (New York, 1938), pp. 110–11.

20. Dorothy Ross, *Origins of American Social Science* (Cambridge, UK, 1991), pp. 95–96.

21. Edward A. Ross, *Social Control: A Survey of the Foundations of Order* (1901; New York, 1929), p. 376.

22. Herbert D. Croly, *The Promise of American Life* (New York, 1909), pp. 139–40. The ongoing quality is clearer in his *Progressive Democracy* (New York, 1914).

23. Albert Shaw, "A Student at Johns Hopkins," in *Elgin Ralston Lowell Gould: A Memorial* (New York, 1916), p. 16.

24. See Thomas L. Haskell, "Professionalism Versus Capitalism: R. H. Tawney, Émile Durkheim, and C. S. Peirce on the Disinterestedness of Professional Communities," in Thomas L. Haskell, ed., *The Authority of Experts: Studies in History and Theory* (Bloomington, IN, 1984), pp. 180–225; Thomas Bender, "The Erosion of Public Culture: Cities, Discourses, and Professional Disciplines," in ibid., pp. 84–106; and Samuel Haber, *The Quest for Authority and Honor in the American Professions, 1750–1900* (Chicago, 1991).

25. See Rodgers, *Atlantic Crossings*, p. 237; Bender, *Intellect and Public Life*, pp. 49–50.

26. On Japan, see Sheldon Garon, *The State and Labor in Modern Japan* (Berkeley, CA, 1987); on the U.S. Bureau of Labor Statistics, see James Leiby, *Carroll D. Wright and Labor Reform* (Cambridge, MA, 1960); on international standards, see Mary O. Furner, "Knowing Capitalism: Public Investigation and the Labor Question in the Long Progressive Era," in Mary O. Furner and Barry Supple, eds., *The State and Economic Knowledge: The American and British Experiences* (Cambridge, UK, 1990), p. 247.

27. Eduardo A. Zimmermann, *Los liberales reformistas: La cuestión social en la Argentina* (Buenos Aires, 1995), pp. 88, 176, 178.

28. Rodgers, *Atlantic Crossings*, p. 237.

29. Alejandro Unsain, *Legislación del trabajo*, 3 vols. (Buenos Aires, 1925–28), vol. 1, pp. 12–13, 135–41, 184; vol. 3, pp. 5, 24, 50, 334.

30. Dawley, *Changing the World*.

31. See Alexander Keyssar, *The Right to Vote: The Contested History of Democracy in the United States* (New York, 2000), pp. 203–205.

32. See Richard T. Ely, *French and German Socialism for Modern Times* (New York, 1883); Jane Addams, *Democracy and Social Ethics*, ed. Ann F. Scott (1907; Cambridge, MA, 1964), p. 176 and passim; Walter Weyl, *The New Democracy* (1912; New York, 1927), p. 160.

33. Quoted in Michael Freeden, *The New Liberalism: An Ideology of Reform* (Oxford, 1978), p. 40.

34. Weyl, *New Democracy*, pp. 278–79.

35. Dawley, *Changing the World*, p. 42.

36. Ibid., p. 4. See also José Aguirre, ed., *Apuntes de legislación industrial* (Buenos Aires, 1915), esp. pref. by Alejandro Unsain and ch. 1 by Cosme Sánchez Antelo.

37. Quoted in Leon Fink, *Progressive Intellectuals and the Dilemma of Democratic Commitment* (Cambridge, MA, 1997), p. 19.

38. Chamberlain quoted in Rodgers, *Atlantic Crossings*, p. 54; Addams, *Democracy and Social Ethics*, pp. 137, 165–66; Churchill quoted in Maria Sophia Quine, *Italy's Social Revolution: Charity and Welfare from Liberlism to Fascism* (London, 2002), pp. 78–79.

39. Seki quoted in Jeffrey Hanes, *City as Subject: Seki Hajime and the Reinvention of Modern Osaka* (Berkeley, CA, 2002), pp. 145–46, 43.

40. Quoted in Freeden, *New Liberalism*, p. 34.

41. Ibid., p. 1.

42. Frederick Jackson Turner, "The Significance of History," in *Frontier and Section: Selected Essays of Frederick Jackson Turner* (Englewood Cliffs, NJ, 1961), p. 17; Weyl, *New Democracy*, p. 165.

43. Hannah Arendt, *The Human Condition* (Chicago, 1958); T. H. Marshall, "Citizenship and Social Class" (1950), in *Class, Citizenship, and Social Development* (Garden City, NY, 1964), pp. 65–122.

44. Woodrow Wilson, "Socialism and Democracy," in *The Papers of Woodrow Wilson*, ed. Arthur S. Link, 69 vols. (Princeton, NJ, 1966–94), vol. 5, pp. 559–63.

45. Janet Horne, *A Social Laboratory for Modern France: The Musée Social and the Rise of the Welfare State* (Durham, NC, 2002), pp. 57, 62, 63.

46. Alfredo Palacios, *El nuevo derecho* (1920; Buenos Aires, 1928).

47. Carroll D. Wright, *Some Ethical Phases of the Labor Question* (Boston, 1903), pp. 65, 33.

48. Quoted in Sean Wilentz, *Chants Democratic: New York and the Rise of the American Working Class, 1788–1850* (New York, 1984), p. 331.

49. Croly, *Promise of American Life*, p. 209.

50. Quoted in Dorothy Ross, "Socialism and American Liberalism: Academic Social Thought in the 1880s," *Perspectives in American History* 11 (1977–78), 25.

51. John Bates Clark, *Social Justice Without Socialism* (Boston, 1914), pp. 2, 3–4.

52. Ibid., pp. 16ff., quotation on p. 25.

53. Quentin Skinner, "States and the Freedom of Citizenship," in Quentin Skinner and Bo Strath, eds., *States and Citizens* (Cambridge, UK, 2003), pp. 21–23.

54. Ira Katznelson, "Knowledge About What? Policy Intellectuals and the New Liberalism," in Rueschemeyer and Skocpol, *States, Social Knowledge, and the Origins of Modern Social Policies*, pp. 23–24.

55. Weyl, *New Democracy*, p. 161.

56. Richard T. Ely, "Industrial Liberty," American Economic Association, *Papers and Proceedings of the Fourteenth Annual Meeting*, 3rd ser., 3 (1902), pp. 59, 60, 61, 64, 65, 63, 69, 78, 79.

57. Quoted in Thomas J. Knock, *To End All Wars: Woodrow Wilson and the Quest for a New World Order* (New York, 1992), p. 17.

58. Quoted in David Rock, *Politics in Argentina, 1890–1930: The Rise and Fall of Radicalism* (Cambridge, UK, 1975), p. 98. On Palacios, see Zimmermann, *Los liberales reformistas*, pp. 55–57.

59. Hanes, *City as Subject*, p. 74 (last quoted phrase is Seki's; others are Hanes's).

60. "Social pacification" is quoted in Quine, *Italy's Social Revolution*, p. 69.

61. Ibid., pp. 58–69.

62. Quoted in Garon, *State and Labor in Modern Japan*, p. 65.

63. Ely, *Ground Under Our Feet*, p. 133.

64. Quoted in Rodgers, *Atlantic Crossings*, pp. 82–83.

65. For Ely, see *Ground Under Our Feet*, p. 133; for Seki, see Hanes, *City as Subject*; for Latin Americans, see Zimmermann, *Los liberales reformistas*, pp. 86–87.

66. Ely, *Ground Under Our Feet*, pp. 134–35.

67. Rodgers, *Atlantic Crossings*, p. 275.

68. See E.R.A. Seligman, "Economics and Social Progress," *Publications of the American Economic Association*, 3rd ser., 4 (1903), p. 6.

69. Quoted in Freeden, *New Liberalism*, p. 9.

70. Ely, *Ground Under Our Feet*, p. 135.

71. The constitution of the Society for the Study of National Economy is reprinted as app. 3 in ibid., pp. 296–99.

72. For Gladden's role, see ibid., p. 140.

73. Ibid., p. 136.

74. Ibid., p. 137.

75. Quoted in ibid., pp. 143–44.

76. Mary O. Furner, *Advocacy and Objectivity* (Lexington, KY, 1975), p. 47.

77. E. L. Godkin, "The Economic Man," *North American Review* (1891), repr. in his *Problems of Modern Democracy: Political and Economic Essays* (New York, 1896), p. 168; William Graham Sumner, *On Liberty, Society, and Politics: The Essential Essays of William Graham Sumner*, ed. Roger C. Bannister (Indianapolis, 1992), p. 231.

78. Godkin, "Economic Man," pp. 175, 174.

79. Sumner, *On Liberty, Society, and Politics*, p. 231.

80. J. D. Pierson, "The Early Liberal Thought of Tokutomi Sohō: Some Problems of Western Social Theory in Meiji Japan," in Kornicki, ed., *Meiji Japan*, vol. 1, pp. 71–72.

81. Garon, *State and Labor in Modern Japan*, pp. 170–72.

82. Quoted in Rabinbach, "Social Knowledge," p. 49.

83. Quoted in James J. Sheehan, *The Career of Lujo Brentano: A Study of Liberalism and Social Reform in Imperial Germany* (Chicago, 1966), p. 78.

84. Zimmermann, *Los liberales reformistas*.

85. Quoted in Pyle, "Advantages of Followership," p. 224.

86. Dirlik, "Socialism and Capitalism in Chinese Socialist Thinking," pp. 136–40.

87. Edward A. Ross, *The Social Revolution in Mexico* (New York, 1923), pp. 106, 109.

88. Weyl, *New Democracy*, p. 17.

89. Dawley, *Changing the World*; Ross, "Socialism and American Liberalism"; and Zimmermann, *Los liberales reformistas*.

90. Dawley, *Struggles for Justice*, p. 100. On the difficulty of defining the border, see Ross, "Socialism and American Liberalism," p. 13.

91. Peter DeShazo, *Urban Workers and Labor Unions in Chile, 1902–1927* (Madison, WI, 1984), p. xxviii.

92. This term is used by Blair Ruble to describe progressive politics in Osaka, Moscow, and Chicago. *Second Metropolis: Pragmatic Pluralism in Gilded Age Chicago, Silver Age Moscow, and Meiji Osaka* (Cambridge, UK, 2001).

93. For the case of France, the origin of most Atlantic world political categories, see Janet Horne, "Le libéralisme à l'épreuve de l'industrialisation: La réponse du Musée Social," in Colette Chambelland, ed., *Le Musée Social en son temps* (Paris, 1998), p. 16.

94. See N. Gordon Levin, *Woodrow Wilson and World Politics* (New York, 1968), for the context following World War I.

95. Pyle, "Advantages of Followership," p. 234.

96. Quoted in Herbert Hofmeister, "Austria," in Peter Köhler and Hans F. Zacher, eds., *The Evolution of Social Insurance, 1881–1981: Studies of Germany, France, Great Britain, Austria, and Switzerland* (London/New York, 1982), p. 279.

97. John A. Ryan, "Summary of Catholic Encyclicals," printed as app. 1 in Ely, *Ground Under Our Feet*, pp. 296–99. Ryan's quoted statement and his quotation from Leo XIII are both on p. 290.

98. John T. McGreevy, *Catholicism and American Freedom* (New York, 2003), p. 142.

99. Ibid., p. 143.

100. James Morris, *Elites, Intellectuals, and Consensus: A Study of the Social Question in the Industrial Relations System in Chile* (Ithaca, NY, 1966), ch. 2.

101. Horne, "Le libéralisme à l'épreuve de l'industrialisation," pp. 19–20.

102. See Christian Topalov, "Les réformateurs du chômage et le réseau du Musée Social (1908–1910)," in Chambelland, ed., *Le Musée Social en son temps*, pp. 283–87.

103. See Horne, *Social Laboratory for Modern France*; Horne, "Le libéralisme à l'épreuve de l'industrialisation."

104. For Italy, see Quine, *Italy's Social Revolution*, pp. 38–39, 69, and passim.

105. John A. Scott, *Republican Ideas and the Liberal Tradition* (New York, 1959), pp. 159, 164.

106. Quoted in Horne, *Social Laboratory for Modern France*, p. 119. See also ch. 5.

107. Scott, *Republican Ideas and the Liberal Tradition*, p. 181.

108. George Weisz, *The Emergence of Modern Universities in France, 1863–1914* (Princeton, NJ, 1983), pp. 309–10. May (Weill) established the school after failing to establish a similar school at the Musée Social as part of the University of Paris.

109. Addams, *Democracy and Social Ethics*, pp. 147, 149.

110. Thomas Bender, *New York Intellect* (New York, 1987), p. 301.

111. Philip Nord, *The Republican Moment: Struggles for Democracy in Nineteenth-Century France* (Cambridge, MA, 1995), p. 246.

112. Gillis Harp, *Positivist Republic: Auguste Comte and the Reconstruction of American Liberalism, 1865–1920* (University Park, PA, 1995).

113. Charles A. Hale, "Political and Social Ideas in Latin America," in Leslie Bethell, ed., *Cambridge History of Latin America* (Cambridge, UK, 1986), vol. 4, pp. 387, 388. See also Charles A. Hale, *The Transformation of Liberalism in Late Nineteenth-Century Mexico* (Princeton, NJ, 1989).

114. W. Dean Kinzley, "Japan's Discovery of Poverty," *Journal of Asian History* 22, no. 1 (1988), pp. 1–24 (quotations from pp. 10, 12); also see the different but compatible account in Harry D. Harootunian, "The Economic Rehabilitation of the Samurai in the Early Meiji Period," *Journal of Asian Studies* 19, no. 4 (1960), pp. 433–44.

115. Philip Nord, "The Welfare State in France, 1870–1914," *French Historical Studies* 18, no. 3 (1994), p. 824.

116. See François Ewald, *L'état providence* (Paris, 1986), pp. 16–18.

117. Rabinbach, "Social Knowledge," pp. 48–51.

118. Robert Castel, *Les métamorphoses de la question sociale* (Paris, 1995), p. 297.

119. Ibid., p. 321. Translation by Emily Marker.

120. See, for example, José Gresti, *Los accidentes del trabajo* (Buenos Aires, 1907), p. 17; Miguel Angel Garmendia, *Jurisprudencia del trabajo* (Buenos Aires, 1918), p. 28. The latter specifically singles out this idea as a "very modern" one. Unsain takes the same position in "Preface" in Aguirre, ed., *Apuntes de legislación industrial*, pp. 10–11, 24–25. See also Köhler and Zacher, eds. *Evolution of Social Insurance*.

121. On the relation between home, gender, and morality in Chicago at this time, see Gwendolyn Wright, *Moralism and the Model Home: Domestic Architecture and Cultural Conflict in Chicago, 1873–1913* (Chicago, 1980).

122. For an outstanding analysis of the relation of gender to the development of the American regulatory state, see Felice D. Batlan, "Gender in the Path of the Law: Public Bodies, State Power, and the Politics of Reform in Late-Nineteenth-Century New York City" (Ph.D. diss., New York University, 2004).

123. See Linda Gordon, "Social Insurance and Public Assistance: The Influence of Gender in Welfare Thought in the United States, 1890–1935," *American Historical Review* 97, no. 1 (1992), pp. 19–54; and Ira Katznelson, *When Affirmative Action Was White: An Untold History of Racial Inequality in Twentieth-Century America* (New York, 2005).

124. John R. Commons, *Myself* (New York, 1934), p. 230.

125. Renaud Payre, "A European Progressive Era?" *Contemporary European History* 11, no. 3 (2002), p. 496.

126. Pierre-Yves Saunier, "Changing the City: Urban International Information and the Lyon Municipality, 1900–1940," *Planning Perspectives* 14, no. 1 (1999), pp. 19–48. Information on New York City mayoral files was communicated to me by Felice D. Batlan of Tulane Law School, who examined these files as part of her research on the emergence of the regulatory state in the Progressive Era and noticed the considerable international correspondence.

127. Arthur Shadwell, *Industrial Efficiency: A Comparative Study of Industrial Life in England, Germany, and America*, 2 vols. (London, 1906), vol. 1, p. 27.

128. Saunier, "Changing the City," p. 21.

129. State of New York, Assembly, *Report of the Tenement House Commission of 1894* (Albany, 1895), pp. 256–59, 566–67.

130. National Conference on Industrial Conciliation, *Industrial Conciliation* (New York, 1902).

131. Unsain, *Legislación del trabajo*.

132. Edward A. Ross, *South of Panama* (1915; New York, 1921), p. 134.

133. Beard, *Administration and Politics of Tokyo*, pp. 5–6.

134. Hanes, *City as Subject*, pp. 198, 208.

135. Zimmermann, *Los liberales reformistas*; Aguirre, ed., *Apuntes de legislación industrial*.

136. Claudio Lomnitz, "Modes of Citizenship in Mexico," in Luis Roniger and Carlos Waisman, eds., *Globality and Multiple Modernities: Comparative North American and Latin American Perspectives* (Brighton, UK, 2002), pp. 276–77; Ross, *Social Revolution in Mexico*, p. 115.

137. E. V. Niemeyer, *Revolution at Querétaro: The Mexican Constitutional Convention of 1916–1917* (Austin, TX, 1974), pp. 101, 114–16; Comisión Naciónal, *Diario de los debates del Congreso Constituyente, 1916–1917*, 2 vols. (Mexico, 1960), pp. 1046, 1043.

138. Garon, *State and Labor in Modern Japan*, p. 17.

139. Alan Knight, "The Working Class and the Mexican Revolution, c. 1900–1920," *Journal of Latin American Studies* 16, no. 1 (1984), p. 77.

140. On the proviso about labor organization, see Garon, *State and Labor in Modern Japan*, p. 43.

141. Kathleen Gibberd, *ILO: The Unregarded Revolution* (London, 1937), pp. 10, 13, 15, 17.

142. Garon, *State and Labor in Modern Japan*, pp. 64, 108.

143. Morris, *Elites, Intellectuals, and Consensus*, ch. 6.

144. Rodgers, *Atlantic Crossings*, p. 269.

145. Beard, *Administration and Politics of Tokyo*; John Dewey, *Character and Events*, ed. Joseph Ratner, 2 vols. (New York, 1929), vol. 1, pp. 149–69.

146. Wright, *Politics of Design*.

147. Pierre Rosanvallon, preface to Chambelland, ed., *Le Musée Social en son temps*, pp. 7–8.

148. Horne, *Social Laboratory for Modern France*, pp. 152–55.

149. Alicia Novick, "Le Musée Social et l'urbanisme en Argentine (1911–1923)," in Chambelland, ed., *Le Musée Social en son temps*, p. 338.

150. Quoted in ibid., Roosevelt's visit, p. 344. Roosevelt's speeches: *Speeches of the president of the 'Museo social argentino' Dr. Emilio Frers and of Col. Roosevelt at the banquet given in the Colón theatre* (Buenos Aires, 1914); *Verdades y verdades a medias, segunda conferencia en el teatro Colón . . . 1913* (Buenos Aires, 1913). See also Zimmermann, *Los liberales reformistas*, p. 76.

151. Novick, "Le Musée Social et l'urbanisme en Argentine," pp. 334, 344.

152. For New York, see Saunier, "Changing the City," p. 39; for Milan, see Patrizia Dogliani, "La naissance d'un Musée Social en Italie," in Chambelland, ed., *Le Musée Social en son temps*, pp. 359–64.

153. Dogliani, "La naissance d'un Musée Social en Italie," p. 360.

154. Hale, "Political and Social Ideas in Latin America," p. 407.

155. Patrizia Dogliani, "European Municipalism in the First Half of the Twentieth Century: The Socialist Network," *Contemporary European History* 11, no. 4 (2002), p. 591.

156. Beard, *Administration and Politics of Tokyo*, p. 13.

157. Kloppenberg, *Uncertain Victory*.

158. See Pierre-Yves Saunier, "Taking Up the Bet on Connections: A Municipal Contribution," *Contemporary European History* 11, no. 4 (2002), p. 518.

159. Moisés Poblete Troncoso and Oscar Alvarez Andrews, *Legislación social obrera chilena* (Santiago de Chile, 1924); Moisés Poblete Troncoso, *Legislación social de América latina*, 2 vols. (Madrid, 1928).

160. Saunier, "Taking Up the Bet on Connections," p. 517.

161. Quoted in Garon, *State and Labor in Modern Japan*, p. 85.

162. Rodgers, *Atlantic Crossings*, p. 242.

163. Saunier, "Changing the City," p. 24.

164. Quine, *Italy's Social Revolution*, p. 77.

165. Quoted in Kenneth P. Pyle, "The Technology of Japanese Nationalism: The Local Improvement Movement, 1900–1918," in Kornicki, ed., *Meiji Japan*, vol. 4, p. 6.

166. Quoted in Rodgers, *Atlantic Crossings*, p. 247.

167. Quoted in ibid., p. 74.

168. Dawley, *Changing the World*, pp. 263–65.

169. Quoted in Ross, *Social Revolution in Mexico*, p. 101.

170. Robert Thurston, *Liberal City, Conservative State: Moscow and Russia's Urban Crisis, 1906–1914* (Oxford, 1987), ch. 5; Ruble, *Second Metropolis*, pp. 280, 285.

171. As an example, I cite the Chilean case, which is both complex and revealing: Peter Blanchard, "A Populist Precursor: Guillermo Billinghurst," *Journal of Latin American Studies* 9, no. 2 (1977), pp. 251–73; Peter Klarén, "Origins of Modern Peru, 1880–1930," in Bethell, ed., *Cambridge History of Latin America*, vol. 5, pp. 625–31; Peter Klarén, *Peru: Society and Nationhood in the Andes* (New York, 2000), pp. 219–25.

172. Joel Wolfe, *Working Women, Working Men: São Paulo and the Rise of Brazil's Industrial Working Class, 1900–1955* (Durham, NC, 1993), p. 28.

173. Jean Meyer, "Mexico: Revolution and Reconstruction in the 1920s," in Bethell, ed., *Cambridge History of Latin America*, vol. 5, p. 181.

174. John Mason Hart, "The Mexican Revolution, 1910–1920," in Michael C. Meyer and William H. Beezley, eds., *The Oxford History of Mexico* (Oxford, 2000), pp. 331, 461–63; Ramón E. Ruiz, *Labor and the Ambivalent Revolutionaries: Mexico, 1911–1923* (Baltimore, 1976), especially ch. 10.

175. Alan Knight, *The Mexican Revolution*, 2 vols. (Cambridge, UK, 1986), vol. 1, p. 431.

176. Hanes, *City as Subject*, p. 7; Garon, *State and Labor in Modern Japan*, pp. 2–3, 8.

177. Werner Sombart, "Why Is There No Socialism in the United States?" *International Socialist Review* 7 (1907), pp. 420–25. (This is the first English publication; the article was published in German in 1905.)

178. "How Neoliberalism Became a Transnational Movement," conference at the International Center for Advanced Studies, New York University, April 2005.

6: GLOBAL HISTORY AND AMERICA TODAY

1. Quoted in Jonathan M. Hansen, *The Lost Promise of Patriotism: Debating American Identity, 1890–1920* (Chicago, 2003), p. 137.

2. Quoted in Ian Tyrrell, "Making Nations/Making States: American Historians in the Context of Empire," *Journal of American History* 86, no. 3 (1999), p. 1031.

INDEX